OPERATION ALBION

Twentieth-Century Battles

Spencer C. Tucker, editor

OPERATION ALBION

THE GERMAN CONQUEST
OF THE BALTIC ISLANDS

MICHAEL B. BARRETT

INDIANA UNIVERSITY PRESS

BLOOMINGTON AND INDIANAPOLIS

This book is a publication of

Indiana University Press
601 North Morton Street
Bloomington, IN 47404-3797 USA

http://iupress.indiana.edu

Telephone orders   800-842-6796
Fax orders   812-855-7931
Orders by e-mail   iuporder@indiana.edu

The paper used in this publication meets the minimum
requirements of American National Standard for Information
Sciences—Permanence of Paper for Printed Library Materials, ANSI
Z39.48-1984.

Manufactured in the United States of America

Library of Congress Cataloging-in-Publication Data

Barrett, Michael B.
Operation Albion : the German conquest of the Baltic Islands /
Michael B. Barrett.
p. cm. — (Twentieth-century battles)
Includes bibliographical references and index.
ISBN 978-0-253-34969-9 (cloth)
1. Operation Albion, 1917. 2. World War, 1914–1918—Campaigns—
Islands of the Baltic. 3. World War, 1914–1918—Campaigns—
Eastern Front. 4. World War, 1914–1918—Amphibious operations.
5. World War, 1914–1918—Naval operations, German. 6. Islands of
the Baltic—History. I. Title.
D552.B3B37 2008
940.4'147—dc22
                                        2007027582

1 2 3 4 5 13 12 11 10 09 08

CONTENTS

MAPS

DATES, TIMES, AND NAMES

In 1917, the Russians still used a Julian calendar, placing them thirteen days behind the remainder of Europe. In Russian documents, the German invasion of the Baltic Islands began on 29 September 1917 rather than 12 October 1917. I have adjusted Russian dates whenever they appear so they correspond to those of the rest of Europe. Different time zones also meant that the Russians were two hours "ahead" of the Germans. Again, I have corrected those so German and Russian times match. If a reader wishes to check the original Russian sources, he or she will have to subtract thirteen days and add two hours from the times listed in the endnotes of this book to get the time and date of an event in the contemporary Russian document.

Many of the place names in this area were German. Both Russians and Germans used the German names, but after the war the Estonians (and other nations) used their own languages to assign place names that are in use today. When first citing a location, I have given its 1917 name (usually German) followed in parentheses by the name in the local tongue. For example, Reval (Tallinn) or Helsinki (Helsingfors) or Arensburg (Kuresaare).

If a person has some importance in this narrative, I usually give biographical details in the text. If a person is mentioned but once or twice in the literature or text, I usually place any biographical data in an endnote.

ACKNOWLEDGMENTS

IN MOST INSTANCES, a single author receives credit for writing a work of history. The reality is that many people contribute to the final product, and I would like to express my gratitude, only hoping I do not leave out anyone.

In the first instance, I must thank Dr. Spencer Tucker, the editor of this series. He invited me to write this book and offered encouragement during the three-year project, and he also provided the contact to Larry Hoffman of Paso Robles, California, who drew the maps. Military history without maps is like painting without color, and Larry did some great work.

In Germany, Martha Caspers and Renate Jansen of the Federal Archive system were instrumental in providing assistance at the Photographic and Military Archives, respectively. In one of those lucky coincidences that often make or break a project, the archivist of The Citadel, Jane Yates, put me in touch with one of the researchers at her institute, Lieutenant Commander Andre Pecher, of the German Navy. Commander Pecher, who was doing research on Vice Admiral Friedrich Ruge, steered me toward some invaluable works by that author, who had participated in Albion. Later, Commander Pecher assisted in helping me get rights to publish some photographs. The library staff at The Citadel, notably Jane Buskirk, Betsy Carter, Deborah Causey, and Kathleen Turner, worked wonders with interlibrary loan. The project might have been stillborn had it not been for my research assistant in St. Petersburg, Elizaveta Zheganina. Drs. Randy Papadapolous and H. P. Willmott put me in touch with her. She opened doors in the Russian State Naval Archive and Naval Museum in St. Petersburg, and the Russian State Military Archive in Moscow, acquiring and translating the Russian records. David Glantz and Dr. Bruce Menning turned me toward some good sources. Katrin Äär, archivist of the Saaremaa Museum in Kuressaare, helped with some photographs and information about the Executive Defense Committee of the Baltic Islands Defense Position.

When it came to editing, Rosemary Michaud, a writer in Charleston, proved indomitable at finding repeated words and turning stodgy prose into what I hope is a readable account that honors the brave sailors and soldiers of both sides who participated in Albion. My colleague Kyle Sinisi proved adept at inserting some degree of consistency in terminology and numbers. The staff at Indiana University Press, led by Bob Sloan, were wonderful to work with from the first day of the project, making the publication process painless. With endless patience, copy editor Carol Kennedy tried to make my writing confirm to the Chicago style.

Financial assistance came from The Citadel Foundation and Dean Al Finch of the School of Humanities and Social Studies at The Citadel.

Finally, my wife, Sara, and son, Michael, offered love, confidence, encouragement, and patience over many years, and it is to them that this book is dedicated.

OPERATION ALBION

CHAPTER ONE

SUBMARINE UC-58, TAGGA BAY, 28 SEPTEMBER 1917

ONCE HE WAS certain the smudge on the horizon was actually land, Lieutenant Karl Vesper ordered his boat to dive. The UC-58, a new mine-laying submarine commissioned only a few months before, submerged and remained on its southerly course. The 400-ton U-boat glided noiselessly under the surface as its engines switched from diesel to electric. Its bow pointed toward Tagga Bay on Ösel Island, some 8–10 kilometers distant. UC-58, product of the Imperial Yard in Danzig and representative of the best in German engineering, had tossed violently as Vesper loitered off the coast waiting for dawn. With sunrise coming at 6 AM, Vesper wanted to be in and out of the bay as quickly as possible so his periscope would not be seen and identified by a Russian sentry.

As UC-58 moved forward, tension rose. Fear began to replace seasickness. The Tagga Bay was some 12 kilometers wide, with enemy coastal artillery fortresses on each side of its entrance. Vesper did not worry too much about the forts. It was mines that worried the skipper and every one of the twenty-five men he commanded. The Russian Navy, vastly inferior in numbers to the Germans, had evened the balance to a degree by its adroit use of mines. Consequently, the Imperial Navy had, up to now, kept the lowest of profiles in the Baltic Sea.

On board UC-58, every sailor held his breath. Each knew the Baltic archipelago, of which Ösel was the largest island, formed the Russian outer defense of the Gulf of Finland, the route to the Russian capital of

Petrograd. With the exception of the Neva River in Petrograd, on whose banks sat the Tsar's Winter Palace and the Russian Admiralty, no place in the Baltic was more likely to enjoy better mine protection than the waters around Ösel Island. Lieutenant Vesper scanned the shore through his periscope as the submarine entered the bay. On his right, to the southwest on a point of land, rose a large beacon, which he knew from his charts marked Cape Hundsort. The beacon soon loomed large in his periscope, but he was searching for something else. Aerial photography had located a Russian coastal battery of medium guns, estimated at 150mm, at Cape Hundsort. Guns of that caliber at close range could bring any vessel to a halt; thus the navy had to know exactly where they were so they could be bombarded and destroyed. Vesper searched for the earthworks and concrete emplacements that characterized Russian fortifications. Just after he passed the beacon, he could see the earthen berms of the battery, and he shouted the bearing to his executive officer. Vesper looked for field fortifications, trenches, any identifying marks. Further down the bay, the steeple of a church appeared, and its location was recorded. A few ramshackle docks indicated the presence of a fishing camp.

Vesper's eyes flashed back and forth between the view in the periscope and his charts, trying to use what he saw to fix his position. He did not want to let his vessel run into water less than 20 meters deep. If the water became any shallower, there was a good chance the submarine could run aground or bounce upward if it hit a rock outcropping, broaching the surface and exposing itself to the Russians. In all likelihood, if that happened the Russians would be too astonished to react, but Vesper had his orders to avoid detection at all costs from no less a personage than Captain Magnus von Levetzow, a high-and-mighty "comer" who had future admiral marked all over him. Vesper, whose rank was the equivalent of an army first lieutenant, had no intention of angering people in high places whose whims could get one sent on dangerous missions like this one.

Passing the 20-meter depth line, Vesper ordered the boat to reverse course and to head north along the east side of Tagga Bay. Here the fir and pine forests had a denser cast, although the rise in elevation from the shore was noticeably less than on the west side of the bay. Despite the magnification of the periscope, he could not see into the woods. They were impenetrable to sight. As he began to emerge from the bay, he came abreast of Cape Ninnast, off to his right. Again, aerial photographs had revealed a battery of medium-size artillery (120–150mm guns) under construction, but Vesper could not see it. The shoreline was thick with trees growing right to the edge. Knowing von Levetzow's curiosity and his orders, Vesper slowed UC-58, but he could not find the fortifications. Disappointed, he motored north into the open Baltic and surfaced 15 kilometers out to sea, safely out of sight of anyone on Ösel Island. Since UC-58 had not hit any mines and disappeared in a blinding flash or billow of water, it was clear there were no minefields. It was 8 AM. The skipper ordered his radio operator to send an immediate four-word message: "Bay reconnoitered. Everything peaceful."[1] Vesper then headed back to his home port of Libau to report his findings in person.

Four days later, on the 2d of October 1917, Lieutenant junior grade Vesper sat in the conference room of the commander of the Baltic Reconnaissance Squadron, Rear Admiral Albert Hopman. While Hopman sat at the table, it was clear he was not in charge. Captain von Levetzow ran the show. He held the temporary position of chief of staff of the Naval Task Force for Special Operations, the ungainly name assigned to the flotilla being assembled to capture the Baltic Islands archipelago in a joint undertaking with the army. As Vesper spoke, capital ships, tenders, steamers, cruisers, auxiliaries, destroyers, minesweepers, hospital ships, and even a seaplane tender steamed toward Libau to form a fleet that would exceed 350 ships. Seaplanes and ground-based aircraft buzzed the skies overhead, while huge zeppelins scoured the Gulf of Riga for Russian movements, movements that would signal that the enemy was aware the Germans were coming.

All eyes around the conference table focused on the U-boat skipper. They knew the two-year veteran of submarine patrols in the Baltic had pushed through when a sister ship, UC-59, was driven back the week before by stormy weather and ran aground.[2] After he gave his report, Vesper fielded questions from those present: von Levetzow and his staff, army officers from the XXIII Reserve Corps, the headquarters of the army forces earmarked for the landing, and officers from the minesweeping flotilla stationed north at Windau. The latter group had ships at that moment attempting to clear the minefields between the Courland coast and the Sworbe Peninsula on Ösel Island—a strait some 20 kilometers wide. The crucial question was the presence or absence of fortifications and minefields in Tagga Bay, the intended landing spot. Lieutenant Vesper reported what he had seen. At Cape Hundsort, a fort whose guns were easily visible from the sea made an easy target, while at Cape Ninnast, there was nothing visible from the surface of the bay. The entire coast, said Lieutenant Vesper, appeared completely peaceful.[3] There were no minefields in Tagga Bay, or at its entrance.

Captain von Levetzow expressed his relief at this latter discovery, which appeared to confirm other intelligence gathered from aerial photographs and spies. Tagga Bay was clear; the operation could proceed. Von Levetzow told those present that as soon as the weather improved, embarkation would begin. The sole German amphibious operation of the First World War, given the code name "Operation Albion," and the largest naval undertaking in the Baltic Sea, was about to begin.[4]

Unfortunately, Lieutenant Vesper was wrong about the mines. They were there, waiting under the surface of Tagga Bay.

OPERATION ALBION

In October 1917, an invasion force of some twenty-five thousand soldiers of the German XXIII Reserve Corps, accompanied by a flotilla of 10 dreadnoughts, 350 other vessels, a half-dozen zeppelins, and 80 aircraft, conducted the most successful amphibious operation of the First World War. Within eight days the islands of Ösel, Moon and Dagö, at the head of the Gulf of Riga, fell, and more than twenty thousand Russians passed into captivity. What is astonishing is that Operation Albion was conducted by military forces with no experience in either amphibious or joint warfare. The assault troops were army soldiers who enjoyed no special "marine" training, and the operation was put together on a month's notice. The naval flotilla was likewise an ad hoc arrangement.

Operation Albion is relatively unknown and often overlooked, largely because it came at the termination of the 1917 campaign season on the eastern front, a front relatively neglected in western historiography. In addition, the far more portentous Bolshevik Revolution overshadows everything on the eastern front in 1917, even the March Revolution and the disintegration of the increasingly hapless Russian army.

Germany's strategy on the eastern front in late 1917 developed an aura of desperation. The March Revolution stoked German hopes that Russia might leave the war, but these proved vain. Even though the Russians were on the ropes and their military forces in revolutionary turmoil, they managed to mount an offensive in Galicia in July. The Germans rolled back the Russians and took more land than they had initially lost, but the Provisional Government failed to get the hint and come to the bargaining table. The High Command grew nervous. The United States had entered the war in April, and by August it was clear that the submarine campaign which had

so angered the Americans had failed to deliver. With the Americans coming, Germany knew it would face a combined English-French-American
offensive in the west in 1918. Only a preemptive assault could shake the
Allies, and the High Command could not contemplate launching such an
attack unless Germany could end the fighting in the east, freeing divisions
to move to France. At the same time, Germany's faltering ally, Austria-
Hungary, labeled a corpse by General Ludendorff, had to be propped up.
For Austria, already engaged in secret negotiations to bail out, an end to
the war in the east might not be sufficient. Austria's Italian front, like a
cancer, had inexorably sapped its strength to the point where its life was
endangered. Without relief, the end was inevitable. The High Command
determined a blow to Italy would give the Austrians relief, and they sent
their mountain warfare expert along with their chief operations officer to
scout out the area during the summer of 1917. Given the green light by
Ludendorff, the Italian Offensive was set to start on the 24th of October.
The divisions trained in the new infiltration techniques earmarked for this
operation came from the west. Ludendorff pulled them from the front in
Belgium and France, which meant that divisions from the east had to take
their place. The fighting in the east had to end.

In the German High Command, as concern over German weakness
in the west grew, Ludendorff thought that an offensive in northern Russia
would cause the Kerensky Government to capitulate. Riga, the third-largest
city in the Russian Empire, lay within easy reach. Ludendorff thought the
shock of losing it would bring the Russians to their senses and the bargaining table. Hedging his bets, a rather unusual step for him, he also planned
to take the Baltic Islands at the mouth of the Gulf of Riga if the Russians did not seek an armistice when Riga fell. Seizing the islands would
put German forces within striking distance of Reval, the linchpin to the
Russian defense of the Gulf of Finland.

Given this situation, a strike at the Baltic Islands, which the High
Command had heretofore discounted for several years, took on new light.
At a minimum, possession of the islands would open the German lines of
communication to newly captured Riga, threatening Russian defenses at
the mouth of the Gulf of Finland and positioning German forces advan-
tageously for conducting a knockout blow if necessary in the coming
spring. At best, capturing the islands could shatter what was left of Russian morale and bring about a collapse. At the worst, the Russians would
fight on, but Germany would be poised to take Petrograd in the spring of
1918. By September 1917, Germany was desperate. The English offensive

at Passchendaele had seriously drained manpower, and a frantic General Ludendorff, fearing that these losses would derail an intended offensive in the west in 1918, gambled that seizing the Baltic Islands might constitute the proverbial straw on the camel's back. Operation Albion was an economy-of-force effort that cost the Germans little and had great potential. Both Field Marshal von Hindenburg and Ludendorff had expectations that Albion might knock a staggering Russia out of the war.

The Germans faced great challenges in Operation Albion: the inexperience of their own military components in working with one another, the approach of winter, the need for haste, and the difficulty in achieving surprise. The German cast contained many names familiar to scholars of the First World War and the Weimar period: Field Marshal Paul von Hindenburg, Generals Erich Ludendorff and Oskar von Hutier and Admirals Prince Henry, Paul Behncke, Erhardt Schmidt, and Wilhelm Souchon.

The Russians had obstacles that towered over those the Germans faced. Revolutionary turmoil almost completely immobilized the Baltic Fleet. The same held true for the army, whose situation was made worse by the election of officers who proved woefully incompetent. Never a Russian strong point, weak logistics had made the islands' defenses a matter of too little, too late. From the Russian side, Westerners know only the names Alexander Kerensky, Alexei Brusilov, and Lavr Kornilov. Given the Soviet demonization of the tsarist period, few Russians would recognize their leaders at the next lower level: Admirals Mikhail Bakhirev and Alexander Razvozov, or Generals Vladimir Cheremisov and Fyodor Ivanov. Perhaps the one exception would be Captain Pavel Shisko, although Soviet histories ignored his postwar sojourn to the West.

If one counts the number of vessels involved, Albion constitutes the largest naval operation of the First World War. The Germans claimed a fleet of some 363 ships and boats; the Russians 151. Most were small craft, namely mine-clearing vessels. Of course, its significance is not the same as the Battle of Jutland, the German attempt in 1916 to lure part of the British fleet to destruction and to break the English naval blockade. At Jutland the English had 150 ships; the Germans 99. The majority of these were large ships. Nonetheless, Albion is not without major significance and interest. It was the largest and most important naval engagement in the Baltic Sea. In what the Germans considered a long shot, what they hoped for happened. The Russians stopped fighting.

With no experience in amphibious warfare, the Germans solved complex organizational command and control problems. On the other hand, mutiny, murder, and an absence of discipline racked Russia's forces, and by the time the operation began, senior officers knew the end was near. In fact, the two leading admirals had already submitted their resignations, yet remained to fight, after discovering that the Germans had put to sea. That the Russians responded as commendably as they did says much about their tenacity and patriotism. Knowing these traits all too well, the Germans approached Operation Albion in a manner that left little room for chance, the fickle goddess of war.

CHAPTER TWO

THE STRATEGIC IMPORTANCE
OF THE BALTIC ISLANDS

WHEN THE WAR broke out in 1914, neither Germany nor Russia felt the Baltic Islands had any significance. France remained the center of interest for the German army. The Imperial Fleet looked to the North Sea and the Royal Navy. The ground forces of Russia did focus on Germany. They planned a two-pronged invasion of East Prussia from Kovno and Warsaw. The small and totally outclassed Russian Baltic Fleet could only huddle in the east end of the Gulf of Finland, circling under the protection of long-range coastal artillery and extensive minefields. By the fall of 1917 matters had changed, and both sides considered the Baltic Islands to be of such strategic importance they were willing to commit themselves to a major battle for their possession. The Germans hoped their seizure would be the final blow to a Russia seething with revolutionary discontent, and even if the loss of the islands did not lead to immediate capitulation, capturing them would breach the Russian defenses and doom St. Petersburg. Between 1914 and 1917, the Russians had taken advantage of the German fixation on the North Sea and had extended their defenses from the easternmost section of the Gulf of Finland to its western approaches, of which the Baltic Islands formed the southern anchor. Firmly ensconced in this region, the Russians now had no choice but to fight because loss of the islands would turn the flank of their western defenses, laying open their capital.

Map 1. The Baltic Theater of Operations

GERMAN STRATEGY IN 1914

Before the First World War, German army leaders believed that in the event of a European-wide war, the decision must come in France. The Great General Staff had studied the problem extensively since the War of 1870–1871, and when France and Russia signed a mutual defense alliance in 1894, the subject assumed an even greater importance. Of the two potential foes, France represented the greater danger. Its political, industrial, and military infrastructure facilitated a more rapid mobilization than Russia could achieve. Russia's backwardness, poor industrial infrastructure, and uninspired performance against Japan in the 1904–1905 war seemed to indicate it would take much longer to activate its forces and bring them to bear. Moreover, Russia's situation was complicated by the fact that it faced two opponents in its western areas, the Germans in East Prussia and the Austro-Hungarians in Galicia and the Bukovina. The German strategy for a general war, embodied in the Schlieffen Plan, reflected these realities by allocating only one of Germany's eight field armies to the eastern front. Confronted by a foe in the west whose mobilization capabilities came close to its own, Germany adopted an "all or nothing" strategy and planned to march seven armies into France in an effort to win a decisive victory before Russia could enter the field of battle.[1]

Germany started the war without an eastern strategy; the mission of the Eighth Army (her sole force in the east) was to defend East Prussia for as long as possible. The Germans wanted to hold the Russians at bay until the armies in the west had crushed France and could thus move east to take on Russia. Recognizing the difficulty if not impossibility of such a task, the General Staff's orders called for the Eighth Army to fight a delaying action against the oncoming Russians. The German commander could even withdraw behind the Vistula River if compelled. As long as Berlin remained intact, any territory lost in the east, however discomforting, would be a temporary loss, to be recovered as soon as France fell.[2]

A similar laissez-faire attitude concerning Russia held sway in the Bendler Block, the new home to the Admiralty Staff. All eyes here looked west, west toward England.[3] German naval policy, which viewed the Royal Navy as the sole rival and threat to the Reich, had led to a catastrophic arms race with England that drove the latter into the arms of France in 1904.[4] Contemporaries and historians agreed that the Royal Navy outclassed the German High Sea Fleet; the only question was the margin of England's advantage. Russia appeared on no one's radar screen. True, Russia had a few obsolete capital ships, and it had ordered some modern and well-designed vessels, but these ships were largely still under construction when war broke out in 1914. The Russians posed no credible threat to Germany, reflected by the absence of any serious German naval planning for operations in the Baltic.

After the war broke out, developments confirmed that the real threat to Germany lay in the west, although in the short run, events in East Prussia proved the accuracy of Moltke the Elder's maxim that no plan survives first contact with the enemy. The unexpectedly rapid Russian advance into East Prussia in August 1914 caused the German High Command, or the OHL from its German initials, to forget its cavalier attitude toward the fate of that province and led to the emergence of Germany's first and most enduring heroes following their victory at Tannenberg, Paul von Hindenburg and Erich Ludendorff. Subsequently given overall command in the east, these two spent the next two years trying to convince the High Command that the war could be won in the east given sufficient resources to implement a strategy of Russia first. Chief of the General Staff Erich von Falkenhayn (1861–1922) rejected the idea and balked at sending units to the east. The fighting that ensued stemmed not so much from any coherent plan but from opportunities arising from campaigns to assist Germany's hapless ally, Austria-Hungary. Nonetheless, by 1916 German-led forces had pushed the Russians completely from Poland. The Reich squeezed out Austria and established a huge military empire in the east.[5] The Brusilov Offensive in the summer of 1916 and the timing of Rumania's defection to the Allied cause later that same year helped to raise sagging Allied morale. Ironically, the situation in 1917 was largely the same with a new cast. Von Hindenburg and Ludendorff had moved west in August 1916 to take over the German High Command, and once in the west, they decided that indeed it was the theater of importance. Their successor in the east, Field Marshal Prince Leopold of Bavaria, got nowhere with his requests for more troops. As Ludendorff wrote when he moved to the west, "We were now reduced to a policy of pure defense."[6]

THE GERMAN STRATEGIC SITUATION
AT THE ONSET OF 1917

The Germans and Turks sat astride the entrances to the Baltic and Black seas, respectively, effectively blockading Russia's most important seaports. The closing of commerce wreaked havoc on Russia. The Russian economy and infrastructure were unraveling and on the verge of collapse. While the Russian army still held, the civilian sector was coming undone.[7] Labor unrest and general governmental ineptitude had crippled the economy. A final push, a nudge, might have done the trick, but the Germans underestimated the situation. Von Hindenburg expected the Russians to make good their losses during the winter months and to return once again ready and willing to battle. He and Ludendorff anticipated a universal Allied offensive effort in the spring of 1917 as soon as the weather and Russian reconstitution efforts permitted.[8]

The Germans were also suffering, despite their great victory in Rumania. They simply did not have sufficient forces to mount an offensive in 1917. Their losses at Verdun and on the Somme in 1916 had shaken the army, and the resumption of unrestricted submarine warfare in February 1917 reflected the German desperation along with deep internal political divisions over the handling of the war. The Germans hoped returning to unrestricted submarine warfare would knock England out of the war before the might of America, sure to enter, could be brought to bear. If England withdrew, France and Russia would follow. Entente offensives on the western front in the spring of 1917 compelled the Germans to remain inactive in the east. When the March Revolution led to the tsar's abdication, the Germans waited to see what developed and hoped that Russia might sue for peace. To their surprise, Russia remained in the war. By the summer of 1917, the increasingly dire strategic situation caused the Germans to focus their efforts in the east in an attempt to force a decision in that theater—one that would free up forces for the coming showdown in the west. By midsummer signs indicated the submarine campaign could not deliver the effect its advocates had promised.[9] The Americans had entered the war as predicted, but they were crossing the ocean untroubled by U-boats, quite the opposite of the Admiralty's sanguine expectations and promises. By 1918 the American presence would be meaningful, and unless Germany could match their numbers, the war was lost. Remaining inactive in the east while waiting for the revolution to unfold would not lead to anything decisive.[10]

THE GERMANS' STRATEGIC SITUATION, SUMMER 1917

By the summer of 1917, however, the Germans had slightly improved their position, to the point that they could attempt to force Russia to sue for peace or to collapse. In the west, the adoption of the "elastic defense," by which units no longer manned the trenches in a continuous, unbroken line, and the withdrawal to the Siegfried Line, which measurably shortened the front lines, freed a number of divisions for employment in the east. Second, in the aftermath of the Nivelle Offensive and mutiny, the French army lay prostrate, incapable of protracted offensive action. The Russian offensive of July 1917, named after War Minister Alexander Kerensky, caught Austria by surprise, and stampeded many of its units. The Germans had anticipated the offensive and took steps to thwart it. They reacted quickly and sent the Russians streaming to the rear. The High Command sent six divisions from the western front to the east. To roll back the Russians and to push their weak government over the edge or to accelerate the spreading anarchy in the Russian army, the High Command ordered two attacks in August at the extreme boundaries of the eastern front: in the south came an offensive in Galicia; the other attack came in the very north in the Gulf of Riga. General Felix Bothmer's Austro-German *Südarmee* rolled General Alexei Brusilov's armies out of Galicia and the Bukovina. In the north, in the first of two phases, General Oskar von Hutier's Eighth Army took Riga on 3 September after crossing the Düna (Dvina) River above the city at Üxküll.[11] The High Command now looked to the second phase of that operation, the conquest of the Baltic Islands.

From 1915 on, the German army had held most of the Russian province of Courland (or Kurland), which formed the western arm of the huge Gulf of Riga.[12] At the head of the gulf, three large islands (Ösel, Dagö, and Moon) sit astride the entrance, forcing vessels to hug the coast of the mainland on either side of the islands. On the south side of Ösel, between it and the coast of Courland, lies the Irbe Straits. The straits are 20 kilometers wide, but sand banks run out from Ösel, forcing coastal traffic to favor the Courland side of the straits. On the opposite side of the gulf, the east side, the Moon Sound runs north-south between the Estonian mainland and the islands of Moon and Dagö. The body of water is narrow, some 7 kilometers between Kuivast on Moon Island and Verder on the Estonian mainland. Both passageways into the gulf are sufficiently narrow to permit interdiction by coast artillery. By 1917, the Russians controlled both the straits and the Moon Sound with land-based artillery, and smaller vessels from their Baltic Fleet used the Moon Sound for entry and exit. Under these circumstances, unless the Germans could gain control of the islands, possession of Riga at the head of the gulf, with its access to the hinterland via the Düna River, was likely to prove more symbolic than useful.

The German navy had long recognized this problem and had proposed taking the islands as early as 1915. In fact, in August of that year, a naval squadron had briefly entered the gulf, rushing through the Irbe Straits, but the size of the Russian minefields, the tenacious Russian defense, and difficulties (principally coaling) inherent in operating far from a fixed-base facility forced a rapid withdrawal.[13] The retreat convinced most admirals of the necessity for capturing the Baltic Islands in order for the Germans to dominate the Gulf of Riga and the eastern end of the Baltic. In fact, taking the islands became the leitmotif of the navy's commander in chief of the Baltic, Admiral Prince Henry of Prussia,[14] the kaiser's brother. Unfortunately, the army cold-shouldered every proposal from the navy for a cooperative undertaking aimed at the islands until the spring of 1917.[15]

By the late summer of 1917, possession of the Gulf of Riga had become a matter of great strategic interest for the Germans, not just for the navy, but for the army as well. The army hoped that its two major blows in the late summer, the rolling back of the Russian armies in Galicia after the Kerensky Offensive and the capture of Riga in the north, threatening Petersburg, would send the Russians to the bargaining table.[16] Capturing Riga meant little, however, unless the lines of communication to it could be used, and that meant opening the entrance to the Gulf of Riga by capturing the Baltic Islands. If that happened, the sea lines of communication to Riga could be employed to stage forces for further inroads into northern Russia. In addition, the western flank of the Russian army's northern front would be turned. The Russians would have to abandon the Estonian coast and retreat to a line anchored on Lake Peipus, halfway to Petrograd. Likewise, from the navy's perspective, possession of the islands allowed them access to Riga. The islands could also be used as staging bases for further forays into the Gulf of Finland and the heart of Russia. If the Germans could take the Baltic Islands, they would turn the flank on the Russians' outer defense position, and in all likelihood, force the Russians to abandon Hango at the extreme southwest of Finland. The central defense position, running from Helsingfors (Helsinki) to Reval (Tallin), might collapse as well.

RUSSIAN STRATEGY IN 1914

Following defeat at the hands of Japan in 1905, Russia embarked on a series of military reforms and reorganization. The subsequent Revolution of 1905 forced similar far-reaching shake-ups in government. A constitution and parliament (Duma) with limited powers was pressed upon an unenthusiastic autocracy. As the government wrestled with how to deal with this new institution, the pace of reform, never vigorous, slowed. The war with Japan had left the government's finances in tatters, and the military was but one of many voices demanding resources. With no one setting priorities, budget battles in the parliament became acrimonious and drawn out. The pace of reform slowed even more. The noted army historian Allan K. Wildman uses terms such as "utter prostration" and "complete disarray"[17] to describe the army; the same terms can be used for the navy.

The tsar saw the necessity for integrating military direction at top levels, and he made two major innovations, neither of which, according to historian Bruce Menning, "fulfilled its initial promise."[18]

The first of the tsar's innovations consisted of a Prussian-style General Staff. The innovation here was to make it independent of the old Main Staff and the War Ministry. It had responsibility for planning and mobilization measures. Its first chief was General F. F. Palitsyn (1851–1923), whose main assistant (senior quartermaster general) was General Mikhail V. Alekseev.[19] The chief of the General Staff acquired direct access to the tsar. The Main Staff retained authority in assignments.

The General Staff fared poorly. Its position outside the War Ministry estranged it from troop concerns; the war minister viewed it as a competitor. Its real weakness stemmed from the inability to assign money to programs, which the minister of war could do. The General Staff could not match money to its plans to make them work. The close ties of Palitsyn and Alekseev to Grand Duke Nicholas did not sit well with the tsar, and after he removed the grand duke from the State Council, Palitsyn went next in November 1908. Nicholas replaced him with General Vladimir A. Sukhomlinov,[20] at the same time taking away the right of immediate access. In 1909, Sukhomlinov became war minister and moved the General Staff back into the War Ministry, which actually proved more efficient in the long run. The General Staff developed Russia's mobilization schemes that carried it into the war.[21]

The General Staff relied on a cautious strategy that stressed the Russian traditional strength, the defense, trading the vast space of their country for time as the vast numbers of active and reserve forces came from all over Russia to where they were needed. General Alekseev wrote the plan. It had two phases. The first consisted of mobilizing and assembling Russia's forces and reserves from garrisons located throughout western Russia. Alekseev recognized that Russia could not concentrate its armies in the vulnerable Polish salient as previous plans had called for. Forces gathering there were too far to the west. A German-Austrian thrust from East Prussia and Galicia could easily cut the lines of communication from Russia and block any retreat. Alekseev recognized that Russia had to mobilize its forces further to the east. In theory Russia was quite exposed during the time period while its forces mobilized and moved to assembly places where offensive operations would begin. In reality, the same held true for Russia's opponents, who were likewise gathering their forces and moving them to the frontiers. What was really new in Alekseev's mobilization planning was the realization that Germany, not Austria-Hungary, constituted the main threat. The tsar approved this outline in 1909 in what was labeled Schedule 18.[22]

A year later, Schedule 19, largely the work of Quartermaster General Yuri N. Danilov (1866–1937), followed. Reflecting both improvements in the Russian forces and growing pressure from France for Russia to attack Germany, Schedule 19 called for a more active defense. Danilov also viewed Germany as the major danger. Stripping Russia's eastern provinces as well as western ones for manpower, Schedule 19 eventually allocated fifty-three divisions against Germany and nineteen to face Austria-Hungary. The assembly of mobilized units occurred further east than in Schedule 18.[23] Ironically, Schedule 19 came under attack from General Alekseev. He now held the position of chief of staff of the Kiev District, which became the southwest front in time of war—and saw the role of his armies, whose mission was to defeat Austria-Hungary, greatly diminished. The proponents of the concentration of forces in the Polish salient also objected to forming the newly called up units and their headquarters far to the east. And significant pressure came from the French to attack by the fifteenth day of mobilization (M+14). The French hoped such an attack would throw the German mobilization off balance and force the General Staff to divert forces earmarked to attack France to defend against the oncoming Russians. All these objections found a sympathetic response from War Minister Sukhomlinov and General Yakov Zhilinski (1853–1918), head of the General Staff from 1910 to early 1914.

Zhilinski devised a modified version of Schedule 19, with versions A and G, and the tsar approved it in 1912. The A version called for taking the offensive against Austria, the G against Germany. In the A version, the southwest front had the lion's share of strength: forty-five divisions in four armies aimed at Austria. The northern front would have two armies with twenty-nine divisions to destroy the German forces in East Prussia and to occupy it. Two additional armies would cover the approaches to St. Petersburg and guard the border from Rumania. The G version simply called for weighting the attack in East Prussia rather than against Austria. Three armies of forty-three divisions would march on Germany, with three armies of thirty-one divisions ensuring that the Austrians did not get into the Russian rear areas. The Russians expected to implement version A; the G version came into existence only if the Germans dispatched a greater than anticipated force to East Prussia. Either version of Schedule 19 was highly ambitious; what doomed both to failure was Russia's pledge to France to attack Germany within two weeks of mobilization. The Russians could simply not meet that date unless they attacked before their mobilization had finished, a risky undertaking. In the same vein, the split of forces left only 60 percent of tsarist forces, at best, arrayed against Austria-Hungary, Russia's primary foe.[24]

The Russians also overestimated how far they had come since the disastrous Russo-Japanese War. While Russia was better prepared, it still was not ready for war in 1914.[25] Its intelligence was poor, and it deployed its forces in Galicia at a great distance from the Austrians, necessitating a lengthy movement to contact that would leave its soldiers exhausted by the time they faced the enemy. Nonetheless, after initial, hesitant engagements with the Austrians, the Russians did rather well in this theater in 1914. By the end of the year, Russian forces had surrounded and besieged the huge fortress of Prezemysl and pushed their opponents from Galicia into the Carpathian mountain passes. Russia's losses were steep; what it inflicted on Austria was far worse: Austria-Hungary had lost 1.2 million, Russia slightly fewer.[26] In East Prussia, the Germans defeated the invading Russian armies piecemeal. The invading Russian Second Army was annihilated; the First, mauled, retreated east back into Russia.

Without an eastern strategy, most of the German energy went into pulling their ally Austria-Hungary's chestnuts from the fire time and again. A German-led breakthrough at Gorlice-Tarnow in May of 1915, aimed at relieving pressure on the Austrian forces who had been pushed into the Carpathians, led to an unexpected rout, and initiated what the Russians called the Long Retreat, which by the end of the year left Germany and Austria-Hungary masters of Poland and the western half of Courland. Here, the Germans advanced to Riga and the Düna River, where the Russians held, blocking the way further north toward Petrograd. Nineteen sixteen proved to be the Russians' year: the surprise Brusilov Offensive, albeit at huge cost, pushed the Austrians back once again into the Carpathian passes by late 1916. Fighting shifted south with Rumania's entry into the war in August; a German-Austrian force poured over the Transylvanian Alps and handily crushed and occupied Rumania in the late fall of 1916. Given their enormous commitments in the south to prop up the stumbling Austria, the German land forces made no effort in 1916 in the north to threaten Riga or the Baltic approaches to the Russian capital. They did not have the strength.

The Russian navy likewise had shown little interest in the Baltic islands before hostilities began in 1914. Of the continental powers, Russia had the least use for a navy, yet geography compelled Russia to consider naval operations in two widely separated theaters: the Baltic and Black seas. The Russo-Japanese War of 1904–1905 had already settled the issue of dominance in Russia's third theater, the Pacific Ocean, in favor of Japan. The Baltic and Black seas were inland bodies of water whose outlets were controlled by neutrals or potential foes. Both bodies of water extended deep into Russia and could not be ignored as potential avenues of approach. In the Black Sea, the Russians faced a threat from Turkey, but here they had a reasonable chance to come out ahead, given Turkey's more serious problems.[27] In the north, most of Russia's foreign trade ran through the Baltic. It had to defend a very long coastline on the Baltic, and its capital sat at its eastern end, vulnerable to naval assault. The Baltic constituted Russia's most important naval theater.

Three neutral nations located at the western entrance to the Baltic, Denmark, Norway, and Sweden, controlled entry and exit from this huge inland sea. In addition, the channels from the North Sea to the Baltic Sea were so constricted and lay so close to Germany that the Germans could interdict or even close them any time they desired.[28] The narrow entry and exit to the Baltic and its proximity to Germany effectively cut off Russia from its most important allies, France and England. The Germans cleverly sidestepped the issue of control of the entrance to the Baltic Sea by constructing a canal, the Kaiser Wilhelm or Kiel Canal, across their section of Jutland. Improvements to the canal completed in the summer of 1914 allowed them to move even their largest capital ships from the

Baltic to the North Sea or vice versa in complete safety within a matter of hours. Finally, even the formidable climate of the Baltic hampered the Russians more than the Germans. Significant sections of the northern and northeastern Baltic froze each winter, primarily the Gulfs of Bothnia, Finland, and Riga, all in Russian waters. For all intents, the winter freeze shut down the Russian navy from January to April. Only Libau (Liepaja in present day Latvia), then at the farthest extent of the Russian western frontier in Courland, largely remained ice-free all winter. It was so remote and exposed that the Russians recognized they could not hold it and planned to abandon it in the event of hostilities.[29]

The cruel hand dealt by geography to the Russians in the Baltic was immeasurably worsened when Russia lost its Baltic Fleet to the Japanese in 1905 at Tsushima. The catastrophe left both the Baltic Sea and the Russian capital sitting at its eastern end undefended, and the war had revealed shortcomings in almost every imaginable area within the Russian navy. In 1906 the Baltic Fleet consisted of only three battleships, one obsolete and two about to be. The fleet had four modern cruisers, twenty minelaying "cruisers" later converted into destroyers, and some sixty-three destroyers of various classes. It could not expect to take on the German High Sea Fleet.[30]

In the aftermath of Tsushima, major reforms should have begun, but political considerations, finances, and the tsar's reluctance to permit necessary administrative reforms made sure nothing happened with alacrity. New ship construction necessarily constituted a long-range undertaking, but the capital's defenses could not wait. In April 1906, navy minister Admiral Alexei Alexandrovich Birilev[31] created a Naval General Staff to solve strategic problems, plan for the rebuilding of the fleet, and manage mobilization. Given the preponderance of young and reformist-minded officers on the new staff, its recommendations were hardly surprising. The first strategic report of the new Naval General Staff, "On the Condition, Re-establishment, and Reorganization of the Navy," called for creating a new Baltic fleet capable of defending the Gulf of Finland and fighting the Germans. While such views found resonance in the Foreign Ministry and numerous interest groups in an excited public, there was resistance from the Army General Staff as well as a few practical-minded officers in the Admiralty.[32]

The new State Defense Council, the second of the tsar's two major innovations to integrate military direction, was charged with developing a unified strategy and dealing with just such divisions. With the tsar's uncle, Grand Duke Nicholas Nicholaevich,[33] at its head, the new council seemed well equipped for its job. Unfortunately, the grand duke, a career cavalry officer, came with some baggage. Not wanting his popular uncle to eclipse him entirely, the tsar had not allowed him a command in the Russo-Japanese War but kept him instead in St. Petersburg in command of forces in Russia. Nicholas Nicholaevich's refusal to institute a military dictatorship in the Revolution of 1905 earned him the tsarina's antipathy, as did his open hatred of Rasputin, whom, ironically, his wife had introduced to the imperial family. The grand duke surrounded himself with a group of "Young Turk" army reformers whose impatience was matched by their lack of political connections and bureaucratic skills. Without a strong personality at its head or the clear authority to provide a single vision or to set priorities for the government, the council's recommendations got lost in the din of competition from numerous agencies.

Meeting in December 1906, it operated under the assumption from the tsar's guidance given in 1905 that the Baltic Fleet would limit itself to securing the coastline, gradually rebuilding the battle squadrons only when resources permitted. Moreover, senior officers in the army saw defending the coastline as their responsibility, one that they should organize and could fulfill by dispatching troops to threatened areas. The concept of an Alfred Thayer Mahan–like navy taking command of the seas, conducting independent operations against the enemy, and above all, draining money from the land service's rebuilding program, found few supporters in the army. This did not sit well with the new navy minister, I. M. Dikov, who proposed in April 1907 a "small program" of construction that would permit the fleet to defend the Gulf of Finland and "allow a free-ranging naval force for the protection of the interests of the empire in foreign waters." Even a small naval rebuilding program had negative budgetary implications for the army. Believing that the army was more important for Russia's defense than the navy, the grand duke gave priority to restoring the army. His State Defense Council shot down the "small program."[34] However impeccable the logic of addressing army requirements first, with money in short supply, the council's recommendation to give priority to rebuilding the army was bound to sit poorly with the naval officers. Somehow, they got to the tsar. By April of 1907, Nicholas II had changed his attitude and endorsed the "small program" to build a battle squadron for the Baltic Fleet. In June, he approved plans to build two battleships, two cruisers, eighteen destroyers, seventy-two torpedo boats, and thirty-six submarines for the Baltic Fleet and four battleships for the Black Sea Fleet.[35] Faced with this untenable situation,

Grand Duke Nicholas tried to win the Council of Ministers to his side and asked them in December 1907 to resolve the impasse. The ministers instead agreed the shipbuilding program was necessary, ending the debate, and indeed, the need for the State Defense Council. The tsar removed the grand duke in 1908 and assigned him to command the St. Petersburg Military District, and in early 1909 abolished the State Defense Council.[36] The new construction program fell victim to politics, financial setbacks, and bureaucratic sluggishness. It took four years to get the small program started, and even longer to get a much larger program of construction, authorized in 1912, underway.[37]

Even had the Duma authorized construction for the Baltic Fleet in early 1907, completion was several years away, and a plan to defend the capital could not wait. In some respects, German sea power posed a more direct threat to the Russians than did the kaiser's formidable armies. While it would take the Russians longer to mobilize their land forces than the Germans, Russia had the space to buy the time to thwart an advance from East Prussia. It would take both sides several weeks to mobilize, and any German army attempting to take St. Petersburg then had to slog its way north through 800 kilometers of enemy territory. On the other hand, without any realistic naval defenses in the Baltic, a German fleet could land troops with impunity just kilometers from St. Petersburg. The Russian General Staff estimated it would take two weeks to mobilize and assemble sufficient forces near St. Petersburg capable of defending it.[38] With German ports within thirty hours of sailing time of St. Petersburg and nothing in the way to stop them, a two-week mobilization period would not save the capital.

Not all naval officers regarded an immediate building program as the solution to defending the capital region. Admiral Nikolai N. Beklemishev, the highly respected chief engineer and designer, had strongly criticized the 1906 Naval General Staff report for being impractical. He insisted the navy's primary mission was to defend against the threat of invasion from the sea. Only after meeting this requirement should the navy address engaging an enemy on the sea. In principle, accomplishing the latter mission called for command of the sea, and Beklemishev recognized that without a fleet, talk of invading the enemy's homeland was fatuous. The navy's first priority was to protect the coastline against invasion. Given the weakness of the Russian naval forces and the time it would take to procure new ships, using mines and submarines offered promise in defending a seaborne invasion.[39]

The use of minefields and submarines as a main line of defense proved anathema to the Young Turks of the Naval General Staff, but the task of defending the Gulf of Finland was immediate, and the practical-minded men won out. The Naval General Staff wrote its first plan for defending the Gulf of Finland in 1907. The staff assumed the enemy would be Germany and Sweden, both of whom would land troops on the north coast of the Gulf of Finland in order to attack in the direction of St. Petersburg. Compounding this bleak assessment, the Russians accepted as a dogma of faith that the disloyal Finns longingly awaited such an invasion as the fanfare to Finnish independence. They anticipated that the Finns would assist the invaders and sabotage the Russian efforts at defense, and they planned to introduce martial law immediately upon mobilization.[40] Neither the landings nor an advance could be prevented or halted in the western portion of the Gulf. Consequently, the chiefs of both the land and naval general staffs agreed that the main task of Russia's armed forces in this area was to defend the Gulf of Finland east of the Gogland Islands. The fleet's mission was to delay for fourteen days any enemy advances into the gulf so ground forces could mobilize and deploy to defense lines on the Kyumen River to the north of St. Petersburg and the river Narva southwest of the capital. To accomplish this mission, the Naval General Staff came up with a scheme using a combination of minefields and long-range guns that had a clearly defensive character.

If mines were set down in sufficient quantity and in a proper pattern, the probability of their detonating against enemy ships was very high. If the average width or beam of the enemy vessels was 50 feet; mines laid every 150 feet apart have a 33 percent probability of detonating against one of the ships attempting to pass through the line of mines. It would take 40 mines with a separation of 150 feet to cover a mile-wide channel. Several rows of mines, offset one behind the other, significantly raise the chances of getting a hit . With four rows of mines with 150 feet of separation, or 160 mines to cover a field a mile wide, the chances of hitting a passing vessel rise to 80 percent. Add two more rows, another 80 mines, and the probability of getting a hit becomes 90 percent. That probability assumes the ship is attempting to penetrate perpendicular to the rows of mines. If the vessel has to approach at an oblique angle, the chances of hitting a mine become greater.[41] The Baltic, and especially the Gulf of Finland, had plenty of shallows and rocky shoals, which forced vessel traffic into relatively narrow channels, making the use of mines an attractive strategy.

Upon the outbreak of war, the Russians planned for their fleet to lay mines north and south of Gogland Island. The cruisers would wait at the mouth of the gulf for the enemy fleet, and when it arrived, they would retreat to the Gogland Island position covered by their battleship squadron. Destroyers located between Helsingfors and Kotka (to the east) would lay mines and hinder the enemy flanks, as would submarines. The battleship division would engage the enemy from behind the minefields and hold for as long as possible in conjunction with coastal artillery on Gogland Island.[42] This position appears on Map 2 as numeral II.

This plan's weakness was all too obvious: it called for abandoning the two key ports of Reval and Helsingfors, which were halfway down the Gulf, and it left the main line of defense dangerously close to the capital. Worse, when tested in 1908, the plan did not work. The Baltic Fleet had too few ships, and poor use was made of them. The bright spot came with the work of the mine division commanded by Rear Admiral Nicholas Ottovich Essen (1860–1915) who sought to enlarge the role of the fleet in the defense of the capital when he became commander of the Baltic Fleet in 1908. Regarded as the ablest Russian naval officer of the First World War and one of the very few naval officers to survive the war with Japan in 1904–1905 with his reputation intact, Essen believed the Germans would not commit their best ships and the major part of their fleet to operations in the Baltic. He accordingly favored a more aggressive course of embarking on raids to mine German home waters and urged moving the defense of the gulf westward. He further planned to deter Sweden from entering the war by threatening to lay mines outside the Swedish fleet's main base of Karlskrona. If deterrence failed, his next step was to attack Karlskrona and Stockholm. These plans were too ambitious for both the Baltic Fleet (which had no modern battleships) and the Naval General Staff, which promptly rejected the plan.[43]

Essen did not give up easily. In 1910 he browbeat the Naval General Staff to add an additional layer or belt of minefields to the defense scheme. He proposed a new line of minefields and artillery much further west, running from Porkkala-Udd in present-day Finland (just west of Helsingfors) to Nargen Island (Naissaare in Estonia) just off the coast of Reval. Essen planned to start his delaying action there, holding out as long as he could before fleeing behind the background defense position centered on the Gogland Islands.[44] In 1912 delivery of new ships strengthened the fleet and allowed Essen to make his stand on the Porkkala-Udd—Reval line of minefields. This new barrier was now designated the main or central

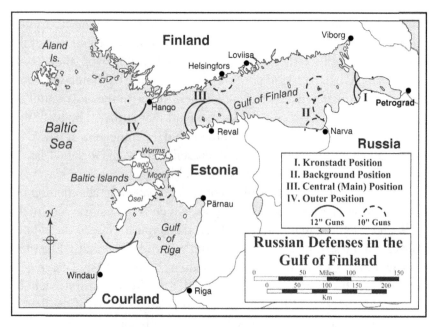

Map 2. Russian Defenses in the Gulf of Finland

defense position, and the fleet was brought forward from Kronstadt to Reval and Helsingfors. The Gulf of Finland was narrower here than on the Gogland Islands meridian, and there were more islands as well scattered about the coastline and the approaches to the harbors, facilitating the placement of shore artillery. Abandoning the Gogland Islands position also meant moving the destroyer force intended to harass the enemy fleet from the north shore of Finland east of Helsingfors. Essen moved the destroyer division far to the west behind the line of rocky islets (skerries) running from the mouth of the gulf at Hango to Helsingfors. He planned to initiate his delaying action at the mouth of the gulf by deploying his battleships and cruisers, where they would engage the Germans and retreat back behind the central position. Smaller vessels (submarines and destroyers) would dash out from behind the Finnish skerries and harass the Germans. Minelaying vessels would block the Moon Sound.[45] The Russians planned to take advantage of the narrow waters in the western end of the Gulf of Finland, which restricted the enemy's maneuverability, forcing him into vast minefields covered by coastal or naval artillery, bringing his advance to a halt. In spite of moving their main line of resistance to the west, the concept of the defense nonetheless remained unchanged, and it amounted to positional warfare. In fact, the Russians were so conservative that the navy came under the command of the army in time of war. Schedule 19 subordinated the Baltic Fleet to the high command, which placed it under the Sixth Army.[46]

On paper, the "Plan of Operations of the Naval Forces of the Baltic Sea in the Event of a European War in 1912" looked good. In reality, it left the initiative with the enemy and it suffered from material shortages. The Baltic Sea fortresses were in sad shape. The War Department (the army) had responsibility for them, and they suffered from neglect. The War Department also opposed modernizing them. The controversy naturally delayed the start of construction. Only in 1911 did work begin, and the Admiralty decided to make Reval its main naval base, designating it the "Reval Fortified Zone." In fact, what moved construction along was Essen's successful demand that the fortresses be placed under his command, which occurred in August 1912. In January 1913, the defense line from the Porkkala-Udd and Reval fortresses became the main defense position of the navy, receiving the name "Fortress of Peter the Great." The 1912 defense plan called for four 14" (356mm) guns in the Surop Islands on the north shore; at Porkkala six guns, and on Makiloto Island, six guns, all of 14" size. On the south shore of the Gulf, Vulf and Nargen islands guarding the approaches to Reval each received four 12" (305mm) guns to protect the harbor. There were also large howitzers in case the enemy broke through, and some forty-six 6" (152mm) guns were placed on the various islands to defend passages. The navy planned a new and large harbor for its battleships at Reval, but until its construction was completed, there were no large docks in either Reval or Helsingfors. Facilities did not exist in either harbor for hull work, necessitating the transfer of battleships or large cruisers to Kronstadt for major structural repairs. Construction on the fortifications and harbors was to finish no later than fall 1917, but delays developed once the war began, and the government had to authorize equipment substitutions. At Nargen and Makiloto islands, the navy authorized three 8" (203mm) batteries of four guns as substitutes for 14" and 12" guns. When war broke out in 1912, the Russians had twelve 8" (203mm) guns; four 6" (152mm) guns; twelve 7.4" (120mm) guns; and eight 75mm (2.95") guns in the central defense position. In the Finnish skerries, they had seven batteries of light artillery.[47]

Ship construction to replace the vessels lost to Japan faced delays in the Duma and in the shipyards. In fact, most of the vessels launched between 1904 and 1909 were destroyers financed through public subscriptions.[48] In December 1907, the navy initiated a design competition for the four battleships that would be assigned to the Baltic Fleet. Actual construction started in 1909 on four dreadnought battleships, borrowing heavily on Italian designs, but they were not completed until December 1914.[49] In 1911 Vice Admiral I. K. Grigorovich,[50] the navy minister, initiated a long-range building program (the short program) that was to culminate in 1920 with eight dreadnought vessels and battle cruisers, along with twenty cruisers and thirty-six *Novik*-class destroyers. The *Novik* class of destroyers was quite advanced and outclassed anything the Germans had. Embracing lessons learned from the Russo-Japanese War and named after a cruiser lost in that war, a *Novik*-class destroyer could reach 38 knots, mounted four 4" guns, and had four torpedo tubes. While political battles in the Duma saw some reductions to Grigorovich's plans, the four dreadnoughts of the *Sevastopol* class (*Sevastopol, Gangut, Poltava,* and *Petropavlovsk*) with twelve 12" guns and the *Noviks* remained earmarked for the Baltic Fleet.[51] The four dreadnoughts arrived during the war, but only fifteen of the thirty-six *Noviks* were commissioned before October 1917. Germany entered the war with nineteen modern capital ships; Russia had none.[52] It never caught up. By 1917, Germany had twenty-four modern capital ships, Russia four. Russia simply could not hope to match German ship construction, which itself attempted to maintain a ruinous 2:3 ratio to the Royal Navy.

Grigorovich also gets credit for ensuring the construction program matched policy. With the Baltic theater having priority, most of the new ships built went there. In the Black Sea, Turkey represented a minor threat, but three dreadnoughts were laid down and delivered to the Black Sea Fleet after the war began. The White Sea and the Pacific Ocean were low priority, and the only new construction they received consisted of torpedo boats.[53]

The Russian Baltic Fleet was still rebuilding when the war broke out. Most of the new craft on order did not become available until 1915–1917. The vast majority of the ships available to the fleet in 1914 were old and outmoded destroyers, torpedo boats, minesweepers, and the like. The Russians had only four available battleships, all obsolescent pre-dreadnoughts: the *Tsesarevich, Slava, Imperator Pavel I,* and *Andrei Pervozvannyi.* The four dreadnoughts delivered in the war were excellent in quality, but they came long after hostilities had commenced and were deep-draft vessels, thus of limited use in the shallows of the Gulf of Finland.

After the start of hostilities, the Russians gradually improved their defense positions once it became obvious the Germans had focused their attention on England and were not likely to force the gulf. Admiral Essen mined the waters of the open Baltic, not just Russia's coastal waters,[54] and the Russians moved their defenses westward toward the mouth of the Gulf of Finland. As early as 3 September 1914, Admiral Essen ordered the commander of the Fortress of Peter the Great (Reval) to stage submarines and destroyers in the Moon Sound region. The aids to navigation (buoys, lighthouses, markers) in the Moon and Soela sounds, turned off or removed in late July, were restored by mid-September as the Russians moved into the region en masse. They began installing coastal artillery at the north and south entrances to the Moon Sound on 22 August. Six weeks later, a battery of four 6" (152mm) guns was on Worms Island at the north entrance to the sound; four 3" (75mm) guns were emplaced on Schildau Island in the middle of the sound; and on Verder Island, at the southern end of the sound, stood a 6" battery of four guns. At the Soela Sound, the Russians began installation of a 120mm battery at the southern cape (Toffri) of Dagö Island.[55]

In 1915, The Russian headquarters in the field, Stavka, reaffirmed the Baltic Fleet's mission to defend the capital and added a requirement to keep the Germans out of the Gulf of Riga. That summer, teams installed two batteries, five 10" guns and four 6" guns, on the south end of Moon Island at Woi. On the mainland, a section of two 75mm guns was emplaced in Rogokyul, a new forward base on the coast just below Hapsal. Work began to dredge the Moon Sound to a depth of 28 feet, which would allow transit of the pre-dreadnought battleships. The Baltic Fleet also allocated three battalions of naval infantry, a squadron of cavalry, and two field artillery batteries to defend the Baltic Islands archipelago. Three infantry battalions went to Ösel: one at the Sworbe Peninsula, the other to the Soela Sound, and the third battalion kept in reserve near Arensburg. The cavalry went to Dagö.[56]

As German entry into the Gulf of Finland began to appear increasingly remote, in 1916 the Baltic Fleet was removed from the army's control. From the onset of hostilities it had come under the Sixth Army, the one responsible for safeguarding the capital. The fleet now came under control of the Naval General Staff. Nonetheless, its mission of denying the enemy passage down the Gulf of Finland beyond the Porkkala-Udd—Reval line remained unchanged. In 1916, the Naval General Staff established an advanced or outer position at the mouth of the Gulf of Finland, anchored on long-range coastal artillery batteries located on Dagö Island and Odensholm Island (Osmussar Island in Estonia) at the south side of the mouth of the Gulf of Finland and Hango and Abo in extreme southwest Finland on the north side of the gulf.[57] They laid more than two thousand mines across the mouth of the gulf and established a base at Kuivast on the east side of Moon Island. Further reinforcements to the region came with the assignment of an artillery division from Reval with six batteries of 6" (152mm) guns and emplacement of long-range 12" guns at Zerel on the Sworbe Peninsula on Ösel Island in 1916. Four 12" guns went in on Cape Takhona on Dagö Island at the same time.[58] When the ice melted in the spring of 1916, minelayers laid six thousand mines in the Irbe Strait. In late 1916, the navy designated the Baltic Island archipelago a "Fortified Position."

All in all, the Russians by early 1917 had established a matrix of positions in the Gulf of Finland characteristic of Russian land defenses. Three layers of minefields covered by coastal batteries formed a formidable barrier behind which their ships could operate, offsetting the German numerical advantage in ships. They also began dredging the Moon Sound between Moon Island and the Estonian mainland to enable their larger ships to use the passage. By 1917, the sound was dredged to a depth of 30 feet, and the pre-dreadnoughts *Slava* and *Tsesarevich* could use the sound, avoiding the hazardous night passage through the Irbe Straits under German fire from the Courland Peninsula.[59]

Summarizing, the Russian naval outer defense position lay at the mouth of the Gulf of Finland. A minefield ran from just north of Dagö Island to Hango in Finland. Long-range coastal artillery (12") at Toffri on the north cape of Dagö Island, facing north, and Abo Island on the north side of the Gulf, facing south, protected the direct approaches to the Gulf of Finland from the Baltic Sea. Entrance into the Gulf of Finland from the south through the Gulf of Riga likewise was blocked by mines and artillery. A fort at Zerel on the southwest tip of Ösel with 12" guns covered the formidable minefields of the Irbe Straits on the west entrance to the Gulf of Riga. The Moon Sound, which ran along the eastern side of the Gulf of Riga between the Estonian coast and the Baltic Islands, was narrow, demanded tricky navigation, and was covered by Russian land batteries ranging from 120mm to 250mm along with mines. The dredging of the Moon Sound in 1916 allowed the Russians an escape should the Germans block the western entrance to the Gulf at the Irbe Straits. Unfortunately, the outbreak of the Revolution in 1917 halted progress on the dredging of the sound at a 9-meter depth. Battleships of the *Sebastopol* class could not pass.[60]

The central defensive position ran across the Gulf of Finland from Helsingfors to Reval. Minefields and coastal batteries located on Nargen

and Vulf islands near Reval and Sveaborg islands on the Finland side constituted the central position. The Baltic Fleet kept its heavy ships in Helsingfors. Smaller ships used in the Gulf of Riga routinely rotated between
Reval and Kuivast. Fighting a qualitatively and quantitatively superior force
from behind defensive positions made sense; it also made for an inherently
conservative defense that took no risks. The Russians rarely left the Gulf of
Finland, and for the most part surrendered control of the Baltic to the Germans.[61] To cite naval historian Paul Halpern, the Russians adopted "a form
of naval trench warfare, with the ships sheltering behind the minefields and
coordinating their fire with the powerful coastal batteries."[62]

RUSSIAN STRATEGY, 1917

In spite of huge losses in 1916, the Russians participated in the Allied war
planning at Chantilly in November 1916 and committed to joining the
Allied 1917 Spring Offensive. Overall, the Allies felt their chances in 1917
were favorable. There were two worrisome unknowns: the continuance of
Russia in the war and the role of the United States. Given these unknowns,
it made sense to try for victory as long as Russia was capable of fighting.
That called for an offensive to which all parties could contribute. To that
effect, the Allies decided at Chantilly to be ready for action in mid-Febru-
ary. General Robert Nivelle (1856–1924) replaced General Joseph Joffre as
chief of the General Staff of the French army. Fresh from a series of successful counterattacks at Verdun, Nivelle adopted part of Joffre's concept
of a joint spring offensive with the English on the western front, supported
by Allied attacks elsewhere.[63] In follow-up to the Chantilly conference, a
large Allied delegation arrived in Petrograd in February 1917 for six weeks
to assess the situation, bolster the Russians, and develop plans for the spring
offensive. The Russian war minister General Belyaev told the delegation in
early February that his country planned to resume the offensive all along
the front in 1917 when weather permitted. General Gourko, chief of the
General Staff, flatly stated Russia could not mount a major offensive until
it raised sixty new divisions.[64] The members of the delegation were skepti-
cal; they left disturbed and not terribly sanguine about Russia's chances.[65]
Indeed, just how well the Russians could have delivered on a series of
offensives is not sure, as they had major problems. No one knew the exact
number of men in the field, although estimates averaged 7 million. The
chiefs of staff of the fronts and armies claimed there were far fewer. Just

how many of these were combatants was a guess, as was the number of deserters, but all agreed there were many of the latter.

Notwithstanding all these problems, the Russians faced 1917 with better prospects than 1916, and the Brusilov Offensive of that year had been the sole Allied bright spot. Owing to the defeat of Rumania in December 1916, the Russian front was now much longer, but its materiel situation had improved slightly. The stocks of arms, ammunition, and equipment were greater than at any time in the war. Supplies from overseas were arriving in appreciable quantities.[66] General Alekseev stated the Petrograd sector before March 1917 was considered "completely secure."[67]

The Russians planned to join the Allied offensive in the spring, but the March Revolution thwarted those plans. Allied plans for a coordinated spring offensive to break out everywhere on the front had come apart when the Russian Revolution began in March. The turmoil in Russia caused the government repeatedly to postpone major engagements. According to General Golovine, a Stavka report in late March said, "We must point out that we are not now in a position to fulfill the obligations which we assumed at the conferences of Chantilly and Petrograd."[68] The Allies nonetheless kept the Provisional Government under extreme pressure both to remain in the war and to mount an offensive to draw off German units from the west. The Western Entente powers had launched an attack in April; a Russian one was to have occurred simultaneously but never materialized. The French attack, called the Nivelle Offensive, collapsed and mutiny broke out, convulsing half the French divisions on line, and leading to Nivelle's replacement by General Henri Pétain. While that same month saw the United States enter the war, even the most sanguine of the Allied leaders knew it would be months before a substantial number of Americans arrived; thus the pressure on Russia to draw off the Germans mounted. The Italians made their contribution in May along the Isonzo River, throwing away 130,000 men—the tenth such failure in that area. Nonetheless, the Russians could not mount any operations as the country began to slide into collapse. After the March Revolution, the Provisional Government changed commanding generals in a vast game of musical chairs. Virtually every front and army command changed three to four times in the spring and summer of 1917, demoralizing and bewildering the troops. In the first half of 1917, the only attack from the Russians came from a small effort to breakout of the Riga bridgehead in January, almost three months before the revolution. The Germans quickly counterattacked to stabilize the lines.[69]

THE RUSSIAN STRATEGIC SITUATION, SUMMER 1917

Matters disintegrated rapidly in the summer of 1917. The Provisional Government, largely due to naval and army minister Alexander Kerensky's impetus, tried to repeat the Brusilov successes of the year before. In fact, Kerensky appointed Brusilov to supreme command, and the latter promptly launched an offensive in July aimed at Lemberg and the oil fields in eastern Galicia. The Russians planned to attack on the Dniester River in what Holger Herwig called "the gambler's last throw: an offensive against Austria-Hungary and Germany designed to show the Allies that Russia was still a trustworthy ally and a Great Power, to uphold Russia's claims for war compensation at Constantinople and Warsaw, and to head off the forces of change and revolution at home."[70] The "Kerensky Offensive" failed with a hint of worse to come. Some units refused to leave their trenches; when the inevitable Austro-German counterattacks began, the Russians put up little resistance, and many refused to fight. When attacked the Russian soldier would fight to defend himself, but overall few soldiers saw the need for offensive actions, and units refused to move from their trenches. Troops ignored orders; many simply left and headed home.[71]

STRATEGIC SUMMARY, 1917

Ironically, at the beginning of the war, the Baltic Islands held little strategic value for either side, but as the conflict lengthened, the importance of the islands grew steadily greater for both parties. The adage "master of the Gulf of Riga is he who possesses Ösel and Moon"[72] summarized the situation as both parties converged in the eastern end of the Baltic Sea in late 1917. The Germans sought to take the islands, opening the Gulf of Riga to military use and capitalizing on using that newly captured city with its port and lines of communication down the Düna River. Possession of the Gulf of Riga would also threaten the right flank of the Russian northern front, forcing them to withdraw to the more defensible line of Narva–Lake Peipus, and simultaneously exposing their capital to ground and especially naval attacks. In light of the revolutionary activity in the Russian army and the erosion of morale, such a move could lead to a route and collapse, thus Russia might have to seek terms. Taking the islands might very well force the Russians to the bargaining table, or, at the minimum, place the

Germans in a favorable position to move in to the Gulf of Finland and take Petrograd the following spring. The Russians, however, had more riding on the islands than just the opening to the Gulf of Riga. If the Baltic Islands fell, the Russian outer and central defense positions in the Gulf of Finland were breached, and the land and sea routes to Petrograd lay open to the Germans. Any German advance on the islands had to be met.

CHAPTER THREE

THE DECISION TO MOUNT OPERATION ALBION

ON THE 18TH of September, 1917, at 10 PM, ten military officers boarded the train from Berlin to Königsberg. No one looked twice. In the third year of the war, uniforms were ubiquitous, especially on the trains heading east to Königsberg, one of the major transfer points to the front lines, hundreds of kilometers further east. Had one paid close attention, however, there were signs that revealed the uniqueness of this group. All but one of the officers wore navy uniforms. Common in port cities, naval officers were definitely a novelty on the rails to the eastern front. The presence of an army officer in their midst stood out as well. As a rule, by 1917 army officers looked down their noses at the navy, regarding it either as a pampered force that sat at anchor in safe and comfortable surroundings or a drain down which countless resources had gone, all to no avail.

Once on board the train, instead of staring morosely into the darkness, as was the wont of most officers returning to the front, they immediately settled into several compartments and got to work, poring over maps and tables. The army officer sat in the middle, pointing at this spot on a map or a line of tabulated data in a folder, as the train clacked across the flats of East Prussia. At Königsberg, the group switched to the line heading north to Courland, and when the train stopped at Memel, the former border crossing town with Russia, two army officers and another naval officer boarded. The latter carried a huge portmanteau of maps and diagrams, and initiated a discussion about rigging a submarine net across a bay on one of the maps. The two army officers, wearing the piping of engineer officers on their uniforms, talked about landing sites and temporary docks. Late in the afternoon, the train halted in the midst of rain and sleet at Libau, the former tsarist naval city on the west coast of Courland. A naval officer awaited them in the cold, and as they got off, they looked at him expectantly. He just shook his head, meaning no word yet, and the tired officers went to their rooms in an area marked "Special Staff" in the headquarters building of the Reconnaissance Forces of the Baltic Sea. No word from Berlin meant the kaiser had not approved Operation Albion, whose plans they had worked on during the long journey from Berlin.[1] But in fact the wheels had begun to move. The kaiser had authorized moving major elements of the High Sea Fleet from Kiel to the Baltic Sea.[2] Every indication pointed toward his approving Albion, and headquarters on both fronts labored under that assumption. Nonetheless, matters had not come this far without false starts, and until the directive was signed, there were no guarantees. Just the day before the staff left for Libau, Wilhelm had abruptly canceled the entire operation. A last-minute snag did not portend well, but until the Special Staff received a go-ahead, Albion, the ambitious plan to end the war in the east, sat stalled.

In August and September 1917 the German army faced a deteriorating situation in the western theater. The Passchendale Offensive in Belgium had begun, the Americans were coming, and the High Command knew it must face an English-French-American storm in 1918. Germany's sole chance lay in launching a preemptive offensive of its own before the Western Allies were ready.

Given the growing Allied preponderance of material and manpower, a German offensive could work only if the war in the east ended and the General Staff could send the eastern divisions to the west. Initially the signs seemed favorable. The March Revolution had paralyzed Russia, and Berlin eagerly waited for the collapse. It never came, and the Russian Provisional Government decided to remain in the war. In July and August, the Germans tried to give the tottering Provisional Government a shove, and an offensive in Galicia in late July sent the Russians fleeing. Russia still staggered, but it had not quit, and another kick shook its very foundations. On September 3rd, the Germans captured Riga, third city of the former Romanov Empire. This blow provoked an abortive military coup against the Provisional Government and set the country on the brink of civil war, and while at this point it resembled a punching bag more than a fighter, it officially remained in the war. The Germans grew desperate. They had already begun preparations for a combined offensive with Austria that they hoped would knock Italy out of the war and resuscitate the faltering Habsburg monarchy. Divisions for the Italian Offensive and the approaching storm in the west could come only from the eastern front, but Russia obstinately hung on. It had to be forced to surrender, or, at the minimum, neutralized. The Germans hoped taking the Baltic Islands, an operation named *Albion*, would accomplish that goal.

BALTIC PLANS BEFORE 1917

After the Imperial Navy called off its efforts to enter the Gulf of Riga in 1915, the commander in chief of the Baltic, Prince Henry, refused to let matters rest. In a memorandum written in February 1916, one of his subordinates, Rear Admiral Albert Hopman,[3] commander of the Baltic Reconnaissance Squadron, urged taking the islands, even if it meant temporarily moving naval infantry from Flanders.[4] The optimum timing for the operation fell sometime between 15 April and 10 May, when the melting of the ice in the Baltic Sea would permit movement into the Gulf of Riga, but before the Russians could reseed the area with mines. The Gulf of Finland and the Gulf of Riga did not ice over uniformly or simultaneously. The Gulf of Finland often froze first, then the Gulf of Riga. The opposite occurred when they thawed, with the Gulf of Riga thawing first, and within the gulf, the Irbe Straits melted before the Moon Sound did. This meant the Germans could move with impunity in the Irbe Straits and Gulf of Riga while the Russian Baltic Fleet was still icebound in Helsingfors and Reval and their smaller craft sat immobile at Kuivast in the Moon Sound.[5]

Prince Henry passed Hopman's memorandum on to the Admiralty, urging a close examination, since it proposed the means for taking the islands without calling upon the army, which was dragging its feet.[6] There is no record of the reaction to this memorandum, but it very likely went nowhere, since its author failed to come up with an answer to the obvious question: if the navy pulled its infantry units from Flanders, who would take their place?

In July of that year, Prince Henry had the commander of his reconnaissance squadron, then Rear Admiral Hugo Langemak,[7] prepare another study on seizing the islands. Apparently the prince had gotten word of an army inquiry concerning the islands.[8] Several months earlier, in March 1916, the chief of the General Staff, General Erich von Falkenhayn,[9] had asked the Admiralty if taking the Baltic Islands would guarantee mastery of the seas in the area, and if so, could the navy then guarantee the lines of communication? The Admiralty Staff responded that the communication lines could be secured by taking the islands, although one could expect occasional losses to shipping from submarines and mines. On the other hand, capturing the islands would not guarantee mastery of the Baltic. Moreover, an operation to take the islands would also require using vessels from the High Sea Fleet, something the navy preferred not to do because it would adversely affect the U-boat war. The Admiralty also said it did not want to be responsible for the operation unless the army thought it essential for support of its land operations. Von Falkenhayn wrote back on the 25th to say that the army accordingly saw no need to take the islands.[10]

Undeterred, both Prince Henry and Admiral Langemak pushed ahead with their proposal. Langemak recommended taking only the Sworbe Peninsula on Ösel and the island's nearby capital, Arensburg. He also advocated blocking the Moon Sound. He argued that these steps would force the Russians to withdraw from the island. If they lost Arensburg, he argued, they could not hold on to the rest of the island because they would have to conduct any further operations from the north and west coast of the island where the water was too shallow to come close to the island. Facilities there were poor or nonexistent, and whatever base the Russians established would be susceptible to German raids or bombardment. In addition, the roads from Moon Island to Arensburg ran close to the shoreline, where they would come under German naval gunfire. As long as Germany controlled the waters around the island, its ships could interdict the roads with gunfire. The Russians would not be able hold the island. Furthermore, said Langemak, once in German hands, the island could easily be defended. The Russians could not attack from the south, and the coast west of Cape Pamerort could easily be defended by submarines. Only the coast east of Pamerort to Moon Island would have to be watched, and that could be done with troops readily available from the units in Courland. Once Ösel was taken, Courland was no longer threatened, so the troops already stationed there could be moved to Ösel. Admiral Langemak thought he could pull off the operation to seize Sworbe and Arensburg with his existing squadron plus two battleships, three cruisers, and a large number of auxiliary vessels from the High Sea Fleet.[11] The need to reinforce the ships available to Prince Henry's Baltic forces constituted the crux of the problem, along with having to find infantry forces. Admiral Reinhard Scheer, commander of the High Sea Fleet, divided between Kiel and Germany's North Sea ports, was loath to dispatch capital ships to the Baltic, fearing that the English would discover the movement and take advantage of the weakened fleet by launching an attack to force the opening of the Baltic.

Prince Henry endorsed the report enthusiastically, but made some important modifications, including expanding the operation. He argued that the undertaking needed only the two battleships from the High Sea Fleet, but more importantly, unless Moon Island were taken, the Russians could continue using the northern route (the Moon Sound) to enter and exit the Gulf of Riga. He advocated taking all of Ösel and Moon islands, and then added Dagö Island for good measure, solely to threaten the Russians from the mouth of the Gulf of Finland. Prince Henry then made reference to the March inquiry from the army, insisting erroneously that the army had offered to provide soldiers for the operation. Of course von Falkenhayn had never offered any units. Such an offer was impossible because the Russians had tied up the Germans with the Lake Narocz Offensive on the eastern front, and in the west, Verdun was raging. Von Falkenhayn was not going to send divisions east. He had none. The Admiralty rejected Prince Henry's plans summarily, stating that the army was simply not going to provide the necessary soldiers; without them, the operation was dead in the water.[12]

1917—PLANNING REOPENED

Spurred by the revolution and the tsar's abdication in March 1917, the German High Command reassessed the situation in the east. The initial reaction was to wait and see if the amazing events in Petrograd would lead to Russia's collapse or withdrawal from the war.[13] At the same time, the German forces in the west were in the midst of a tricky withdrawal behind their new Siegfried Line, and a month later they had to cope with huge Entente offensives at Arras and the Chemin des Dames. By the end of April, the High Command felt it had weathered the immediate crisis in the west. It became clear, however, that although revolutionary activity continued to convulse Russia and had seriously reduced its military effectiveness, it intended to remain in the war. The army now could no longer hope to wait the Russians out. The Germans also discovered in late March that the new Austrian emperor Karl had secretly tried his hand at negotiating peace with France at Germany's expense.[14] Berlin knew the Austro-Hungarian army had suffered staggering losses, but the Germans thought their ally was quick to cry wolf. The exposure of Karl's inept diplomacy had to give the High Command jitters over Austria's ability or willingness to persevere in the war for much longer. Forcing Russia out of the war would relieve the pressure on Austria-Hungary.

On the 15th of May, 1917, Major Georg Wetzell (1869–1947), the operations officer of the High Command, met with his navy counterpart, the new chief of the Operations Section of the Naval Staff, Rear Admiral Walter Freiherr von Keyserlingk (1869–1946). Von Keyserlingk had just moved to this position from the High Sea Fleet, where he had commanded the battleship *Kaiser* during the Battle of Jutland in 1916 and had been acting second-in-command of the Fourth Battle Squadron for most of the spring of 1917. In addition to his fleet experience, he had served in 1906–1907 on the General Staff in its deployment section, experience that was to prove invaluable. Finally, von Keyserlingk belonged to Admiral Reinhard Scheer's inner circle. Scheer, who commanded the High Sea Fleet, had grown increasingly critical of the Admiralty's leadership, or, in his mind, its lack of leadership. Scheer chafed at Berlin's hesitancy to send his fleet to sea to take on the Royal Navy. Von Keyserlingk's appointment in such a key position became the first step in placing Sheer's followers, and ultimately the admiral himself, in control of the Admiralty.

Wetzell was relatively new to his job as well. A taciturn General Staff Corps officer serving in the Fifth Army as an operations officer, Wetzell had impressed Ludendorff when the latter visited the hellhole of Verdun. Ludendorff moved him in December 1916 to the same position on his staff, which he held until the fall of 1918. Wetzell's main claim to fame came from planning the Caporetto campaign of October 1917, which knocked Italy out of the war for a year. The two officers met in Bad Kreuznach, where the High Command had established its headquarters. Based on the notes von Keyserlingk brought to the meeting, one can deduce that Wetzell had advised him a few days earlier that the army might be able to find troops for a landing on the Baltic Islands and inquired if the navy could help. Undoubtedly the admiral gasped in surprise. After all, the navy had promoted this operation since 1915, to no avail. Von Keyserlingk brought with him a document entitled "Considerations about Exercising Military Pressure on Russia to be Accomplished by an Assault on Ösel,"[15] in which he had written out the steps the navy needed to take, along with the likely number of ships necessary to ensure the operation's success. The admiral agreed that the strategic reasons for the operation were quite sound. The shock of losing Ösel Island, the key to the Russian's forward defense line, might just cause the collapse of military resistance and then the government. Failing that, the navy would have Ösel as a future staging base for attacks toward either Reval or Petrograd or both.[16]

Von Keyserlingk mentioned he had to have adequate lead time to procure steamers for moving the soldiers and their equipment to the island, but his strongest reservation came from fears that the operation might somehow deflect support from the crucial submarine campaign against the Allies. Nonetheless, there must have been mutual interest or agreement, for the next day von Keyserlingk and Wetzell were joined by Admiral Henning von Holtzendorff, chief of the Admiralty Staff, and General Erich Ludendorff, quartermaster general of the High Command. Von Holtzendorff (1853–1919) was under pressure. He had been recalled from forced retirement in 1915 and appointed to head the Admiralty Staff. A striking figure with an enormous snow-white beard, he had clashed with Admiral Tirpitz in 1913 over the latter's building program. After coming from retirement, he became a convert to Tirpitz's calls for unrestricted submarine warfare. Criticism was also mounting that the fleet was ill-used, or worse, not used at all.[17] Prior to the war, all parties had expected a Trafalgar-like battle pitting England's Grand Fleet against the upstart German High Sea Fleet. The one engagement off the coast of Denmark (the Battle of Jutland in 1916) that led to the clash of both fleets had been disappointingly inconclusive. The public clamored for action. National treasuries had not been emptied in order to have vessels sit at anchor. Von Holtzendorff knew this, of course, because he overheard the mutterings within his officer corps over their inaction. Despite the rather spectacular number of sinkings to date in the recently reopened unrestricted submarine campaign, the admiral also knew that the Allies showed no signs of cracking, nor had the supply of men and materiel moving across the ocean to the front slowed.

At this meeting von Holtzendorff offered to move forces from the High Sea Fleet into the Baltic, but only if the potential reward was substantial, and as examples he cited the collapse of Russia or the seizure of Ösel Island. Furthermore, any operation would have to be weighed against the impact on the U-boat campaign, his top priority. Ludendorff concurred, reassuring the admiral that the army did not want to weaken the submarine campaign. Von Holtzendorff said he would conduct a feasibility study about the prospect of the landings and review the planning data with Prince Henry, along with ascertaining what naval assets might have to be pulled from the North Sea theater to support the operation. In turn, von Holtzendorff wanted to know if the army would provide one or two divisions. Ludendorff refused to commit the army to the operation. He replied that from the army's perspective, "this is only a contingency plan; its practical execution does not come into play." He did leave a door open, however, noting that Russian resistance was weakening.[18]

Nothing came from this meeting. Apparently Ludendorff's reluctance to assign actual army units to the operation stopped everything. The next meeting between the army and navy to discuss a joint operation did not come until August 14. The reason for the delay between May and August is not known, but in all likelihood having to respond to the Kerensky Offensive in early July set back the German timetable. The Germans had then responded with an offensive of their own that had surprising results, virtually clearing the Russians from Galicia and the Bukovina. The success may well have led the Germans to pause, hoping this might be the end for Russia. In addition, physical conditions slowed the Germans. Destruction in the Russian rear area had severely hampered the German advance.[19] In the same vein, when the July Days erupted in Petrograd, leading to the resignation of Prince Lvov and Kerensky's takeover of the Provisional Government, the Germans once again did little, hoping the Russians would withdraw from the war. Little fighting went on, but Russia nominally remained in the war.

In any event, Wetzell and von Keyserlingk again met in Bad Kreuznach on the 14th of August. Before the meeting, Ludendorff had called his former operations officer, Colonel Max Hoffmann, now filling Ludendorff's prior position, chief of staff of the supreme commander in chief, east, to ask his views about operations in the Riga area. Ludendorff told Hoffmann the German offensive in Galicia was grinding to a halt. Ludendorff wanted to know if Hoffmann was in favor of transferring operations north to Riga and the Baltic Islands. Hoffmann "was all for it," but of course he wanted more units, namely the six divisions the High Command had sent from the western front for the Galicia offensive.[20] The meeting in Kreuznach on the 14th seems to have been the logical follow-up with the navy to Ludendorff's call to Hoffmann. From the onset then, the campaign to take Riga incorporated a plan to seize the Baltic Islands.

Later that day, Wetzell and von Keyserlingk were joined by von Holtzendorff and Ludendorff. The notes of the meeting do not permit knowing exactly what plans lay on the table, but the army brought up the Riga-Ösel plan. When an operation bogged down, shifting the attack to another area of the front was a standard method of keeping the enemy off guard. By this time in the war, the Gulf of Riga had a greater political than military value. By the late summer, the High Command was getting nervous. The surprising Russian resurgence in the Kerensky Offensive had forced the Germans to send divisions from the west to the east, the opposite of what Ludendorff wanted. The cost of fighting in the east had gone up, not down. In this situation, the strike at the Baltic Islands and Riga took on new importance. As Admiral Scheer pointed out in his memoirs, the first German effort to enter the Gulf or Riga "was broken off at the end of August [1915], as at that time the army had no troops available to support the entrance of the Fleet into the Gulf of Riga, and no importance was attached then to the possession of the town. [In 1917,] besides the desired opportunity of confronting the enemy with the Fleet . . . the conquest . . . of the Baltic Islands, was of importance."[21] Taking the islands would secure sea lines of communication to Riga, threaten Russian naval bases in the Gulf of Finland, and provide the army a forward base of operations from which to threaten Petrograd.

Wetzell presented the navy with a major change to the plan: the army wanted to take Riga first, and if that did not cause the Russians to collapse, then taking Ösel would follow. Ludendorff wanted to know what support the navy could provide for the capture of Riga. Von Holtzendorff proved less than enthusiastic. Citing the danger from the extensive Russian minefields at the mouth of the gulf (the Irbe Straits) along with the numerous mines floating in the Gulf of Riga, the navy offered only a few aircraft and U-boats from the Baltic forces belonging to Prince Henry. Von Holtzendorff was not going to risk any of the capital ships from the High Sea Fleet for an operation that offered great uncertainty with no immediate gain for the navy. On the other hand, the admiral said that "the navy could guarantee complete support if the conquest of Ösel came first [before that of Riga]."[22] Making Ösel the top priority implied clearing the minefields in the Irbe Straits first and then the ones in the Gulf of Riga, which if Ösel fell into German hands could be accomplished without interference from the Russians. The capture of Ösel would give the navy a base for staging mine-clearing sweeps. Von Holtzendorff did not want to risk any capital ships by entering the Gulf of Riga until the mines were neutralized.

Major Wetzell demurred on taking Ösel first, adding it was simply too late as well as too difficult at this point to change the plans for the assault on Riga. He indicated that the army was satisfied with the level of naval support (the planes and submarines from Prince Henry's Baltic forces) under these conditions, and he added that the army planned to move on Ösel after Riga fell—probably around the beginning of October. Ludendorff, however, interrupted to point out that all their planning depended on the situation in the west,[23] meaning the English assault at Passchendaele which began on 31 July and had already bogged down. In other words, if the English threatened to break through in Flanders, there might not be troops for the Baltic Islands undertaking. Ludendorff was worried. In his memoirs, he said the turning back of the English offensive on the 31st of July had cost "very considerable losses in prisoners . . . and a heavy expenditure of reserves," although on the 10th of August the Germans had repulsed another assault with great loss to the enemy and little to themselves. He also said nothing regarding his concerns about the efficacy of the ongoing submarine campaign. Ludendorff was beginning to have doubts the navy would fulfill its extravagant promises.[24] When the meeting broke up, von Holtzendorff nonetheless felt sufficiently certain about the likelihood of the operation against Ösel to alert the Sea Transport Section of the Admiralty about the probability of having to form a flotilla at Windau on the coast of Courland.[25]

The army went ahead with its plans and took Riga on the 3rd of September, turning the Russian northern flank. The Russians retreated north and northeast to the Aa River line. The Germans came after them, but in a desultory manner. Unlike the Düna River at Riga, which was a formidable obstacle, where the Russians had held out for two years, the Aa presented no challenge. The Russian position could easily be forced, but to little strategic avail. The Russians would simply retreat northeast, requiring more German units to pursue them, something Ludendorff could not afford. On the other hand, the loss of the Baltic Islands and the threat to their naval defense lines in the Gulf of Finland might bring about the collapse of their war effort, especially given the revolutionary turmoil within the country. Taking the islands was a classic economy-of-force measure: a division or two would be all that was necessary, and the consequences perhaps decisive. The alternative, pushing the Russians from the Aa, would require more divisions and would likely end in a fruitless pursuit into the interior of Estonia. While the navy had all along wanted the islands, von Hindenburg in his memoirs leaves no doubt that the decision to take the islands came from the army at this time, to which the navy responded favorably with all its resources. The goal was to threaten the naval base at Reval and to place pressure on Petrograd. Ludendorff said the same: "The blow was aimed at Petrograd . . . it was bound to make an impression there."[26]

After the army entered Riga, von Holtzendorff had another meeting with the High Command in Bad Kreuznach about the Ösel undertaking—probably on the 6th of September. The navy, he said, needed twenty-five days to put together the fleet for the operation, and time was running short. He asked if the army still wanted to make a landing in the Baltic Islands. Von Holtzendorff's notes say "the High Command," which likely meant Major Wetzell, replied positively. The army also wanted the navy's assessment about the feasibility of the operation and whether or not the landing could be accomplished by the end of September.[27] Von Keyserlingk got to work at once. The next day, he called one of his assistants, wanting him to get in touch with Transport Section of the Admiralty Staff to see if shipping could be arranged to move a reinforced infantry regiment without its heavy equipment or horses to Ösel.[28]

Another meeting occurred either later that day or the next, because the admiral called his office in Berlin on the 8th with more questions and instructions about the operation. He told his staff that the next meeting for the operation would occur on the 11th, in Berlin, and officers from the High Sea Fleet; the commander in chief, Baltic; the army unit conducting the landing; the Admiralty Office; and the navy's Air Section would attend. Von Keyserlingk advised his people to keep the following parameters in mind. The army planned to use sufficient troops to eliminate the chance of failure, so the High Command had raised the strength of the landing force from a reinforced regiment to a reinforced division without its horses. The landing would take place at Tagga Bay on the north coast of Ösel or Aristent Bay on the island's west coast. The port of embarkation for the landing force would be Windau in Courland. In addition to transport vessels for the division, minesweepers to clear the Irbe Straits were needed, along with aerial photographs of the fortifications on Sworbe and elsewhere. Other considerations, said von Keyserlingk, were

1. unloading of the troops under the protection of cruisers and destroyers
2. security of troops against Russian ships coming from the northeast
3. reduction of the fortifications on Sworbe with battleships
4. ship-to-shore bombardment of area around Arensburg from the Gulf side
5. aerial attacks all over the island.[29]

THE NAVAL TASK FORCE STAFF AND THE WAR GAME

Von Keyserlingk faced two delicate tasks. First in immediacy was assembling a special staff for the operation. The staff would pick up the planning issues and war game the feasibility of the operation. The operation was going to be sizable, involving a large number of vessels of all types. The High Sea Fleet was certainly capable of conducting it, but the North Sea and west coast of Germany could not be left unguarded, nor the submarine campaign neglected. Nonetheless, substantial elements of the High Sea Fleet would be needed for the operation, and a logical step would be to assign all the planning to its experienced staff. While logical, however, it was neither politically wise nor practical. The operation was going to occur in the eastern edge of the Baltic Sea, which came under the responsibility of the commander in chief, Baltic, Prince Henry. He could not be ignored. Unfortunately, his headquarters had neither the experience nor the size nor the ships to run the operation. Nonetheless, the leaders of the High Sea Fleet could not come barging in on a senior admiral's area of responsibility and simply take over. The same held true for the Admiralty Staff. It could get away with interfering in Price Henry's area of operations, but it was not organized to conduct naval operations.[30]

Von Keyserlingk decided to form a special, ad hoc staff for the coming operation. He wanted someone on it from his office, along with representatives from the Admiralty Staff, the High Sea Fleet, and the Baltic commander's staff. Although von Keyserlingk had extensive experience, including recent service with the High Sea Fleet, he had to ask the fleet or theater commanders for nominations.[31] He asked Admiral Scheer to suggest some officers, and knowing Scheer's chief of staff, Rear Admiral Adolf von Trotha, who happened to be in Berlin, he asked his assistance as well. Von Trotha immediately bombarded the High Sea Fleet staff in Kiel with a flood of instructions, telling them in minute detail whom and what to send to Courland.[32] Scheer responded immediately as well, nominating Vice Admiral Erhardt Schmidt to command the operation and Captain Magnus von Levetzow to serve as chief of staff.[33] Von Keyserlingk eventually created a task force staff for the operation, consisting of the following officers:[34]

1. Captain Magnus von Levetzow, chief of staff;
2. Lieutenant Commander (*Korvettenkapitän*) Dietrich Meyer-Quitlingen; operations;
3. Lieutenant Commander Tegtmeyer; logistics;
4. Lieutenant Rudolf Firle; destroyers, torpedo boats, aviation;

5. Lieutenant Louis Kiep; navigation and the landings;
6. Lieutenant junior grade Christ; signals and communications;
7. Lieutenant junior grade Richard Schreiber; comptroller;
8. Lieutenant Rennecke; admiral's aide de camp.

They came from all walks of the fleet. Admiral Scheer had recommended Captain von Levetzow. He was both a logical and a personal choice. Scheer had come to regard von Levetzow as an officer destined for a great future, and he included him among his favorites (like von Keyserlingk), whom he tried to place in key positions to assure a planned takeover of the Admiralty. Von Levetzow had skippered the heavy cruiser *Moltke* from 1913 to 1916, and in early 1916, when Scheer replaced Admiral von Pohl as commander of the High Sea Fleet, he "begged" to have von Levetzow as his operations officer on the fleet staff.[35] Lieutenant Commander Meyer also came from the fleet. Entering service in 1895, he was on the staff of the High Sea Fleet, the operations officer. He later went to Berlin with Scheer and von Levetzow in 1918. He too was in Scheer's inner circle.[36] Lieutenant Firle was von Keyserlingk's pick, and he enjoyed considerable fame as the officer who sank the English battleship *Goliath* at the Dardanelles. He had later fought at Jutland, and as a rising star, went to the Admiralty Staff.[37] Lieutenant Kiep was the odd one out, having no visible ties to Scheer, von Keyserlingk, or von Levetzow. He originally served on the *Ostfriesland,* a battleship assigned to the High Sea Fleet in Vice Admiral Schmidt's First Squadron, where he seems to have caught the admiral's eye.[38] The latter moved Kiep to his staff. Lieutenant Commander Tegtmeyer came from Prince Henry's staff.

The members of the Special Staff traveled to Berlin as fast as they could. On the afternoon of the 11th, von Levetzow, Firle, and Kiep met in the Admiralty Staff conference room along with Prince Henry's chief of staff, Rear Admiral Ludolf von Ußlar.[39] They discussed the operation. The army wanted to take Ösel and Moon islands. Because there were enemy fortifications at the mouth of the landing site, Tagga Bay, surprise was essential. In addition to attaining surprise, another important issue was having a landing force of such strength as to guarantee overwhelming the enemy. This meant moving a large number of people and ships at night through unmarked German and Russian minefields. The undertaking was going to be huge, and several officers had reservations about the operation. The officers from the High Sea Fleet (von Levetzow, Meyer, and Kiep) were strong advocates for the undertaking, and they persuaded their colleagues to go along with them. After much discussion, Kiep said the three of them "agreed to take on this responsibility, probably because we felt in the last analysis it would not be right for the navy, if given the opportunity for an operation this size, to say it could not do it."[40]

On Wednesday, the 12th of September, the Special Staff and officers from the Admiralty conducted a formal review of the proposed operation. The review took the form of an exercise well-known to the Germans, namely a war game (*Kriegsspiel*). The Special Staff assumed the operation was to take Ösel Island with an independent but sufficiently strong force under naval leadership facing a Russian division of 14,000 with high-quality naval support. The requirement to attain surprise posed the first major problem. This dilemma had several elements. The fleet had to clear the mines around Ösel prior to landing any troops. The Russians would detect any new minesweepers introduced into the area and discern that something was underway. The Germans nonetheless felt they could pull off the necessary mine clearing with the minesweeping assets already assigned to the Baltic commander. The Russians were used to seeing these boats; their presence in the waters around Ösel would not trigger any alarm. Once the German fleet started to assemble for movement to the island, surprise was lost. It would take three days to load and assemble the fleet off the coast of Courland, where the Russians had many spies. The Russians could not fail to detect the movement of so many ships. With luck the Russians would be uncertain about which of three likely destinations the Germans were heading to: the Aaland Islands between Sweden and Finland, Reval, or Ösel Island. Loading and assembling the fleet posed substantial risks. If the Russians reacted quickly, they could move their submarines to an area north of Libau or even run block ships into Libau harbor and render it useless. Nonetheless, these scenarios were deemed unlikely. Instead, the Russians probably would reinforce the two capital ships they had at the Moon Sound and lay more mine barriers around the island.

These last steps would not be welcome, but if they were all the Russians undertook, the German landing force could approach the coast undetected. The fortifications at the mouth of Tagga Bay were a major problem, especially if they had howitzers. In any event, capital ships would have to bombard and silence them. Next, the Germans had to secure and break out of their landing lodgment area the first day. If the army failed to break out, then artillery and machine guns would have to be landed so they could blast a way through the Russian lines, further slowing a German breakout. Meanwhile, the Russians would not be standing still. The war-game group estimated it would take the Russians at least a day to react and send reinforcements. The Russians could not arrive until the second day of the operation at the earliest, but if the Germans had failed to break out, the Russian reinforcements would appear just when the German artillery and heavy equipment was going ashore. The chaos would be fatal. The Germans could prevent such an interruption by blocking the Soela Sound so Russian ships could not get to Tagga Bay via the Kassar Wiek (Kassar Inlet) on the north of Ösel Island. To speed the landing, a senior and experienced naval officer from the Admiralty had to be in charge of every three or four of the transports. The transports were requisitioned civilian vessels, so the Admiralty Staff was expected to provide officers with extensive experience. Extra portable or ship-mounted floodlights would allow around-the-clock unloading. The final steps that the war game indicated the Germans needed to take were logical ones, namely to reinforce the harbor at Libau from any surprise Russian attack; to start daily reconnaissance flights over the islands; to bomb the heavy battery at Zerel; to start mine-clearing operations to open the Gulf of Riga by sweeping the Irbe Straits; to assign light cruisers to the escort fleet; to station light ships to facilitate navigation near Tagga Bay; and to bring a seaplane tender so there would be planes in the air over the landing zone. Finally, they suggested the army landing force commander sail on the flagship. After all these issues were aired, the officers concluded that the risks were acceptable.[41]

Technically, the army officers were not on the Special Staff, but they began to arrive in Berlin as the war game was unfolding. From the High Command came Major Wetzell, already well-versed in this project, although he was also balancing his time between planning for the Ösel undertaking and the upcoming Italian (Caporetto) Offensive. From Prince Leopold's headquarters, in charge of the entire eastern theater, came its chief of staff, Colonel Max Hoffmann (1869–1927). A bear of a man towering over 6'4", Hoffmann was the most knowledgeable officer in the army when it came to Russia. First in his class at the General Staff Academy, he received as a reward a half-year sabbatical in Russia to master the language, which he did. Accompanying the Japanese in the War of 1904–1905, he had seen the Russians fight, and he returned to Berlin to take charge of Russian intelligence on the General Staff. From the beginning of the war he had served only in the east. When Ludendorff went to the western front in 1916, Hoffmann took his place as chief of staff. The promotion required special arrangements, for the position called for a general officer, and Hoffmann was too junior then to promote. As a result, Colonel Hoffmann had generals working for him, indicating just how unique the army thought he was. He brought along his assistant, his operations officer, Major Friedrich Brinckmann.[42]

Also coming from the east was Captain Erich Otto Volkmann, the General Staff officer of the Forty-second Infantry Division, a division from Strassburg (Alsace), which held a section of the line on the Aa River, just northeast of Riga. Volkmann hailed from central Germany (Halle, Thuringia) and entered service in 1900 after completing gymnasium studies. As the General Staff officer, in effect, he served as chief of staff for the division. His modest rank did not reflect his real authority. After eight years of service, all lieutenants took a comprehensive examination, and the top three hundred were assigned to the Kriegsakademie (War College) in Berlin for a rigorous three-year training course in General Staff duties. About two hundred finished the course and were seconded to the General Staff Corps, a separate branch of the army. They received accelerated promotions, literally the "fast track" of the army, indicated by the fact that its members had carmine piping on their uniforms and wore bright carmine stripes on their pants, both of which also marked the uniforms of general officers. About 90 percent of the army's generals came from the General Staff Corps. Chiefs of staffs, from division through army, had their own chain of communication, and their opinions always received studied consideration. Commanders listened to their chiefs; they had all been there.[43]

The Eighth Army's operations officer, a major, had Volkmann report to him in Riga before he went to Berlin. Volkmann opened the conversation with "Pleasant or unpleasant news?"

"Pleasant. Guess."

"France?"

"No."

"Italy?"

"No. Try amphibious."

The major looked at the astonished Volkmann, and said, "Your division will work jointly with the navy to conquer Ösel. . . . Out of a hundred divisions, only one gets the toss for an amphibious operation, something unknown in this war." The major then added that the Forty-second Division would entrain at once in Riga for movement to Libau. Volkmann, on the other hand, was told to be on the morning train for Berlin to report to the War Ministry and the Admiralty.[44]

COMMAND ARRANGEMENTS

Naming the commander of the operation became the next thorny issue. Two services were involved, which suggested a joint task force with the obvious assignment of separate command responsibilities on water and land, with an admiral and general in charge respectively, but that did nothing to resolve the issue of the overall command. As far as the army was concerned, the Gulf of Riga fell within the operational boundaries of the Eighth Army; thus it became that headquarters' responsibility to determine the units and commanders to take part in the assault. The Eighth Army assigned the XXIII Reserve Corps as the senior army command element. The corps was one of the first reserve headquarters activated in the fall of 1914 to command the waves of recruits volunteering in the euphoria following the declaration of war. It saw its baptism of fire in the bloody fighting at Langemarck (First Battle of Ypres) in October–November 1914. It had recently held a sector in the west on the Chemin des Dames during the Nivelle Offensive in April 1917, then went east. The actual unit providing the forces for the landing was the Forty-second Infantry Division, originally from Strassburg.

The navy faced more complicated issues. The Baltic Islands archipelago clearly lay in the geographic area of Prince Henry, the commander in chief, Baltic. Prince Henry wanted to command the operation. The sticking point was that virtually all the major ships would have to come from the High Sea Fleet in Kiel or Wilhelmshaven. To assure a margin of safety in reducing the forts at the mouth of the Tagga Bay and to force entry into the Gulf of Riga, perhaps half of the High Sea Fleet would have to support Albion. Prince Henry had only a reconnaissance squadron assigned permanently to his command, which included a few cruisers, destroyers, mine-clearing boats, and submarines. Under the best of circumstances, stripping half the assets of the High Sea Fleet and assigning them within Prince Henry's theater under a different commander was awkward, but Prince Henry's experience in combat with so many ships was negligible. He had commanded what became the High Sea Fleet from 1906 to 1909, but at that the time it was much smaller, and he had been shunted off to the position of inspector of the navy following clashes with the powerful Admiral Tirpitz. When the war broke out, the kaiser made his brother the commander in chief, Baltic, a newly created position. Admiral Georg von Müller, the head of the Naval Cabinet, which recommended personnel assignments, balked at this one, telling the kaiser on 30 July 1914 that the

"Prince did not possess the necessary qualifications." The kaiser agreed but noted that the Baltic Sea was a backwater and tried to rectify matters by giving Henry an excellent staff. Von Müller later admitted Henry did a good job.[45] Nonetheless, backwater or not, the area belonged to Prince Henry, he wanted the job, he had performed well as Baltic commander, and he was the kaiser's brother.

Von Levetzow, Meyer, and Kiep agreed. They felt Prince Henry should be in charge since he commanded the Baltic theater. On the other hand, they wanted a forceful subordinate admiral to lead the fleet that would transport and secure the landing force, and that admiral should have "full freedom of action while standing on the bridge of his flagship."[46] The three voiced these ideas to von Keyserlingk right after the war game on the 12th as they left for Kiel and the fleet. No sooner had they arrived, however, but they were immediately recalled to Berlin for a meeting the next day, as the operation had come under fire. The Naval Cabinet had weighed in, declaring the operation too risky. Prince Henry also showed up at this meeting, and he insisted that the entire operation fall under his command. He also rejected flatly the notion of a special staff for the operation.[47]

Von Keyserlingk was livid. He thought he had put everything neatly together, and now Prince Henry threatened to throw the cart off the track. Prior to Prince Henry's visit, von Keyserlingk had prepared the order for the kaiser's signature appointing the officers of the task force staff and outlining the general command arrangements. He wanted the naval staff to be responsible for preparing the directives for the operation. The commander in chief, Baltic, would exercise theater command, while the actual execution of the operation would come under the command of the High Sea Fleet.[48] Henry's obstinacy threatened all the work to date. Von Keyserlingk fired off a memorandum that afternoon or evening to Admiral von Holtzendorff. The army, von Keyserlingk pointed out, wanted this operation, and "we agreed to it on the 11th." Prince Henry and his chief of staff, he complained, want to run this affair themselves with their own staff. This completely went against what the Admiralty believed best.

> "The operation is too important," wrote von Keyserlingk, "to experiment with a new command relationship. The Admiralty's future prestige lies on this operation. The question is simple: should the Commander-in-Chief, Baltic, place his flag on a ship and assume total responsibility for this operation in conjunction with his own staff or should the headquarters of the High Sea Fleet assume this responsibility with its own staff or a special one, relegating the Commander-in-Chief, Baltic, to a side role between this [special] command and the Admiralty?"[49]

While von Holtzendorff pondered these issues, the next morning (the 14th of September) Prince Henry went to see Admiral von Müller, head of the Naval Cabinet, where he brought up "the question of command in the Ösel operation. He expressed the greatest misgivings about the whole venture."[50] The prince then went back to the Admiralty, where he submitted a memorandum entitled "Reservations against the Ösel Undertaking," expressing his apprehensions. He voiced three major concerns: timing, the specific military situation, and the general situation. With respect to timing, the prince argued that the oncoming winter weather would hamper all aspects of the operation, but particularly mine clearing. In addition, supporting an occupation force afterward on the island would be tricky. He expressed the greatest respect for Russian mine warfare and felt that, militarily, everything worked in the enemy's favor. He mentioned—the only one to do so—Gallipoli and the lack of German experience in army-navy operations. From a wider perspective, he feared that England would get wind of their plans and try to force an entry into the Baltic, what the Germans called "Case J." He felt that waiting until spring was the best choice—that if the situation in Russia was allowed to develop further, the islands might come to Germany anyway. Rather oddly, however, at the end of his report, he grudgingly admitted that the operation might succeed, and he urged that if it were carried out, maximum force be used, no matter the cost, and insisted that Moon Sound be taken as well.[51]

Henry's memorandum stirred the waters, but worse was to come. The prince next went to his brother and expressed his misgivings about the operation.[52] This step created a major flap. As a theater commander, Prince Henry came under the Admiralty and did not have the authority, the so-called *Immediatvortrag*, to report directly to the emperor. Only three people held that prerogative in the navy: the head of the Naval Cabinet (Admiral von Müller), the state secretary in the Navy Office (Admiral Eduard von Capelle), and the chief of staff of the Admiralty (von Holtzendorff). In fact, on the 14th of September, von Holtzendorff, who had not yet seen Prince Henry's memorandum, had briefed the kaiser on the Ösel operation. The chief told the kaiser why the navy planned to land at Tagga Bay and not Arensburg. He indicated that Prince Henry's Baltic forces would handle the reconnaissance of the island and the softening up of Russian positions. Overwhelming the Russian fortifications at the mouth of Tagga Bay, added von Holtzendorff, would take stronger ships, and these could come only from the battleship squadrons of the High Sea Fleet. He also gave two reasons for entering the Gulf of Riga. The first was to interdict any Russian

naval reinforcements coming along the south side of the island. The second reason was to support with gunfire army troops advancing east across
the island, since the latter were going to land without their own artillery in
order to achieve surprise through a speedy advance. The battleships had to
follow the army's advance from the south side of the island. The waters on
the north side were too shallow for large ships. While he stressed the need
for surprise and overwhelming force, and acknowledged the extra difficulties posed by the lateness of the season, von Holtzendorff nonetheless said
he supported mounting the operation now. "How well the Russians [will]
resist and the effects of the weather this late are unknowns," he added, "but
the chaotic situation in Russia, on the verge of breakdown, helps us. There
are risks but also rewards and success reinforces our position in the area."[53]
Von Holtzendorff's notes made no mention of the command structure,
nor did he mention that there was some dissension within the navy about
the operation. As a result, when the kaiser heard from his brother later that
day that there were officers with some reservations about the operation, he
was not happy.

Meanwhile, the army grew impatient with what seemed like intermina-
ble wrangling over elementary issues. In the first combined army-navy staff
meeting on the 15th of September, Major Wetzell handed the navy staff
officers the draft of an operation order that designated the Eighth Army's
commander, Lieutenant General Oskar von Hutier, to be in charge of the
operation. Wetzell's logic was inescapable: the navy's role was to support
the army in the operation. In fact, the army had suggested the undertaking in the first place. In addition, the islands lay within the Eighth Army's
area of responsibility, and after their capture, the Eighth Army would have
to garrison them. In the draft of the operation order, both the admiral in
charge of the special task force and the general commanding the landing
forces came under von Hutier's authority. The admiral was responsible
for transporting the army to the islands and security en route; once they
were ashore, responsibility passed to the army to take and later occupy the
island.[54] The staff officers agreed to this solution. The arrangement offered
von Holtzendorff an escape from the dilemma posed by Prince Henry's
obstinacy. Von Hutier was a lieutenant general; Prince Henry an admiral.
An admiral was not going to serve under a lieutenant general. Moreover,
the supreme commander in chief of the eastern theater (Field Marshal
Prince Leopold of Bavaria) had already agreed to this arrangement; thus
Henry would not be able to get Prince Leopold named as overall commander and argue that the navy needed to match ranks by appointing an

admiral to command the special fleet. The rank issue also kept Admiral Scheer out of the picture. Later that day Wetzell prepared a letter suggesting this arrangement and had it personally signed by Field Marshal von Hindenburg, who passed it on to von Holtzendorff, who saw that it went to the kaiser.[55]

With that out of the way, all von Holtzendorff thought remained was to name a vice admiral to command the special fleet. Scheer had recommended Vice Admiral Erhardt Schmidt, commander of Battle Squadron I, on the 13th, a logical choice. Schmidt was the senior vice admiral in the navy, had been in charge of gunnery training, and had comported himself and his battleship squadron well in all the major engagements of the war. He knew the Baltic; he had led the fleet to Ösel in 1915. Supporting Scheer, Captain von Levetzow also pushed hard for Schmidt's selection. The two knew each other well from working together many years earlier.[56]

Von Holtzendorff must have breathed a sigh of relief on the 13th, thinking that all the bickering about position had finally come to an end. Then Prince Henry went to his brother. Von Holtzendorff and von Keyserlingk were summoned on the 17th to Potsdam for a meeting with the kaiser, as was Admiral von Müller from the Navy Cabinet. To everyone's horror, the emperor abruptly cancelled the operation, "declaring he had not been informed of the High Command's intentions."[57] Somehow, the astonished admirals undid the damage and convinced their sovereign that indeed the High Command and Admiralty stood unified on the undertaking. On the next day, to prove their point, they produced a joint directive for the kaiser's approval, signed personally by both Field Marshal von Hindenburg and Admiral von Holtzendorff.[58]

While von Holtzendorff wrestled with the problem of who would command the operation, the navy task force staff had started working with their army counterparts, now joined by Colonel Hoffmann from Prince Leopold's headquarters. The parties had discovered that while they fought on the same side, they spoke a different language. For example, Captain Volkmann from the Forty-second Infantry Division and the specialists in the Sea Transport Section tried to put together a loading plan. The navy wanted to load the transport vessels with an eye toward making the maximum use of the space in the ships, while Volkmann told them that the loading order should be based on the operational requirements once ashore. Confusion reigned. Volkmann claimed he was at his wit's end, given the fact that the navy refused to accede to the army's need to land certain units first. At one point they all conceded that they had reached a stalemate. The next day dawned clear, however, and they agreed to toss out everything and start from scratch. From that point, Volkmann said, things went smoothly. When he left Berlin three days later on the 18th, he felt that at least they had an outline for a loading plan, and in fact it was printed that day.[59]

That night, the 18th, filled with misgivings, the task force staff and Volkmann left for Libau. The officers departed Berlin without knowing if the emperor had approved the operation. Prince Henry's meddling had thrown a cloud over matters, and with the kaiser due to leave for a state trip to Rumania and Bulgaria the next day,[60] there was precious little time to get his authorization. The officers also understood that their highest leaders had great expectations for the operation. There was nothing in writing, but the pressure was there. Colonel Hoffmann, normally quite affable, had snapped at Volkmann during their first meeting. The morning after the captain's arrival in Berlin, Hoffmann took him to breakfast at the Hotel Adlon, one of the city's most famous and posh. All eyes were on Hoffmann's huge figure as he entered the dining room, the only colonel in the army with the oak leaves to his *Pour le Mérite*. "One knew," thought Volkmann, "that the plans of many battles on the Eastern Front had materialized from his mighty skull." Volkmann sat in a shabby field uniform and listened to the conversation around him. The two then took their coffee in an empty corner in the hallway where no one could overhear them. Hoffmann asked Volkmann if he had any reservations about the planned operation. Volkmann thought it best to keep silent, so he simply said, "the division will do what is expected of it."

Hoffmann's thick eyebrows arched and he glared at Volkmann, saying, "Little monk, little monk, you are walking a difficult path."[61] Volkmann noticed the cold glance of the colonel and felt the implied threat. "If the navy brings us safely over the sea, we'll take responsibility for the rest," he replied. "I certainly hope so," snapped the colonel; "the fighting in the East must end. The forces in the East are needed for the West. Your division has the honor to strike the last blow against Russia."[62]

Such remarks were not typical of Hoffmann, who actually had a well-earned reputation for a sense of humor, not for bludgeoning. He must have felt the pressure from the High Command to end the war. Navy Lieutenant Kiep, however, did see the famous Hoffmann wit as the group prepared to leave for the front. "Along with many of us," wrote Kiep, "Hoffmann had his reservations about the undertaking," but as the staffs prepared to head out, the colonel said, "if the operation failed, then we would spread the news through radio messages that not a single German ship had been at the Tagga Bay and that the Russians must be mistaken, just as they had done at the Doggerbank!"[63]

The task force staff, Volkmann, and the navy's liaison officers to the landing forces arrived in Libau on the 19th.[64] An anxious two days passed while von Levetzow and his colleagues waited to hear from Berlin if the kaiser had finally approved the undertaking. The Special Staff finally received the go-ahead early in the morning of the 21st of September. The kaiser had signed the directive ordering the Eighth Army to take the Baltic Islands:

> In order to control the Gulf of Riga and for the purpose of affording protection to the flank of the field forces in the east, the islands of Ösel and Moon will be captured in a joint attack by the land and naval forces; moreover, the Great [Moon] Sound will be blocked so that hostile naval forces cannot pass through it.[65]

Albion had received the green light.

CHAPTER FOUR

THE ISLANDS AND THEIR DEFENSES

GEOGRAPHY

THE LAST ICE age was not kind to the Baltic islands. Glaciers scoured the terrain, leaving it flat and largely featureless. The land was low, with the few higher elevations usually located on the north part of the islands and facing west, subsiding gently to the south and east. When Lieutenant Vesper nudged his submarine into Tagga Bay, he gazed up at the highest point on the islands, at bluffs on the west side of the bay rising some 60–75 feet above sea level. The islands were heavily forested, with breaks for small villages and the occasional meadow or individual farm. The trees were the dense mix of species expected at high latitudes, namely pines, birches, aspens, and junipers. At least half the trees were deciduous, and the leaves had turned to a pale yellow-green and were starting to drop when the Germans arrived. In the fall, the climate was cool and damp, and September and October of 1917 were uncommonly stormy. Until the temperature rose, morning mist was pervasive and persistent, severely restricting long-range visibility. Underlying the poor-quality soil were limestone and karst, which contribute to poor drainage. Consequently, the few naturally open areas were largely bogs or fens. Between the dense forests and the boggy areas, movement was restricted to roads.[1]

The main roads on the islands were mostly packed gravel and narrow. Heavy wagon loads left debilitating ruts in the rainy season, hampering trafficability. Arensburg (Kuressaare), on the south side of Ösel, was the capital of the island and the hub of its road network. The main thoroughfare on the island ran along the south shore from Arensburg to the causeway near Orrisar and then to Kuivast on Moon Island. The causeway united Ösel and Moon Islands. Built of stone around 1910, it was a meter or two above sea level and about two to three meters wide, and it permitted two-way traffic between the islands. Alongside the Arensburg-Orrisar main road was a secondary unpaved one that ran further north into the interior of the island and ended at Orrisar. Another main road ran north from Arensburg toward Cape Pamerort, the northernmost tip of the island. Just below the cape, the road split. The road branching to the left headed due north to the cape and the nearby village of Pamerort. The right junction turned into a dirt road and ran along the north coast of the island, with a view of the Kassar Wiek, a huge and shallow inlet bordered by Ösel, Dagö, and Worms islands and the Estonian mainland. This northernmost road hugged the coast, turning south at the village of St. Johannis, and it also ended in Orrisar. An important secondary road left Arensburg heading northwest to Kielkond, located midway on the island's west coast. Finally, the road to the Sworbe Peninsula ran southwest from Arensburg. The northernmost section of the peninsula where it joined the island was extremely narrow, 2 kilometers across, but it soon widened to 8 kilometers for the rest of its length. The peninsula extended some 32 kilometers from the mainland to its tip at Zerel.

Secondary roads linked the main roads. These roads were also made of packed dirt and were used mostly by farmers to move animals and wagons. Rocks abounded. Streets in Arensburg and some of the larger villages were cobblestoned, as was the road from Kielkond to the seaplane station at Papensholm.[2] Over the centuries, the islanders had gathered the large boulders and rocks from the fields and used them for construction, usually for churches and the walls that delineated fields, as in New England. Near villages, the stone walls lined the shoulders of the roads. Villages and farmers' fields tended to cluster near the main roads, especially those running from Arensburg to Orrisar. The northern and central areas of the island, west of the road to Pamerort, were empty.

From a military perspective, the topography and terrain of the island favored neither side. There were no river lines or heights presenting formidable obstacles. In only one aspect did the land favor the defenders. The density of the forests coupled with the boggy nature of the islands forced both sides, but particularly the Germans, who hoped to make good time, to restrict their movements to the roads. Well-placed Russian artillery or machine guns, taking advantage of the limited mobility of the marching infantry columns, hemmed in by dense trees, stone walls, boggy ground, and swamps, could wreak havoc on the advancing Germans.[3]

THE INHABITANTS

The thin soil on the islands made for hard living. Despite its exceeding 2,600 square kilometers in size, only fifty-five to sixty thousand people inhabited Ösel before 1914. The economy was based largely on agriculture and fishing. Herring constituted the mainstay of the population during the winter.[4] Very little money was in use, and payment in kind was common. Prices and rents were extremely low. The island's little horses enjoyed regional fame, as did its meats and cheeses. The only town of any size, and the commercial, administrative, and government center of the island, was Arensburg, with five thousand inhabitants.[5] For the most part, the remainder of the inhabitants lived in small villages of twenty houses or so, or on the countryside in individual farms. There were some 131 manors or estates left from preindustrial times on Ösel, 10 on Moon, and two dozen on Dagö.[6] The importance of serfdom to the agricultural magnates had, in fact, led to strained relations. The large landowners on the islands were mostly German in origin, dating from the Middle Ages. The same held true for the few merchants and the Lutheran clergy. This gentry class became known collectively as the Baltic Barons, while the commercial and professional classes, all ethnic Germans or Germanized Estonians, were called German Balts. Alexander von Buxhövden, who owned estates on Moon, supervised the civil administration of that island and Ösel. Because of their ties to Germany, the Baltic Barons came under suspicion during the war, and many feared for their lives and property. On Ösel, most estate owners moved from their manors to Arensburg, feeling safer in the capital than out in the countryside. The Russian government also evacuated a number of what it thought were German sympathizers to the mainland, including one of the island's four supervisors, a Baron Toll, in 1915. Another indignity for the Baltic Barons came with the closing of the island's German language newspaper, the *Arensburger Zeitung*, in 1915.[7]

The vast majority of the islanders were Estonian peasants. Relations between them and the Baltic Barons could be described by only one word: hate. Although they were on the outer edge of the empire, Russia's Baltic provinces (Estonia, Courland, and Livonia) had not proven immune to rising nationalism. Estonian nationalism was decidedly anti-German in nature. Despite two centuries of Russian rule, Baltic Barons governed the land with an iron rod. They had exploited the indigenous peoples through centuries of rule, regardless of the nominal rulers: the Brothers of the Sword, the Teutonic Knights, the Swedes, and now the Russians. Conservative and devotedly Lutheran (after the Reformation), they also controlled parishes, and later commerce and the professions. The Russian presence in Estonia was minimal, and the tsar's administrators allowed great local autonomy until the reign of Alexander III (1881–94). In return, the Baltic Germans and Barons served the tsarist system with considerable loyalty,[8] while simultaneously keeping their ethic identity and culture relatively intact.

In the late nineteenth century, as indigenous (Estonian) nationalism developed, the tsarist government of Alexander III found it expedient to channel it against the Baltic Barons. Given the centuries of ethnic exploitation and concomitant hatred, this was not hard. The harvest came during the Revolution of 1905, when agrarian and nationalist reform movements joined in violent attacks on German estates. One hundred eighty-four manors were torched in the three provinces; mobs murdered eighty-four Baltic-Germans, with many Lutheran pastors in that number. Had the violence not been associated with the nationwide 1905 Revolution, the tsarist government might have overlooked it. That revolution came close to toppling the autocracy, and it responded brutally, in Estonia alone executing 908 revolutionaries, deporting thousands to Siberia, and setting ablaze hundreds of peasant holdings. Many of the army expeditionary units carrying out these reprisals had Baltic-German officers, which certainly was not overlooked by the natives.[9]

The islanders had no use for the Russians, either. Brutal Russification drives from the previous two decades, along with excessive wartime requisitions of livestock (50% in 1915) generated antipathy. In addition, the Russians had forced about half of the males of military age to work on fortification projects, while civilians from the west and northwest of Ösel had been evacuated. Finally, soldiers stationed on the islands had a history of abusing the local populace.[10] Without a stake in the victory of either side, the natives simply stood back during the upcoming invasion; they are not mentioned once in either German or Russian accounts.

When the First World War broke out, the Baltic provinces remained loyal to the tsar. As the German armies moved into the east, many locals fled, especially from Lithuania and Latvia, emptying the countryside. While the German occupation regime on the mainland, the OBEROST, introduced many public health and infrastructure improvements, it became clear that the purpose of these was not to improve the lot of the natives but to raise productivity for German exploitation.

The March Revolution and Provisional Government changed everything. The inexorable waning of Russian authority and military discipline led both to burgeoning nationalist movements that called for regional autonomy and to a reconsideration of loyalties on the part of the German Balts. The Kerensky Government tried to harness some of the nationalist sentiment rather late in the game by creating an Estonian Regiment, but any warmth toward that regime faded when the regiment was sacrificed in its first engagement. When German forces took Riga in September 1917, German Balts began to think the unthinkable—coming home to the Reich and becoming part of the empire.[11]

THE WATERS AROUND THE ISLANDS

Unlike the topography, the hydrography of the islands clearly favored the defenders and played a significant role in military operations.[12] The islands were relatively young and still rising from the ocean floor. Consequently, most of the water surrounding the islands was shallow, restricting the passage of ships close to the shore. Approaching the archipelago from the west, shallows, shoals, and reefs extended from 2 to 8 kilometers into the Baltic. On the south side of Ösel, the shoals ran out even greater distances into the Gulf of Riga. The coastline was littered with rocks, magnifying the danger and difficulty of navigating close to the shore.

Between the mainland and Dagö, Ösel, and Moon Islands was the Kassar Wiek Inlet, running some 40 kilometers from its western entrance at the Soela Sound and its eastern end at the Moon Sound. The water in the inlet was shallow, limiting passage to destroyers and smaller craft. Battle reports from both sides frequently mentioned groundings. The Soela Sound, separating Ösel and Dagö, was slightly under 5 kilometers wide, full of rocks, and under 3 meters in depth. Neither the Russians nor the Germans attempted to navigate it at night. The Russians had not mined the Kassar Inlet, and they had left a channel through it and the Soela Sound so their torpedo boats could rapidly get to the Baltic or the western side of the Gulf of Riga. At the eastern edge of the Inlet, a chain of small islands and rocks extending southeast from Dagö compelled vessel traffic heading east to close on the north side of Moon Island. Once a ship rounded the north

side of that island, it was in the Moon Sound and fully visible to the Russian
fleet anchorage near Schildau Island. The Moon Sound had naturally deep
water (over 10 meters) only at its southern terminus. The deep water ended
just north of Schildau Island. The sound had to be dredged north from
Schildau to just west of Worms Island, with a channel running to the east
so vessels could enter Hapsal and Rogokyul on the mainland. Batteries on
Worms Island and the mainland protected both of those harbors. The lower
section of the Moon Sound likewise came under shore-based artillery fire
from Moon and Verder on the mainland. The Russians were deepening
the channel in the sound to 10 meters when the Germans invaded. Most
vessels except the largest dreadnought-type battleships could navigate the
Moon Sound, but to do so called for a skilled captain. When the cruiser
Admiral Makarov arrived from Lapvik (Finland) in the middle of the battle
of the Moon Sound, its captain would not run the sound unless accompanied by a tugboat. If he grounded his ship, he wanted to be able to pull it
off and not block the sound.[13] The dredged channel was very narrow, 70
meters wide, and it meandered to avoid rocks. Passage through it at night
was not possible.

Only on the northwest corner of Ösel Island were there places suitable
for landing a large number of troops. Three bays permitted deep-draft vessels to approach close to the shore: Filzand, Tagga, and Mustel bays. Filzand
Bay was on the west corner of Ösel, and if vessels hugged the north side of
the bay, they could sail to within 3 kilometers of land. The only suitable
place to land there, however, was occupied by a Russian seaplane station,
ruling out that approach. Tagga and Mustel bays on the northwest shore
offered the best prospects. Tagga was the wider and deeper of the two.

THE LAND DEFENSES

As the Russians extended their defenses for the Gulf of Finland further
westward during the war, they soon incorporated the Baltic Islands into
their planning and fortifications. First came long-range artillery to cover
the minefields integral to their defense schemes, then came infantry units.
The long-range coastal artillery stationed on the islands had the main role.
If the gunners did their job, German ships could not approach the islands
to discharge any troops.

The first heavy artillery came in 1915 at the south end of the Moon
Sound. The Russians installed five 10" (254mm) long-range guns at Woi,

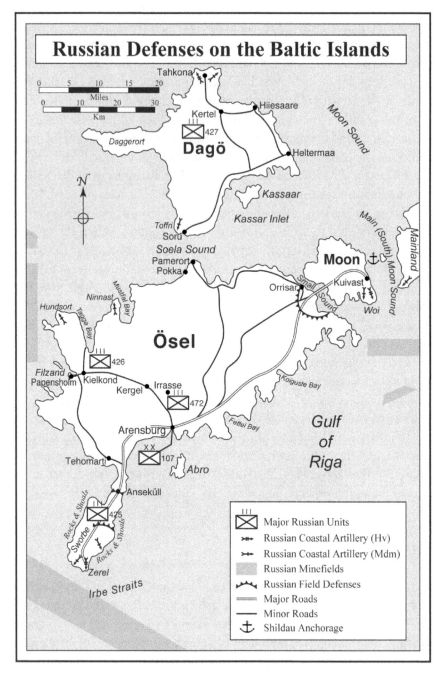

Map 3. Russian Defenses on the Baltic Islands

together with a battery of four 6" (152mm) smaller guns, designed to cover minefields. Together the mines and guns were to prevent an enemy from entering the sound. These guns were actually naval pieces, doing double duty defending the coast from shore batteries as well from Russian warships. The 10" guns on Moon were the same as guns on the older, pre-dreadnought warship the *Slava*, and they could hurl a 500-pound projectile 20 kilometers. A detachment of two 75mm naval guns went in 1915 to guard Rogokyul, where construction was underway for a forward staging base for the growing number of ships assigned to protect the Moon Sound–Irbe Straits area. After moving such a large number of vessels into the area, the navy formed them into a separate command, the Naval Forces in the Gulf of Riga. That summer, Admiral V. A. Kanin, Baltic Fleet commander, had his sailors lay 2,200 mines in the Irbe Straits and 150 more off the southern end of the Moon Sound. Following the German incursion into the Gulf in August of 1915, Kanin assigned responsibility for guarding the Irbe Straits to the Naval Forces in the Gulf of Riga. In addition, the Sixth Army commander (under whose authority the Baltic Fleet then came) approved moving the old battleship *Slava* from Reval to the Moon Sound on a permanent basis. In case of another German foray into the gulf, the *Slava* was to block entry into the Irbe Straits by adroit use of the minefields and its own firepower. In 1916, an artillery division of six 6" (152mm) guns went to Moon Island. Work began on installing four 12" (305mm) guns at Zerel on Ösel Island. Eventually this became Battery #43.[14] On each side of these huge cannons, protecting their flanks, stood batteries #40 (four 120mm guns) and #41 (four 130 mm guns). They formed the Eighth Battalion of the Artillery of the Coastal Front, a navy organization that reported directly to the Fortress of St. Peter in Reval, the headquarters of the land components of the naval defense of the Gulf of Finland. A Captain First Rank Knyupfer commanded this battalion from its onset in 1916. According to Commander Dimitri Fedotoff-White, who was at Zerel in June 1917, it was "due to [Knyupfer] whose energy and remarkable administrative qualities the Zerel batteries were constructed in such an amazingly short time"[15] A similar four-gun battery (#39) of 12" guns went in at Cape Tahkona on Dagö. The 12" guns were mounted on Russia's latest dreadnought-type battleships as well, and their maximum range with a 1,000-pound projectile was 33 kilometers.[16]

Responsibility for the defense of the Baltic archipelago lay with the navy. By late 1916, the Naval General Staff had allocated sufficient assets in the islands to call the region the "Fortified Baltic Islands Defense Position."

Its commander was Rear Admiral Dimitry Aleksandrovich Sveshnikov. Born in 1864, Sveshnikov appears to have had no special credentials for this position. He had commanded a gunboat and two cruisers prior to the war, but what he did in the war is not certain. His admiral's commission is dated 11 October 1916 and probably reflects the importance of the Baltic Islands Defense Position. His predecessor held the rank of captain first rank.[17] He reported to the commander of the Peter the Great Fortress in Reval. Sveshnikov established his headquarters at Arensburg.[18]

The main force he had at his disposal was the 107th Infantry Division. Formed in May of 1915 as a unit of the Forty-second Army Corps in the Sixth Army (then responsible for defending Petrograd), the division had four infantry regiments: the 425th (Kargopolsky), 426th (Povenetsky), 427th (Pudozhsky), and 428th (Lodoinopolsky). The names come from the Russian custom to assign the name of a city, province, or river, or occasionally an honorary colonel's name, to a regiment.[19] Located first in Reval, then Hapsal, the division saw its subordinate regiments shifted about. In 1916 the First Brigade Headquarters and the 426th Regiment went to Ösel, probably near Arensburg. Two weeks later, the 425th Regiment went to Sworbe to guard the long-range artillery units at Zerel. In November of that year, the division headquarters and the 427th Regiment moved to Hapsal, and the entire unit came under the command of Admiral Sveshnikov's newly created Baltic Islands Fortified Position. In January 1917, the division received an additional artillery brigade. An artillery brigade had six batteries, each with eight 76mm field guns, a total of forty-eight.[20] With its two brigades of artillery, the 107th Division now had ninety-six 76mm guns. At the end of February, the division headquarters and its last two regiments moved to the islands. The 427th Infantry Regiment went to Dagö; the headquarters and the 428th Infantry Regiment went to Ösel. Brigadier General Fyodor Matveevich Ivanov commanded the 107th Infantry Division, and Sveshnikov placed him in charge of the Western Defense of the island. The admiral gave him parts of the 118th Infantry Division as well. The headquarters of the division and two of its regiments, the 470th (Dankovsky) and 472nd (Massalsky), came under the 107th Division in April 1917.[21] At the time of the invasion, only one of the division's regiments, the 472nd, was on Ösel. The 470th Regiment was still on the mainland.[22]

Fyodor Matveevich Ivanov was new to the 107th Division. He became the division commander on 5 May 1917, having served over thirty years without any great distinction. After entering the army in 1884 and becoming an officer a year later, he spent the bulk of his career in the Warsaw region, his home. Ivanov was commissioned in the Twenty-fifth Reserve Infantry Regiment, later renamed the First Warsaw Fortress Infantry Battalion, clearly indicating its role as a second-line garrison unit. Ivanov slowly rose through the ranks. The fact that he neither saw service in the war with Japan nor attended the General Staff Academy seems to have slowed but not harmed his progression. In December 1909 he was promoted to colonel and took command of the Twenty-ninth (Chernigov) Infantry Regiment. The Chernigov Regiment's headquarters was Warsaw. On the eve of the war he took over the 114th (Novotorzh) Infantry Regiment, which he led until promotion to brigadier general in 1916. He commanded the brigade headquarters in the Forty-fifth Infantry Division.[23] In 1916 the division was stationed in the Reval area and was the reserve division for the northern front. Its mission was to defend the rear areas to include Reval if the enemy succeeded in landing on the eastern side of the Gulf of Riga.[24]

Consequently, General Ivanov knew the Baltic islands well. He had made a thorough reconnaissance a year before in May of 1916, just as he came aboard the Forty-fifth Division. He had been charged with making an assessment and plan for the islands' defense. He understood that their loss would compromise the Russian position in the Gulf of Riga. The Sworbe Peninsula had to be held at all cost. If it fell, the Germans could enter the gulf at will and block the southern Moon Sound entrance. Unfortunately for the general, Sworbe was not the only vulnerable place he had to concern himself about. If the Germans succeeded in landing anywhere on Ösel, they could take the Zerel batteries from behind, where they were defenseless. Ivanov identified the likely landing spots along the west and northwest coasts. Coming ashore here would greatly facilitate a rapid German advance to Sworbe. Tagga Bay came up frequently in his report, as did the Daggerort Peninsula on Dagö.[25]

With his 425th Regiment he moved to the island permanently in March–April 1917.[26] Ivanov assessed the mission given him by Sveshnikov, which was to defend the western half of Ösel, roughly west of a line running from Pamerort on the northernmost part of the island to east of the capital, Arensburg, on the south side. Based on the positioning of his units, Ivanov had concluded that a German amphibious landing constituted the greatest threat. Tagga and Mustel bays were the most likely candidates for a landing site on Ösel. Although his major task constituted the protection of the Sworbe Peninsula, he knew from his reconnaissance of the island and study of its hydrography that the Germans could not land there. The northwestern coast offered the Germans the best landing sites and protection from weather for their fleet, and Ivanov located the bulk of his division to defend that area.

General Ivanov had an infantry division with reinforcements of artillery and cavalry at his disposal. Nonetheless, he had to defend a huge area and faced an enemy who had both the initiative and the capability to conduct landings. There were several suitable places where the enemy could come ashore, and Ivanov knew he did not have sufficient forces to guard even the likely spots, let alone all of them. The Russian general recognized that a static defense aimed at holding on the beaches at the likely landing places would fail catastrophically if the Germans broke through. If they penetrated his defenses and cut his lines of communication (and retreat) to Orrisar, his division would be lost, and the Germans could then leisurely reduce the forts at Sworbe.

Instead, he decided to delay, trading space for time as he withdrew to the east while he waited for reinforcements from the mainland. This solution was his only realistic choice, and it took advantage of the one feature of the island's terrain that favored him, namely the exposed "avenues" framed by the narrow roads, dense woods, boggy terrain, and stone walls over which the Germans had to advance. He instructed his units to take advantage of their knowledge of the island's road network and terrain. The bogs and forests would make it "impossible for the enemy to advance in force between the roads." When the Germans came to a Russian position at a crossroads, they would have to halt and group their forces for a frontal assault on the Russian position. To avoid bloody losses, they would need to prepare their attack carefully, something that would take a lot of time, which is what the Russians needed in order to bring up more soldiers. Ivanov stressed holding the road junctions and the secondary crossroads that linked the main ones. These crossroads would permit the Russians to move their forces rapidly, to great advantage against the Germans. If the Russians could hold the Germans at the road junctions while moving reinforcements laterally between main roads via secondary ones, they could gradually retreat eastward toward the terminus of all the roads at the Orrisar Causeway. The key, he wrote, was to prevent, at all costs, the Germans from moving east faster than his own forces and getting to the causeway before the Russians could. Implicit in this scheme was the likelihood Ivanov would have to leave the garrison at Sworbe on its own. If the Germans broke through the Russian lines, Ivanov had to move east to the causeway. Abandoning the Sworbe defenders was not as drastic as it sounds. The narrow neck of the peninsula would offset the German numerical advantage, favoring the defenders. As long as they held out, the German fleet could not enter the gulf, and the Russian navy could supply the garrison indefinitely, allowing "General Winter" to come to the rescue.

The Russian general's method of controlling his delaying action and withdrawal was to create four phase lines, where units were to hold until permitted to withdraw further east. The first ran from Kielkond to Piddul, a village just southeast of Tagga Bay. The second line ran parallel to the first but to the east, from southwest of Kielkond northeast to the village of Kergel. The third line ran from Arensburg on the road to the village of Karris, and the final phase line from Fettel Bay (east of Arensburg) to Orrisar.[27]

To facilitate the plan, Ivanov divided his half of Ösel into three defense sectors. The first, which he assigned to Colonel Gvaita and most of his 426th (Povenetsky) Infantry Regiment, ran from Pamerort to Rotzikull, encompassing the northwest of the island. This section included the two bays (Tagga and Mustel) favorable to landings. In Tagga Bay Gvaita stationed two (of his three) battalions of infantry, two light batteries, and two machine gun teams.[28] Ivanov gave Colonel Gvaita some extra artillery, namely a brigade of four additional batteries and some engineers. The engineers came to help construct a line of fortifications running across the base of the Hundsort Peninsula. Ivanov wanted three lines of trenches and berms, running west from Kekhill (Kehila) at the bottom of Tagga Bay to Kurrifer (Kurevere) on Kielkond Bay, facing opposite Filzand Island. By sealing the base of the peninsula, Ivanov apparently hoped to thwart any landings in either Kalange Bay on the tip of Hundsort Peninsula or on the west side of Tagga Bay.[29]

The second sector was a low-threat area, judging from the number of troops assigned. The division commander placed Lieutenant Colonel Yakhimovich, commander of the Third Pogranitschnaya Border Guards cavalry, in charge, giving him two platoons of infantry from the 426th Regiment, two hundreds of his own cavalry, a medium artillery battery (100 mm), and a platoon (two guns) from the Reval Artillery Brigade.[30] While the colonel's sector ran from Rotzikull to Eri, roughly 38 kilometers (not counting the estuaries between Rotzikull and Cape Melaido), the area that had General Ivanov's closest attention ran from Cape Mukhanina (Muha nina) to Eri, a distance of about 8 kilometers. The estuaries in this sector on the northwest coast were shallow and rocky, with only Attel Bay (Atla laht) offering any possible landing site. The same held true for the west coast, and neither Attel Bay nor the coast west of Cape Mukhanina offered any protection against the prevailing westerly winds, ruling out these sites as likely landing spots.

Sector 3 comprised the Sworbe Peninsula, and Ivanov assigned the 425th (Kargopolsky) Infantry Regiment to the task. Its commander was Colonel Sherekhovsky, but by the time of the invasion, a Colonel Borsakowski had replaced him.[31] His regiment had orders to focus on the west coast of the peninsula. Combat Engineers attached to his command dug two lines of trenches across the southern tip of the peninsula. The south line ran from Yamma to Myassa (Jamaya-Massa); 3 km to the north the second line ran from Kaunispe to Otsa. Both trench lines faced north, defending against an enemy coming from that direction, heading south down the peninsula. Ivanov gave the 425th Regiment a battery of 76mm guns from the Reval Artillery Brigade, along with a 105mm battery. If the enemy failed to show in the Irbe Straits or was driven off, the Eighth Battalion of Naval Artillery, which manned the long-range gun batteries at Zerel, had orders to assist the 425th Infantry Regiment in its defense of the peninsula.[32]

The reserve force, the 428th (Lodeinopolsky) Infantry Regiment, came under the command of Colonel Charnotsky. Ivanov planned to station the regiment near Kergel (Kärla) village just off the main road running from Kielkond to Arensburg. The site was strategically chosen. It permitted the division commander to move reinforcements quickly to the 426th Regiment in Sector 1 at any of the critical locations, especially Tagga Bay. The reserve force was also in a good position to support Sector 2, which had the fewest units of any sector. General Ivanov located the headquarters and staff of the 118th Infantry Division at the Medel Manor, just to the east of the 428th Regiment, about 8 kilometers north of Arensburg. Sector 3, the Sworbe Peninsula, was the furthest from the reserve. It was not a probable landing site; thus when positioning his reserve, Ivanov gave Sector 3 little concern. He knew that if he could thwart the landings, Sworbe was in no danger. If the Germans succeeded in landing, then Sworbe was on its own for a while. He located the artillery park at Padel, about 4 kilometers south of the 428th Regiment on the Kielkond-Arensburg road. In Arensburg he formed a motor pool with some trucks and two armored cars. The general sited his field hospital at the eastern end of the island, at Peude Manor. Finally, Ivanov withheld two infantry companies and a cavalry hundred for local security duties in Arensburg, where he had his headquarters.[33]

Ivanov had developed that plan in March–April. In October, when the Germans landed, his units and their dispositions had changed. In principle, the defense plan remained the same. The main change affected the division reserve. Initially, Ivanov wanted to use his own division's 428th Infantry

Regiment as his reserve, but that regiment never seems to have made it to Ösel. Instead, Sveshnikov replaced it with Colonel Arekhov's 472nd (Masalsky) Infantry Regiment,[34] two battalions of which Ivanov placed in Sector 2, running from Rotzikull to Cape Mukhanina. These units beefed up this sector considerably. The remaining two battalions of the regiment formed the nucleus of the reserve, reinforced by the Sixth Battery of the Field Brigade of the Artillery of the Land Front of the Emperor Peter the Great Fortress, the First Battery of the 107th Artillery Division, the Fourth Hundred of the Arensburg Cavalry Frontier Division, and batteries #47, 48, and 49. The major change in stationing reserve units came with locating the two infantry regiments in Medel with the headquarters of the 118th Division as opposed to Kergel.[35]

The actual strength of the defending infantry units when the landing came is a matter of conjecture. Authorized strength was 60 officers and approximately 2,600 men per infantry regiment. On the day of the invasion, 12 October, the division commander reported slightly lower numbers: 425th Regiment—2,472 men; 426th Regiment—2,885 men; 427th Regiment (on Dagö Island)—2,435 men; and the 472nd Regiment with a further 2,435 men. The strength of the naval artillery units and the artillery reinforcements assigned to the 107th Division is not known. There were quite a few of these naval artillery units. Besides the Eighth Naval Artillery Battalion at Zerel, there were separate naval artillery battalions manning the guns at Hundsort and Ninnast, along with other battalions on Dagö and Moon islands. On Ösel, General Ivanov also had four hundreds of the Arensburg Frontier Cavalry Division, reported as 552 strong.[36]

The real question, of course, was the actual strength on the ground, which was not necessarily the same number as those reported as assigned to the unit. In units of the Imperial Army, desertion had taken a toll in 1917, and there is no reason to think the 107th Division or any of the units on the islands was an exception. In fact, Captain Reek, Sveshnikov's chief of staff, bemoaned the discrepancy between reported figures and actual ones, grumbling that the Baltic Islands Fortified Position had always suffered manpower shortfalls. Nonetheless, he cited only the 472nd Regiment for having "considerable discrepancy" in numbers. He said the unit's real number of effectives was 1,440, not the 2,435 men carried on the rolls.[37] Reek did not say where these numbers came from, nor does he complain of similar differences in the other units, so all that can be safely said is that at least one of his major units was at 60 percent strength. Complicating matters is a report from the "Paymaster" of the 425th Infantry Regiment at

Zerel, made after its surrender, in which he states the regiment had 3,500 soldiers.[38]

On Dagö, the Russians had one heavy and three medium batteries of coastal artillery, which, combined with the minefields to the west and north of the island, constituted the first line of defense. If these weapons did their job, the Germans would not get close to the island. On the northern-most point, at Cape Tahkona, sat four 12" guns, Battery #39, safeguarding both the island and the southern approach to the Gulf of Finland. Just a few kilometers to the east was Battery #38, four 6" guns (152mm) fac-ing northeast. With their counterparts in Battery #30 on Worms Island, they sealed off the northern entrance to the Moon Sound. Battery #47, located midway on the north coast of the Daggerort Peninsula, watched the western approaches to Cape Tahkona, while Battery #34, consisting of four 120mm guns sited at Cape Toffri on the southern point of Dagö, overlooked the Soela Sound. All of these units came under the Second Coastal Battalion. Standing orders called for all the naval artillery to join their land counterparts in the defense of the island once they had driven off the invading fleet, or if there were no suitable targets.[39]

The 427th Infantry Regiment was responsible for the island's land defense. Based on the allocation of resources, the commander feared the southwest side of the island constituted his Achilles' heel. He labeled the area his Middle Battle Region, running from Mardianee Estate (on Hunds Wiek Bay) to Cape Serro at the southern tip of the island, and he assigned three of his four infantry battalions to guard this region. In addition to the infantry, he added a cavalry troop, twelve extra machine guns, and a com-pany of combat engineers. On the north and northwest corner of Dagö, from the Iooranna (Joeranna) Estate on the northwest of Cape Tahkona to Kertel on the east side of the cape, an area which he called the Right Battle Region, the colonel assigned one infantry battalion, extra light artillery, six machine guns, and a few cavalrymen and engineers. In most cases, the trees grew close to the shoreline, so the engineers worked to establish a series of small roads running perpendicular from the shoreline to the main highways paralleling the coast, allowing units to deploy in the tree lines on the coast in case the Germans attempted to come ashore. Observation towers were ordered for key places on the coastline. Islanders attempted to dig several lines of trenches near likely landing spots, but the high-water table forced the construction of berms. Finally, a chain of modest hills ran along the east to west axis of the Daggerort Peninsula, widening to form two groups of hills, one in the middle of the peninsula, and the other where the peninsula joined the main part of island. In the region of the first group the Russians envisioned positions that would block the roads leading inland from the western edge of the peninsula. In the region of the second group of hills, the Russians planned a line of fortifications to crossing the neck from Luidalo Bay on the north side to Hunds Wiek Bay on the south side, which would enable them to seal off the entire Daggerort Peninsula. The regimental commander held back one infantry company for his reserve.[40]

Along with the plan for defending the two islands, Admiral Sveshnikov and General Ivanov asked for more soldiers and an extensive amount of construction and engineering effort. The plans included constructing observation posts, roadblocks, trenches, obstacles, blockhouses, and pill-boxes, clearing lanes of fire, and siting anti-aircraft guns at road junctions, but most of these fell through. A lack of money, a shortage of time and manpower, and the turmoil created by the chaotic conditions of the revolution all combined to thwart General Ivanov's best designs. In case his forces failed to repel the Germans on the shore, Ivanov wanted to hold from a line running from Fekkerort to Sakla, but "a great amount of work was needed to fortify this line, and [an] even greater amount of forces were needed to defend [it]; we had neither and did not have an opportunity to obtain either."[41] The army then proposed a line utilizing the lakes in the center of Ösel to flood certain areas, shortening the line and reducing the amount of labor and soldiers needed to prepare things. Work had not started when the Germans came. The final line, the bridgehead at the causeway terminus from Moon Island, was designed to provide an exit for the Russian forces on Ösel. Three infantry battalions and eight artillery pieces were allocated for this position, which was centered on an impassable swamp that bisected the line. It was completed at the time of the invasion. Aircraft flew from the mainland to Ösel, which had several air stations: Papensholm, Zerel, and Arensburg. The aircraft came under the direct control of the Baltic Fleet commander, a "situation [that] was completely abnormal," according to Sveshnikov's chief of staff. He complained that "the commander of the [Baltic Islands] position, one which had strategic significance, did not have authority over the only workable intelligence means for the position—aviation."[42] Matters fared no better on Dagö. Locating the defense lines was never resolved, and construction accordingly never began.

Sveshnikov asserted that he had insufficient forces to defend the islands. On March 18th, he wrote the naval staff asking for more forces. He stated that he could not defend the islands without the return of the 428th Infantry Regiment. He demanded additional field artillery and supplies, especially grenades, saying his soldiers had none. He asked for more reserves as well, but indicated the best place for them was Hapsal on the mainland. The naval staff was sympathetic and arranged for the return of the 428th Regiment. In addition, they got the army to pledge two additional regiments (the 470th and 472nd), more artillery, and a brigade of infantry to form a reserve. Unfortunately, this state of affairs did not last long, and Stavka countermanded the return of the 428th Infantry Regiment, while the 470th Regiment remained on the mainland in a state of disarray. Even had 470th been battle-ready, Stavka had no plans to send it and turned down an additional request for cavalry as well.[43] What made matters worse was the fact that Sveshnikov had to use his soldiers for construction projects because he could not hire sufficient numbers of civilian laborers. This state of affairs virtually put an end to any effort to conduct training. Adding insult to injury, the Provisional Government required the army to pay soldiers engaged in construction the going rate of civilian workers, but the government did not have enough money to pay all of Sveshnikov's laborer-soldiers. As he reported, some got paid and some did not; the product was discontent.[44]

THE SEA DEFENSES

Defending the islands from the sea and the waters around them lay in the hands of two admirals, Alexander Vladimirovich Razvozov and Mikhail Koronatovich Bakhirev. Razvozov was a mine warfare and destroyer specialist who had served with distinction in the Pacific Squadron at Port Arthur in the Russo-Japanese War. A captain second rank in 1914, he served the first two years of the war mainly in charge of destroyer squadrons (the Second, Fifth, and Ninth), and was promoted to captain first rank in late 1915. He was in charge of the Baltic Islands defense when naval minister Alexander Kerensky selected him in July 1917 to command the Baltic Fleet, with promotion to rear admiral. A junior captain, he jumped over half the captains in the Russian navy with his promotion to flag rank.[45] Although he was very young (thirty-eight), "officers and men, all alike, were glad . . . because he seemed like the right man in the right place in those troubled times. . . . [He] knew how to influence the crews, and even demagogues from different committees and soviets."[46]

As commander in chief of the Baltic Fleet, Razvozov had official responsibilities that covered the entire Baltic, but in reality, his major concerns were defending the gulfs of Riga and Finland. His fleet came under the operational control of the army's northern front, charged with defending all the approaches to the capital in Petrograd.

Razvozov wanted Mikhail Bakhirev to take charge of protecting the waters around the Baltic Islands. On the surface, getting Bakhirev to come on board looked formidable. For starters, he far outranked Razvozov. In fact, he was a vice admiral and the senior officer in the Russian navy in the summer of 1917. The disparity in rank was quickly overcome with surprising ease. First, Bakhirev wanted to fight, and the two ignored any issues arising from seniority and rank. Bakhirev had an impressive combat record dating back to the Russo-Japanese War, and in December 1914 he earned his admiral's flag following a successful cruiser engagement with the Germans. He had commanded the cruiser and battleship brigades of the Baltic Fleet, and was currently in charge of the mine defenses of the Baltic Sea. Second, the junior admiral in the Baltic Fleet had the responsibility of defending the Baltic Islands. Anticipating the German invasion, Razvozov knew he would have to reinforce that region, and he had a concern that if admirals from his cruiser or destroyer divisions arrived with reinforcements, they would be reluctant to work under an admiral junior in rank to them. To get around this problem, he asked Bakhirev if he would wear "both hats," namely his current one in charge of mine defenses along with taking on responsibility for the Baltic Islands defenses. Bakhirev agreed, and Razvozov issued the orders on the 2nd of August.[47]

What proved more difficult to overcome was Kerensky's lack of enthusiasm for Bakhirev,[48] but Razvozov pulled it off. Kerensky had once considered naming Bakhirev to head the Baltic Fleet but found his uncompromising devotion to the monarchy unacceptable. Bakhirev's attitude had surfaced when Admiral Nepenin, the commander of the Baltic Fleet, had declared his support for the Provisional Government following the tsar's abdication. Bakhirev balked, expressing reservations about serving the revolutionaries of the Provisional Government. He told Nepenin, "today they will demand that power should go to the Tsarevich, tomorrow they will no longer content themselves with this and will claim a republic, and after tomorrow they will bring Russia to ruin." Nepenin appealed to Bakhirev's patriotism and wrung a concession to "remain, but only until the end of the war."[49] Equally unappealing to the puritanical regime, Bakhirev's private life teetered on the scandalous, for he drank hard and occasionally appeared in public with women of dubious reputation. In spite of these faults, both Admiral Razvozov and his colleagues recognized that he "was a sailor to the marrow of his bones." One of his subordinates wrote, "who in the Navy did not know . . . [him], who did not love him and did not look upon him with the greatest respect! Always even, calm, self-possessed, in the moments of danger he never lost his presence of mind and was always irreproachably brave."[50]

To defend the islands, Bakhirev had at his command two pre-dread-noughts, the *Slava* and the *Graschdanin* (formerly the *Tsesarevich*), built in 1903 and 1905 respectively. The *Slava* had its main guns replaced during the war, and to universal astonishment, they could outrange the latest German dreadnoughts. In addition, Bakhirev had two cruisers (two more arrived during the battle), three older gunboats, twelve first-rate *Novik*-class destroyers, and fourteen older destroyers, along with a dozen torpedo boats and a large number of minesweepers and some steamers. He also had three British submarines.[51] The majority of Bakhirev's ships were based at Kuivast on Moon Island, and all his deep draft vessels anchored at Schildau Island, about 3 kilometers north of Kuivast in the sound. The torpedo boats and smaller craft could also use Hapsal and Rogokyul on the mainland, along with a pier at Sworbe and the harbor mole at Arensburg.

Integral to the Russian defenses were the heavy land-based guns on the Sworbe (Zerel) Peninsula on Ösel, at Cape Tahkona on Dagö, and at Woi on Moon Island at the south entrance to its sound. These positions, along with many others employing smaller artillery, were carefully sited to take advantage of the many reefs and shallows around the islands. In the waters surrounding these emplacements were minefields, which kept German battleships from drawing close enough to reduce the Russian forts. The land-based artillery could shoot further than the ships' guns. German efforts to sweep the fields, thus allowing their ships to close in, all failed, as the smaller vessels inevitably had to withdraw under the hail of heavy Russian gunfire. In 1916, the obsolete *Slava* by itself, hiding behind the minefields at Sworbe, had held off Admiral Schmidt's superior fleet of five battleships and eight cruisers for several days.[52]

What Bakhirev could not count upon, despite having to face a far larger German fleet, was much help from Admiral Razvozov and the Baltic Fleet. Two factors tied Razvozov's hands. First was his mission to ensure that the enemy did not enter the Gulf of Finland, which necessitated keeping the bulk of his ships near the gulf's central or main defense position. Second, none of his capital ships could navigate the Moon Sound. They drew too much water.[53]

REVOLUTIONARY RUSSIA AND MILITARY COLLAPSE

There can be no question that the war was both a cause and a catalyst in the March 1917 riots in Petrograd, which led to the toppling of the Romanov dynasty and the demise of the tsarist government. The sufferings, privations, and reverses during the three years of the war had exposed the deficiencies of the government. The ultimate justification of monarchism, to provide military leadership from its elites, had come up visibly short. While all the military monarchies failed and paid the ultimate price, Russia was the first.

The signs of discontent had appeared long before the Petrograd riots of March 1917. Army morale plummeted in the late fall of 1916, in spite of an improved materiel situation. The average soldier knew all too well the real costs of the successful Brusilov Offensive, and war weariness pervaded the ranks. Several mass mutinies occurred in the army in late 1916, but all of these focused on purely military matters such as orders for attacks seen as suicidal by the soldiers. Officers were disobeyed but not murdered; their control of military matters was not questioned.[54]

In the fleet, discontent was equally manifest. Winter months were inactive ones, owing to the freezing of the eastern Baltic Sea. The ships literally froze into the ice for three to four months, and the numbing cold reduced everything to a state of torpor. With the fleet largely at anchor at Helsingfors and Reval, and a few vessels in repair at Kronstadt, sailors had time on their hands. Stavka's strategy of protecting Petrograd from behind a series of defense lines in the Gulf of Finland also ensured that summer was as stagnant as winter. Fearful of losing an engagement to the larger German fleet and thus opening the capital to invasion, the much smaller Russian fleet made no significant effort to confront the Germans on the high seas. Thus, for most of the war, the bulk of the Baltic Fleet sat at anchor. Morale consequently plummeted, resentment festered, and the ships' officers used "make work" projects to keep their sailors busy. The goal was to prevent further disturbances like the mutiny that had taken place on the new dreadnought *Gangut* in 1915, largely as a result, it was believed, of the crew not having enough to do.[55] The newly appointed (September 1916) fleet commander in chief, Vice Admiral Nepenin, known as a martinet, planned to deal with these issues by waging a more active campaign in 1917. With his ships frozen in, however, he could not move until April, and during the winter months the involuntary service, poor morale, low pay, and hostile officer-enlisted relations grew into a volatile combination awaiting a spark.

The spark came in the form of the March Revolution. This time more than a refusal to obey orders was at stake. Indeed, the garrison soldiers in Petrograd turned on their officers and murdered many. Neither civil nor military authorities could contain the conflagration, and within a few days, the three-hundred-year-old Romanov dynasty was gone. In some areas of the front, and in the Baltic Fleet, military authorities unwisely sought to withhold notice of the tsar's abdication, pending resolution of the crucial question of the emperor's successor. An event of this magnitude could not remain under wraps,[56] and once word leaked out, sailors and soldiers, believing their superiors were deliberately concealing political news in the hopes of reversing it with military measures, revolted and murdered scores of officers. From Helsingfors on the 17th of March, Baltic Fleet commander Admiral Nepenin telegraphed that mutinies had broken out in the battleship brigade, and "the Baltic Fleet as a fighting force no longer exists." Mutineers murdered more than fifty officers and petty officers that night, as sailors ran across the ice from vessel to vessel, hunting down officers. A sailor killed Nepenin the next day.[57]

The political machinations leading from the March Revolution to the Bolshevik coup in November 1917 lie outside the scope of this work. What is of concern, however, is the effect of the imposition of revolutionary democracy within the armed forces and on military operations, especially in the Baltic Fleet and the units on the Baltic Islands. The new government, the old officers, and the newly elected officers tried to initiate democratic reforms from above, while ship committees and soviets, called into existence by the Petrograd Council (Soviet) of Workers and Soldiers Deputies' famous Order Number One, sought guarantees against counter-revolutionary backsliding while instituting further reforms from below.[58] Clashes inevitably followed.

Copies of Order Number One, calling for the formation of unit and ship committees, appeared at the Baltic Fleet and the northern front within four days of its publication, and almost immediately thereafter it reached the other fronts. The senior officers, who grasped its implications, were stunned. "Cursed be the man who conjured up this abomination," wrote General A. I. Verkhovsky, a future war minister and Red Army commander. Even though the Provisional Government managed quickly to disseminate the important proviso that Order Number One was limited to the Petrograd garrison area, soldiers and sailors everywhere imbibed the spirit of the order with respect to a loosening of discipline.[59]

The Provisional Government and Stavka cautiously moved in the same direction, making unit and ship committees official and authorizing elected disciplinary courts.[60] The committees received authority to supervise distribution of supplies and to regulate matters of accommodations and feeding. When Alexander Kerensky took over the army and navy portfolios in May, he continued these efforts. His Declaration of Servicemen's Rights recognized full civil and political rights for servicemen and ended saluting. Other orders allowed the elected ships' committees to determine and administer punishments for disciplinary infractions. The committees also administered meals and public funds and supervised finances and supply, while a joint committee of officers and soldiers or sailors oversaw work details and recommended promotions and leave policies. Naval officers still operated the ships; army officers continued to direct ground operations.[61]

Over the next several months, the sailors of the Baltic Fleet gradually grew more politicized. Soviets appeared in the harbor and shore installations, and ships' committees developed in the fleet units. All in all, in the Baltic Fleet there were over 500 ships committees, 200 port ands shore soviets, and 150 committees in coastal defense units, and another 80 committees existed at intermediate levels, namely brigade and division levels. Many of the delegates to these soviets were apolitical, but as the summer came, radicals and activists took over, vying for power. The force of the future, however, was the Bolshevik wing of the Social Democratic Party, which after Lenin's arrival in Petrograd in April had a coherent program that attracted more and more adherents. Lenin unequivocally called for an end to the war and rejection of the Provisional Government.[62]

In April, the crews of the *Graschdanin* and the *Admiral Makarov*, sitting at anchor in the Moon Sound, called for electing a soviet of deputies from the Baltic Fleet. What resulted was the Central Committee of the Baltic Fleet, or Tsentrobalt, located in Helsingfors. The committee acknowledged its duty to support the motherland, but its assertion that it had the authority to approve any order concerning the "internal and administrative life of the fleet" created a dual command structure. One the one side stood the navy hierarchy of admiralty, fleet headquarters, ship divisions, and individual ships; on the other side were ship committees, shore installation soviets, and Tsentrobalt. The new arrangements were awkward, with Tsentrobalt exercising a middle position of coordinating the actions of the individual ship committees and passing on to them the directives from its higher organ, the Naval Section of the Petrograd Soviet. The fleet commander had to issue Tsentrobalt's resolutions in the form of orders to the fleet, but he could disagree with any and appeal them to the navy minister before ordering their execution. Officers remained in charge of operations, navigation, and the technical aspects of ship handling. Tsentrobalt managed the self-government and administrative sphere, and the two jointly dealt with refit work, promotions, and other personnel actions. The delineations left ample room for confusion, which soon developed.[63]

While not as well organized as their naval counterparts, soldiers formed unit committees that, in effect, constituted a counterweight to the army hierarchy. As the months wore on, discipline steadily deteriorated. In April and May, soldiers at the front believed peace was imminent. What stirred these rumors is not known, but units balked at returning to or entering the trenches. Actions that might provoke enemy retaliation or hinder peace were denounced. Soldiers assumed the darkest possible interpretation of the orders given to them by their officers, which led to an increasing number of mass refusals to obey commands. Conflicts between officers and soldiers occurred more frequently, and while violence was not yet the norm, the arrest of officers by unit committees grew more frequent. During the Easter holidays, the enemy initiated mass fraternization. The Germans and Austrians spread leaflets urging peace and shouted that they would hold their fire if the Russians would. Large sections of the front became dormant, and the trenches became a sieve as German agents and provocateurs traveled with impunity behind the Russian lines in order to "neutralize Russian regiments by engaging them directly in peace negotiations."[64]

While the military services struggled with trying to democratize themselves by adopting revolutionary measures forced upon them in the midst of an active war, the Provisional Government squandered its moment of genuine popularity. It had not pushed the revolution far enough, the war still raged, and the economy disintegrated. Wildman's extremely well-documented work makes it clear that fraternization and "chronic defiance of command authority" had not abated, hampering the preparation and later execution of the Kerensky Offensive.[65] When the offensive finally opened in Galicia in early July, the garrison in Petrograd rioted and the Baltic Fleet reacted badly. The *Petropavlovsk's* ship committee called for removal of the government's "capitalist" ministers and for the transfer of all power to the soviets. The *Slava's* committee agreed and urged calling off the offensive. When disturbances in Petrograd broke out on the 16th and 17th of July, thousands of sailors went into the city in support of rioting soldiers who refused to move to the front. The slogan "all power to the soviets" grew in magnitude and volume. The agitation in Petrograd slowly died out, but the so-called July Days took a heavy toll. Staggered by the events, Prince Lvov resigned as minister-president on 20 July and relinquished power to Kerensky, who managed to restore a semblance of order by taking strong measures.[66]

The crews and ships of the Baltic Fleet played a significant part in the revolutionary unrest, but the key question becomes measuring what effect, if any, the revolutionary activity had on the fleet's readiness and its later performance in the Baltic Islands campaign. In the first place, readiness is not a concept easily measured. There are materiel and personnel aspects to the equation. Materiel in the Baltic Fleet was never a strong point, forcing a purely defensive strategy from the onset. Many shipbuilding contracts were cancelled in April 1917 for lack of funds, and revolutionary activity by yard workers disrupted refit work. Nonetheless, sufficient fuel oil, ammunition, mines, and torpedoes were at hand. Coal stocks were low and often of poor quality, but since there had been little naval activity in 1917, what existed more than sufficed. Retirements, dismissals, elections, and murders created a shortage of about 10 percent of the fleet's officer billets. From the lower deck's perspective, the revolution and the activities of the ships' committees and soviets likely raised morale, but the politicization, challenging of orders, and assertion of claims to ratify the appointment of officers all undermined readiness.[67] Second, after the initial shock over the mutiny and murders receded, there was really no choice but to go on. The Provisional Government had a mantle of legitimacy, and it continued the war. As spring came and the fleet emerged from its hibernation in the ice, and officers and sailors became accustomed to the new and awkward relations, training slowly resumed, and vessels went to sea, although not always without incident.

The army's readiness for battle had also declined because of revolutionary activity. Order Number One had had the same effect as in the navy, and all along the front, unit committees and commissars contested the authority of the official military hierarchy. The July, or Kerensky, Offensive had illustrated the anarchy that ruled at the front. During a remarkable conference held at Stavka on the 29th of July 1916, the front commanders poured forth a litany of complaints to Kerensky, now head of state as well as minister of war and the navy. Every commander saw the disintegration of discipline, brought about by unit committees and encouraged by the stream of directives and orders from the Provisional Government, as the root cause for the army's collapse. The generals cited example after example of breakdowns, such as forty-eight battalions in the Tenth Army refusing to advance during the July Offensive, while unit committees had removed fifty commanders in another front. General Denikin of the western front needled Kerensky by recounting that every soldier in the Twenty-eighth and Twenty-ninth divisions had pledged to fight when the minister inspected the units, but as soon as he departed the units passed a resolution not to advance. "The failures at the front," summarized supreme commander General Alexei Brusilov, "stem from the fact that we have no discipline." The generals' solution called for dismantling all the steps taken toward democratizing the army. After a pathetic defense, Kerensky indicated that many of the changes could not be reversed, adding "he who cannot reconcile himself to the new order . . . should resign." Two days later, Kerensky replaced Brusilov with General Lavr Kornilov.[68]

While the navy had responsibility for defending the Baltic Islands, geographically they lay in the area of the Northern Front, which had the worst reputation concerning the breakdown of discipline. It was part of what Kerensky called the "rotten corner" running from Petrograd to Reval to Riga. The Twelfth Army, located in Riga and anchoring the front on the Gulf of Riga, had a particularly bad record in late 1916. The revolution did not improve matters. In early March the Twelfth had separate soviets for officers and soldiers, which took the initiative in setting up similar organs at lower levels, and by the end of March, it had the most advanced unit committee system of all the armies. The Bolshevik element was strong within this region, especially in the "naval and military installations that guarded the littoral of the Finnish and Riga Gulfs [which] were more a part of the revolutionary nexus of the cities than that of the front." Within the Twelfth Army, the officers had lost control in many units.[69]

What drove both the fleet and army into the hands of the radicals was the Kornilov Affair. On the 9th of September, General Kornilov ordered one of his generals to occupy and disarm the capital. Kerensky immediately dismissed Kornilov, and civil war threatened. The fleet backed Kerensky, and when sailors from Kronstadt rushed to defend Petrograd, Kornilov's men hesitated, and the putsch collapsed without bloodshed. The damage was catastrophic. The sailors now viewed all officers as counterrevolutionaries, as secret sympathizers with Kornilov.[70] It did not matter that Admiral Razvozov had clearly supported Kerensky; in fact, he sent two destroyers from Reval to Petrograd to support the government. The admiral and his chief of staff, Rear Admiral Prince Mikhail Cherkassky,[71] even signed loyalty oaths to the Kerensky Government. In fact, most naval officers did, but four on the *Petropavlovsk* refused and were summarily shot by the ship's committee.[72] Open hostility existed between sailors and officers across the fleet, and officers feared for their lives amidst rumors of a St. Bartholomew's Night.[73] Tsentrobalt and the ship committees slipped into the hands of the radicals. Admiral Razvozov, weary and discouraged by all the infighting with Tsentrobalt and the numerous ship committees, decided to resign, fearing for the lives of his staff. On the 6th of October, he went to Petrograd and offered his resignation to navy minister Admiral Verderevsky, stating, "I'm exhausted and can do nothing more."[74] Soviet-era historian Achkasov says Admiral Bakhirev submitted his resignation at the same time, citing "demoralization . . . and interference in operational matters by ship and regimental committees."[75]

The Kornilov Affair had the same poisonous effect in the army as it did in the Baltic Fleet. Prior to the affair, the officers had naturally promoted the prowess of Kornilov as the supreme commander in order to raise confidence. Once Kornilov was accused of treason and prosecuted, the soldiers viewed those who had spoken well of him as counterrevolutionaries, and, "as a consequence," wrote the commander of the Sixth Siberian Corps, "the situation of the officer personnel has become very difficult. . . . There is a complete lack of authority and . . . the possibility of an open rebellion against the officers is not to be excluded." Matters became so grave that even the Petrograd Soviet, now in the hands of the Bolsheviks, called for an end to the lynching of officers.[76] On the 24th of September, General Verkhovsky, the new (from 15 September) minister of war, gave a thoroughly alarming report to the leaders of the Socialist Revolutionary Party about the disintegration in the army following the Kornilov Affair. General Alekseev, who led the Stavka, resigned, fuming over Kerensky's prosecution of Kornilov as a traitor and the martyrdom of the officers at the hands of the soldiers. He explained his position to a reporter from *Russkoe Slovo* on 26 September: "I can state with horror that we have no army."[77]

Just how this situation translated to the units of the 107th Division or Admiral Bakhirev's ships in the Gulf of Riga on the eve of the invasion is not entirely clear, although it does appear that the jostling for control between unit and ship committees and senior officers in the Gulf of Riga and on the Baltic Islands paralleled similar developments in the army and fleet as a whole. In late March a Soviet of Soldier Deputies of the Baltic Islands Defense Position was organized. Paralleling the activities of its soviets on the mainland, the soviet seems to have concerned itself with administrative matters relating to communication and welfare issues. The soviet published a newspaper, the "Proceedings of the Moon Sound Defensive Position," to keep soldiers informed about revolutionary activities and "to support the new Government in organizing and arranging internal affairs of our homeland and in leading the war to a victorious end." In addition to military news and government announcements, the newspaper even had a classified section. Articles combating alcoholism appeared regularly. The soviet had an executive committee which met much more frequently than the full soviet, but both groups published their activities in the "Proceedings." Starting with issue #13, 24 April 1917, the executive committee took over editorship of the "Proceedings." Chairman of the executive committee was Senior Lieutenant Prestin; editor of the "Proceedings" was Second Lieutenant Gladkov.[78]

Like its counterparts across the Northern Front, the executive committee spent an inordinate amount of time organizing itself for revolutionary activities. Prestin and his group took a month to decide they would merge their organization with the many construction workers on the island, forming the Soviet of Soldiers and Laborers Deputies for the Moon Sound Defensive Position. After much debate, this group rejected participation by the peasants, implying that they were not sufficiently revolutionary.[79] The guidelines for the new soviet were drafted and publicized in early July and approved by the soldiers at the eighth meeting of their soviet, held on the 19th of July. The summer had seen the radicalization of soviet activities everywhere, and the Baltic Islands proved no exception. For example, in the original guidelines drafted in July for the combined soviet of soldiers and laborers, the soviet's chief mission was to "carry out to the masses of population (soldiers, workers, peasants and citizens) the beginning of the people's sovereign rule." Added to this function a month later and reflecting the growing politicization was that of "organizing soldiers, workers and peasants for the purpose of coordinating their activities in terms of defending and broadening the achievements of the Revolution and implementing these achievements." The deputies to the new soviet elected the ubiquitous Lieutenant Prestin as chairman, and the organization held its first meeting on the 13th of August.[80] Besides Prestin, other Executive Committee members were Lieutenants Gladkov and Tapilin; official Kriz; sailor Fedorov; and soldiers J. D. Machlin, Fomin, Shamaev, and Gusev.[81] According to the Germans, who got their information from sympathetic islanders, Prestin and Machlin dominated the group. Supposedly Prestin was a Latvian who was "strongly Russified," while Machlin, an officer candidate from the 107th Infantry Division, was Jewish and allegedly had served in the German military before the war. The Germans assessed Machlin as clever and energetic, and although nominally the second in charge, they thought he was the driving force in the division's soldiers' committee. They noted he had more or less taken the citizens of German background, along with their property, under his wing.[82]

During the summer of 1917, reverses on the battlefield coupled with war weariness and disillusion with the Provisional Government's progress in ending the war and implementing the revolution saw soviets aggressively challenge unit commanders for the control of operations. Initially the Arensburg Soviet focused on getting out correct information about the manner in which the war was unfolding. For example, in contrast to a rather bland official report about the evacuation of Riga, which avoided both the significance of the move and the breakdown in discipline exhibited by the retreating units, the Executive Committee covered the disaster unflinchingly, adding that "being in the know of events" the Executive Committee would "inform military units and civil population through newspaper and special issues, without concealing the truth, about the actual state of events."[83] But the Arensburg Soviet also asserted its presence into the realm of military operations. In response to the fall of Riga, the soviet ordered its counterparts at lower levels to assign commissars to the various headquarters on the islands. The Arensburg Soviet delegated ten of its members to form a Military Bureau to work in Sveshnikov's headquarters.[84]

The Kornilov Coup caused great excitement, and the Executive Committee printed a special edition of the paper which contained an appeal from Admiral Sveshnikov on the 10th of September urging calm and pledging support for the Provisional Government. Nonetheless, the underlying tension between the senior officers and the soviet broke into the open. Just five days after Admiral Svesnhikov had rallied to Kerensky's side, the Arensburg Soviet urged its members "to immediately establish control over all telegraph and telephone machinery" and to report all counter-revolutionary activities to the Executive Committee.[85]

Revolutionary activity had crippled some of the division's smaller units. The two regiments from the 118th Division, the 470th and 472nd, hardly contributed to the islands' defense, given their state of decay. When the 472nd Regiment arrived on Ösel in April, Sveshnikov was appalled. He immediately informed the Northern Front Headquarters that the unit "is in an extremely unsatisfactory state both in terms of internal order and battle readiness." The commander, he reported, had no staff, and mere ensigns commanded the battalions and companies. The regiment came with only 1,200 soldiers, half its authorized strength, and while en route to the island, the soldiers and even some officers robbed and looted civilians. Internal administration had collapsed.[86] Its sister regiment, the 470th, was to have accompanied it to Ösel at that time, but Stavka refused to allow it to leave, deeming it in an even worse state of readiness!

It is even harder to gauge the mood on Bakhirev's ships. The *Slava* had wintered in Helsingfors in 1917, and when ordered to move to the Moon Sound in late June, the lower deck angrily demonstrated. The crew called for the *Andrei Pervozvannyi* or the *Imperator Pavel I* (now renamed the *Respublika*) to go instead. These were dreadnoughts of the *Sevastopol* class, newer and larger, but their deep draft did not permit passage of the Moon Sound. In fact, these ships had seen little action, which really caused the crisis. "Let them taste the smell of gunpowder and experience some fighting," cried the *Slava*'s crew. After the captain again reminded them that the newer ships drew too much water to navigate the Moon Sound channel, tempers quieted and the *Slava* weighed anchor and sailed.[87] It was unusual for the lower deck to question sailing orders, and on the surface, one might conclude that such questioning represented revolutionary activity that undermined readiness. On the other hand, an alternate reading of the sailors' gripes indicates an element of natural frustration. Their ship had borne the brunt of battle while others sat in the harbor. The crew demonstration seems to reflect more battle-weariness and self-pity than a challenge to authority. When reminded of the logical reason why their ship had to go, they settled down.

Another incident of insubordination, quite minor, infuriated Admiral Stark, the commander of the Gulf of Riga Destroyer Division. Just prior to the onset of Albion, the destroyer *Pobeditel* steamed at flank speed past Stark's anchored flagship, rocking it severely. Of course a reprimand followed, to which the crew on *Pobeditel* signaled, "The fleet is informed that the commander of the destroyer division is seasick."[88] Was this revolutionary insubordination or simply the cheeky attitude of a high-spirited crew?

After the German invasion, Admiral Bakhirev wrote that the ship committees were out of control and had far exceeded their authority. Political intrigue thrived. Ship committees met on an almost daily basis, and there were similar meetings for shore facility units. This activity, Bakhirev explained, undermined morale and sabotaged readiness. Crews became excessively concerned about their safety. He cited examples of crews wearing life vests when safely outside of areas where either enemy ships or mines could be expected. When the Eleventh Destroyer Division arrived for a periodic rotation in the Gulf of Riga, its anchorage was at Arensburg, but the crews demanded a screen of picket boats for their security while in this safe harbor. The admiral wrote that the committees interfered in everything, to include operational matters, to which they had no claim of authority. Their representatives insisted on being present for the decoding of operational orders, and after discussing these, they occasionally refused to obey them. Worse, said Bakhirev, the committees would decode political telegrams first and spend hours discussing them, delaying action on telegrams containing operational matters. Bakhirev stated that he had argued with the committees all summer about this, and finally, in late July, matters came to a head, when Tsentrobalt asked Admiral Razvozov to authorize ship committees to take control of operations. He refused. He mentioned this episode to Bakhirev, but what Razvozov did not relay, according to Bakhirev, was Tsentrobalt's claim that the sailors in the Gulf did not trust their admiral.[89]

THE EVE OF INVASION, FALL 1917

As the importance of the Baltic Islands grew in the Russian strategic plan for defending the gulfs of Finland and Riga, they took steps to fortify and defend the region. Eventually a reinforced infantry division garrisoned Ösel and Dagö. The unit received substantial amounts of extra light artillery that General Ivanov allocated to the two main defense sectors. Nonetheless, given the huge area of the islands and the complete absence of terrain features aiding the defenders, Admiral Sveshnikov's forces were inadequate. The requirement to hold the Sworbe Peninsula and its coastal artillery, located at the extreme southwestern end of Ösel, vastly complicated the conduct of a rational defense. The key terrain on the island, the causeway terminus at Orrisar, lay almost 100 kilometers away at the opposite end of the island from Sworbe. If Orissar fell, the Russians would be trapped and would quickly run out of supplies. The division commander worked out where the German landing would come and tried to weight his forces accordingly. He planned to limit the German penetration, and if that failed, to retreat slowly east while waiting for reinforcements. Such a course of action meant temporarily abandoning the troops on Sworbe to fend for themselves until the Russians were capable of mounting a counterattack to recover the island. The plan relied on the infantry regiment and the extra artillery allocated to the peninsula's defense holding the narrows at the northern end against a German assault. As long as the 12" guns at Zerel at the southern end kept the German fleet from entering the Gulf of Riga, the Russians could supply and reinforce Sworbe indefinitely from the sea. Unfortunately, such a defense scheme required good communications and sangfroid, both of which proved in short supply. The communications on the island were poor and distances considerable.

The naval defenses offered more hope. From the admirals to the seamen, they represented the best available. Razvozov and Bakhirev had proven themselves, as had most of the ships at Bakhirev's disposal. Bakhirev could not match the number of German dreadnoughts, but he had tools that helped to mitigate the German advantage, namely the mine-fields covered by the shore-based coastal artillery at key passage points. Unfortunately, revolutionary activity brought into question the efficiency and morale of his crews, and the critical element of trust between leaders and led no longer existed. In June, Admiral Razvozov had made a highly favorable impression on a U.S. admiral, Glennon, during the latter's visit to Rogokyul. Dimitri Fedotoff-White, a Russian officer who had spent two years in the Gulf of Riga and who made the rounds with the American Commission as a translator, left Rogokyul profoundly discouraged. What troubled him was the "evident lack of assurance," from Razvozov and his captains, that "they would be able to ward off the impending attack of the German fleet on the islands in the Gulf of Riga."[90]

People were the great unknown. The civilian population was not the issue. With the exception of a few ethnic-German sympathizers, the local populace remained indifferent, aloof, and largely invisible. The question was the Russian soldier and sailor and to what degree he had fallen vic-tim to war weariness and revolutionary propaganda. The Russians forces were not the same after the March Revolution. Discipline had collapsed. No Russian officer could be certain what his soldiers would do—even if attacked. The same held true for the fleet, where officers had more than ample reason to look over their shoulders. On the eve of battle, the necessity of having to watch one's back could not have been comforting. Against an enemy as determined, adept, and resourceful as the Germans, confidence faltered, and the Russians could only hope "General Winter" would once again come to their rescue.

Fortunately for Russia, navy minister Verderevsky had not acted immediately on Bakhirev's or Razvozov's resignations, and while he waited, news arrived from Libau that the German fleet had put to sea, bringing the operational concerns to the front. Razvozov asked that his resignation be put on hold as he raced back to Helsingfors and his ships.

Navy staff for special task force on the *Moltke*. *Bundesmilitärarchiv, Nachlass Schmidt,*
N-291/36b.

Tagga Bay: infantry being towed ashore. *Bundesmilitärarchiv, Nachlass Schmidt,*
N-291/36b.

a. General Hugo von Kathen.
b. General Ludwig von Estorff.
c. Vice Admiral Erhardt Schmidt.
d. Vice Admiral Paul Behncke.
e. Captain Magnus von Levetzow.
f. Captain von Winterfeld.
g. Commander Hugo von Rosenberg.
h. Lieutenant Max Doflein.
i. Lieutenant Colonel Kurt Fischer.
j. Commodore Paul Heinrich.

Assault troops on B 110. SM Torpedo Boat B 110, 58, #2.

German transport steamer. Note how high it is riding. The Germans could load cargo vessels only to half capacity because Tagga Bay was so shallow. *Bundesmilitärarchiv, Nachlass Schmidt, N-291/36b.*

Congestion in Libau harbor. *Bundesmilitärarchiv, Nachlass Schmidt, N-291/36b.*

German infantry loading at Libau. *Bundesarchiv-Koblenz, 46-2005-0159.*

Going below deck. *Bundesarchiv-Koblenz, 46-1970-074-24.*

"Gulasch Cannons." Feeding on board from field kitchens. *Bundesmilitärarchiv, Nachlass Schmidt, N-291/36b.*

The battleship squadrons
headed for Ösel.
*Bundesmilitärarchiv,
Nachlass Schmidt,
N-291/36b.*

Tagga Bay: unloading
horses from the hold.
*Bundesmilitärarchiv,
Nachlass Schmidt,
N-291/36b.*

CHAPTER FIVE

THE INVASION

THE DEPARTURE

AT FOUR IN the morning on the 11th of October, Lieutenant General Hugo von Kathen, the commander of the XXIII Reserve Corps, ate breakfast. Of medium build and height, von Kathen was clean-shaven except for a full "handlebar" moustache. Popular before the war, especially since the kaiser sported one, the style had fallen into disfavor, probably because of the problems of hygiene in the field. In any event, the moustache gave the general a distinguished, if rather old-fashioned, air. He was sixty-two but carried his age well. Born in 1855, he entered the army in 1873 in one of its guard regiments. After graduating from the War College, he held the usual command and staff positions as he moved up the ladder. Promoted to major general in 1910, he commanded an infantry division and was the governor of the Fortress of Mainz, a post normally held just prior to retirement. The war revived his career. He was given command of the XXIII Reserve Corps, a new headquarters for controlling the wave of units raised since the beginning of the war. The XXIII was thrown into the maelstrom of Ypres in November 1914, remaining in the salient for eighteen months. The corps later saw action on the Somme and the Chemin des Dames during the Nivelle Offensive. Transferred to the eastern front in the summer of 1917, von Kathen led his corps in the Galician Offensive of July 1917, then in the capture of Riga.[1]

His chief of staff, Colonel Erich von Tschischwitz, with whom he had worked closely for the last three years, joined him. Von Tschischwitz had entered the army in 1889 and later attended the War College. Early in his career his extraordinary record there, especially in tactics, had garnered him attention. He graduated with the highest honor awarded: the notation "especially suited for the Army General Staff." One of his superiors in the war wrote, "He belonged to those men by whom 'weigh then venture' was kept in proper perspective in the war. He never bragged; he never lightly dismissed difficulties. By temperament more serious than cheery, he gave his commanders excellent support." When the war began, he was a lieutenant colonel and the operations officer of the Third Reserve Corps, which took part in siege of Antwerp. Later that year, he became chief of staff of the newly formed XXIII Reserve Corps, and he remained with that unit from 1914 on.[2]

After the two officers finished breakfast, a couple of staff officers joined them, and they left the hotel. In a steady downpour of cold rain, a chauffeur took them through silent, empty streets to the docks. For the most part, the troops and their gear were already on board the vast armada that filled the harbor and roadstead. The loading had finished at 9 PM the night before, although troops of the assault force were still climbing aboard some of the destroyers and smaller steamers. As the first to unload on the island, they boarded last. They had also decided to forgo sleeping gear in order to minimize what they had to carry, since they would have no vehicles. They had spent the night on shore in whatever places were available, and as the general and his small entourage watched, they hastened up the narrow gangways to the steamers. The empty streets, unnaturally silent, came as a bit of a shock. Over the last three weeks, as twenty-five thousand soldiers and as many sailors had arrived in Libau, chaos, confusion, and, above all, noise had ruled. Loading and landing exercises had filled the daylight hours of the last three weeks, while the evenings had seen sailors and soldiers crowding into the town's taverns, good-naturedly debating which service was the best.[3]

Boat #63 awaited General von Kathen and his party at the landing. They boarded at 5:30 AM, and the petty officer steered the launch toward the *Moltke*, the fleet flagship, which rested at anchor a half an hour away in the roadstead just outside the steamers and cargo ships. The *Moltke*'s skipper, Captain Hans Gygas,[4] met the group at the head of the boarding ladder, welcoming the dignitaries aboard. Admiral Schmidt was busy directing the movement. There was no speech—Schmidt simply lifted his glass and offered a toast to the army. That was sufficient. As one participant later wrote, "the atmosphere and the confidence the services had in one another could not have been better for all intents and purposes."[5]

To the unaccustomed eyes of the army officers, an amazing scene came into view as the dawn slowly unfolded. Stretching to the horizon were ships, large and small, tiny and tall. Inside and outside the harbor mole, ships bobbed everywhere. Battleships, cruisers, destroyers, cargo ships, colliers, oilers, ammunition ships, hospital ships, and countless smaller craft covered the inner harbor and the roadstead. The clank of mechanical machinery accompanied the last few pieces of cargo coming aboard from lighters. As the booms swung in and out over the decks, sailors and soldiers hurriedly lashed down the cargo and hatches. Deck parties weighed anchor, and the torpedo boats and the three steamers carrying the assault troops steamed slowly by the *Moltke*. To the west, the telltale fire direction centers sitting atop the spindly masts that marked the largest warships seemed to rest on a cloudbank of smoke. One knew there were ships under those masts, but none could be seen through the thick, acrid coal smoke. Slowly, dark shapes moved in the cloud. Bows, guns, turrets, bridges, and funnels pulled clear of the smoke, dragging the dark, billowing clouds with them as they cleared away slowly to the northwest. The Third Battle Squadron, five of Germany's newest battleships, fell into line behind the assault force. The *Moltke* followed, then the Fourth Battle Squadron with its five more dreadnoughts. From the east, a zeppelin (LZ 20) appeared and took station over the fleet.

A day's sail ahead of the fleet was a horde of small boats, the von Rosenberg flotilla. The navy had already cleared the passage to Ösel of mines, but Lieutenant Commander Hugo von Rosenberg's force went ahead, making one last sweep in case there were any "floaters" or last-minute surprises left by enemy submarines. Von Rosenberg's craft were small and slow and mine clearing could not be rushed, so he had left at noon the day before the fleet pulled out to allow for the slow speed of his ships.

Operation Albion had finally begun.[6]

THE WINDOW OF OPPORTUNITY

The High Command came within hours of canceling Albion. The critical military situation in the west demanded divisions from the east. The Italian front had priority. The High Command stood poised to launch a campaign in the Julian Alps aimed at neutralizing or knocking Italy out and giving Austria-Hungary some sorely needed breathing room. The planning was far advanced; the operation scheduled to start on the 24th of October. This operation also came late in the season in an area known for harsh winter weather, which added to the pressure to get it launched before the winter arrived. The campaign planned for Italy also involved use of the new infiltration tactics, which required specialized training. The divisions with this unique training could be committed to the operation only if replacements from the east took their place. The shuffling of units was underway by early October. If the XXIII Corps and Forty-second Division were not used for Albion, they were needed in France.

Even without the pressure of the impending Italian operation, the season had its own dictates. Fall had just started, but at high latitudes it is short, and winter comes much earlier than the calendar suggests. The previous winter had been one of the worst on record, and the fall season in the Baltic was known for storms. An early onset of the stormy season would halt mine-clearing operations, and unless the way to the Baltic Islands and the entrance into the Gulf of Riga were cleared of mines, the operation could not prudently proceed. Winter would bring its own problems, principally ice, which brought navigation to a halt. Faced with these constraints, the Germans had a very narrow window of opportunity. From the 18th of September, when the kaiser approved mounting Albion, the Germans had almost four weeks in which to launch it before the weather or other operations compelled them to call it off. Keenly aware of these difficulties, the Berlin planning group had set 27 September as the date for commencing the operation.[7] Weather and operational demands sabotaged this schedule.

Captain von Levetzow, the Special Staff, and Captain Volkmann from the Forty-second Infantry Division had traveled together from Berlin, arriving in Libau on the 19th. The next day, Colonel von Tschischwitz from the XXIII Corps arrived and made it clear that any and all dealings between the army and navy went through him. Why he had not been in Berlin is not known. He should have been there. The army had planned from the onset to put a corps headquarters in charge of the operation. When Volkmann was first told that his unit would provide the troops for the landings, the Eighth Army's operations officer made it clear that "a corps headquarters will have overall command of the landing forces. . . . You will read all about it."[8] Colonel Hoffmann had mentioned in Berlin that General von Kathen would be in charge of the operation, so it was known as early as 18 September that the XXIII Corps had received the nod.[9] The absence of the Eighth Army's chief of staff from the meetings in Berlin is more easily explained. The Eighth Army was between chiefs. A new chief was en route from Antwerp to take the position; the outgoing one had just been promoted and was leaving to take command of a unit.

Von Tschischwitz also wasted no time in calling for major modifications to the operation. When army and navy officers had discussed the concept of the landing during their meetings in Berlin, both Wetzell and Hoffmann believed army forces should hold a beachhead around the landing site at Tagga Bay against Russian attacks while the navy sailed around Ösel and forced an entrance into the Gulf of Riga. Once that was accomplished, an undertaking that might last five to ten days, the landing forces would move south to Arensburg to link up with the fleet, making the island's capital their joint base of operations. The army would then move east toward Orrisar and the causeway to Moon Island, supported by naval gunfire from ships sailing along the south side of the island.[10] Von Tschischwitz balked at this concept and spent most of the day convincing Captain von Levetzow why it would not work. The colonel argued that holding a beachhead around Tagga Bay posed too great a risk. The Russians would have time to react, he said, and would send reinforcements from the mainland, either via Moon and the causeway or by sea. He wanted to move away from the beachhead as soon as possible, directing the troops toward the east to wrest the causeway from oncoming Russian reinforcements. In addition, von Tschischwitz said he expected support from naval gunfire as his soldiers moved across the island, and at the causeway itself once the troops arrived there. This assistance, he added, came in addition to backing up a column of cyclists he planned to send to capture the batteries at Sworbe on the day of the landing. Von Levetzow listened carefully, and after dinner that evening, assembled his staff and told them he agreed with von Tschischwitz. What this meant, he stated, was that "the entire operation can only begin when the Commander of the Reconnaissance Forces, Baltic [Admiral Hopman], is just about finished clearing an entry passage into the Gulf of Riga that the battleships can use. Only when this requirement is met will the undertaking be set on a secure foundation." He then gave Admiral Hopman the assignment to use all means to clear a passage into the gulf for the warships.[11]

This change greatly complicated matters. Instead of focusing its efforts on transporting the XXIII Corps to the landing site, then turning to the problem of entering the Gulf of Riga via the Irbe Straits, the navy had to break through the straits within a day or two of the landing so it could support the soldiers as they raced across Ösel toward the causeway to Moon. The navy could not approach the causeway from the north side of Ösel because the Soela Sound and Kassar Wiek Inlet were too shallow for large vessels. The navy had to clear a passage to Tagga Bay through the mine-fields in the open ocean in order to accomplish the landing, and it had to sweep a channel in the Irbe Straits between Ösel and Cape Domesnes for its battleships much sooner than anticipated.[12] In fact, both areas had to be cleared simultaneously for this new plan to work.

This development more or less doubled the mine-clearing require-ments and, along with the impossibly bad weather that forced the mine-sweepers to remain in harbor, nearly capsized the operation. Meanwhile, von Tschischwitz informed Eighth Army of the changes he and von Levet-zow had made, and that raised eyebrows. The next day (23 September), Colonel Hoffmann and Colonel Frotscher,[13] the new Eighth Army chief of staff, arrived from Riga to discuss things. "Unsympathetic" was the word used to describe the displeased Hoffmann's attitude. He held to his notion that speed and surprise would overcome everything. He wanted the landing force to hold the area around Tagga Bay until the navy breached the Irbe Straits. When ships could approach Arensburg from the south, the landing forces would send a column of cycle troops to Arensburg and then along the road to Orrisar to block the Russians from withdrawing across the causeway. Infantry columns would simultaneously head down the Sworbe Peninsula to take the Russian batteries at Zerel from the land side.

Von Tschischwitz, joined by Volkmann, reiterated his opposition. Tak-ing Moon in itself was not a major problem, given the decay of the Russian army, but getting to the island might well be, especially if the Russians blew up the causeway. Von Tschischwitz argued that waiting in the beachhead while the navy sailed around the Sworbe Peninsula and forced an entry into the gulf would forfeit surprise. It would take too long to clear those minefields in the Irbe Straits. The Russians could bring in reinforcements from land via Moon Island or from the sea. Waiting also gave the Russians time to move from Arensburg to the causeway terminus at Orrisar. Pushing them back from the causeway, if they had an opportunity to dig in, would be a difficult task, but what would make it nigh impossible was the fact the Germans would have no artillery support. To gain speed, the landing forces planned on coming ashore without artillery. As long as the battle for the island was fluid, the element of surprise remained on the German side. If they sat and waited for the navy to clear the entrance to the Gulf of Riga, they would lose it. Taking on a fortified defensive perimeter around the causeway bridgehead without artillery support would not work.

Hoffmann could not convince either von Tschischwitz or Volkmann to consider any other alternatives, so he grudgingly went along. At the end of the meeting, Admiral Schmidt notified the Admiralty that "Albion will be postponed until mine clearing operations are sufficiently along that the entry of naval forces into the Gulf of Riga during the first days of the operation can be assured so that we [the Navy] can guarantee the Army assistance in capturing Arensburg and providing effective support in the advance toward Moon. Complete agreement among [Navy], 8th Army and the XXIIIrd Corps; the Chief of Staff of the Commander-in-Chief, East, says he'll go along [with this plan]."[14]

During Captain Volkmann's trip to Berlin to discuss the planning for Albion, his division, the Forty-second, left the front and moved to Libau, where the staff had set up headquarters in a hotel. Volkmann rejoined them there and filled in his commander, Major General Ludwig von Estorff, on what had transpired in Berlin as well as the discussions in Libau with the Navy staff and von Tschischwitz. He briefed the general like a nautical expert on loading, mentioning cargo holds, lighters, gangways, coaling, and the like. "Those are the details," said the general who sat with his stiff leg resting on a foot stool, "now let's get to the main point." As Volkmann relayed the plan of the land operation, he noticed the general's attention became focused, "like that of a falcon hovering over its victim, waiting for the final plunge." When he finished, Volkmann mentioned that Colonel Hoffmann had confided to him in Berlin that people in the highest circles had expectations that the division would strike the final blow in the East. The general's face reddened a bit, and with a sudden movement he ran his hand over his forehead. "In that case, we must give the Russians a crushing blow. It will not suffice merely to drive them from the island."[15]

Ludwig von Estorff (1859–1943) was the general to do just that. He came from Hanover. He attended the War College in Berlin, and upon graduation in 1894 went to German Southwest Africa (Namibia) for several years in the colonial army, the Schutztruppe. He then served in Germany's East African Colony and went back to Southwest Africa during the Herrero War and Hottentot Rebellion.[16] He was wounded three times in Africa and had thus seen a good bit of combat before World War One. He returned to Germany in 1911 as a colonel in command of a regiment, and when promoted to brigadier general in 1912, he took charge of a brigade in Metz. He was with that unit when the war broke out and was badly wounded in the Frontier Battles. A bullet shattered his knee, causing the leg to become stiff and lame, but he worked his way back on the active list and returned to field service in 1915. He joined the 103rd Infantry Division, seeing action in Galicia and Serbia. The division moved to the western front in 1916 and took part in the last stages of the Verdun Campaign. Now a major general, he was given command of the Forty-second Infantry Division in late 1916. The division was in the east and fought with great distinction in the counteroffensive in July 1917, clearing out the Bukovina and Galicia. The division next moved north to Riga in the campaign to capture that city. Crossing the Düna on 1 September, the division reached the Aa River by the 5th and settled into trenches until it moved to Libau. The division's performance in the summer of 1917 earned von Estorff the *Pour le Mérite*, Prussia's highest military award. The men of the division, mostly Alsatians, idolized him. They called him "the Old Roman," clearly in deference to his patrician appearance. Thin, always erect, and with a white goatee and full mustache, he looked distinguished.[17]

THE OPERATION PLAN

While the navy started the mine-clearing operations at the mouth of the Gulf of Riga, Colonel von Tschischwitz and Captain Volkmann worked on the operation plan. As the Russians had already observed, the geography and hydrography of Ösel dictated landing on the island's north or northwest coast. The mission of capturing the guns on the Sworbe Peninsula and the island itself posed a relatively straightforward military problem. The solution called for landing on the north coast, marching southwest to capture Sworbe, then moving eastward, driving the Russians off the island. Once Sworbe fell, the navy could enter the gulf safely and support the advancing soldiers with its guns, sailing along the south coast of the island. Unfortunately, Colonel Hoffmann's expectation that the operation would constitute the final blow to the Russians transformed a relatively simple operation into a dilemma. A spectacular victory, one that would knock the Russians out, implied not just taking the island but annihilating or capturing all the defenders, stunning the Provisional Government and causing it to capitulate. The Germans could destroy or capture the Russian forces only if they could block their avenue of retreat to Moon Island and the mainland. The weak link for the Russians was the causeway at Orrisar, the major exit from Ösel to the mainland and safety. If the Germans could get to Orrisar before the Russians, then it was over. Unfortunately for the Germans, numbers, geography, and time—virtually everything—militated against them.

In the first place, the invading Germans numbered about the same as the Russians, and if nothing else the war had taught that the attackers needed to far outnumber the defenders. Second, the key features whose capture would likely permit the Germans to attain their goals, namely the guns at Sworbe and the causeway at Orrisar, lay at opposite ends of the island. If the Germans marched directly from the landing site at Tagga Bay to Sworbe, they could bring about the quick demise of the fortifications there, opening the Irbe Straits to the navy. However, in the several days this operation might take, the majority of Russian soldiers located in the west and center of the island would retreat eastward to Moon Island, blowing up the causeway after they crossed, ending any hopes for a smashing victory. On the other hand, if the Germans tried heading in the opposite direction, namely heading from Tagga Bay to the causeway terminus at Orrisar, hoping to get there before the Russians and blocking their retreat, time was against them. The bulk of the Russian soldiers were closer to the causeway than were the Germans. Even if the Germans arrived at the causeway before the Russians, they could find themselves in a bad spot. To attain the speed they needed to get across the island first, they planned to land without their artillery, which meant in all likelihood that when they got to the bridgehead, the Russians would have artillery and the Germans would have none. The Germans had anticipated this scenario, and they expected the navy to arrive off the coast and shell the Russians, but the navy could not get through the Irbe Straits to help until the fort at Zerel on the Sworbe Peninsula was neutralized.

To have any hopes for a "crushing blow," the Germans decided to mount operations aimed at taking Sworbe and cutting off the escape to Orrisar simultaneously. From an operational and logistical perspective, such an effort constituted a divergent attack, one in which the attacking forces moved further away from each other with every step they took toward their goals. In other words, as they closed on their objectives, the German columns moved farther apart, precluding any possibility of aiding each other. By splitting their forces, they also ran the risk that each column might be too weak to do its job. Every staff college in every army taught officers that victory came from converging forces on the enemy from different directions, overwhelming the enemy, who had to divide his strength to meet each attack.

Scrutinizing their maps, von Tschischwitz and Volkmann racked their brains for answers, for a way to resolve their nightmare. The first glimmer of hope seems to have come from the colonel. From his long service in France and Belgium, he knew the army had converted a brigade of infantry into bicycle troops. The unit was located in Belgium. Von Tschischwitz asked the High Command to let him have it for the operation, and he told Volkmann on the 26th of September they would have use of the cycle troops. The brigade had in excess of five thousand men, and it took several days to move from Belgium to Libau.[18] The first cyclists, along with their commander, Brigadier General Alfred von Quadt,[19] began arriving at the end of September. They ended up playing the key role in the operation.

The troops attacking Sworbe had to cover the greatest distance from Tagga Bay, and until they got there and eliminated the fort and its huge guns, the navy could only float impotently at the entrance to the Gulf of Riga. To accelerate this operation, von Tschischwitz initially planned to dispatch the cyclists to Sworbe. Its capture, however, would solve only half the problem, leaving the vast majority of Russians remaining in the center of the island free to head east and escape. Von Tschischwitz decided he would send a column of infantry toward Arensburg in order to interdict the roads from it to Orrisar before the Russians could retreat eastward. If the infantry could block the two roads leading from the capital to Orrisar, getting to the bridgehead first would not be quite so critical. This approach was logical to the point of being obvious, and General Ivanov's plans for the defense of the island had anticipated exactly such tactics.

On the 27th of September during a planning meeting, von Tschischwitz, von Levetzow, and their staffs discussed a secondary attack at Pamerort. The Germans thought the Russians had a battery there controlling the Soela Sound, although aerial photography later threw that assumption into doubt.[20] Landing at Pamerort would confuse the Russians, silence the battery (if there was one), and allow the Germans to establish an observation and signal station on the cape. The station would provide warning of any Russian naval vessels coming through the Soela Sound to threaten the landings. The navy planned to put three hundred men ashore with some ten machine guns to take the town and the cape. The army welcomed the concept and agreed to send some specialists along, namely some signalmen and gunners who could operate any captured artillery. Captain von Winterfeld, commander of the Eighteenth Storm Company, was named to command the army units.[21]

Over the next few days, von Quadt's cycle brigade arrived in Libau, and Volkmann became aware of its capabilities. He realized that with their speed and mobility, the cyclists could be put to use in the center of the island, operating behind the Russian lines, as well as heading down the

long road to the fort at Zerel. Once the German columns turned onto the
Sworbe Peninsula, the Russians there were trapped. On the other hand,
if the Russians evaded or got behind the German roadblocks on the roads
from Arensburg to Orrisar, the mobility of the cyclists might permit the
Germans to reach the causeway before the Russians did, preventing their
escape. At the staff meeting with the navy on the 29th, Captain Volkmann
asked if he could add an additional four hundred cycle troops to the Pamerort landing force. Their mission, he explained, was to move into the interior
of the island and harass fleeing Russians.[22]

It is not certain when Volkmann had his epiphany, but at some point
after his initial request for the four hundred cyclists, he realized that they
could be put to far better use than harassing the Russians behind the lines.
Volkmann later wrote that he thought hard about what General von Estorff
had said about dealing the Russians a decisive blow; Volkmann understood
the general's remark was more than a wish. It was a command, and in order
to carry it out, one would have to cut the retreat off at Orrisar to prevent the
Russians from escaping to the mainland. Volkmann got out his maps and
measured the distance between Tagga Bay and Orrisar and between Arensburg and Orrisar. The Russians had the shorter route to Orrisar; one would
have to fly to beat them to the causeway. Nonetheless, if Volkmann could
block their retreat, the entire division would be captured or destroyed, a
decisive blow. Strategy, he noted, rarely emerged fully formed, like Athena
from the head of Zeus. His plan gradually formed as he pondered how to
fulfill von Estorff's desire to annihilate the Russians, and the final shape
came to him out of the blue one day. The cycle troops, he realized, could
race along the north shore of Ösel to Orrisar much faster than the Russians
could retreat on the roads in the middle of the island. A speedy advance
along the island's coast would enable the Germans to take Orrisar by a
coup de main, as the bridgehead would most likely be lightly defended.

Volkmann went to von Estorff and briefed him about the plan in detail.
Volkmann later admitted he suddenly got cold feet, wondering if one thousand soldiers would prove sufficient to hold the causeway. The Russians, he
knew, would eventually have a huge preponderance of numbers at the end
of the causeway, and their fear would invigorate their efforts. The Germans
would have only light weapons along with a limited amount of ammunition. The division would have to get reinforcements to the bridgehead
without much delay. Von Estorff thought about the plan carefully. "We
can never escape risk," he finally said, "but boldness almost always pays
off. I'll take the responsibility."[23] Armed with von Estorff's willingness to

take the risk, at the daily staff meeting on the 2nd of October, Volkmann added one thousand cycle troops to the Pamerort landing force.[24] Their mission was to speed along the north shore of Ösel from Pamerort to the causeway and seize the bridgehead at Orrisar. If the situation permitted, they could send patrols across the causeway to Moon Island to ascertain enemy strength.[25]

A few days later, on the 8th of October, Volkmann asked to add another three hundred soldiers to von Winterfeld's force, embarking them on the *Castor*, one of von Rosenberg's vessels. He wanted more cycle troops. Von Rosenberg said there was room for them, so von Levetzow agreed.[26]

With the plan for the landing at Pamerort complete, von Estorff briefed his subordinate commanders carefully. He went through the operation in detail, just like a large war game, saying he wanted them to know his intentions so that if he could not get orders to them in time, they would know what his concept and plans were and could act accordingly. He urged them to be bold and aggressive and said he would stand behind their battlefield decisions.[27]

Although it took some time to work out that part of the operation with its potential for a "crushing blow," the staffs worked on the other issues as well. They had to plan in detail the sea journey to Ösel and the landings in Tagga Bay and as well as Pamerort. In addition, ships' crews and soldiers had to rehearse their roles. None of them had ever participated in an operation like this one.

Laying out the sea journey proved to be the easiest task. Schmidt's staff devised the order in which the ships would sail to the islands and anchor once they got there. Security and standard tactical considerations dictated these arrangements.[28] Minesweepers had to go first, and that task fell to Lieutenant Max Doflein and Lieutenant Commander von Rosenberg. Because the sweeping process was slow and tedious, their sweepers would have to depart twenty-four hours ahead of the fleet. Accompanying them were the small steamers *Donau*, *Castor*, and *Coburg* and some torpedo boats, carrying the 1,600 cycle troops and 150 or so sailors and soldiers that would land at Pamerort. Von Rosenberg's force would continue to a location off Pamerort once his vessels got to Point White, a waypoint 11 kilometers north of Tagga Bay.

At the head of the main fleet, the assault landing force led the way. The landing force consisted of Lieutenant Commander Heinecke's Second Torpedo Boat Flotilla, the tender *Blitz*, and the steamers *Corsica* and *Equity* carrying the initial assault landing force of some 3,600 soldiers.[29] Behind them came the two battleship squadrons with the *Moltke* sandwiched in between. Next, in the *Emden,* was Commodore Heinrich, whose light cruiser flotilla provided security to the transport fleet, which came next, fourteen ships in all, then the logistical tail of ammo ships, cargo carriers, water tenders, two hospital ships, a couple of oilers, and the *Santa Elena,* a seaplane tender. The *Santa Elena* was actually a converted tramp steamer, with hangers and cranes, that served as a mother ship to the seaplanes. The crew used cranes to lower the planes over the side and serviced them along-side when they returned after flights. When major repairs were needed or the weather turned sour, the *Santa Elena's* crew retrieved the planes and stored them in the deck hangers. On both flanks of the fleet, cruisers, destroyers, and minesweepers kept watch for submarines, and overhead zeppelins performed the same duty. The German fleet numbered some 363 vessels, a force that was larger than the combined German and English fleets that met at Jutland the previous year.[30]

The initial phase of the operation called for landing on both sides of Tagga Bay at dawn with an assault force of 3,600 soldiers. Carried on Lieutenant Commander Heinecke's flotilla of torpedo boats, the motor launches of the battleship squadrons, and the *Blitz, Corsica,* and *Equity,* the assault landing force would enter Tagga Bay ahead of the two battleship squadrons, relying on darkness and surprise to get past the Russian forts at the bay's mouth. The steamers, torpedo boats, and launches carrying the assault troops had to precede the battleships—the battleships were going to steam in circles near the forts to keep them under continuous fire, and the vessels carrying the assault landing force either would find it impossible to get by or would have to pass under an exchange of gunfire. If the troop-carrying craft went first, they might proceed past the forts without being detected. If the Russians saw them and opened fire, the assault landing force flotilla would simply hold off while the battleships moved forward and took on the forts. The real danger arose if the Russians fired just as the assault landing force passed by the forts. In that case, they would have to run the gantlet and take the losses. Fortunately, the Russians' guns were positioned facing seaward, so if the Germans succeeded in getting past without detection, they were safe from those guns.

Of course, the Germans were not sure exactly what awaited them ashore. Their intelligence had detected a number of artillery batteries in the woods on both sides of the bay, but these were division-level guns (76mm) whose value was reduced by the wooded areas lining the bay. The Russian guns could wreak havoc on the anchored steamers and launches, but the woods that gave them cover also limited their effect on the German infantry, who once ashore would enjoy the same cover. In addition, Heinecke's torpedo boats carried 105mm guns. His job was to suppress the Russian artillery in the woods near the landing sites. Just before the fleet arrived at the anchorage in Tagga Bay, special troops from the Tenth Shock Battalion (commanded by Major Sluyter) would head ashore in two parties, one to take the fort at Hundsort from the land side, the other to do the same at Fort Ninast on the opposite side of the bay. Two battalions of the 131st Infantry were to go ashore at Ranna (Veere) on the west bank; two from the 138th at Kalasma on the east side of the bay. These units had the mission to go as far inland as the line Laege-Pidul-Abdul, securing the area and forming a defensible perimeter around the beach area.[31]

Once the beach was secure, the remainder of the force would enter Tagga Bay and come ashore. Simultaneously, the Germans planned to reduce the batteries at the mouth and sides of the bay and bombard the seaplane station at Papensholm as soon as feasible. Taking the latter would both immobilize the few Russian reconnaissance aircraft and provide a base for German aircraft, especially land-based ones flying over from the mainland. The first major objective for the division was to capture Arensburg, blocking the retreat of any enemy forces from the capital northeast toward Moon. At the same time, an infantry regiment (the 131st) was to march overland and capture the Russian fort at Zerel on the tip of the Sworbe Peninsula as quickly as possible.[32]

The secondary landing at Pamerort by von Rosenberg's flotilla and the cycle troops aimed at confusing the Russians about the location of the main landing, plus it allowed some of the cycle troops to start out 30 kilometers closer to their destination, the bridgehead of the causeway at Orrisar, than had they landed in Tagga Bay. In addition, seizing control of Cape Pamerort would enable the Germans to dominate the western end of the Soela Sound and the Kassar Inlet. After taking the cape and any enemy fortifications there, the sailors were to hold the cape while the two battalions of cycle troops headed inland, one toward Arensburg, the other toward Orrisar.[33]

To throw the Russians off guard further and to make them think that additional landings were planned, naval feints and bombardments were staged at Toffri (on Dagö Island) on the north side of Soela Sound and against the batteries at Zerel.[34] Once the landing force was safely ashore, the fleet was to force an entry into the Gulf of Riga through the Irbe Straits and support the ground force in the assault upon Arensburg. In addition,

naval gunfire was to assist the army regiment attacking the Sworbe Peninsula. After Arensburg fell, the fleet planned to transfer its base of operations
to that city. From there, the navy would provide protection for ground
forces advancing up the southeast coast of Ösel toward Orrisar. When the
assault on Moon came, the navy was to enter the Great [Moon] Sound east
of the island and drive out the Russian fleet.[35]

THE PREPARATIONS

The artificial harbor at Libau accommodated the transport fleet as well as
the bulk of the torpedo boats and support ships. Admiral Schmidt staged
the capital ships at the Putziger Wik near Danzig, and they arrived only
on the morning of 11 October to escort the landing fleet up the coast.[36]
The mine-clearing squadrons anchored further up the Courland coast at
Windau.

The navy had no transport ships. A few civilian steamers had been
kept in a partial state of readiness at the navy yard in Danzig. The ships
were earmarked for contingency operations, *Fall-J* and *Fall-N* (Case-J and
Case-N). Alarmed by the vulnerability of their important commerce in
the Baltic and the defection of Rumania to the Allied side in 1916, the
Germans developed plans (cases J and N) to seize Denmark or to blockade the Swedish coast in case Sweden joined the Allies. The steamers at
Danzig were kept semi-seaworthy for such contingencies,[37] largely by can-
nibalizing parts from other interned vessels. These ships and more or less
any cargo ship that still floated became a suitable candidate for Albion's
transport fleet, and the Admiralty chartered vessels indiscriminately. One
group was chartered in Kiel; another came from Danzig along with the
three or four *Fall-J* steamers, and a few were picked up in Hamburg. The
yard in Danzig made getting the vessels ready for sea a top priority, even
using prisoners of war to coal the ships, but given the urgency to have
them in Libau, they sailed in a shockingly bad state. Most had no charts or
even compasses, and one ran aground! Crews were drafted from warships
undergoing repairs, army combat engineers were pressed into service as
winch handlers and deckhands, and retired merchant mariners were hired.
Schmidt commandeered officers from the Admiralty Staff, organizing the
vessels into groups of three (a group per regiment) and assigning an officer
to each group. Hustled into a convoy, ships broke down or could not keep
up when they left Danzig for Libau, and the formation fell apart. The

stragglers struggled in one by one, to the horror of Captain Fuchs, the fleet commodore. Ranging in size from 1,700 to 12,000 tons, the smaller ships had insufficient deck space for efficient loading of cargo. The larger ones, if fully loaded, drew too much water to enter Tagga Bay or Arensburg Bay, so they sailed only half-loaded during the operation.[38]

The crowding of the ships in the harbor at Libau merely added to the chaos, which was colossal. Few of the soldiers had the foggiest notion of what to ship and how to stow equipment for an assault. Army units arrived with far more equipment than required or expected,[39] and the appearance of the XXIII Corps staff, which had not participated in the initial planning in Berlin where the loading plan was devised, led to further revisions of the plans.[40] In practice, moving the horses proved the most time-consuming and difficult part of the shipping operation. Large, wooden boxlike stalls with an opening at one end were constructed for each horse. Once it was goaded into the box, the horse and portable stall were winched aboard and stowed below deck. Thinking the departure for Ösel might come any day, no one made any effort to move the horses once on board, but when it became apparent the delays were endemic, the horses had to be moved for health and sanitation reasons. The horses were divided into two groups, and every forty-eight hours the horses on board were taken ashore, while the ones on shore went aboard. Hygiene requirements also affected arrangements for the infantry units. They moved on board the steamers initially, but postponements to the operation made the living conditions intolerable, and the officers moved the troops into tents and billets ashore. The mobile field kitchens remained on board, however, and the soldiers marched from shore to ship daily for meals.[41]

The poor weather that hampered the minesweeping and delayed the operation proved a blessing in disguise insofar as the transport fleet was concerned. Lietenant Friedrich Ruge, whose torpedo boat was part of a flotilla tasked to disembark the assault landing force, wrote about the exercises. At first the infantry practiced loading and unloading without any equipment. Once that was mastered, then came the same drills carrying personal weapons, then machine guns, mortars, and associated gear and supplies. Full-scale dress rehearsals went on along selected beaches. In the evenings, soldiers and sailors had to attend slide-show lectures illustrating the islands' fortifications, presented by intelligence officers.[42] Nonetheless, the first major rehearsal on 29 September apparently did not go well, for Admiral Schmidt relieved the transport flotilla commander, Captain Fuchs. Schmidt felt Fuchs became overly involved with minute details and lost sight of the larger picture. He replaced Fuchs with Captain von Schlick, the commander of the cruiser *Straßburg*.[43] The subsequent arrival of two specialized Army units helped matters greatly. The first was the Pioneer Landing Company (PILAKO), which came from Rumania. This unit specialized in combat bridging operations, but prior to leaving Rumania, it had operated ferries on the Danube. The haste with which it moved from Rumania precluded bringing any of its equipment. The navy assigned it to stevedore duties, namely loading and unloading the horses and transporting them to the beach. After a day or two on the job, its commander told Captain von Schlick it would take a miracle to unload everything within ninety-six hours, even in good weather conditions, in Tagga Bay.[44] Next came the Ninth Pioneer Battalion from the Elbe River. Its men constructed floating docks, pontoon bridges, and gangways for cargo discharge.[45]

An operation the size of Albion could not remain secret. Once the Germans set up their forward staging base in Libau, it became evident that a huge operation was underway. With the constant loading-unloading from the transports and the amphibious assault landing rehearsals along the shoreline, the only uncertainty remained the exact destination, and one hardly needed much speculation to divine it. A very junior navy officer said it did not take much thought to figure out the force was headed for the Baltic Islands. Seaman Richard Stumpf, assigned to the battleship *Helgoland*, anchored in Wilhelmshaven several hundred kilometers to the west on the North Sea, wrote in his diary on the 27th of September that the entire city was abuzz with excitement about the planned operation to take Ösel from the Russians. He knew of the troop transports being readied, adding, "We would all like to give the Russians a thorough beating."[46] Within the army units, even at the company level, most soldiers knew the destination.[47]

The Germans did develop a deception plan aimed at convincing the Russians that the invasion was headed either for the eastern coast of the Gulf of Riga to link up with the Eighth Army or into the Gulf of Finland.[48] The exact details of this plan have not survived. To avoid pinpointing the landing site, reconnaissance flights were prohibited from flying over Tagga Bay.

WEATHER, MINES, AND TIMING

One hundred sixty kilometers up the coast at Cape Domesnes, where the fleet of minesweepers labored, the concern was, as always, the weather. Based at the small port of Windau just south of the cape, the minesweepers played out the frightening drama of clearing the Russian minefields. Even in the best of conditions, the undertaking was dangerous. The mines did not float but were anchored below the surface at varying depths, invisible to vessel traffic. In shipping lanes, mines would be set at a depth of 15–30 feet, in the hope that deep-draft vessels would run into them. In shallow waters, mines were set at a depth of 4–6 feet below the surface. The mines detonated on contact. The Russians laid their mines in patterned rows, each row offset from the one in front of it, the concept being that a ship that passed between two mines in one row would hit a mine in the next row since it was offset by half the distance between the mines. Intervals between mines varied, but they usually ran 200–400 feet. However, minesweepers could not count on the mines remaining in the methodically laid patterns that would facilitate clearing once the sequence of mines became apparent. Storms and currents caused the mines to drift, upsetting the schemes in which they were laid, making it that much more difficult to clear a channel. The winter freeze likewise moved the mines about and caused some to break free. Once free from their mooring anchors they drifted until they washed on shore or hit an object with sufficient force to detonate.

To clear the mines, specialized vessels were used. In open water, minesweepers went first. These were craft of 150–200 tons, operating in pairs, and towing a steel cable abreast between them. Dragged below the surface at a designated depth, the cable was designed to snag a mine's anchor line. Once in contact, the cable cut the anchor line with mechanical or explosive cutting devices. Freed from its anchor, the mine would bob to the surface, where it would be destroyed. Sweeping demanded the best in seamanship and navigation. If the minesweepers failed to navigate in overlapping rows, an area reported clear might in fact not be, with calamitous results awaiting those vessels entering a presumably clear area. In shallow waters, much smaller boats were used in a similar manner since the mines were anchored quite close to the surface. In many cases, the sweeping cable would snag on a rock outcrop in shallow water, necessitating several sweeps of the same area. The small boats drew less than 3 feet of water, but their diminutive size made them more vulnerable to enemy gunfire and to detonating mines. In the event of bad weather, the small boats could not be used because the danger of foundering was too high. The process was slow, tedious, and, above all, dangerous.[49]

The Germans had to clear two very different channels. The first ran north from Libau through the open ocean, roughly parallel to the coast of

Courland, turning to the northeast as one passed Ösel, then due east at the 58°40' N parallel. The Germans designated the end of this channel "Point White," and it lay 11 kilometers north of the mouth of Tagga Bay. Not all of the ocean west of Ösel was seeded with mines, but both Germans and Russians had laid fields near the island that had to be cleared. The second channel ran into the Gulf of Riga between Ösel and the mainland, through the Irbe Straits. Shoals, fog, rocks, and wrecks made for tricky navigation at any time, and the channel had a dogleg. Large ships had to enter from northwest of the mouth of the straits from about the 58°N line, heading southeast for 19 kilometers until about 5.8 kilometers north off the coast of the Courland mainland, then turn sharply to the northeast, running parallel to the mainland for some 29 kilometers until clear of Cape Domesnes. This channel constituted the sole entry into the gulf from the west for large vessels. Consequently, both sides had mined the Irbe Straits extensively. Making matters worse, most of the Irbe Straits came under the range of the Russian 12" guns at Zerel.

Lieutenant Max Doflein was in charge of clearing the open sea passage from Libau to Tagga Bay. He commanded the Second Mine Reconnaissance Flotilla, a unit of the High Sea Fleet. He arrived in Libau from Kiel on the 21st of September, bringing most of his flotilla, some twenty craft in all.[50] Admiral Hopman's minesweeping units had the responsibility for clearing the Irbe Straits. Two factors worked to his advantage. First, his men knew the waters after operating in the region for three years. Second, the Russians knew Hopman's ships; seeing them in the Irbe Straits would be business as usual. The Russians would immediately notice any different vessels and might conclude the Germans had something underway. The Germans did not want to draw attention. Hopman had two full mine-clearing divisions, the Third and Fourth (twenty-two vessels) along with the Third Mine Reconnaissance Half Flotilla, with fifteen vessels, for a total of thirty-seven.[51]

Doflein's Second Flotilla had the marginally easier task of clearing the sea-lane to Ösel. With larger, oceangoing trawlers, Doflein's sailors could remain at sea on most days in conditions that kept Hopman's men in their smaller craft in the harbor. By the 2nd of October, Doflein reported that his mine-clearing craft had swept a channel some 2.4–2.7 kilometers wide to Point White, the rendezvous point for the fleet north of Tagga Bay. Meanwhile, the units clearing the Irbe Straits had the harder job, and miserable weather kept them in port on most days. Clearing a mined channel under the best of conditions was dangerous. Add steep seas, cold weather, slippery decks, shallow waters, and enemy fire, and the operation moved at a snail's pace. Weather was the most formidable obstacle. "Oh, how often we cursed that weather," said Lieutenant Commander Franz Wieting, in charge of one of the mine-clearing flotillas.[52] With winds and storms coming from the west, the Irbe Straits became a lee shore, adding the chance of being driven ashore and smashed to pieces to the litany of woes. The entries in the special fleet's Daily War Diary catalog the stormy days: 21–22 September, no minesweeping owing to winds; 25 September, same; 26–27 September, winds 6–7 on Beaufort Scale, no mine-clearing operations; 28–29 September, wind and weather led to operations being canceled. Admiral Hopman wrote that he often railed at the weather god as he looked out his window every morning to see nothing but miserable weather and storms. The 1st of October saw the small craft flotilla hard at work, although the Russians fired salvo after salvo from Zerel on the small craft. Wind and rain forced cancellations from the 2d to the 6th of October. At this point, some of Doflein's smaller vessels had gone to help Hopman, but the miserable weather slowed their work as well.[53]

Worse, Colonel Frotscher, the Eighth Army's chief of staff, arrived from Riga the morning of the 4th of October with a telegram from Ludendorff. That general understood the situation, and he minced no words. "Giving consideration to how far along the [fall] season is," wrote the quartermaster general, "as soon as the weather permits, I want you to carry out the operation without waiting for completion of the clearance of the channel to Arensburg."[54] This was an order. Aghast, von Levetzow and Frotscher worked on a reply for Eighth Army commander General von Hutier[55] to send to his cousin. The navy was not going to send its battleships into the Irbe Straits until they were clear of mines, and the XXIII Corps was not going to land until the navy could come around the island and provide fire support. "I am in total agreement," wrote von Hutier to Ludendorff, "with the Special Task Force Staff that before we commence embarkation [for Albion], our measures for clearing the entry into the Gulf of Riga must be far enough along so that they can be completed during the Operation to guarantee the scheduled movement of the 2nd echelon to Arensburg along with the timely assistance of the fleet in the Moon Sound. To do this, 3–4 days of good weather are required before the onset of loading." Over the next few days, a flurry of phone calls ensued between Colonel Frotscher and Colonel Hoffmann, in which von Hutier and his staff tried to get the deadline extended. On the 6th, Hoffmann called to say that after talking with the High Command, the "lateness of the season is forcing a decision.

If the operation has not commenced by the middle of October, you had better count on it being cancelled."[56]

The same day, a Russian mine sank torpedo boat T54, with a loss of eight sailors and three wounded. On boat T60, a mine detonated after being taken on board, killing one and wounding three. Another vessel (M31) was lost that night to mines. One sailor was killed. Once again, bad weather kept the smaller craft in harbor, and even the larger vessels returned after the T54 sank. The state of the seas also forced the cancellation of a landing exercise for one of the groups of the assault landing force.

Von Hutier and Schmidt feared the worst, namely that the High Command would indeed cancel the operation. Schmidt fired off a telegram that afternoon to Admiral von Holtzendorff in Berlin, advising him that although the weather forecast looked favorable for launching the operation, in the event the weather did not cooperate, he and von Hutier did not want to give up the operation. He promised to energetically argue the case for the operation vis-à-vis the commander in chief, east, and the army High Command. That night General von Hutier returned, dejected, to Riga.[57]

PASSAGE TO ÖSEL

The fleet and the army stood poised, leaning forward, ready to go, but the weather conspired against them. Von Hutier had gone back to Riga; Schmidt spent his time preparing memoranda that argued in favor of pushing back the High Command's deadline to cancel the operation. Then the weather rapidly improved. On the morning of the 7th of October, Admiral Hopman called from Windau to say the second Mine Searching Flotilla had made fairly good progress on the previous day before the sinking of the T54 put an end to its operations. He also indicated that all his minesweepers and related craft had put to sea that morning. The weather outlook was good for the next few days. He said he anticipated making substantial progress that day. In fact, his forces might reach Point F, a location in the Irbe Straits from which the remainder could be cleared in hours. In other words, his forces could sweep the rest of the straits in far less than the ninety-six hours it would take to load the fleet and sail to Ösel. The two operations would run concurrently. The placing of markers in the channel entering the Gulf of Riga had begun that morning, he told Schmidt. On the 8th, Hopman reported that after he had spoken with Admiral Schmidt the day before, his smaller craft had had to turn back because of high winds, but nonetheless everyone was back at sea as he spoke. At 5 PM that afternoon, Hopman called back to report his progress. He had reached Point F. Enthused, Admiral Schmidt immediately called Eighth Army Headquarters to request permission to commence embarking the soldiers the next morning, the 9th of October. Albion could begin, he reported. The reply shocked him. In light of the situation, the High Command had now reserved for itself the authority to give the green light. Colonel Frotscher had to call the High Command at Bad Kreuznach and get permission. After an anxious hour, Schmidt finally heard what he wanted: do it. Embarkation would commence on the 9th of October, and the fleet would sail for Ösel on the 11th, marking the first day of Operation Albion.[58] Over the next several hours, the orders to embark at dawn went to every vessel and headquarters. Two days later, with the vast armada poised, Admiral Schmidt and General von Kathen boarded the *Moltke* and the fleet put to sea.

The passage of the fleet along the coast of Courland to Ösel went according to plan. The fleet could travel no faster than its slowest party, the troop transports, about 10 knots. The distance from Libau to Tagga Bay was 187 nautical miles.[59] The zeppelins ranged to the east and west, and as far ahead as the entrance to the Gulf of Finland, looking for Russian vessels or aircraft. There was almost no chance of stumbling into any enemy warships; submarines were another thing and caused the greatest concern, especially the squadron of English submarines known to operate from Finland.[60]

General von Estorff had assigned his leaders to different vessels in case the fleet ran into problems. Von Estorff sailed on the *Königsberg*, the flagship of Admiral Reuter, whose cruisers protected the transport fleet. Von Estorff's brigade commander, Colonel Willi Matthiass, went with Captain Volkmann on the B98, the command ship of Lieutenant Commander Oskar Heinecke, whose Torpedo Boat Flotilla II carried units of the Assault force, far in advance of the transport fleet. The assault force would go ashore several hours ahead of the main body, and von Estorff wanted Volkmann on the spot in case anything went awry. Matthiass, of course, would go ashore with the assault force to direct the battle.[61]

During the daylight hours, the trip up the coast was pleasant, at least for those on the larger ships. Von Tschischwitz, on the *Moltke*, found a stateroom and went to sleep until the fleet anchored, missing the excitement that came later that night. On the smaller vessels, things were different. Lieutenant Friedrich Ruge, on B110 in Heinecke's flotilla, wrote with

Schadenfreude that as the fleet headed northwest, the swells grew and the roll became more pronounced, causing many soldiers' faces to go white, and more than a few headed for the rail "to give the sea God his due."[62]

As night fell, the fleet entered the minefields and slowed appreciably. After midnight, the weather deteriorated. The wind and seas rose. In spite of slowing, at 2 AM the fleet ran into Lieutenant Commander von Rosenberg's mine-clearing ships and the landing force earmarked for Pamerort. Despite a twenty-four-hour head start, von Rosenberg's pace was slow and painstaking. His sweepers labored along at 3 knots.[63] On the heels of the assault landing force came the rest of the fleet, which slowed to a snail's pace and began to bunch up. At this rate, the ships would close on Ösel after sunrise. Volkmann, who had engaged in conversation all night with Lieutenant Commander Heinecke, overheard him say, "Something has to give. If we land in broad daylight, we'll all be shot dead!" On the *Moltke*, the tension was palpable. Lieutenant Kiep, the navigator, recalled how difficult it was to see von Rosenberg's or Doflein's vessels. They carried a white running light that was shielded in such a fashion that it could be seen only from astern, but the weather reduced visibility drastically. The fleet stood poised to run over its own minesweepers and proceed into an unmarked minefield. It was 2 AM.

Admiral Schmidt did not hesitate. "Continue course," he said. "Radioman—make signal to the minesweepers: Give way immediately for the fleet. Pull in your gear."[64] Upon receiving that transmission on Volkmann's boat, the signal officer told the skipper, "The fleet commander says to proceed without the minesweepers. He has ordered that the sweepers give way so the battle fleet can pass." "A hard call," said Heinecke, "if we have bad luck, we'll lose ships and men. We're now in the middle of the minefields."[65] A tall and taciturn man who made his own luck, Heinecke had entered the navy in 1897 and led the Fifteenth Torpedo Boat Flotilla with great skill in the Battle of Jutland. His reward was command of the Second Flotilla, the newest and largest flotilla, which he led until the end of the war.[66]

An hour later, the fleet arrived at "Point White," a rendezvous point 11 kilometers north of Tagga Bay, marked by a submarine. Navigator Kiep had a hard time seeing the blinking light on the submarine, largely due to the fleet being several kilometers off course because of the strong winds. Kiep said he openly sighed with relief when the head of the fleet passed the U-boat, and Schmidt finally gave signal to anchor.[67] For the next hour, last-minute preparations were completed. On the battleships, crews hosed down the bags of coal stacked on the decks and passageways. The ships carried tons of extra coal for themselves and the torpedo boats, as no one knew how long they would remain in the area. Expecting to come under Russian gunfire, they wet down the coal to reduce the danger of explosion or fire.[68] The Third Battle Squadron lowered its motorized launches, and the troops of the assault force riding on the battleships went over the side and into the launches. At 0400, the signal came to weigh anchor and move in.

Two special assault, or storm, companies of the assault force on torpedo boats B112 and V 100 led the way into Tagga Bay. They were followed by the motor launches carrying the first assault wave, Heinecke's flotilla carrying Captain Volkmann's second wave of assault forces, then the transports *Corsica*, *Equity*, and *Blitz*, carrying the remaining battalions of infantry from the 131st and 138th Infantry Regiments—about 3,600 soldiers in all. At 0430, Heinecke's torpedo boats, loaded with over a hundred assault troops on each, left Point White and began to move into the bay. Heinecke could not see the motorized launches from the Third Squadron. "If I go without them," he said to Volkmann, "we'll be short 700 men." As the minutes ticked, the tension rose. At 0440, Heinecke said, "I can't wait any longer; let's go!" Just then the motorized launches arrived, having had a much longer journey under unexpectedly bad conditions to the rendezvous, and the flotilla moved south into Tagga Bay. After a few minutes that lasted forever, Heinecke said between clenched teeth, "The Russians seem to be asleep. The shore batteries can no longer do us much damage, since we've passed Hundsort and Ninast."[69] Dawn came rapidly, and soon the Germans could make out details on the land: trees, bushes, houses, and fishing smacks, and finally, at the landing spot on the east side, a few hundred meters past the village of Kalasma, trenches and barbed wire.[70]

Von Tschischwitz, on the *Moltke*, had a different picture. When the cruiser began to move at 0440, he could see nothing because of the fog and darkness. As the ship neared the bay almost an hour later and the skies lightened a bit, the fog thinned and slowly began to dissipate. It was still raining. From the bridge he could see emerging from the murk first the deck and the bow of the cruiser, then the water rushing by, and finally then the stern of the *Corsica* in front of him carrying the Second Battalion, 138th Infantry Regiment. It came last in the combined fleet of twenty steamers, torpedo boats, and minesweepers carrying the assault force. As the sky lightened, to the west (his right), three battleships of the Fourth Squadron faintly slipped in and out of the fog, paralleling the *Moltke* and moving into place to bombard the battery at Hundsort. To the east (left) were the four battleships of the Third Squadron, heading for their places to fire on the fort on Cape Ninast. Out of sight were the battleship *Bayern* and the light cruiser *Emden*, steaming to join von Rosenberg's flotilla off Pamerort.[71] The Admiralty had permitted a reporter to sail on one of the battleships. Watching the assault force entering Tagga Bay, he could not believe the Russians failed to see the German vessels. The assault force, he wrote, "extended far into the bay—as far as he could see."[72]

Further into the bay, at the head of the column, Heinecke said, "We've really had a piece of great luck." Dropping anchor, he added, "We're in. Whether we remain here is something we'll find out within the next few minutes." A bit later, at 0520, Volkmann heard a dull, faint sound. "A mine," said the vessel commander. "Now the dance will start!"[73]

On board the *Moltke*, they heard the same explosion. A staff officer ran to von Levetzow and said, "The *Bayern* has begun to fire at Toffri."

"Open fire," said von Levetzow, and the command was relayed. Von Tschischwitz interrupted. He urged von Levetzow to wait, saying it was possible the enemy in the bay had not heard the far-off shooting. Surprise was everything—the longer one could wait . . .

Von Levetzow agreed, adding, "It will take a while [for my ships] to return fire." As he turned to countermand his order, the guns of the battleships in Squadron IV, opposite Cape Hundsort and its fort, opened up.[74]

CHAPTER SIX

ÖSEL, 12–13 OCTOBER 1917: THE CENTRAL ISLAND

FILZAND LIGHTHOUSE, 12 OCTOBER

ARTUR TOOM WAS the first to hear the German guns firing the morning of the 12th of October. He was the lighthouse watchman at Filzand (Vilsandi) Island, on the west coast of Ösel at the mouth of Kielkond Bay. When he heard the shooting, just before 6 AM, he raced up the 120 feet to the deck at the top of his lighthouse to see the cannonade. The rain and fog obscured everything at first, and he could discern only the direction from which the noise came—Cape Hundsort. The cape lay to the northeast, some 13 kilometers across the peninsula of the same name, and marked the entrance to Tagga Bay. He knew a Russian fort with a battery of 6" guns guarded the entry to the bay.

Within fifteen minutes the weather lifted a bit, but all he could see was "shell explosions along the entire shore of the Hundsort cape." He could not raise the fort by telephone, and no one else that he reached in the nearby village of Kielkond had any idea what was happening. Soon Toom had his own problems. Three German destroyers steamed right past him and, around 8 AM, opened fire at the seaplane station at Papensholm, 3 kilometers away across Kielkond Bay. A Russian seaplane swooped in at the same time and landed in front of his pier. Toom rushed to the dock. The pilot, Lieutenant Telepnev, got out, shouted excitedly that the Germans were landing, and told Toom to alert the men at the seaplane station. "There are six transports near the shores of Tagga Bay and they are landing troops," said the lieutenant, and "three large vessels are at the entrance to

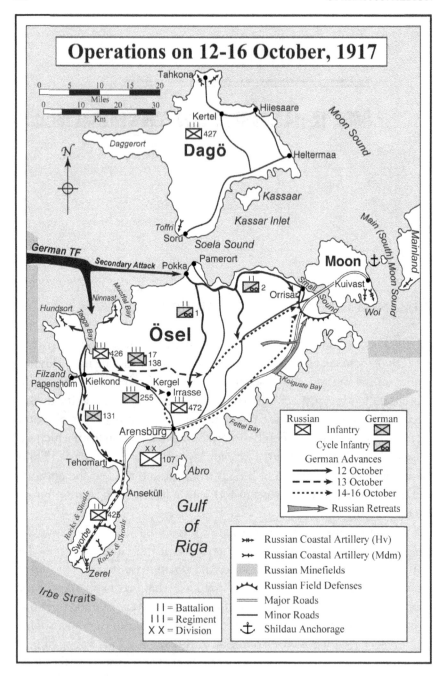

Map 4. Operations on 12–16 October

the bay, three destroyers are in the Kielkond Bay and two vessels are north-west of Filzand [Island]." Toom got through to both the seaplane station and Admiral Sveshnikov's headquarters and relayed the lieutenant's message, but with the seaplane facility under fire from the German destroyers as Toom spoke, Telepnev's report had probably lost some of its immediacy.[1] The officer jumped back into his plane and gunned it just as four German fighters began to attack. The Russian pilot got off successfully and disappeared into the low clouds.

The rain moved back in, obscuring visibility from the lighthouse, so Toom sent a man to a cottage on the other side of the island to see and report what was happening. The lighthouse keeper kept reporting ship movements all morning. At 1 PM, just as the telephone connection with the seaplane station was lost, the three German destroyers headed back out to sea, where they joined a large number of other vessels. At 3 PM, Toom saw that Papensholm was burning, and he decided to abandon his lighthouse and island. After setting his own papers on fire, and noticing that to the north the ocean was full of ships, he cast off from the lighthouse pier at 5:15 PM.[2] The German invasion had started.

TAGGA BAY, 12 OCTOBER

By the time Artur Toom spotted the bombardment of Hundsort, the Germans were already ashore and making for the fortifications at the mouth of the bay. Two launches landed shock troops from the Tenth Storm Battalion just below the forts. The members of this elite battalion raced through the woods, hoping to get to the batteries before dawn. Meanwhile, further down the bay, the flotilla sailed past several fishing camps. A dense mixture of trees and undergrowth started almost at the water's edge, blocking the view inland. A small wooden tower marked the church, the one reported by Lieutenant Vesper in his submarine reconnaissance. No movement was noted—the Russians seemed to be sleeping. The long line of torpedo boats, launches, and steamers, some thirty-eight in all, safely passed the forts and moved to the middle of Tagga Bay, where they began discharging their cargo of gray-coated infantrymen. As the flotilla approached the landing site, the cutters cast off and rowed to shore. The infantry jumped out when the water was chest high and ran ashore. First ashore was Captain Justi's company of the 138th Infantry Regiment. From the enemy came nothing.[3]

The battleship *Bayern*, far out at sea from Tagga Bay, inadvertently unleashed the shooting. The *Bayern* did hit a mine at 5:07 AM, but that explosion probably was not the one the deck officer on the *Moltke* had reported to Captain von Levetzow. The *Bayern* was then too distant, kilometers away near the coast of Dagö Island. The noise from a mine would in all likelihood not have been audible to the sailors or soldiers in Tagga Bay. Commodore Heinrich's flagship, the *Emden*, was much closer to the *Bayern* at that time, and his lookouts heard no explosion.[4] In all likelihood, the sound heard on the *Moltke* came from *Bayern*'s main guns when a few minutes later the ship fired on a purported submarine. Finally, there was also a good chance the explosion came from within the bay itself, because Lieutenant Vesper of UC-58 had erred when he made his reconnaissance. There were Russian mines in Tagga Bay.

The last vessel in the parade transporting the assault landing force was the steamer *Corsica*, an interned British prize. It carried the Second Battalion of the 138th Infantry Regiment, destined for the east side of Tagga Bay. At 5:10, a huge water spout erupted from behind the *Corsica*. "Mines!" shouted sailors.[5] It let off a huge blast of steam and abruptly pulled out of the line of ships, flashing the signal that it had hit a mine. Admiral Schmidt did not know of the *Corsica*'s plight until thirty minutes later, but the officers on the *Moltke*'s bridge might well have mistaken either the noise of the steam jet or the small explosion as coming from a mine out to sea, where they knew there were both mines and vessels. In any event, Captain von Levetzow gave the two battleship squadrons and the Second Reconnaissance Group the order to commence firing.[6]

The Russians had awaited the Germans. Long before the Germans began concentrating ships and men at Libau, the Russians suspected an effort to enter the Gulf of Riga. When a U.S. commission, led by former secretary of war Elihu Root, visited the Gulf of Riga in June 1917, Russian naval officers could not assure the Americans that they "would be able to ward off the impending attack of the German fleet on the islands in the Gulf of Riga."[7] Army officers had their own fears about a German offensive. Although the islands were important, their concern centered on the area behind the Twelfth Army, an area that stretched from the front line on the Aa River north of Riga at the southern end of the Gulf of Riga to Baltic Port in the north. The distance was great, the roads were primitive, and the countryside was empty, although that description held true for most of Russia. What made this region unique, however, was the fact that a German breakthrough in this area offered them access to Reval and eventually the Russian capital of Petrograd. The city lay 300 kilometers distant and winter would soon arrive, but one thing the Russians had learned in this war was not to underestimate the Germans.

General Vladimir Cheremisov's Northern Front had responsibility for the area.[8] In addition to exercising operational control over the Baltic Fleet, Cheremisov had three armies, the Twelfth, First, and Fifth. They were arranged from northwest to southeast more or less along the Aa-Düna River line. Until this point, the Gulf of Riga had been an asset protecting the Russian rear, but if the Germans successfully forced entry into the gulf, its eastern shores became an undefended flank. All of General Cheremisov's armies were in the wrong place and facing the wrong direction if the Gulf of Riga became a theater of operations. His Twelfth Army, the northernmost one, which had just been pushed from Riga to Valk, would have to be responsible for this enormous area. It was also the army that, as historian Allan K. Wildman noted, had the most advanced revolutionary committee system of all Russian armies. Its units seethed with revolutionary fervor, and in many, the officers had lost control.[9]

Lieutenant General Dmitry Pavlovich Parsky commanded the Twelfth Army and the vast empty spaces behind his sector of the front leading toward the capital.[10] Geography divided his area of responsibility into two zones. The northern zone, running along the coast of Estonia from Baltic Port on the Gulf of Finland to Pernau at the midpoint of the eastern shore of the Gulf of Riga, was filled with bogs and low areas, rendering very difficult the inland movement of a major force. The southern zone ran from Pernau to the current front line on the River Aa. The terrain in this area was more congenial to transportation and movement. A landing in this region threatened the immediate rear of the Twelfth Army and the entire northern front. The invaders could either roll up the rear of Cheremisov's three armies or strike inland for Dorpat (Tartu), cutting the northern front's lines of communication and threatening Reval.

General Nikolai Nikolaevich Dukhonin,[11] the head of Stavka, had advised Cheremisov as early as the 23rd of September that German landings were imminent, identifying a breakthrough into the Gulf of Riga as the likely objective.[12] Admiral Razvozov's Baltic Fleet had responsibility for defending the Gulf of Riga, the Baltic Islands, and the coastline from the Aa River front to Petrograd. If the Germans got past the fleet and landed on the mainland, Cheremisov's three armies would have to hold them. Of course, the general knew of the revolutionary disturbances in the fleet and how thinly spread its forces were on the Baltic Islands. Nonetheless, beset with his own difficulties from revolutionary militancy and already directly engaged with the Germans, all he could do was to pass on Stavka's intelligence about German activities and order contingency planning in case the Baltic Fleet failed.

Russian prisoners later told Colonel Tschischwitz the German preparations at Libau were well known to them. The Russian soldiers had been on varying levels of alert since the 25th of September. For days the landings had been expected. Admiral Sveshnikov "ordered the soldiers to sleep without undressing and [for commanders] not to grant leaves to anyone."[13] On the 3rd of October, army officials on Ösel told Admiral Bakhirev they expected a German landing that day. On the 10th of October, the Baltic Fleet staff told Sveshnikov the Germans would put to sea the next day.[14] Exhausted by the constant vigilance, however, the Russians finally lowered their guard. The miserable weather also gave them a false sense of security. When, after three clear days (9–11 October), no Germans appeared, the Russians concluded the invasion was canceled.[15] The bad weather and poor visibility on the night of the 11th and 12th of October offered further reassurance, and the soldiers relaxed. The arrival of 12" shells from the Fourth Squadron into the Russian fort at Hundsort shattered their illusions.

The incorrect assumption that inclement weather would keep the Germans home put the Russians off guard, a state from which they never completely recovered. On the afternoon of the first day of battle, Sveshnikov's chief of staff, Captain Reek, presented a picture of a headquarters overwhelmed by the speed of the German operation. "The battle is developing too quickly," he told Colonel Kruzenstiern, chief of staff of the land defense forces. "The losses in units are undoubtedly high, according to the reports. . . . Events are unfolding like lightning and the enemy forces outnumber ours."[16] Spread thinly on the ground and caught by surprise and the speed of the German assault, the stunned Russian defenders committed their forces piecemeal, a recipe for certain defeat.

Not all the Russians were sleeping. At 5:27 AM a radio listening post picked up von Levetzow's order to open fire and relayed it immediately to Sveshnikov's headquarters, stating that a "German Commander-in-Chief gave some brief orders to the IV and III Squadron and II Reconnaissance Group."[17] According to Tschischwitz, a Russian artillery observer on the west bank saw the German ships enter the bay and ran to his battery commander, woke the sleeping officer, and reported what he had seen. "Those are our ships; let me sleep!" was the response from the officer, who was awakened by German soldiers a few minutes later.[18] Although colorful, this story is highly doubtful. Who could sleep through a barrage of 12" shells coming down? On the other hand, it does serve to illustrate that the Germans got their assault force into the bay before the Russians reacted.

After the Germans opened up, the Russian gunners at the head of the bay returned fire almost immediately, aiming at the *Moltke*. When they looked over their parapets, it was right in front of them, looming large. The battleships were further out to sea, and almost impossible to pinpoint in the impenetrable haze.[19] The first Russian salvo had the direction of the *Moltke* but landed 100 meters short. The German cruiser returned a broadside, and the next Russian rounds went just over it. The Russians had it bracketed, and the third salvo landed next to it, showering the deck with seawater. "These fellows can shoot well!" shouted a German officer as he scuttled behind a turret. The *Moltke* continued to fire, as did the dread-noughts in Squadron IV, and within a few minutes the fort was silenced. One could see only smoke where it was located. The stench from the guns lingered in the air.[20] The first German rounds had penetrated the bunker of Gun 2 in the fort, causing an explosion and putting the weapon out of action. The second salvo brought down the observation tower. The Russian report of the action acknowledged that "the enemy fire was so effective that after the first salvos the battery could not return fire and the crew had to leave." The same scenario transpired with the Third Squadron, which fired on the fortifications at Ninnast on the eastern side of the bay. The Russians in Ninnast never returned a single shot toward the fleet, although they held off the Germans attacking from the land side with small arms fire until 10 AM. By 6:20 the naval barrage at the entrance to Tagga Bay ended, with Schmidt ordering the battleships to cease fire.[21] Admiral Sveshnikov's headquarters reported that "Batteries #45 and #46 [Hundsort and Ninnast] were lost from the very beginning of the battle; they were destroyed by the first dreadnought salvos."[22]

Further down the bay, when the mine went off next to the *Corsica*, Volkmann wrote that everyone in the assault force looked toward the ship. Then the horizon lit up, followed by the sounds of heavy gunfire. They knew that the bombardment of Ninnast and Hundsort batteries had started.[23] Responding to the German fire, several Russian batteries, carefully concealed in the woods, opened fire on the assault force from both sides of the bay. Battery 2 of the 107th Division occupied the west bank. One of its platoons of guns defended the Hundsort fortifications from the sea, and another sat camouflaged at Ranna, overlooking Tagga Bay. Directly opposite on the east side of the bay and facing west, stood the Third Battery in the village of Kalasma with two of its platoons. A third platoon was to the north near Cape Merris. Each site had an observation tower. In the vicinity of the bay, the Russians also had a reserve of three infantry companies, a death company, and a machine gun company.[24]

The Russians let loose shrapnel on the torpedo boats and the landing sites. Infantry and machine gun fire likewise sounded from the woods. Heinecke's torpedo boats returned fire with their 88mm and 105mm guns, lashing the shore. As the sun rose, one could see the surface of the bay covered with small boats making for the shingle beaches. Had the Russians kept their nerve, Volkmann thought, they could have made each round and sweep of their machine guns count. Instead, their fire went high and the shrapnel burst too soon, while their artillery shells plunged dramatically but harmlessly into the water between the boats. The first wave of assault troops quickly went over the side of the torpedo boats into cutters, which were towed ashore. In the excitement, the cook on the B110 also went overboard into the water, having forgotten to let go of the line securing the cutters to his ship. Soon the noise of the ships' guns lessened, and eventually it ceased. Despite the enemy fire, the landing parties went ashore from the torpedo boats and the *Blitz* and *Equity*.[25]

The 131st Infantry Regiment landed on the west bank, the 138th on the east. In the forest, troops found the cover to assemble and head for the Russian batteries. The 138th Regiment captured the Russian artillery after fighting at close combat. It took hand grenades and cold steel to dislodge the Third Battery of the 107th Division, but at that point the Russians retreated through the woods. On the opposite side of the bay, the Russian defenders did more damage to the torpedo boats than their comrades on the eastern side accomplished.[26] Nonetheless, the 131st Regiment forced the Russians from their positions. At the head of the bay, the storm troopers seized the forts and brought their prisoners to the beach.[27] "A defeated bunch, these Russians," Lieutenant Commander Heinecke said to Volkmann. "I wouldn't have thought they'd let us off so lightly."[28] A more religious observer noted, "For sure, the dear lord favored black-white-red today."[29]

The Russian defense was handled poorly. Colonel Gvaita, commander of the 426th Infantry Regiment and the area around Tagga Bay, simply sat in Mustel with a reserve force of three companies and never budged. No one could explain why. According to the captain in charge of Battery 3, Gvaita was "completely ignorant about what was happening in Tagga Bay." For three and a half hours the Third Battery constituted the sole defense of the eastern side of Tagga Bay, and "there was complete inaction from the units of the 426th Regiment at the moment of the enemy landing . . . completely inexplicable . . . incomprehensible." Some units bolted. For example, a machine gun company had moved north to Cape Merris, near the fort at Ninnast, then fled at the first sign of the German infantry. On the west side of the bay, the Second Battery had fought for a half hour, but after its commander, a Lieutenant Golvesev, was killed, the soldiers broke. Captain Reek summarized the situation, writing that "in the region of Tagga Bay, only eight light pieces of ordnance resisted the enemy landing while the infantry did nothing."[30]

On board the *Moltke*, following closely behind the assault force, Schmidt saw the *Corsica* begin to list. He sent a staff officer over in a small boat to investigate. He returned to say that the vessel had run into a mine, reporting that the damage that had occurred was not that serious. Schmidt ordered the two torpedo boats accompanying the *Moltke* to pick up the 850 soldiers on the *Corsica*. The infantry got off in good order, despite the shells whizzing overhead and a worsening list. The *Corsica*'s skipper then ran it aground to await a salvage team.[31]

Admiral Schmidt next ordered Lieutenant Commander Doflein's minesweeping flotilla into the bay. To everyone's shock, thirty-five mines were pulled up. All the ships but *Corsica* had providentially sailed through an opening in a minefield. Lieutenant Kiep, who had laid out the course for the fleet in the chartroom at Libau weeks before sailing, noted years later that it was simply happenstance that his route and the gap in the minefield coincided. Admiral Schmidt was more succinct. "Fortune willed it," he said.[32]

Schmidt and Kathen did not waste time. Even while the battle raged in the woods at the south end of Tagga Bay, they ordered the steamers carrying the main body of infantrymen to move near the entrance to the bay.[33] Around 6:30 AM the first vessels appeared at Point White. Doflein's small craft were still at work when the steamers with the main force began to move from Point White into the bay at 8:15. The commander of Reconnaissance Group II, Rear Admiral Ludwig von Reuter,[34] led the way in his flagship, *Königsberg*. He reported that one could still hear firing from the forest on both sides of the bay and that shrapnel shells still flew about.[35]

Volkmann had himself rowed over to von Reuter's flagship, where von Estorff and his staff waited. Volkmann reported on events, and the general took command of the forces. The sound of firing from the shore grew more distant, and reports came back that the landing site was secure. By 10 AM,

Russian resistance in the Tagga Bay area had largely ceased. The leading German forces had moved about 3–4 kilometers inland[36] and were making good forward progress. Volkmann told von Estorff that reports from the landing at Pamerort indicated that matters had likewise gone well there. The Germans now had to count on one of two probabilities. The Russians could launch a counterattack with reinforcements from Arensburg, aimed at pushing the Germans back into Tagga Bay. The other probability was that the landing at Pamerort, in the rear of the Russian defenses, might unnerve them to the point where they would pull their forces south to Arensburg in order to head for Orrisar as rapidly as possible. Unknown to the Germans at the time, the landing at Orrisar had achieved precisely that effect. In the words of the Russians, the Pamerort landing force "brilliantly accomplished its task . . . it destroyed the rear and occupied the Orrisar bridgehead, creating a hopeless situation which [the] disorganized and demoralized remnants of the 107th Division could not overcome."[37]

The German operation plan called for securing the Tagga Bay landing area, unloading their equipment, and proceeding first to Arensburg and then to Orrisar. That put enormous pressure on the Pamerort landing force, now heading for Orrisar. That group would have to hold the bridgehead at the causeway for some time—perhaps for as long as a day or two. Volkmann and von Estorff discussed the situation, arriving at the conclusion that to wait and complete the unloading of all the supplies and equipment could prove fatal to the Pamerort-Orrisar force. The decision to move without essential equipment or the units' combat trains (field kitchens, sleeping gear, ammunition, and provision wagons), especially the artillery, was a hard one. The three batteries that had been labeled essential were still not ashore. Experience in combat had taught the Germans how crucial it was to have artillery. Von Estorff knew he had to engage the Russians decisively within one or two days, three at the most, if he hoped to annihilate them. He had faith that his soldiers could make a long march without clean clothes and hot meals.[38]

The general decided to head inland at once, trying to intercept the Russians just north and east of Arensburg. Von Estorff gambled that if he could move extremely fast, his men could reach the Arensburg–Orrisar road before the Russians did, and destroy them. If he could accomplish this task, there would be only disorganized stragglers arriving at the causeway. If he did not block the road in time, von Winterfeld's detachment of storm troops and cyclists would be in for a hard time.

As the two officers looked over the landing site from the deck of the *Königsberg*, the enemy's response was patently disorganized. It was best to strike now, von Estorff told Volkmann, and allow the Russians no time to regroup. "The regiments should march immediately," said the general. "The machine gun companies must come when they can." Volkmann wanted to hold back at least until the commanders could get their horses, but the general said no, that would take hours. Instead of waiting in the beachhead area for the main body of soldiers to unload, Volkmann took his cue and dispatched the lead regiments inland. The 131st headed southwest toward Kielkond and Papensholm. To the east of the Bay, the 138th broke through the confused Russians and marched in a southeast direction, toward Arensburg and the roads leading from it to Orrisar.[39]

Von Estorff's regiments took off on foot, fanning out, marching further and further from each other, fighting and pursuing Russians through the birch and pine forests. They pushed all day, rarely slacking, until they reached their objectives late that night. The 131st took Kielkond by 2 PM, and, after a brief engagement, the Russian seaplane station at Papensholm by 3:30.[40] The Germans captured several aircraft, along with some slightly damaged buildings and hangers. Much of the airfield remained serviceable. The Germans immediately flew in aircraft from the mainland and began to conduct operations the same day. To the east, Colonel Willi Matthiass led his Sixty-fifth Brigade (the Seventeenth and 138th Infantry Regiments) through the woods, taking Karro and Mustel (10 kilometers inland) respectively before halting for the night. A thirty-five-year veteran of military service, Matthiass could get the most from his soldiers. His wartime career had consisted entirely of commanding infantry units, first Reserve Infantry Regiment 46 in more than seventy-three separate engagements in both the western and eastern fronts, then Infantry Brigade 65 (of the Forty-second Division) from 1916.[41] Matthiass knew when to push his men and when to allow some slack. After breaking the Russian resistance on the shore, the colonel marched his regiments inland toward their objectives, but he occasionally looked the other way. As one observer noted, "For the most part, the numerous pigs and geese brought about more delays than the Russians did. Every private as a matter of faith assumed an inalienable right to one of these animals."[42] Things became more serious as the Russians recovered their breath and resistance stiffened. Following the Sixty-fifth Brigade came the 255th Reserve Infantry Regiment. That unit left Tagga Bay at noon, leaving behind its field kitchens and ammunition supplies, which the soldiers did not see again until the operation was over. The regiment marched along desolate roadways until 8 PM. Soaked to the skin by the incessant rains, the soldiers bedded down for the remainder of the night at the village of Irro. A "squalid cottage" was the term used by one officer.[43]

Back in Tagga Bay, General von Estorff finally went ashore at nightfall. He used a peasant's farm for a headquarters. The farm was filthy and reeked from the remains of slaughtered animals and dead Russians in the courtyard. In the bay, unloading continued unabated under the lights of the fleet. Uneasy horses screamed, and their handlers shouted back in response. Volkmann said later that he was amazed to find himself in the midst of this huge operation. He was particularly proud of the fact that, in the end, it had not cost thousands of German lives. Planning, boldness, and surprise had all played a role, he thought, as had luck.[44]

ARENSBURG, 12 OCTOBER

About the time General von Estorff decided to move his regiments inland without waiting for their full complement of weapons and logistical trains, Admiral Sveshnikov was giving the bad news about the invasion first to Admiral Bakhirev, his immediate superior as commander of the naval defense of the Gulf of Riga, and then to Baltic Fleet commander Admiral Razvozov. At 9:39 AM Sveshnikov had reported that "the enemy with unknown forces landed in the region of [Tagga Bay], I sent two regiments and one death regiment against them. Our forces in the Tagga Bay region amount to 2 infantry battalions, 2 light batteries, 2 machine-gun crews."[45] Bakhirev merely said he would ask for an additional naval death battalion.[46] Admiral Razvozov let General Cheremisov, the commander of the northern front, know about the grave situation. Razvozov indicated that he had issued orders for positioning submarines and other naval forces near the islands. In addition, he said, "I am sending the naval death battalion from Reval to the islands as quickly as possible," and he indicated he was giving thought to moving the 173rd Infantry Regiment to Ösel as well. The garrison at Sworbe, he indicated, had orders to hold at all costs. He concluded by asking General Cheremisov if he could send these reinforcements to Ösel.[47]

Sometime during the day, Razvozov also went to the *Poliarnaia Zvezda* (*Polar Star*), the former imperial yacht, which the Tsentrobalt had seized for its use. A newly elected Tsentrobalt had convened on the 7th of October. Thoroughly bolshevized, it chose as its chairman storekeeper Pavel Dybenko, a long-time follower of Lenin. Razvozov informed the assembly of the German landings, asking for support. Dybenko said he told Razvozov the delegates said, "'In battle your order is law.'" They also affirmed that "'anyone who dares not obey a battle order will be considered an enemy of the revolution and will be shot.'"[48]

Meanwhile, General Cheremisov radioed back to Razvozov within two hours, informing the admiral to make use of the 173rd Regiment as he saw fit. Further, the general indicated he had ordered the Estonian Regiment and a brigade of the Forty-fifth Infantry Division along with an artillery division (all at Reval) to entrain for Hapsal. If necessary, he would send the division's remaining units. Cheremisov then added that he had received reports that indicated units in the 107th Division had not performed well on the battlefield or had simply fled. He would not tolerate such behavior, and he concluded with a stern warning that he expected commanders and soldiers to remain calm and to take strong measures against panic and defeatism.[49] Later that same day, General Lukirsky, the northern front's chief of staff, passed on two bombastic telegrams from Alexander Kerensky, Russia's acting head of state. He exhorted the soldiers and sailors to remain steadfast. The message for the fleet was pointed:

> Russia is expecting heroic work from the Fleet for its salvation. . . . The time is coming when the Baltic Fleet has an opportunity to stand up for the honor of the Motherland and the great precepts of freedom and revolution and to prove that it is worthy of them. . . . Let everybody remember that the Motherland, which is going to live not only today, will not forgive criminal thoughtlessness or intentional treason. Let the terrible crime of the *Petropavlovsk* be redeemed.[50]

On Ösel, General Ivanov knew that if he did not stop the invasion on the shores of Tagga Bay, the island was in jeopardy. Telephone lines were down. Communications had collapsed. He had no idea that Colonel Gvaita's 426th Infantry Regiment had already failed. He did not get word of the German landing at Pamerort until 11 AM or thereabouts.[51] While in the dark, he did what seemed logical under the circumstances. He ordered units from his reserve regiment, the 472d, to move toward Tagga Bay from their positions at Kergel on the Arensburg–Kielkond road. This order placed the Russians on a collision course with the advancing Germans. Confused reports about chaotic conditions filtered back to the 107th Division headquarters, so around noon General Ivanov sent his deputy, Brigadier General Vladimir Nikitich Kolbe, to the Tagga Bay area.

A veteran with over thirty-five years service, Kolbe had seen combat crises before, and he knew the units of the 107th Division well, having been its brigadier for eighteen months. He had served in Manchuria in the Russo-Japanese War, where he commanded a rifle regiment in action. When the war with Germany began in 1914, he led a brigade in the Twelfth Siberian Rifle Division. He seems to have spent most of the war in the vicinity of Petrograd, although he had taken over the brigade headquarters in the 107th Division in April 1916.[52]

Kolbe had to use the Arensburg–Kielkond road to get to Tagga Bay, and he came across signs of calamity almost immediately. As he passed through Kergel, the fortified position for the division reserve northwest of Arensburg, units from the 426th Regiment, fleeing south, tore past him. Their infectious panic overwhelmed the few reserve forces remaining in Kergel, and they joined in, running pell-mell. As the mob streamed toward Padel, the next village, the disorganized soldiers collided headlong with two companies from the 472nd Infantry Regiment moving in the opposite direction. These units had left Arensburg with Kolbe but had fallen behind him as they marched on foot toward Tagga Bay. The sight of their fleeing comrades shook them badly, bringing their column to an immediate halt. Their regimental commander, Colonel Arekhov, tried to rescue the situation, but his entreaties to get back in line and to head toward the enemy fell largely on deaf ears. Fortunately, he also had with him a battery of field guns from the division's artillery park, and the gunners unlimbered their guns on the road. They aimed their pieces on the highway, blocking any further retreat. The frightened soldiers reluctantly stopped and began to entrench.[53] Nonetheless, by late in the day, one group of Russians (mostly those from the west side of Tagga Bay) had fled to the villages of Semmern and Padel, just south of the defensive position at Kergel, only 15 kilometers from Arensburg. A second group, from the eastern side of the bay, coalesced at the village of Saufer, 10 kilometers further to the north and on a secondary road leading to Arensburg.[54]

Sveshnikov, his staff, and the executive committee of the Islands Defense Soviet assembled in their headquarters at the bishop's castle in Arensburg, around 4 PM. By this time, the Russians were aware of the landings in their rear at Pamerort, and they recognized the grave danger posed by this potential threat. They knew German cycle troops had come through Laisburg (a village below Pamerort) and had intersected the Arensburg–Orrisar road, and Sveshnikov had sent a force to block them. What the Russians did not know at this time, however, was the whereabouts of the other cycle battalion, now closing in on Orrisar, the causeway, and their escape route. Sveshnikov wrote that when he met with Ivanov and Kolbe, he knew only that German cyclists were on the Arensburg–Orrisar highway. His orders to Ivanov to have the garrison units of the 107th Division break through the cyclists operating in the division's rear areas in order to secure the critical position at Orrisar indicate he did not know that the village already was in German hands. He admitted what information he had was "partly inaccurate and received with significant delay."[55] Captain Reek summed up the problem, saying, "[We tried to concentrate] at Tagga Bay, but were not on time, also [we had to face] a dreadful threat in [our] flank, rear and [Pamerort]."[56]

Accounts of this meeting in the bishop's castle indicate it resembled a council of war in which a majority carried the day rather than a commander giving crisp orders and providing definitive guidance to a staff. Phrases such as "to save the 107th Infantry Division" reflected the pessimism of the moment and the gravity of the situation. The group recognized that the forces near Tagga Bay could no longer hold their positions, even the ones planned for the phased withdrawal toward Orrisar. Instead, the group concluded that General Ivanov should immediately take the remnants of his division and march them to Orrisar, breaking through any Germans he might encounter along the way. Once there, he should secure the area and wait until help came from the mainland via Moon Island. The forces at Sworbe would simply have to hold. Finally, the group decided that they should leave at once for Hapsal on the mainland and organize reinforcements arriving to rescue the 107th Division. The consensus was that Sveshnikov best knew the entire situation, and he should move to Hapsal as soon as possible.[57]

Generals Ivanov and Kolbe arrived at the castle a couple of hours later, coming from the battlefield. They briefed the admiral about the artillery losses, the absence of reserves, the refusal of some units to follow orders, the panic, and the failure of the fleet to put up resistance to the enemy landing. The navy, complained Ivanov, further allowed the enemy to break through the Soela Sound, which resulted in the landing at Pamerort. The generals said it was impossible to eliminate the enemy. "On that account," said Sveshnikov, "I ordered all garrison units, except those on the Sworbe Peninsula . . . to break though to the fortified position at Orrisar. I set the objective of keeping the Orrisar bridgehead (which covered the causeway to Moon) in our hands to allow the reinforcements [arriving from the mainland] to move to the offensive."[58]

Meanwhile, further reports of reverses had gotten back to General Cheremisov at northern front headquarters. He was unhappy with the performance of all concerned and made it clear in a radio message sent to Razvozov at 9:21 PM.

> Our troops on Ösel are not resisting. That's going to allow the enemy, after landing his forces, to defeat our soldiers and take the island. I suggest you issue an order to the 107th Division commander to immediately concentrate as many troops as possible in the location of the enemy's landing and to start a decisive counterattack against the troops on the shore. I am also asking you to demand that your subordinate naval commanders undertake more offensive [minded] actions at sea against enemy ships.[59]

It is not certain if General Ivanov knew of Cheremisov's order to counterattack, but at 10:30 PM he issued Order #18 to his division, outlining the next day's tasks. Counterattack was not on his agenda. Ivanov told Colonel Gvaita to round up whatever troops he could from his former region around Tagga Bay and slow down the Germans in the morning. General Ivanov expected Gvaita to hold a line running from Karrishof to Udofer, towns on the northern road from Arensburg to Pamerort. Colonel Arekhov's 472d Regiment, the division reserve, was split up. A Lieutenant Colonel Prokopovich was given three companies from Arekhov's regiment and told to assemble in Udofer, and at dawn to move north on the road toward the coast at the Kassar Inlet. While not clearly stated, apparently their mission was to ensure that the German force that had landed at Pamerort did not use this road. Arekhov had to send three additional companies to Orrisar to protect the causeway bridgehead, and with whatever was left of his regiment, Ivanov told him to halt the Germans who were expected to come from Kielkond toward Arensburg the next day. The 425th Infantry Regiment remained at Zerel to protect the batteries.[60]

Sveshnikov's chief of staff, Captain Reek, sketched the situation in a telegram to Admiral Bakhirev and Admiral Razvozov and neighboring army units. He admitted the 426th and 472nd Regiments were falling back toward Arensburg under enemy pressure, and he expressed concern about the threat to his rear areas from the German force that had landed at Pamerort. He indicated Sveshnikov had committed all his reserves and regarded the situation as "critical."[61]

A later telegram hinted at disaster. Captain Reek stated that the 472nd Regiment had pulled back from the region west of Arensburg to cover the retreating forces, whose "objective was to break through to Orrisar and occupy the Orrisar position."[62] In other words, the Russians suspected or knew that the Germans already blocked the only avenue of escape from the island, and unless the 107th Division could smash through the lines, it was doomed. While the Russians did not know for certain that von Winterfeld's forces held Orrisar until just after midnight, the language of the telegram indicates that someone at Sveshnikov's headquarters knew or suspected the Germans already held Orrisar and the bridgehead.[63] Finally, Reek told General Ivanov to send his reports directly to Hapsal in light of Sveshnikov's impending move to the mainland.[64] Sveshnikov departed on the gunboat *Chrabry* at 1 AM (13 October) for the base at Kuivast.[65] A second vessel, the *Elba*, accompanied *Chrabry*. The *Elba* carried the headquarters personnel and their baggage and families.

Captain Reek remained behind for a few more hours, operating from a makeshift command post on the pier at Rommassare, Arensburg's port area. Lieutenant Prestin, the head of the soviet's defense committee, likewise stayed, and the calmness of his reports and actions could not have contrasted more unfavorably with those of the rattled Sveshnikov. Prestin radioed the Baltic Fleet headquarters, explaining that reports indicated the Germans had landed near Orrisar and had cut the road from Arensburg. He was not certain about the accuracy of the reports, but he said that if the road to Orrisar was blocked, he planned to stay in Arensburg until the last possible moment, then he would blow up the bishop's palace and try to escape on a torpedo boat.[66] Prestin left the island that night or the next morning. He fought heroically on Moon Island a couple of days later.

Sveshnikov's hasty departure did not sit well with any of his superiors. Razvozov immediately radioed Sveshnikov on the *Chrabry*, telling him "you should stay with the headquarters on Moon to support firm communications with the troops on Ösel." Sveshnikov had meanwhile arrived at Kuivast, and went on board the *Libava*, where he met with Admiral Bakhirev, who was not known to mince words. What they discussed is unknown, but Sveshnikov then radioed Razvozov, saying, "I can't issue any orders here on Moon [Island] because of the lack of direct communication with Hapsal, the rear and Dagö. I have no reserves on the islands, . . . I'm asking to go to Hapsal. I'm on the transport *Libava* waiting to hear from you."[67] Sveshnikov spoke with Razvozov a few hours later, and the ground force commander once more poured forth a litany of reasons why he should depart for the mainland:

"I'm asking for permission to go to Hapsal," begged Sveshnikov, "because there is no communication with Moon Island at the present time. My objective is to transfer and organize reinforcements. I don't think we can expect any rallying from the troops left [on Ösel]. I have no communication with the division commander, who is probably at Nei-Level. No communications with Arensburg as well. We must begin a new operation on Moon. For this purpose I need an infantry division, an artillery division, and no less than 2 cavalry regiments. I don't expect much from the regiments of the 118th Division.

Razvozov's terse reply indicated his disgust and desperation: "Go to Hapsal. Defend the causeway by any means."[68]

Admiral Bakhirev, who had spoken with Sveshnikov when he was on the on the *Libava*, took more forceful action. Bakhirev impounded the steamer *Elba* with all of Sveshnikov's headquarters personnel and their baggage when the vessel showed up in Kuivast. The same storm that suspended the German unloading operations in Tagga Bay gave him an excuse for the delay, but Sveshnikov recognized what was happening, and became livid. He cabled Bakhirev, saying he had issued instructions to have the ship sent from Kuivast to Hapsal. "My directions were canceled," fumed Sveshnikov, "and the transport ship was delayed in Kuivast for 24 hours and is still there. The families . . . and my headquarters personnel are probably starving on the *Elba*."[69] Bakhirev never responded; he was busy fighting the Germans.

General Cheremisov, the northern front commander, also weighed in with a radio message to Razvozov. The 107th Division, he wrote, had clearly collapsed. The only energy its officers and men displayed consisted of fleeing to Orrisar to save their skins. No one, he fumed, tried to resist the Germans. Consequently, he wrote, those who failed to fight should "be tried by a revolutionary court." Second, he urged senior officers to sack subordinates who had failed to display sufficient energy and decisiveness. Third, he announced he was putting General Nicholai Vladimirovich Ghenrikson in charge of the land forces on the Baltic Islands. "Sworbe," he wrote, "must be held at all costs and Ösel Island should be cleared of the enemy by all means, even if it involves losing all the troops." Finally, he instructed Razvozov and Bakhirev to provide better support to the army.[70]

The new commander of the land forces, General Ghenrikson, came from Finnish stock. Born in 1871, he entered the army in 1891, serving in the routine assignments of a junior officer in the infantry. Admitted to the Nicholas General Staff Academy in 1898, he went to the staff of the Warsaw Military District following graduation. He remained in this area until 1910 in a variety of staff positions. By 1910 he was a lieutenant colonel and held several staff jobs at Kronstadt until transferred to the Army General Staff in 1912. In 1914 he was given command of the Twenty-ninth (Chernigov) Infantry Regiment, but was recalled to the Warsaw Military District staff on the outbreak of hostilities in August 1914. In 1915 he took over the 202nd (Goriisky) Infantry Regiment, and he was wounded severely later that year. In 1916–1917 he served on the staff of the northern front headquarters, being promoted to brigadier general in December 1916. He commanded the 109th Infantry Division from late April 1917 until General Cheremisov assigned him on the 6th of October to take over the duties of commander of the land forces, Baltic Islands defense. He arrived at Hapsal on the 13th of October.[71]

Ghenrikson displaced Sveshnikov. Initially, his responsibilities seem to have focused on the eastern shore area of the Gulf of Riga, but Cheremisov's radio message of 14 October to Razvozov changed that. Ghenrikson now had responsibility for the islands, and he wasted no time in attempting to set up a defense to hold the Germans.

He issued his Order #1 on the 13th of October, calling for Ivanov to hold a line running from Arensburg north to Cape Pamerort. He wanted Ivanov to push the Germans back to the west, clearing them from the island, even to the point of restoring direct communication with the 425th Regiment on the Sworbe Peninsula. He told General Martynov, the 118th Infantry Division's brigade commander, who was on Moon Island, to hold it and the bridgehead at Orrisar. Coming from the ranks of the hereditary nobility, Martynov had enjoyed a smooth start to his career until he was dismissed from the general staff academy in 1903 from what was termed "domestic circumstances."[72] He recovered his career by getting assigned to the Foot Guards in 1908, where he remained until the eve of the war, when he was assigned to command a battalion in the Sixty-ninth (Ryazan) Infantry Regiment. Wounded in 1914 and then again in 1915, he had an outstanding war record for bravery, and went on to command the Seventy-first (Belevsky) Infantry Regiment in 1916 and a brigade in the 118th Infantry Division in 1917. Promotion to brigadier general came in August 1917.[73]

Ghenrikson obviously did not know the Germans already occupied Orrisar. Reinforcements, he explained, would arrive on Moon the next day, namely the Reval Naval Death Battalion, the 470th Dankovsky Infantry Regiment, and the Second Detached Reval Frontier Cavalry Hundred. The 471st Kozelsky Infantry Regiment was moving to Hapsal and would then be sent to Moon. Ghenrikson told Martynov to use these soldiers to clear the eastern side of Ösel and link up with General Ivanov and the 107th Division.[74] Reflecting a poor understanding of the progress of the Germans and the collapse of the defenses on the island, Ghenrikson's Order #1 was already overtaken by events.

Cheremisov's assignment of responsibility to defend the Baltic Islands to Ghenrikson left Sveshnikov with his title (commander of the Baltic Islands defense position) intact but little else. He no longer had the slightest authority over units on the islands or ashore, which he soon discovered. Realizing he was through, he acknowledged that "I was in fact dismissed. . . . All my activities were narrowed down to blindly following the orders and assisting transportation of the troops sent to the Islands."[75]

ARENSBURG, 13 OCTOBER

Late on the night on the 12th, from his farm headquarters, General von Estorff gave orders to his regiments to move the next morning toward the Orrisar–Arensburg road in two columns. The 255th Reserve Infantry Regiment was to take the southern road, while Colonel Matthiass's Sixty-fifth Brigade moved along the northern road. The units started at dawn on the 13th of October. The 255th Regiment soon encountered resistance from Colonel Arekhov's 472d Regiment that took several hours to crush. Later, during the afternoon of the 13th, the 255th took a break at Irrasse, a village 10 kilometers north of Arensburg. A Russian cavalry squadron suddenly appeared, coming from the village of Hanjalla to the west, and tried to break through to the east by galloping through the village while the tired Germans smoked and milled about the public fountain. The Russian cavalry squadron commander led the rush. The Germans were astounded at this foolhardy attempt in broad daylight. One lieutenant described the action to a naval officer friend. "In columns—you would have described them like ships following one after the other in a review at Kiel—the dragoons rode through the village. Our men stood in the gardens [of the homes] and mowed the poor guys down," killing and severely wounding many. "The main street was full of human and animal corpses." Most of the Russians, including the badly injured commander, were captured.[76]

Infantry Brigade 65 (the Seventeenth and 138th Regiments) had no initial resistance after leaving the beachhead area until the afternoon of the 13th, when it encountered Russians near the village of East Karmel. The Germans had one artillery battery leading their lengthy column. When the brigade encountered the Russians, the artillery opened up at 800 meters, yet it still took an assault with hand grenades to route the enemy. The 138th Regiment alone took one thousand prisoners, eight cannons, and several machine guns, along with the Russian commander, Colonel Gvaita of the 426th Regiment. The Russian report that went to General Ivanov's headquarters the next day could only surmise that "[Colonel Gvaita's] group was surrounded, and we don't know what happened there."[77] The brigade then marched to Putla and Mustla, where the two regiments bivouacked for the night. The Germans now sat astride the north road from Arensburg to Orrisar.

Earlier that day (the 13th), von Estorff's headquarters moved from the peasant farm on Tagga Bay to a ruined country estate just north of Arensburg. Adding greatly to the uncertainty of the situation for von Estorff's staff was the fact that the division's units kept moving further and further apart. Volkmann feared that if the Russians concentrated their forces at Arensburg and waited, choosing the right moment, they could fall on and destroy any of the individual German regimental columns. The regiments were too far apart to come to each other's aid, and only one regiment had any artillery with it.[78]

Toward evening, General von Estorff became aware of the fighting at Orrisar.[79] While he mulled over this news and its implications, Volkmann received a report from a wounded soldier, Deputy Officer Meyer. He said he had been on a long-range patrol that had gone into Arensburg from the north-northeast side. Very little destruction was visible, and the city appeared empty of Russians except for a Colonel Popow, the commandant of the town. Meyer said his patrol promptly took him prisoner and demanded the keys to the city, which Popow surrendered. Under questioning, the colonel said some ten to twelve thousand Russians had left Arensburg the evening before [12 October], heading for Moon Island. To the southwest, a further five thousand Russians were still on the Sworbe Peninsula.

Growing visibly faint, Meyer mumbled that he had also questioned local residents, who confirmed the colonel's information. Volkmann handed the exhausted deputy officer a few cigarettes and gave him a pull from a bottle of cognac. Revived, Meyer added that as he sat down to compose a message to the division headquarters, Russian stragglers or rear guards attacked the building where he was and opened fire. The Russians captured his comrades and wounded him in the melee. He got away, he said, only by crawling through a garden and stealing a horse.[80]

In fact, the Germans had narrowly missed witnessing a scene of terrible humiliation that would have confirmed their growing sense that their enemy was beaten. When Meyer's patrol wandered around Arensburg, the Russians discovered it. Just to the northeast of the city, on the road heading to Orrisar, Colonel Arekhov had formed the shaken remnants of several companies from his 472nd Regiment. They had fought the delaying action for several hours that morning against the German 255th Infantry, and the survivors were forming up to march to Orrisar and what they thought would be safety. Standing guard between the struggling infantry and the town of Arensburg was the First Battery of the 107th Division.

Townspeople told the commander of the artillery battery about Meyer's patrol—that there were seven German scouts in the city. The artillery commander decided to take care of the Germans and tried to round up some soldiers from the 472nd to assist his few gunners, but the soldiers refused. He tried to get them to give him their rifles, explaining that his men had only revolvers and swords, and they needed rifles to go after the Germans. The soldiers refused to give up their arms, so the artillery officer went looking for Colonel Arekhov. As he approached the command post, chaos ruled. Soldiers milled about, some in single file, some walking behind officers, others just standing in crowds. Many sat on the ground, eating rations from tin cans. After being apprised of the situation, Colonel Arekhov had his officers form the soldiers into units, and he asked for volunteers to roust the German patrol. No one stepped forward. In vain the officers implored the troops, and efforts to shame them failed. The soldiers refused to hand over their arms to the artillerymen, who did volunteer to enter the town. "If the gunners are so brave," sneered the soldiers, "they can advance by themselves." From the officers came oaths and curses, which provoked the response that "this is not the old regime and you can't shout at us." Disgusted, the battery commander gathered his men, and along with a few volunteers and Colonel Arekhov, went into Arensburg and attacked Meyer's patrol, capturing two Germans. The others, including Deputy Officer Meyer, escaped. Some approaching Germans saw this and opened fire. The battery commander then ordered his unit to move back out of town until it got out of range. The disorganized units of the 472nd Regiment had remained alongside the Arensburg Road the entire time, witnessing this episode. As the artillerymen approached their comrades, "all the remaining infantrymen raised white flags on their rifles and in one moment the road bloomed with white flags." Worse, the retreating Russian artillery had drawn German attention and small-arms fire, and as it neared and passed by the lines of Russian infantry, they opened fire on their comrades, apparently hoping to stop the movement that had attracted enemy fire.[81]

The battery commander had decided the situation was hopeless, so he spurred his men and horses on, past the standing Russian infantry, and headed up the road to Orrisar. Colonel Arekhov and his staff followed, abandoning the stragglers. The incessant rain and the passage of the bulk of the 107th Division the day before had made the road ahead a quagmire. The exhausted and starving horses struggled in the mud, towing the guns and caissons. In addition, they were burdened by wounded or sick soldiers riding on top of the equipment, who refused to dismount.

At some point in the night Colonel Arekhov and his staff rode past the gunners. Alarmed, the artillery commander sent some scouts to find him, but they soon returned to say the colonel had gone into the woods to detour around the road, supposedly blocked by Germans. At this point, the battery commander said, "the horses refused to go further, and so our three guns would not fall into enemy hands, we decided to destroy them."[82]

Within a few minutes of the conversation between Volkmann and Deputy Officer Meyer, a reconnaissance plane landed at the headquarters of the division. The pilot sought out Volkmann and reported that he had seen heavy fighting at Orrisar. It appeared, he said, that the Russians had taken the entrance to the causeway.[83] This report confirmed von Estorff's and Volkmann's worst fears, namely that the Russians might overwhelm von Winterfeld's force and escape to safety across the causeway to Moon. It was nightfall, however, and Orrisar was 50 kilometers distant. They felt they could do nothing about that situation until morning. As for Arensburg itself, signs indicated that the Russians had abandoned it, so Volkmann ordered the Sixth Cycle Battalion, the division reserve, to make a night march and take it that evening. The battalion did so and confirmed Meyer's information. The city was deserted.[84]

Volkmann met with General von Estorff for fifteen minutes, and gave his orders to the staff. "The regiments will continue their advance toward Orrisar at dawn tomorrow." An officer interrupted to ask why the troops could not be ordered to start right then. Even if half or two-thirds of the men fell out, he argued, the remaining third would make all the difference between a happy or unhappy ending for von Winterfeld's men.

Volkmann thought about it. On the day of the landing, the division's regiments had marched and fought long past midnight. The same held true for the present day (the 13th), and the infantry units had yet to reach their objectives and night bivouac sites. There was a risk that to continue the march would further exhaust already drained troops. Still, the division was tough; it had never failed. This was the time, Volkmann decided, to demand the greatest sacrifice.[85]

He directed his staff to strike the last paragraph of his orders, and went to speak with General von Estorff. Both officers understood that to order their troops to move toward Orrisar without a night's rest was asking for heroics. They faced a 50-kilometer march in cold weather on poor roads—after having two days of the same under their belts. They had had no dry clothes or hot meals since landing on the island. Nevertheless, von Estorff quickly grasped the situation and ordered the march to continue "at once."[86]

A few minutes later Volkmann returned and dictated to the staff, "Success beckons. We must deploy every last element of the division. We have to help the troops at Orrisar. The 65th Infantry Brigade marches at midnight through Taggaser to Orrisar and to Moon. Leave your kits behind. Take only your assault packs! The immediate dispatch of volunteers [to mark the way] is authorized. At the same time and in the same manner Reserve Infantry Regiment 255 will march through Mustla-Kongrossa in an effort to hit the enemy from the rear. Infantry Regiment 131 will continue its assault on the Sworbe Peninsula. The division staff will leave at dawn through Arensburg to Hasik" for Orrisar.[87]

Colonel Berring's Infantry Regiment 255 broke bivouac at 1:30 AM and marched all night in the rain and deep mud, carrying their commander, whose foot was injured, in a horse-drawn wagon. They took a break at 9 AM when they reached the southern Arensburg–Orrisar road. The regiment took a second rest at 5:30 PM. One of the regiment's officers, Lieutenant Backer, described the scene:

> Later that night came the orders to move out just after midnight. Winterfeld's Section was in a jam at Orrisar. Off we went. And then came a day, a red letter day. For 25 hours we marched 53 kilometers! Roads, I say, what roads?! But let's say no more about them. We marched the entire time either through furrowed fields or along roads in mud up to our thighs. I felt sorry for our men. They could not lie down during the breaks because it rained pretty much the entire time.[88]

The regiment had orders to advance until encountering the enemy, which it finally did around 1 AM near Kapra, just below Orrisar, on 15 October. Given the exhausted state of his soldiers, Colonel Berring wisely refrained from fighting in the dark.[89]

Colonel Matthiass and the Seventeenth and 138th Infantry Regiments were already on the northern Arensburg–Orrisar road when they received orders to move out. The roads turned to rivers of mud that sucked at the legs of the advancing soldiers. Despite conditions, few faltered, because "like an electric spark, the worn-out troops suddenly realized that despite two days of marching in constant rain, with washed out roads and no replenishments or food, a huge victory beckoned. Each was ready to expend his last ounce of energy."[90] The tired soldiers picked up the pace. As General von Kathen expressed it, "Every officer and soldier knew what was at stake. Everyone urged, 'On!'"[91]

CHAPTER SEVEN

ÖSEL, 12–16 OCTOBER 1917: THE ISLAND'S ENDS

ANSEKÜLL, THE SWORBE PENINSULA

"Keep in mind," said Lieutenant Colonel Kurt Fischer, commander of Infantry Regiment 131, "this is an effort to save German lives." With those words, First Lieutenant von Oppen, accompanied by several soldiers and a translator, headed south at 8 AM on the 14th from the village of Tehomarti toward the Russian lines. Colonel Fischer had assigned to von Oppen, the regiment's operations officer, the difficult job of convincing the Russian soldiers and sailors on the Sworbe Peninsula to surrender. Fischer promised the Russians an armistice, internment rather than imprisonment, and no forced labor in return for surrendering without destroying their artillery. As he started south, von Oppen knew that he would run into a Russian roadblock within a few kilometers, just below the village of Anseküll. A patrol from his unit had made that discovery the day before. Beyond that, he knew only that over three thousand enemy sailors and soldiers were on the peninsula. von Oppen later said that only as he left the safety of friendly lines did it dawn on him how important his mission was. Thirty minutes later, as he approached the roadblock and called out for a safe passage, the Russians opened fire, forcing him and his men to dive for cover.[1]

While von Oppen and his party huddled in front of the Russian defenses, back up the road at Tehomarti, Colonel Fischer and the rest of the regiment waited for them to return and the navy to arrive. The soldiers were tired. On the morning of the 12th, the regiment had encountered stiff resistance when it landed at dawn on the west side of Tagga Bay. After overrunning the Second Battery of the 107th Artillery Division, Fischer's men marched southwest toward their main objective, the seaplane base at Papensholm on the west coast of the island. The village of Kielkond stood in the way, some 5 or 6 kilometers from the base, and the 131st Infantry had a hard fight to clear Russians out of field fortifications on the east edge of the village.[2] By midday, the Germans had routed the defenders and headed for the aerodrome. At the same time, the three destroyers that had bombarded the seaplane base during the morning headed out to sea as the infantry arrived. In spite of the shelling and a hasty Russian attempt at destroying the facilities, the Germans captured the station largely intact. The Russians flew three aircraft to safety at Arensburg; seven others were damaged and abandoned. The hangers and aprons remained serviceable, and the Germans began to move in, flying aircraft over from the mainland. "Tops" was how the new station commander characterized how his personnel felt about their new arrangements after they had moved in.[3]

Meanwhile, Colonel Fisher had kept his men on the move, pushing south down the road from Kielkond to Monnust. He set up a bivouac that night at Tawi, an insignificant village, having marched close to 30 kilometers. A hard-driving man, Fischer had almost thirty years of service behind him. A major and regimental adjutant when the war broke out, he had fought in the 1914 Marne Campaign and had commanded the 131st Regiment with great distinction in the east since 1915. Unknown to him, General von Estorff had recommended him for Prussia's highest decoration, the *Pour le Mérite*, for exceptional heroism in the recent campaign in East Galicia, where he had a horse shot out from under him while he was leading a charge, and for his handling of the crossing of the Aa River in the just completed Riga Campaign. The kaiser approved the award while the fighting at Ösel was underway.[4]

The next morning, Fischer set out for the Sworbe Peninsula. Most of the villagers on the way proved quite friendly, and advised the Germans that a short while before Russian troops had gone by, apparently marching from Arensburg to Sworbe. By nightfall, the regiment arrived at a village named Tehomarti. This village lay at the top of the Sworbe Peninsula, and with that area now in German hands, the Russian garrison on the peninsula could not escape. The Russians knew their garrison at Zerel was now cornered. Admiral Razvozov radioed to urge resistance. "Comrades, be strong, we're with you, count on our help!"[5]

SWORBE, 14–15 OCTOBER

Not knowing exactly what faced him, Fischer ordered his men to bivouac on the spot when they arrived at Tehomarti. Later that night a battery from the division's own Field Artillery Regiment 8 arrived to join Fischer's regiment.[6] On the morning of the 14th, after dispatching Lieutenant von Oppen, the 131st Regiment advanced to the roadblock. With the ocean on one side and a swamp on the other, the possibility of outflanking the Russian position at Anseküll looked doubtful, leaving Fischer little choice other than a frontal assault. Even with the newly arrived artillery, that strategy promised high casualties, hence Fischer's sending von Oppen to parlay, a decidedly long shot. Fischer had other cards to play just in case. Before leaving Tehomarti, he had radioed the *Moltke* and asked for a squadron of ships to provide naval gunfire. Admiral Schmidt had sent the Fourth Battle Squadron (the dreadnoughts *Friedrich der Große*, *Kaiserin*, and *König Albert*) to cover the advancing soldiers. Squadron commander Vice Admiral Wilhelm Souchon[7] immediately weighed anchor and sailed around Filzand and the west end of Ösel, but the ships were still hours away when Fischer's forces ran into the Russian fortifications at Anseküll.[8] Fischer expected Souchon to arrive around 3 PM,[9] which gave von Oppen plenty of time to negotiate with the Russians.

Two Russian companies (the Fifth and Seventh of the 425th Infantry Regiment) manned the roadblock at Anseküll. They were determined to hold the line. The day before, as they occupied the position, one of the officers reported that "their [soldiers'] mood was serious. They calmly expected . . . to be killed."[10] These soldiers had pinned down von Oppen's group the morning of the 14th. Only by holding up their hands like deserters could von Oppen and his party get the shooting to stop. After disarming the Germans and hearing that they had come to negotiate a surrender, a Russian officer swore, ""You sons of bitches! You want to talk to us about committing treason!"" Russian soldiers then blindfolded the Germans and stole their overcoats, sending them in freezing rain south in a small horse-drawn vehicle. The hapless Germans were soon soaked to the skin and began to shake from the cold. At 3:30 PM they arrived in Torkenhof, a manor some 17 kilometers south on the western side of the peninsula. Their captors turned them over to a soviet, which seemed to be in charge. Several senior officers, among them the regimental commander of the 425th Regiment, Colonel Borsakowski, and the commander of the Eighth Naval Artillery Battalion at Zerel, Captain First Rank Knyupfer, also came to hear the

German negotiators.[11] Von Oppen relayed his commander's terms, chief among them that if the Russians surrendered without destroying any of their equipment, Fischer would ensure that they would be interned and not forced to do any work against their will.[12]

During the several hours it took for von Oppen to get to Torkenhof, Colonel Fischer held his regiment in place while nervously waiting for his negotiating party to return. As time passed, he grew increasingly concerned. Around noon two planes from Windau landed and reported that five Russian destroyers were nearby in the Gulf of Riga. Fischer concluded that the destroyers were standing by to evacuate the Russian garrison, but he had no idea where the Fourth Squadron was, so he asked the pilots to find Admiral Souchon and tell him to hold his fire unless the batteries at Zerel fired at him. In the afternoon the Germans could hear heavy gunfire to the south. Souchon had apparently taken on the fort or vice versa. Neither scenario boded well for von Oppen.

Admiral Souchon's squadron had been steaming in circles off the peninsula since arriving at midday. Foul weather with attendant poor visibility and the unknown situation prevented him from doing anything until later that day. Around 2 PM, he engaged in a short duel with the 12" guns. The Russians initiated the action. The first salvo from Zerel flew over Souchon's ships; the second fell just short—perfect bracketing. The Germans expected a hail of fire, but only one further shot was fired, which hit one of the German ships. Then silence. Unknown to the Germans, the Russian sailors manning the guns had mutinied and refused to serve their guns. They insisted that the ammunition was too heavy and claimed that they had done enough work for the day. Despite the threats of their officers, the sailors refused to fire, saying that saving their lives was now the most important consideration. The Russian report states that only one gun actually engaged the Germans. The other crews had panicked and ran.[13]

At Kuivast, Admiral Bakhirev received the news of the mutiny almost at once and relayed it to Admiral Razvozov, telling him that the naval gunners had fled. Razvozov telephoned his liaison at the northern front headquarters, Captain V. M. Altvater,[14] to advise him of this calamity. Razvozov indicated that the Zerel battery crew left their guns and retreated to the western side of Sworbe. He was clearly beside himself, adding that if the batteries had really surrendered, he would order the nearby battleship *Graschdanin* to shoot them down. The admiral proved as good as his word; at 3 PM Bakhirev radioed the battleship and reported the gun crew had abandoned the 12" guns. The "Commander of the Fleet," he said, "orders you to destroy the battery at all costs." The *Graschdanin* fired twelve salvoes of four rounds each into the battery. Only the arrival of a torpedo boat from the fortress with the incorrect news that the guns were destroyed halted the shelling. Two hours later the captain of the *Graschdanin* radioed Admiral Bakhirev that "the battery was destroyed" and torpedo boats were evacuating personnel. The *Graschdanin* brought back some of the mutinous gun crews, and Bakhirev commented that none had wounds.[15] The crew from Battery #43 later ended up at Reval. Alexander Kerensky, head of the Provisional Government and supreme commander, blamed the loss of Moon Island on this mutiny and ordered a special court martial for the crew.[16]

Meanwhile, General Cheremisov tried to minimize the catastrophe, telling Razvozov "not to worry too much about the loss of the Sworbe Peninsula and the Zerel battery . . . [and instead] continue the concentration of forces on Ösel, and tomorrow, the 16th, decisively attack the enemy and clear the island."[17] Even though Sworbe was lost, Cheremisov told Razvozov to send ships to the Irbe Straits to impede the German occupation of the Gulf of Riga. Cheremisov either did not know what he was talking about or failed to comprehend the significance of his loss. Without the guns at Zerel, minefields and two old battleships could not keep the Germans from entering the Gulf of Riga. Once that happened, the *Slava* and *Graschdanin* would be hopelessly outclassed by the modern German dreadnoughts.[18]

Meanwhile, ignorant of the mutiny at Zerel and fearful for his intermediaries, Fischer decided to advance down the road toward Zerel from Anseküll. The Russians greeted his regiment with a barrage, stopping the Germans in their tracks. Two Russian batteries controlled the town's streets, and their cannon fire caused a team of horses drawing the regiment's flamethrower to bolt, wrecking the equipment. With nightfall coming, Fischer decided to cease operations until the next morning.

All afternoon the members of the soviet in Torkenhof had blasted von Oppen with revolutionary propaganda, avoiding any serious negotiations. The Russians argued that if they lost Ösel they would lose control over the eastern Baltic, and they told him they would not be a party to that, vowing to fight to the last bullet. "If you want to avoid unnecessary bloodshed," they said, "get off Ösel at once!" The Russians prepared to send him back to Anseküll, but they suddenly changed their minds, saying they could not guarantee the safety of the German party in the darkness. Angry Russian soldiers might ambush and murder them.[19]

While the deputies in the soviet berated von Oppen, the garrison commander advised Admiral Razvozov by radio that his units still held the Anseküll line, but "the state of affairs is very serious. We need help now!" He begged for reinforcements, namely, two battalions of infantry and some ships. Razvozov and Bakhirev knew they had no soldiers or ships for Zerel. Their priority was salvaging what they could at the east end of Ösel and holding on to Moon Island. They faced major difficulties in moving units just 8 kilometers across Moon Sound. Bakhirev radioed back and urged calm; help would come, he promised. The platitude failed. The sailors begged Bakhirev, "Comrades, we can't hold out, we are asking for help by morning."[20]

In Torkenhof, the soviet locked von Oppen and his companions in a nearby hospital for the night. Six sentries guarded the Germans, and one officer guarded the sentries. While the prisoners worried about their safety, the naval gunners who had refused to engage the German battleships that afternoon meandered into Captain Knyupfer's headquarters in Mento. Most came from Battery 43, the 12" guns, and said that they had left their posts because of the "impossibility of resisting the entire German fleet with four guns." They claimed that the Germans had put two guns out of action and that the magazines were unprotected against enemy fire; there was a chance they could blow up at any moment. The gunners were also unhappy about the absence of the Russian fleet. Captain Knyupfer countered each grievance with arguments, exhortations, and various attempts at giving orders to get the sailors to change their minds, but to no avail. More sailors from the other batteries arrived. Initially opposed to abandoning the fight, they soon reversed course and threw in their lot with the crew of Battery 43. At this point, an army officer named Moginov, the paymaster of the 425th Infantry Regiment, announced he could not accept this cowardice.

"I stated as bluntly as I could," he later reported, "that this group of people had no authority to make any decisions since 3,500 soldiers of the 425th Regiment are currently guarding the Zerel Batteries. For this reason, if the gunners abandoned Zerel and left for safety on a transport, they would betray and dishonor the Kargopolsky (425th) Regiment." Moginov pointed out that the regiment protected them as they spoke—permitting them the opportunity to discuss surrendering. A decision to surrender, he said, could not be made without representatives from the regiment having their say. "Everybody, of course, agreed." Another meeting with the proper representatives was held at 5 AM that morning (15 October). This group came to the opposite decision—everyone should return to their guns. For a while, the sailors did so, but later that morning the crew of Battery 43 again walked away.[21]

SWORBE, 15 OCTOBER

Just after the second meeting broke up and the sailors returned to their guns, at 6 AM, von Oppen and his companions, again blindfolded, were driven in the wagon back to Anseküll. They arrived in the middle of a skirmish. Fischer had mounted a breakthrough effort, and the 131st Infantry Regiment was attacking the village.

The Russians were planning to release von Oppen and his party so they could get across no-man's land as best they could, when one of their battalion commanders suddenly rushed up and stopped them. He said that he had just received a phone call from Zerel indicating the units there had changed heart. Immediately after the German party had left Torkenhof that morning, the Zerel soviet received word from all its units but two, stating that the men wanted to surrender. Zerel was lost, they claimed, so why die? The officers had opposed quitting. The commander of the 425th Infantry, Colonel Borsakowski, "cried like a baby" when he heard his troops planned to capitulate.[22]

The Russians now became courteous, waving light-color flags to halt the fighting. They told von Oppen they would meet with a German negotiator at a neutral place at 3 PM. One of the Russian officers accompanied von Oppen back to Colonel Fischer's command post. Von Oppen had spent twenty-eight hours behind the Russian lines; thus his appearance was accompanied by great relief. The Russian officer requested an armistice in order to meet with someone empowered to negotiate with them, preferably Fischer, and to be allowed time to consider offers.[23]

Fischer wrote a quick response to the Russians, giving it to von Oppen to take back. The regimental adjutant, First Lieutenant Dormagen, went along with von Oppen. Fisher wrote that he could not offer an armistice because naval operations were underway, and he could not stop them. Instead, he offered them an opportunity to surrender with good terms. If the Russian units on the peninsula would form up unarmed on the road between Zerel and Salm, flying white flags, he would guarantee his previous offer of internment. Fischer had an important proviso: the Russians could not destroy the massive 12" guns at Zerel. Finally, he agreed to allow a few men in each of the regimental and battalion soviets to retain their arms to maintain order.[24]

In the midst of these negotiations, General von Kathen had arrived at Fischer's command post. Von Kathen told Fischer he could count on getting a heavy artillery battery that night, and he added that his radio monitors had intercepted a Russian message calling for ships to come to Zerel. "Things haven't changed," he said to Colonel Fisher. "We have to render the batteries at Zerel harmless as soon as possible so the fleet can enter the Gulf." This news confirmed Fischer's suspicions. He felt the Russians were delaying so they could evacuate as many of their sailors and soldiers as possible from Zerel. He decided to take advantage of the lull and began to move his regiment south from Anseküll. At 6 PM, von Oppen and Dormagen met him in the small village of Kaimri about 5 kilometers south of Anseküll and told the colonel the good news. The Russians had agreed to capitulate at 8 AM the next day, the 16th of October.[25]

SWORBE, 16 OCTOBER

During the night of the 15th–16th, at 8 PM, 28 officers and approximately 1,200 soldiers surrendered to Fischer's Second Battalion. At 2 AM, another Russian claiming to be a plenipotentiary appeared in the German lines, confirming that the Russians would adhere to the terms of the capitulation. At the same time he handed Colonel Fischer a note from his Russian counterpart, Colonel Borsakowski of the 425th Regiment, who begged for some cigarettes, a request not easily filled.

At 8 AM on the 16th, Fischer's regiment moved out, heading down the road toward Zerel. As the Germans marched toward the end of the peninsula, Captain Knyupfer radioed Bakhirev begging for transports to get his men off before the Germans arrived.[26] Unaware of this duplicity, Fischer gave orders not to fire on Russians showing white flags; otherwise the regiment had orders to attack aggressively. Two hours later the German regiment bumped into the bulk of the 425th Infantry. The Russians stood silently by the roadside, displaying white flags, waiting to surrender. Fischer approached the Russian commander and said, "I regret your military misfortune," to which one of the Russian's staff shouted, "Why won't this Russia die because it cannot live? When will this torture end?" a reference to the confusion bought about by the revolution.

When the Germans got to Zerel, they discovered the batteries were unserviceable. Various pieces of the locking mechanisms on the guns had disappeared, which rendered them unusable. There was no visible damage from naval gunfire, fire, or bombs. The tally of prisoners and captured materiel from Sworbe was impressive: 150 officers and 5,100 soldiers, along with 54 machine guns, 27 light and 8 heavy artillery pieces, 150 wagons and 500 horses, four 305mm canons, four 150mm cannons, 20 antiaircraft guns, and 10 revolver-type cannons.[27] Before Fischer arrived, the Russians did evacuate some of the garrison. Most of the mutinous sailors from Battery 43 returned to Kuivast on the *Graschdanin* and a transport. The Germans did intercept one tug pulling a barge full of sailors and soldiers from Zerel and took everyone into captivity.[28]

PAMERORT AND ORRISAR, 12 OCTOBER

On the eastern side of the island, matters had not unfolded as smoothly for the Germans. General von Estorff had hoped to defeat the Russians in the center of the island near Arensburg by cutting off their retreat to the east. Recognizing that his scheme might not succeed, the general had hedged his bet. He planned to land a company of elite storm troopers and a battalion of cyclists at Cape Pamerort, with the mission to move east and block the Moon Causeway bridgehead at Orrisar. Commander von Rosenberg's torpedo boat flotilla, protected by the battleship *Bayern* and cruiser *Emden*, would land the cyclists and soldiers at Pamerort. Commodore Heinrich was in charge of the operation. The *Emden* was his flagship.

Both ships left the fleet at Point White at 0400 the morning of the 12th of October to link up with von Rosenberg at Pamerort, 40 kilometers to the east. Heinrich sent *Bayern* toward Dagö Island to silence the Russian battery at Cape Toffri, which controlled the entrance to the critically important Soela Sound. The commodore took the *Emden* to cover the Pamerort landings. The *Bayern* planned to lurk offshore in the dark, waiting for Captain von Levetzow to give the fleet the command to open fire. Just after 5 AM, Heinrich wrote in his logbook that he could barely make out Cape Toffri to the north, across the Soela Sound, and at 5:15 his lookouts reported seeing flashes around the *Bayern*. Oddly, they did not hear anything. *Bayern* had had bad luck. First it ran into a mine at 5:07 AM. The damage turned out, on later inspection, to be quite serious, but at the time the captain thought the buckling to the hull was minor and pressed on with his mission. Second, the flashes seen by the *Emden* indeed came from the *Bayern*, but not from the mine strike. The *Bayern* had fired on what its commander thought was an enemy submarine. Admiral Schmidt had given clear orders that only he would authorize engaging the enemy once the fleet got to the islands. While the *Bayern* had jumped the gun, and Admiral Schmidt made a point later of taking its skipper to

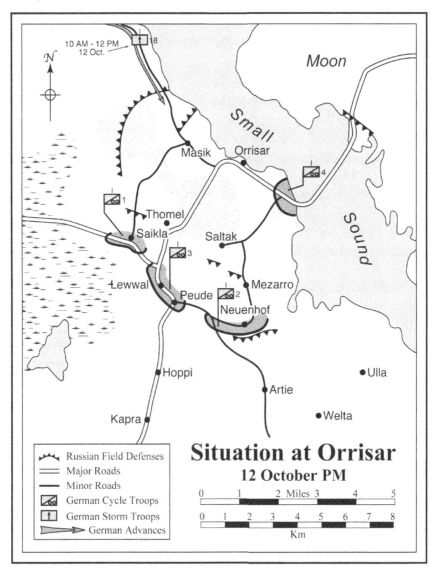

Map 5. Situation at Orrisar, 12 October

task for this breach of his orders,[29] the damage was done. The crew on the *Moltke* heard this noise, which prompted them to open fire, followed by the battleship squadrons.

Ironically, while in Tagga Bay the fleet engaged in a duel with the fort at Hundsort, initiated by *Bayern*'s unauthorized shots at the purported submarine, neither the *Emden* nor the *Bayern* commenced firing at Toffri for another half hour. When *Bayern* struck the mine, *Emden* could not help; *Emden* was lowering its boats for von Rosenberg's use. As soon as the boats were free, Heinrich headed for Toffri. Once he got to the *Bayern*, both ships headed for the shoreline.

The *Bayern*'s captain, Heinrich Rohardt, could not make out the location of the Russian battery, and he was reluctant to approach too closely, being unsure of the depth of the water. He sent two small trawlers from von Rosenberg's force ahead of his ship to sound the waters. Rohardt also sent two torpedo boats in support of the trawlers. As they advanced slowly taking soundings, torpedo boat A28 approached to within two nautical miles of Toffri at 6 AM. Fully alerted by the noise at Tagga Bay, the Russians saw the vessel and began to shoot, straddling it with their first rounds. A second series hit on the stern, but flashes from the guns had betrayed the battery's location, and *Bayern* and *Emden* cut loose. Their first salvo landed on target. The battery at Toffri nonetheless continued to return fire. The German guns pounded the shoreline, firing almost six hundred rounds at the battery. Toffri was quickly silenced without its guns causing further harm.[30]

Meanwhile, at 7 AM, the sailors of von Rosenberg's flotilla, along with the First and Second Cycle Battalions, and Storm Company 18, went ashore at Pamerort. They found neither the expected battery nor any enemy. The First Cycle Battalion then went south toward Laisberg,[31] 8 kilometers distant. The village formed the junction of the coast road and the highway leading to Arensburg. The battalion headed south toward the main Orrisar–Arensburg road, hoping to cross it and block any Russians retreating from Arensburg. Despite the bad weather, the First Cycle Battalion made good progress on the gravel roads, occasionally coming across Russian cavalry patrols, who quickly took flight. Only around dusk did they encounter strong resistance as they completed their mission, having covered 40 kilometers and crossed the two roads leading from Arensburg to Orrisar.[32]

The Second Cycle Battalion and the Eighteenth Shock or Storm Company, under Captain von Winterfeld,[33] came ashore around 10 AM.[34] Shortly after landing, von Winterfeld found a number of farm wagons assembled for a church festival. Confiscating these, he used them to carry his machine guns. Once they discovered there were no Russians near Pamerort, the Germans set out for Orrisar, almost 40 kilometers away.[35] The cyclists left first, rapidly leaving behind von Winterfeld's force, which moved on foot along the north shore toward the Moon Causeway. The cyclists arrived at Orrisar at dusk, having made good time in the rain, and completely surprised the Russians quartered in the various homes and farms of the village.

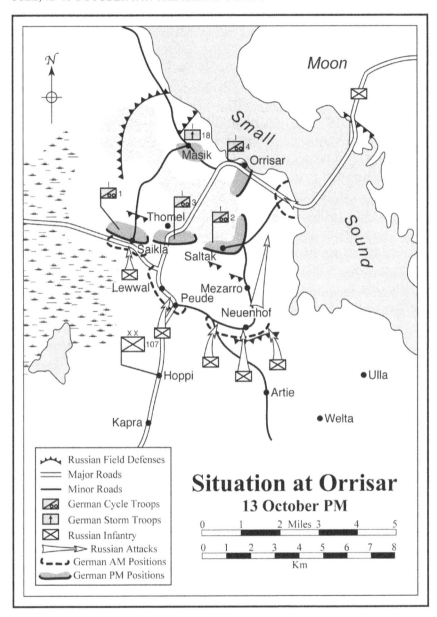

Map 6. Situation at Orrisar, 13 October

They captured the garrison of fifty to eighty soldiers along with the treasury of the Arensburg regional government (200,000 rubles) just as the Russians were taking it across the causeway to Moon, the mainland, and safety.[36]

The Germans secured the bridgehead at the Orrisar end of the causeway and sent a patrol across to Moon. Lively Russian resistance turned back the patrol just 30 meters from Moon Island. Had the Germans been able to break though this roadblock, they could have taken Moon Island because the Russians had no troops there. Only forty men held the key position at the Moon side of the causeway.[37]

At midnight, von Winterfeld's soldiers and the machine gun company from the cycle battalion arrived. He took over the command and set up a perimeter around the causeway bridgehead. The captain set out three of his cycle companies in a semicircle around the bridgehead: the First at Saikla, the Second at Neuenhof, and the Third at Lewwal. Von Winterfeld kept his own Eighteenth Storm Company at Thomel as his reserve. Cycle Company 4 held the causeway bridgehead.[38] As the night wore on, the German leader could only hope the remainder of the division had thwarted the Russians along the Arensburg–Orrisar highway; otherwise, he and his men faced a bleak morning.

ORRISAR, 13 OCTOBER

The garrison and trains units of General Ivanov's 107th Division left Arensburg on the evening of the 12th. The division's field hospitals and logistical units led the way. The next morning, after an all-night march, at Lewwal the Russian column stumbled into von Winterfeld's Third Cycle Company, which opened fire with its machine guns. The Russian escorts fired off a few shots, but the devastating machine gun fire hammered everyone and everything to pieces. The few survivors immediately ran for cover in the roadside ditches. Next, a column of 130 cars and wagons carrying the officers' goods and baggage, along with wives and female "friends," arrived. The soldiers escorting this group returned a good fire for fifteen minutes, and then they abruptly surrendered. The scene was chaotic—cars, trucks, and wagons shattered by fire lay crisscrossed on the road along with dead horses, wounded horses, and dead and dying Russians. The Germans rounded up about five hundred stunned prisoners and sent them north up the coast road to St. Johannis, 10 kilometers away.[39] The word meanwhile went back down the Russian convoy: the enemy held the bridgehead at the causeway. The Germans had picked all the low-hanging fruit. The Russians were alerted and would no longer be taken by surprise.

Their infantry came on the scene next. They appeared in small units in front of all three cycle companies, attacking at 11 AM. The lengthy front, terrible weather, and poor coordination hindered a breakthrough. Complicating matters, around noon the Fifth and Sixth Cycle companies staggered into the German perimeter. They had gotten lost the day before and bogged down on a bad road, and they ended up riding in circles. They arrived exhausted. Von Winterfeld had no choice but to allow them to rest. At that moment, they became his reserve. His situation was not good. He had three weak companies of cycle troops trying to hold a front 7 kilometers long. His supplies were going fast, especially ammunition.

Several Russian units soon broke in behind the cyclists and began to take shots at runners moving between von Winterfeld's units. They engaged the reserve forces at Thomel village. Von Winterfeld needed to eliminate this breakthrough, but his forces were too weak. Soon the infiltrating Russians cut von Winterfeld's ties with his Fourth Company on the bridgehead. The captain tried to get to the causeway to see what was happening. When he went through Orrisar, he saw Russians walking around the village. In addition, Russian artillery batteries on Moon Island began firing on the cycle company at the Orrisar bridgehead. Von Winterfeld switched the cycle company with his own storm company, ordering the Fourth Cyclists to Orrisar—just over a kilometer away but not under fire from Russian artillery.[40]

At 7 PM, sections of the Second Cycle Company at Neuenhof on the left wing were driven out of their positions by a large Russian attack supported by artillery. This left a substantial gap between the Third Cycle Company at Lewwal and the Storm Company on the causeway bridgehead. Von Winterfeld ordered the Second Cycle Company to move in the direction of the manor at Saltak to plug the gap. The Russians next took the bridgehead under fire and attacked Saltak in large numbers. To the defenders, the attack on Saltak seemed to mark the most serious effort at a breakthrough yet, its ferocity signifying the Russian desperation. A lengthy night fight developed. Fortunately for the Germans, farm buildings behind the Russian lines caught fire, making silhouettes of the advancing infantry against the flames. Von Winterfeld also moved the remnants of the Fourth Cycle Company back from Orrisar into the gap. At that point, the Russians stormed across the causeway from Moon. The opposing forces were only 40 yards apart at the bridgehead, tossing hand grenades at each other. The combat lasted for

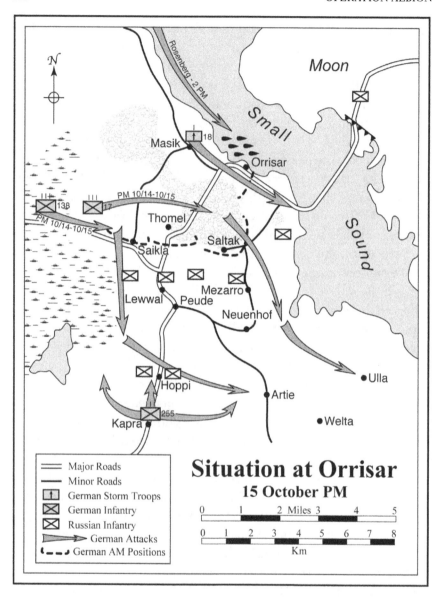

Map 7. Situation at Orrisar, 15 October

three and a half hours. Captain von Winterfeld recognized the gravity of the situation. The bridgehead was the key to success, but it was slowly slipping from his grasp. His men were down to ten rounds each.[41]

Forced to retreat, he moved his soldiers from the bridgehead to the north side of the road running from Orrisar to the causeway. The Russians did not pursue. While the causeway to Moon Island stood open, he had his machine guns sweep its entrance from time to time, so the Russians could not use it to flee to Moon in large numbers.

On the morning of the 14th, the Russians attacked again. They came forward in a northerly direction toward Thomel across the highway. Von Winterfeld threw in his last reserves against the Russian cavalry—the two exhausted cycle companies that had arrived the day before.[42] While the Germans momentarily held their own, von Winterfeld knew the Russians had further plans for their enemy.

ORRISAR, 14 OCTOBER

On the 14th of October, Volkmann and General von Estorff left for Orrisar, hours behind their regiments. Their car kept sinking in the mud, but when they finally caught up with the marching infantry columns, Volkmann got bad news from a pilot. The night before, he said, a Russian counterattack had driven von Winterfeld's men from the bridgehead, allowing the enemy access to the causeway, and they had escaped to Moon. The Forty-second Division had no chance to catch the retreating Russians because they had had too great a head start from Arensburg. There would be no "crushing blow." There would be no glorious, blood-soaked victory and thousands of prisoners. Von Estorff and Volkmann faced a terrible disappointment with equanimity.[43]

The division's regiments knew nothing of this development. At noon, they had heard the sounds of cannon fire and quickened their pace. The cannon shots came from both the Russians and the Germans. In mid-afternoon, Lieutenant Commander von Rosenberg had entered the Small Sound with his Type A II torpedo boats. These were the shallowest-draft boats in the German inventory with any kind of artillery. Drawing 8 feet, they carried two 88mm guns.[44] He knew von Winterfeld needed help. Von Rosenberg put an officer ashore, around 2 PM, with orders to find the cyclists. Von Rosenberg and his crews on the six boats waited nervously in the middle of the Sound. About two hours later, von Rosenberg's officer returned, saying Captain von Winterfeld was in a tight spot. The Russians had forced him from the bridgehead at the Ösel end of the causeway, and the armored cars visible on the causeway were Russian. Von Rosenberg's vessels promptly took them under fire, claiming hits on two cars and forcing the third to run for cover back on to Moon Island. Von Rosenberg also sent some small arms ammunition to von Winterfeld, whose men had run out.[45] Had the navy not arrived at that moment, the beleaguered Germans would have had to either retreat further or surrender.

At the same time, the van of the Forty-second Division, the Seventeenth Infantry Regiment, and Battery 6 of the Eighth Field Artillery Regiment approached the villages of Taggaser and then Saikla, on the right flank of von Winterfeld's defense line as it faced south. Down the north coast road from St. Johannis came the Fifth Cycle Battalion, having ridden along the north shore of Ösel since landing at Tagga Bay on the 12th. The road from Thomel to Orrisar was under Russian machine gun and artillery fire. The infantry arriving from the west sought cover while the cyclists appeared from the north and passed through Masik.[46]

The situation looked bleak for the arriving Germans, but things had not gone well for the Russians. Their attack had commenced that morning around 8 AM, but it unfolded in a rather desultory manner. After an artillery barrage fell on the German lines, Russian infantry advanced to the north side of Peude Church and a company from the Massalsky (472nd) Regiment moved into Kirka village. German machine gun fire brought that advance to a halt. At 10 AM the Russians resumed their artillery fire, this time on the village of Lavala, but their infantry balked at advancing. The commander of the Third Battery of the 107th Division, whose guns had provided most of the resistance at Tagga Bay two days earlier, reported that "the entire infantry, which occupied a position to the right of the road from Peude leading to [the causeway] began to retreat . . . one-by-one the soldiers of the Massalsky Regiment passed by my observation post. When I stopped them, they said that they were on their way to get more ammunition." When told the Germans had retreated from their positions, the Russian soldiers still refused to move forward.[47]

Later in the day the Russians assembled a makeshift force from the remains of their 426th and 472nd Regiments, and attempted one last breakthrough effort. The assault started around 5 PM, but once again, "the infantry didn't do anything." At this point, around 6 PM, the leading German units coming from Arensburg arrived.[48]

The commanders of the lead German battalion (First Battalion, 17th Infantry Regiment) and the Sixth Battery (Field Artillery Regiment 8) recognized the danger—they saw the Russians soldiers nearing the causeway from the Ösel side and the armored cars leaving the causeway on to Ösel. The regiment's mortar officer called for immediate artillery support because the cyclists were defenseless against armored cars. The battery commander went forward to reconnoiter, first telling his runner to have his unit move forward at a gallop.

He found an excellent position in a park at Orrisar, and his battery moved in, unlimbering the guns and opening fire. Within seconds rounds began to land near the leading armored car as it circled around the cyclists' position. The car stopped, turned, and fled back over the causeway, followed by the others, all chased by artillery shells. Meanwhile, the regiment's Second and Third battalions marched up as darkness began to fall, moving along both sides of the road from Orrisar to the causeway. By 7 PM the causeway terminus was in German hands again. The Russian breakthrough had failed. The Seventeenth Infantry Regiment dug in on the left side of the bridgehead; the 138th Regiment had moved to the right side.[49] The fighting continued sporadically as night wore on, picking up briefly as the 255th Regiment arrived at 1:30 the morning of the 15th. Lieutenant Backer described the scene:

> Our 11th Company, sent out as an advanced guard, ran into the enemy around 0130. A spirited fire fight developed, the bullets flew, a real joy. What was not so nice was that the regiment was in a march column [strung out] on the highway. We tried to develop the situation in the fog and darkness [but] no one knew where any company was, and the companies were looking for the staffs. Headline: night fight! You can't imagine what it is like until you have been there! We can laugh about it now, but then it was a unique situation.[50]

The fighting then dropped off with only the odd round here and there piercing the night, and finally it stopped. There were few captives.

A dejected Volkmann refused to believe the prisoners who said that very few Russians had gotten over the causeway the night before. The mood in the division staff plummeted.[51] The Germans were exhausted, and their brutal forced march now seemed in vain. Commanders tried to find barns and farms in which to bed their soldiers, but most of the men slept in the open as best they could, too tired to spend much time searching for cover in the dark.

ORRISAR, 15 OCTOBER

General Ivanov's headquarters was near the village of Peude, southeast of the bridgehead. His subordinate commanders brought in their reports that night, and they contained a depressing litany of troubles. Soldiers refused to conduct patrols. Others had simply left their lines and were wandering about. The commander of the ad hoc mélange of units that had taken on the Germans told the division chief of staff that his men had abandoned the trenches. The chief's response was to ask the assembled officers to man the machine guns, which they did. "The situation at this time," wrote the Third Battery's commander, "was considered hopeless."[52]

General von Estorff had established his headquarters just south of Peude Village. The next morning, the 15th, Volkmann and the staff processed paperwork listlessly, hardly saying a word. Battalion and company commanders tried to assemble their scattered units, while stragglers came up the road from Arensburg. Sporadic fighting continued as Russians tried to escape the tightening German noose. Opposite the 255th Regiment, now in good order, the Russians launched several breakout efforts, but as Lieutenant Backer said, the Germans "cut them down; smeared 'em."[53]

A bit later a patrol reported that Russian ships stood off the southeast coast of Ösel, by Kubyssar, trying to evacuate their troops. Von Estorff ordered some artillery to fire on the ships and to repel them. A field artillery battery slowly responded, but exhaustion showed as the horses and men departed at a walk for the bay. When the unit arrived at Kubyssar, the commander observed a small Russian flotilla at anchor. Captain Second Rank Chetvertukhin from Admiral Bakhirev's base at Kuivast had taken charge of this desperate expedition to assist General Ivanov and his soldiers. Chetvertukhin's forces consisted of the minesweepers *Gruz*, *Kapsyul*, *Kramvol*, *Minrep*, and *Udarnik*. Captain Shevelev, in charge of the destroyers covering the force, sent the torpedo boats *Deyatelny* and *Delny* to the Moon Sound, while *Rezvy* and *Retivy* covered the shoreline in Kubyssar Bay.

The German battery opened fire from its shore position, but the Russians returned fire and silenced the outnumbered German guns. Unfortunately for the Russians, the valiant effort proved in vain. None of their soldiers were waiting. A small party sent ashore found only weapons and cartridges, but no soldiers waiting for evacuation.[54] Fearful of drawing more attention, the Russian flotilla soon left.

At the Forty-second Division's headquarters, as Volkmann worked, a company of infantry from the 138th Regiment marched by, led by its commander, Lieutenant Walter Flex. He saluted some of the senior officers hanging around the headquarters. Volkmann recognized him, waved, and came out to talk. The little lieutenant was a national treasure. A philosopher who had tutored the Bismarck grandchildren, Flex had volunteered at the onset of the war and had served most of it in the front lines with the 138th Regiment. His book *Wanderer between Two Worlds*, written in spare moments in the trenches, was the first German novel of the war. Its protagonist was an idealistic infantry lieutenant with a copy of Nietzsche in his knapsack. Eclipsed later by Jünger's *Storm of Steel* and Remarque's *All Quiet on the Western Front*, Flex's work is virtually forgotten today, yet over a million copies were printed in the war years alone. The High Command had transferred Flex to its propaganda section, but he had wrangled his way back to his regiment in time for the Galicia and Riga campaigns. Volkmann claimed that he had extracted a commitment from the famous author to join the division staff after Albion, when, the lieutenant said, the "great adventure of the summer" came to an end. Volkmann ran out of the headquarters to remind Flex when he saw him go by. "The big adventure is over," he shouted. "You must now leave your company."[55] Flex nodded, but his unit had orders to mop up the remaining Russian resistance. Thirty minutes later he was mortally wounded while mopping up some of the remnants of the 107th Division.[56] Counting Flex, only three German Army officers fell in Operation Albion.

By afternoon the fighting died down. The Forty-second Division headquarters had again moved, this time to a peasant's farm, closer to Orrisar. As Volkmann went into the house, his operations officer reported he had three Russian generals and some staff officers in tow. "Don't joke with me," said Volkmann. "Get ready to move out. We are leaving in 5 minutes."

"Wait," said the officer. A group of prisoners appeared, guarded by two German soldiers with fixed bayonets. A Russian officer with general's shoulder boards on his uniform approached Volkmann. He saluted. "I hope you are not alone?" said Volkmann as he returned the salute.

"I'm afraid there is nothing left for me [to do] but to tell my division we are prisoners," said General Ivanov.

"Your division?" asked Volkmann. "We thought you had escaped."

"Unfortunately, no," said the Russian.

Earlier that morning, the general had assembled his few remaining officers, informing them he would soon have to surrender. Some of them wanted to try to break through the German lines on their own, which he authorized. In fact, he gave them his blessing, only asking them to tell

Russian authorities what had happened if they succeeded in escaping.[57] Two soldiers did succeed in getting away, fleeing in a boat. A torpedo boat picked them up, and they explained that most of the officers in the headquarters, including the division and brigade commanders, had forced their way to the church in the village of Peude, where the Germans surrounded them. The headquarters personnel fought until ammunition ran low. Taking into account the hopeless situation, Ivanov told the soldiers to scatter and get away as best they could. They reported that Ivanov was either killed or captured.[58] In reality, after authorizing his soldiers to surrender or flee, General Ivanov had waited for the Germans, who captured him and took him to von Estorff's command post.

Volkmann immediately ran to get General von Estorff, and when he arrived, Ivanov offered his sword to him. Inexplicably, in light of his subsequent cold treatment of the Russian, von Estorff refused it. Ivanov explained that several of his officers had their families with them, and in the revolutionary conditions that existed, he worried about their safety. Von Estorff replied rather coldly, "They will get whatever relief regulations prescribe for imprisoned officers." The Russian general was led away.

The two German officers were quietly jubilant. "Well, Volkmann," said the general, "I have had many great days, but never such a proud one as this!"[59]

The general's enjoyment was short-lived. Volkmann had not exaggerated when he had told his staff the division would move in five minutes. The Seventeenth Infantry had orders to take Dagö Island, while the 138th could see its next objective across the causeway on the far side of the Little Sound: Moon Island.

While the Germans issued their official communiqué announcing they had taken the island on the 16th, General von Kathen pointed out in his account that "within four days (12–15 October) Ösel was in our hands; its garrisons were almost all taken prisoner.[60] The official announcement was more bombastic:

> Ösel is completely ours. At Zerel, the enemy carried out demolitions to prevent the use of the heavy batteries. Remnants of enemy on Ösel reduced to a few hundred men, who may escape by water transport, but we have captured all their arms and equipment. The enemy frequently offered stiff resistance, and in isolated instances mounted strong counter-attacks, which were crushed with heavy losses. Attacking enemy border guard forces ripped to pieces. Prisoner and materiel accounting underway.[61]

CHAPTER EIGHT

THE CAPTURE OF MOON AND DAGÖ ISLANDS

THE SIGNIFICANCE OF MOON ISLAND

THE RUSSIANS UNDERSTOOD the importance of Moon Island. Moon formed the midway point between Ösel Island and the Estonian mainland. If they lost control of the causeway bridging the two islands, they could neither withdraw any of their forces nor bring in reinforcements. If Moon fell, with its anchorage and shore facility at Kuivast, the larger Russian bases in Hapsal and Rogokyul became untenable. The Germans would certainly bring in artillery and close the narrow Moon Sound, forcing the Russian navy from the Gulf of Riga and threatening the entire coastline from Riga to Reval.

With their forces spread rather thinly and in disarray following the invasion, Bakhirev and Razvozov naturally concentrated their energies on defending the islands and protecting the ships under their command. Admiral Razvozov immediately ordered reinforcements to Moon Island once he became aware of the German landings on the 12th of October. The reinforcements consisted of two regiments (the 470th Dankovsky and 471st Kozelsky) of the 118th Infantry Division, the Reval Naval "Death Battalion," and some cavalry units. He had also asked the northern front commander for assistance, and General Cheremisov ordered the Twelfth Army commander to send reinforcements to Hapsal.[1] In the long run, however, most of these reinforcements mutinied, refused to entrain, would not fight, and in one fashion or another, sabotaged the efforts to reinforce the island. The Reval Death Battalion provided the major exception.

General Cheremisov's northern front had responsibility for all north-west Russia. The threat to the coastline posed by the loss of the islands captured Cheremisov's attention. Long cognizant of the potential calamity if the Baltic Islands fell into German hands, Cheremisov had initiated plans for such a contingency. While he had committed to sending reinforcements to the beleaguered islands as early as the day of the landings, his attention remained on the shoreline and the rear area of the Twelfth Army. To his credit, he kept his priorities in order. He proved willing to commit reserves to defend Moon as long at that was feasible. The moment it became clear the defense could not hold out, Cheremisov cut his losses and tried to salvage what he could.

Geography divided the landmass behind the Twelfth Army into two distinct regions. The northern zone ran along the coast of Estonia from Pernau at the top of the Gulf of Riga to Baltic Port on the Gulf of Finland. It was filled with bogs and low areas, rendering the inland movement of any major force very difficult. Cheremisov assigned responsibility for defending this region to the Baltic Fleet, which of course had few land units. The southern zone ran from Pernau to the current front with the Germans on the River Aa. The terrain was more stable, and existing transportation networks facilitated military movements. A landing in this area was both more probable and more serious. The invaders could either roll up the rear of the Russian front or strike inland for Dorpat, threatening both the lines of communication for the northern front and the key port and rail junction of Reval.

In the planning stages, Cheremisov had indicated his headquarters would control the rear areas just behind his armies. In the Baltic Fleet's region, north of Matzel Inlet, Cheremisov formed a "Baltic Islands Land Defense Forces," commanded by General Ghenrikson. This headquarters came under the control of Admiral Razvozov and his staff, and its function was to defend the shoreline that fell under the Baltic Fleet's responsibility, namely the coastline from Cape Spithamm (Spitkhamna) to just below the Matzel Inlet.[2]

Ghenrikson and his staff arrived in Hapsal late on the 13th of October. Unfortunately, Admiral Sveshnikov showed up there at the same time, although his headquarters staff did not make it until the 16th owing to storms and delays.[3] Sveshnikov had worn out his welcome with Admiral Razvozov and General Ghenrikson by his inept handling of the invasion and his departure from Arensburg without orders. Ghenrikson simply muscled him out of the way, a tactic supported by Cheremisov, who reiterated that Ghenrikson had command of all "the land forces on the Baltic Islands" on the 14th of October.[4] While Sveshnikov sat in Hapsal until after Moon fell, he no longer exercised any command authority. Sveshnikov recognized that he had been sacked, and felt he had received shabby treatment. He asked for a transfer to Reval, which Razvozov approved.[5]

Ghenrikson's Order #2, issued on the 16th of October, outlined the defense of Moon and Dagö Islands. He instructed all units remaining on Moon, Dagö, and Worms islands to defend their positions, and he placed General Evgenii Nikolaevich Martynov in charge of the forces on Moon Island. To defend the shores on the mainland, Ghenrikson appointed General Gustav Aleksandrovich Kreitner, who commanded the brigade of the Forty-fifth Division, which Cheremisov planned to move closer to the coast from its location at Reval. Kreitner came from Lithuania, and had spent the majority of his career in the 178th (Ust-Dvinsk) Infantry Regiment, which belonged to the Forty-fifth Division, a regular division. Before the war, the division was permanently garrisoned in Penza, 480 kilometers east of Moscow, although its four regiments (177–180) recruited from Estonia and Latvia. He rose through the ranks of the regiment, commanding it from 1915 to 1917, when he became the brigade commander. Promotion to brigadier general followed almost immediately in August 1917.[6] Kreitner's assistant was Colonel Aleksander Tõnisson,[7] commander of the newly formed Estonian Regiment.[8] Two battalions of that unit went to Moon Island, but Tõnisson and his third battalion remained on the mainland along with General Kreitner. General Kreitner's area of responsibility ran south from Cape Spithamm to just below Hapsal. From Spithamm to Reval, the commander of the Naval Fortress at Reval was responsible.[9]

Because the terrain north of Pernau was so unstable and soggy, the area to the south from Pernau to the active front lines promised to be the key sector if the Germans invaded the mainland. A German landing here would permit them to wreak havoc in the rear of the Twelfth Army. The army commander, General Parsky, thought the Germans would first have to take the Baltic Islands for a staging area before they could mount any further invasions along the coast. He figured an operation of such magnitude would take at least five to seven days. He also concluded that the Germans would then land if at all near Hainash (Ainazi) in the southeast corner of the Gulf of Riga. While that area offered no protection for the German fleet in case of bad weather, once ashore the landing forces had the freedom to roll across the communications lines in the rear of the Russian armies on the northern front. Another option for the Germans was to head inland directly for Dorpat and Reval. If the Germans did land near Hainash, the Thirteenth Corps would have the lion's share of the work. Its "objective . . . will be to defend the right flank and rear of the army from the shore side, and then join with the [Twelfth] army against the enemy, advancing [both] from Riga and from the shore side." Parsky directed his corps commanders and their staffs to determine where they would concentrate their units to take maximum advantage of the road network and to use natural terrain features that favored them.[10]

REINFORCEMENTS

When the Germans landed on Ösel there were only forty Russians soldiers defending the causeway on Moon,[11] and when Admiral Bakhirev discovered on the 13th of October that Winterfeld and his forces held Orrisar, he became alarmed, fearing that the Germans would try to seize this key to the island. He rushed a ragtag group of soldiers and sailors culled from *Slava*, *Graschdanin*, *Bayan*, and shore facilities to the causeway and told them to hold it at all costs. Bakhirev's timing was perfect, and on the morning of the 14th, his unorthodox band actually counterattacked and recaptured the bridgehead at Orrisar on the Ösel side of the causeway. Lieutenant Prestin, who had arrived from Admiral Sveshnikov's headquarters in Arensburg on the 13th, personally led this attack.[12] Later that afternoon, reinforcements from the 470th Regiment and the Reval Naval Death Battalion arrived to carry the brunt of the effort.

Captain Pavel Ottovich Shisko[13] commanded the Reval Naval Death Battalion. Even before the war began, Shisko had an enormous reputation. As a junior officer he was assigned to the staff of the Pacific Fleet in 1904 when the Japanese War started, but he could not report for duty because the Japanese had besieged the headquarters at Port Arthur. Twice he attempted to break through the enemy blockade in an antiquated and leaky steamship in order to bring supplies to the beleaguered garrison. His bravery caught the attention of a public reeling from its unexpected defeats at the hands of so-called inferiors. After Port Arthur fell to the Japanese, Shisko returned to Russia and found a billet on the battleship *General Apraksin*, part of the Second Pacific Squadron, which was heading for the Pacific with the Baltic Fleet. He participated in the Battle of Tsushima, where his ship was lost and he was captured. After the war's end, he was assigned to Vladivostok, coming to public attention again by single-handedly quelling a riot there in

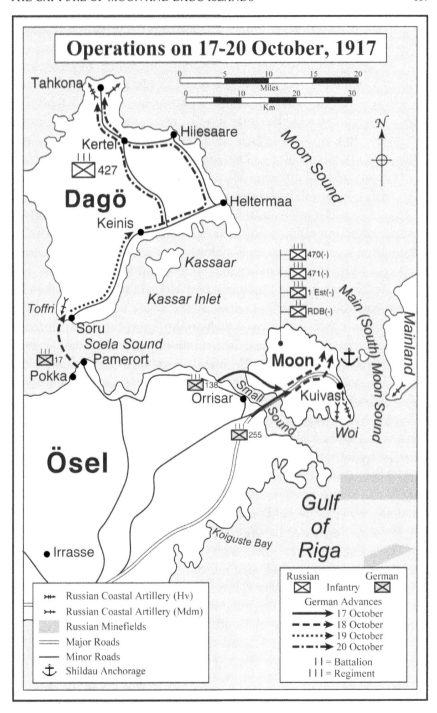

Map 8. Operations on 17–20 October

1907. In the first years of the war, he commanded the destroyers *Engineer-Mechanic Dmitriev* and *Gavriil.*

The Death Battalion encountered some difficulties traveling from Reval to Moon Island. Captain Shisko stated that he got the word to move to Ösel the day of the German landings, namely the 12th of October. His sailors, he reported, let out a "huge hurrah" when they heard of their mission and set to work loading their equipment on a train. Shortages, especially draft animals, delayed matters, and the battalion, some six hundred sailors strong, did not arrive on Moon until two days later, the afternoon of the 14th. Shisko still had materiel problems, and he had to go begging for ammunition. He went aboard the destroyer *Silny* in Kuivast and took all the revolver ammunition. In addition, he commandeered horses, carts, ammunition and weapons at gunpoint from the mobs milling around the port of Kuivast waiting or begging for transport to the mainland. The Death Battalion arrived on the causeway at Moon the morning of the 15th and was engaged in the fighting that day.[14]

Other units began to arrive at Moon, but most came in piecemeal fashion. Chaos, confusion, anarchy, and mutiny best describe the situation. The Twenty-fifth Cossack Regiment, apparently located north of the Gulf of Finland, feared traveling by sea. The officers asked to be routed on trains through Petrograd, but Baltic Fleet chief of staff Captain Cherkassky refused, complaining that honoring this request would waste precious time. Worse, Cherkassky had to tell Admiral Razvozov that the first echelon of the 471st Infantry Regiment, sent from Reval, had arrived in Hapsal and refused to get off the train. The unit's third echelon stopped its trains in Kegel (to the southwest of Reval) and was "behaving outrageously."[15] In the end, only two battalions of the regiment's three made it to Moon Island. Further south, the three battalions of the 470th (Dankovsky) Regiment, had arrived at Verder for transport to Moon. During the night of the 13–14th of October, one battalion mutinied and refused to embark. The soldiers then fled. When Third Battalion moved to the dock, soldiers in one company refused to board, shouting they were being taken to a trap on the island. They would never get there, they cried, because enemy submarines would sink the ferry, and they would drown. The battalion commander, Lieutenant Colonel Rudnev, quelled the riot only after he secured the assistance of a sailor, a "Comrade Brezgunov," who came from the soviet formed from the garrison unit at the fortress at Verder. Brezgunov calmed the mutineers and convinced them to embark. "From that moment," wrote Rudnev, "this deputy was always with me."[16] Nonetheless, as in its sister regiment coming from Hapsal, only two of Dankovsky's three regiments made it to Moon.

The Third Battalion's disturbance delayed their departure until dawn on the 14th, but at that time the unit crossed the Sound to Moon on a ferry. Once ashore in Kuivast, Colonel Rudnev departed for the opposite side of the island to catch up with his other companies, which had already landed and moved out. At first, things looked normal, but as he headed west across the island toward the causeway, he

> began meeting soldiers, first one-by-one, then in groups. They were soldiers from different units, many without weapons . . . running from the position [at the causeway], saying the most incredible things. Notwithstanding my and my deputy's entreaties and pleas to return [to their positions], all were moving and running toward the pier at Kuivast. The further we went the more frequently we saw soldiers and the larger their groups became. They were all panic-stricken, fearing for their lives. . . . They would not listen to me or [my] deputy, saying "if you really want to, go and fight yourself."[17]

The advance elements of the Death Battalion reported the same scenes, except they added that the soldiers fleeing from Ösel threw their ammunition away and buried their weapons by the roadside.[18] As Rudnev approached the Ösel–Moon causeway, he discovered why the soldiers were fleeing. He had arrived about the time Lieutenant Commander von Rosenberg's small flotilla of torpedo boats took the causeway under fire, aiming for the armored car. The Russian commander said that by this time he had managed to turn around some 250–300 fleeing soldiers, but then an armored car pulled up, and a voice from within shouted, "'Comrades, . . . the Germans have landed on Moon Island and are moving toward Kuivast.'" At this point, "everyone bolted. No matter how much I shouted . . . nothing helped."[19]

FIGHTING AT THE CAUSEWAY

The causeway lay open, and Rudnev prepared for a German assault. The colonel placed his men in trenches prepared long before the operation, then manned some abandoned artillery pieces, training them on the narrow road exiting the causeway. Assisted by two other officers, and the battalion's telephone section, some seven in all, the colonel's party sat by the guns, waiting for the Germans, certain they would attack in great strength. Fortunately the scouts and lead elements from Shisko's Death Battalion arrived at nightfall. Rudnev sent them across the causeway to hold and widen the bridgehead at Orrisar. The colonel also brought up his battalion to the Moon side of the causeway, and planned to march across in the morning, the 15th of October. At 4:30 AM, Shisko arrived and surveyed the situation. He told Rudnev he was going to pull his men back from the Orrisar bridgehead and back across the causeway to Moon. His men were "weary," and he said he would have his soldiers reoccupy the bridgehead the next afternoon after they had rested. Rudnev vehemently objected, but Shisko put this suggestion to a vote, and his men approved. "I disagreed," wrote Colonel Rudnev, but "I couldn't do anything. The Commander of the Death Battalion was in charge." Rudnev moved three of his companies to a nearby village for some rest; the fourth remained with Shisko at the causeway.[20] Shisko withdrew his men from the Ösel side of the causeway, which now belonged to the Germans.

Both Rudnev's and Shisko's battalions sat out most of the action on the 16th. Shisko did send a patrol back across the causeway, but it met with an ambush, losing twelve men. The Germans captured two and killed the rest. The Russian uniforms told the story. On their black shoulder boards, they had a silver skull; the buttons on the coats were death's heads. The Germans now knew they faced a death battalion.[21] Meanwhile, German torpedo boats in the Small Sound (between Ösel and Moon islands) and larger craft at its north end kept up a heavy fire on the Russians, forcing them to stay low.

During the afternoon of the 16th, most of two battalions of the Estonian Regiment arrived in Kuivast. As the Estonians unloaded, they were pushed back by soldiers fleeing from the island and trying to board the vessels. Off to the side but crowding the pier area were some units from the 470th and 471st Regiments. They just stood there, according to an astonished Lieutenant Rebane, a staff officer in the Estonian Regiment. The Estonians struggled through the crowds to get off the pier and out of the harbor area. They set up bivouac in a field near Kuivast, and General Martynov visited them that evening. Shortly afterward, their orders arrived. The Estonian First Battalion received instructions to occupy the west side of Moon Island just north of the causeway to the end of the island. The battalion marched to its assigned position the morning of the 17th of October, accompanied by its regiment's scouts and machine gun units. Shisko's Death Battalion actually sat astride the causeway bridgehead and the road that went across to Ösel. The Second Estonian Battalion moved to the middle of Moon, where it remained in reserve.[22]

When the First Estonian Battalion arrived near the causeway, it moved into the area next to Colonel Rudnev's battalion. The two units kept as low a profile as possible, not wanting to attract attention, because German torpedo boats in the Small Sound continued to bombard the shore near the causeway. The two companies of Shisko's Death Battalion closest to the causeway suffered heavy casualties. A couple of officers took over the artillery pieces that Rudnev had used the day before and returned a rather desultory fire.[23]

COLLAPSE IN KUIVAST

Back at Kuivast, the situation had collapsed into chaos. More stragglers and deserters arrived, wandering aimlessly about the harbor and quay. Most came from the units of the 107th Infantry Division, which had disintegrated on Ösel the day before, and they were joined by the survivors of the Eighth Naval Artillery Battalion, the one that had mutinied at Battery 43 on Zerel. The battleship *Graschdanin* and the transport *Zimmerman* had brought most of these sailors to Kuivast.[24] At 6 AM that morning more units from the 470th Dankovsky Regiment had arrived from the mainland and joined this volatile brew, gathering in a nearby field. Around 7 AM, word spread that a German battleship squadron was closing on Kuivast from the south. Panic set in, and the soldiers ran for the transports. The defenseless Russian transports immediately left, steaming a few kilometers north and anchoring on the north side of Schildau Island. Instead of German ships, however, a few German airplanes appeared, and the soldiers and sailors crowding the port facilities hid in nearby woods and bushes. The planes attempted to bomb the two or three small vessels remaining at the quay.[25] When the bombs fell, the soldiers and sailors who had hidden in the nearby bushes and woods rose and fled in panic. One of the 470th's officers, Captain Krotkov, attempted to establish order, but "neither shouts nor the whistles of the officers could stop the soldiers. Wagons, machine gun packs, people were running all over the field; I hadn't seen such a panic in over two and half years." After the planes left without doing any damage, the soldiers remained huddled in a forest.[26] They apparently remained there until later in the day, and when General Martynov abandoned the area and moved his headquarters north, they straggled after him.

THE GERMAN CROSSING TO MOON

The Germans made several efforts to cross the causeway to Moon on the 16th but were driven back each time by Russian fire. In addition to the resistance from the units on the shore of Moon opposite the Germans, the Russians also employed the large guns on their ships anchored on the far side of Moon in the Kuivast or Schildau roads. The shell fire for the 12" guns of *Slava* chased von Rosenberg's A II boats from the Small Sound.[27]

The mission to take Moon belonged to Colonel Matthiass's Sixty-fifth Infantry Brigade, now consisting of the 138th and 255th Infantry regiments and some assorted support units.[28] The Seventeenth Regiment, normally part of the brigade, had already left for Dagö Island. Matthiass's plan called for von Rosenberg's flotilla to transfer a battalion of the 138th Infantry from Pallipank on Ösel during the night of the 17th across the Small Sound to Kienast Island, a glorified sandbar connected to Moon. Aerial reconnaissance during the afternoon of the 17th by a Lieutenant von Klenck indicated that the Russians were withdrawing from Moon and that very few remained. The lieutenant estimated about 100–120 of the enemy were still on the island,[29] a wildly inaccurate estimate as matters later unfolded. Nevertheless, Kuivast harbor was largely empty. General von Kathen ordered an immediate crossing, and the motorized launches ferried the Sixth Company, 138th Regiment, across the Small Sound at 4 PM. The plan called for several of von Rosenberg's A II boats to lay a smokescreen, but the wind suddenly shifted, and the forty-five-minute crossing took place in sight of the enemy, who failed to react. In addition, the company commander had the sailors drop his men off a few hundred meters north of the planned landing site, the village of Keggowa. The army wanted to land near some higher ground that offered a commanding view of the landing site, but an unexpected consequence arose when the launches could not find a channel that led close to the shore. The soldiers had seen Russian cavalry and infantry on the shore, so they took no chances and jumped out of the launches into waist-high water, wading ashore through knee-deep mud and shingle. The remainder of Third Battalion followed at intervals later that night.[30]

THE RUSSIAN WITHDRAWAL

Actually, the Russians had decided to withdraw most of their troops from Moon, but they had not yet implemented this plan. Their capitulation at Zerel on the 16th had opened the Gulf of Riga to German capital ships, making the Russian presence there untenable. As a German squadron closed toward the northeast side of the Gulf, near Pernau and the Moon Sound, northern front commander General Cheremisov realized the danger and called Admiral Razvozov at midday on the 17th of October. He told his naval counterpart that the concentration of Russian forces (seven battalions) on Moon Island made sense only if the island could be used as a springboard for retaking Ösel.

> At the present time," he said, "it seems we can't count on this any longer. . . . Concentrating forces on Moon doesn't make any sense. Considering the enemy's ability to fire at the island, it can't be defended. If we can't hold the Moon Sound, [and it doesn't look promising,] given German naval superiority, then all the forces concentrated on Moon are going to be captured. . . . I think that we should leave only one or two battalions . . . the rest of the troops should be transferred immediately to the mainland . . . to counteract enemy landings and to cover the roads to Reval.[31]

Razvozov remained noncommittal. He said that as they spoke Bakhirev was battling the Germans to see who would control the Moon Sound, and he wanted to wait for the outcome, to talk to Bakhirev before doing anything. Both Razvozov and Cheremisov, however, had greater concerns. Razvozov was worried about his bases at Hapsal and Reval and about getting his ships out of the Gulf of Riga, while Cheremisov fretted about the undefended coastline from Riga to Reval. He told Admiral Razvozov that he needed all the highways kept clear for troop movements. He added he had ordered the Forty-fourth Division to Reval to guard it, and he was moving two army corps into this region. The situation, he said, "was serious but . . . far from hopeless." Nonetheless, he repeated his order to get the army units off Moon as fast as possible, and Razvozov now concurred. Cheremisov concluded by telling the admiral to remind General Ghenrikson to be sure to focus his efforts on protecting the roads on the mainland leading to Reval. Cheremisov did not think Ghenrikson should try to defend the region by locating all his forces on the coastline. It is necessary, said Cheremisov, to organize the defense differently than on Ösel. Ghenrikson should not disperse his units along the shoreline. Instead, he should concentrate them inland in a few key locations so they could decisively and simultaneously attack any enemy landings with all their strength from different directions.[32]

The arrival of the German ships (Admiral Behncke's two dreadnoughts and Hopman's two cruisers) in the south end of the Moon Sound on the 17th had caused Admiral Bakhirev to move his transports and small craft north of Schildau Island. That brought them temporary safety but left Kuivast completely exposed. Unable now to use the facilities there to embark his forces for transport to the mainland, General Martynov had no choice but to move his base of operations further north along the east coast of Moon Island. Around 3 PM, General Martynov called Colonel Rudnev and explained that the German navy had succeeded in forcing its way into the Gulf of Riga and was headed for the Moon Sound. The general ordered Rudnev to dispatch a reconnaissance force to the northern part of Moon to scout out defensive positions for his own unit (Third Battalion, 470th Regiment), the Death Battalion, and the Estonian Battalion near the villages of Moisakyull and Tuppernume. As soon as darkness fell, said Martynov, Rudnev should march his men to the new area, and be ready to blow up the causeway in the morning. Martynov also added that he was relocating his headquarters to Raugi on the northeast side of Moon. Raugi had a small pier. Late in the afternoon of the 17th, Martynov gave orders for the units on Moon to fall back to the north end of the island. The general divided his forces into two groups. The first fell under Shisko's command and consisted of the Death Battalion, the Second Battalion of the Estonian Regiment, and Rudnev's battalion. Colonel Mironov led the second group, composed of two battalions from the 471st Regiment, the Second Battalion of the 470th (Dankovsky) Regiment, and the First Battalion, Estonian Regiment.[33]

The first German unit to cross to Moon, the Sixth Company of the 138th Infantry Regiment, had arrived at Keggowa, about 6 kilometers northwest of the causeway. Meeting no resistance, the unit cautiously moved toward the causeway, and the rest of the Second Battalion soon followed. From Ösel, the Eighteenth Storm Company simultaneously came across the causeway, but Russian machine gun fire prevented the soldiers from getting any closer than 600 meters from the end. Von Rosenberg's flotilla approached the causeway and opened fire with 88mm guns, setting ablaze a manor on the shore that contained ammunition. It blew up, taking with it an abandoned armored car. Only around 2 in the morning (of the 18th of October) did Shisko's Death Battalion abandon its positions, permitting the 138th Infantry to fire off the three white flares indicating the causeway was clear. In the morning, the rest of the Sixty-fifth Brigade crossed to Moon and headed to the northeast corner of the island, where the Russians sat, trapped and listless.[34]

THE RUSSIAN SURRENDER

While the rearguard battled it out with the Germans at the causeway, the units under Shisko and Mironov marched to Moisakyull and Tuppernume, bombarded the entire time by German artillery.[35] Colonel Mironov's group of forces disintegrated as it approached Raugi. Captain Krotkov of the Second Battalion, 470th Regiment, wrote afterward that the march to Raugi "was carried out in complete disorder. Those were robber gangs retreating, not soldiers." Martynov ordered the two battalions from the Kozelsky (471st) Regiment to secure the area near Raugi and to dig in. One of the battalions balked; its commander came shamefaced to Martynov in the dark to report that his men had decided to surrender and refused to move into a defensive perimeter. The soldiers, he said, justified their refusal to fight by insisting that "sooner or later they will be captured, and by defending themselves, they would only get more people wounded." An angry Martynov sent that commander back, but an hour later, around 10 PM, a delegation from the regiment's soviet appeared at Martynov's headquarters, declaring that they were not going to fight. Nothing Martynov nor his staff said changed their attitude. "With tears in his eyes," wrote Krotkov, "the general asked them to fulfill their duty. . . . But they kept repeating, 'we do not have artillery and we are not going to fight without it.'"[36]

The same two battalions also tried to subvert the Estonians. Lieutenant Rebane, of the First Battalion, Estonian Regiment, had dealt with rumors all day. His men believed the Russians had sent them to Moon solely to get them killed. In the evening, after getting his troops settled in a forest bivouac near Raugi, Rebane went to a meeting in Martynov's headquarters. Lost, the lieutenant stopped to ask directions from a group of soldiers arguing animatedly. They said they had no idea where the headquarters was located, but they asked Rebane what regiment he came from. Upon hearing that he was from the Estonian Regiment, the soldiers asked him to convey to that unit's soviet that the "regimental soviets in the Kozelsky and Dankovsky Regiments had . . . decided not to fight but to surrender right away when the enemy appears tomorrow. Your [unit's] soviets should discuss the same issue and come up with their decision." Disgusted, Rebane rejected the suggestion, telling the soldiers he was an officer and this was none of his business. When he found Martynov's headquarters, he discovered the general still had fight in him. He had "decided not to surrender, but to fight on with the few who would."[37]

The mutineers proved true to their words. At dawn the next morning, the 18th of October, as the Germans drew close, soldiers from the Death Battalion awakened Colonel Rudnev with the alarming news that there were no friendly units on his left flank. The soldiers who had been there the night before had vanished.[38] Rudnev and his men faced Germans to the front and the ocean to the rear. Captain Chelishev of the Tenth Company assessed the situation: "We did not have any way out. Break through forward? Where? Retreat, but where? Behind us . . . there was water and we could not expect rescue." He reported this situation to Colonel Rudnev, who saddled his horse and left at once for Martynov's headquarters. Approaching the command post, to Rudnev's horror, white flags were everywhere. He found Martynov, surrounded by his staff, depressed and moaning, "The situation is critical. Soldiers are refusing to take up positions." The general said he did not want to cause unnecessary bloodshed and told Rudnev, "I am forced to order you to tell your battalion, the Death Battalion, and the Estonian Battalion, to lay down their weapons." Martynov then burst into tears. Rudnev mounted his horse and pushed through the crowds of soldiers milling about the headquarters. He berated them, saying, "If you want to surrender, at least destroy your weapons." The crowd shouted back, "Why should we break the guns? We shouldn't—the Germans will be nicer to us if we don't." Disgusted, Rudnev rode back to his battalion.[39]

When he arrived, the situation had deteriorated further, and he came across a face-off between his men and those from Shisko's Death Battalion. At first, the Death Battalion had sent a team over and proposed that if any of the Dankovsky soldiers did not want to surrender, they could join with the Death Battalion, which intended to fight to the end. While the soldiers mulled this over and awaited the return of their commander, a rumor circulated that "the Death Battalion will not let [the] soldiers surrender and will fire at those who do." Rudnev defused the situation by telling his men that Martynov had ordered them to destroy their weapons rather than lay them down, adding that this was not his decision. Instead, he suggested they negotiate with the Germans, proposing that the regiment would not fight if the Germans would allow them to leave for the mainland with their arms. If the Germans did not go along, the Third Battalion, Dankovsky

Regiment, would resist to the last man. Apparently the unit soviet and the soldiers agreed, because Rudnev sent some emissaries to negotiate with the Germans. In the middle of the talks, however, minesweepers and torpedo boats under the command of Captain Chetvertukhin (on the *Gruz*) arrived from Schildau and took off most of the battalion. In fact, Bakhirev had organized the effort the day before, and Chetvertukhin and a covering force of destroyers from the Thirteenth Division hovered north of the island, unable to get close to Moon because they had no shallow-draft vessels. These did not arrive until after dark, and navigation then was too dangerous. They had to wait until the next morning.[40]

Around 1 PM, the Death Battalion discovered that the brigade headquarters had surrendered, but General Martynov had encouraged those who wanted to fight to join Shisko's forces. Few did. Instead, numerous soldiers waving white flags rode by on horses they had commandeered from the brigade headquarters. They tried to seize a couple of sailors from the Death Battalion to use as hostages to turn over to the Germans to win good faith. The Death Battalion's soldiers tried to pull down the white flags. Meanwhile, the Death Battalion tried its own negotiations with the Germans. Emissaries from the battalion told the Germans they would not fight if promised transport to the mainland. Suspecting the Russians were playing for time so they could evacuate men from the island, the Germans replied that the Death Battalion had thirty minutes in which to surrender. When the time elapsed, the 138th and 255th Regiments attacked. Shisko heroically rallied his forces by standing in their midst with a red flag tied to his rifle, exhorting his men to fight on. Wounded, he soon went down in the smoke and confusion. Adding to the German dominance, von Rosenberg's flotilla arrived off the coast and poured artillery and machine gun fire on the hapless Russians. Most of the Death Battalion's sailors were killed or captured, to include Shisko. Only 120 of their 600 got off Moon during Captain Chetvertukhin's evacuation, and 60 more escaped in smaller craft before von Rosenberg drove off the rescuers. Lieutenant Backer of the 255th Regiment admitted the Death Battalion put up a good fight; otherwise, he characterized the fighting on Moon as "nothing special."[41]

With Shisko and the Death Battalion routed, the fighting ended. The Germans captured some 5,000 Russians on Moon Island. Most of the Russian prisoners came from the 470th and 471st Infantry Regiments, but the Germans also captured 16 officers and 1,582 soldiers from the two Estonian battalions. Those two units lost an additional 20 officers and 150 soldiers killed on Moon Island.[42]

THE DECISION TO TAKE DAGÖ ISLAND

The Germans had not originally planned to take Dagö Island. After the landing on Ösel and the battles in the Soela Sound, they changed their minds. The Germans actually went ashore at Dagö on the first day of the landings, the 12th. They knew they had to silence the Russian battery at Toffri in order to assure access to the Soela Sound, but the landing operations at Tagga Bay and Pamerort required every available landing craft, including the launches from the navy ships and the lifeboats from the civilian steamers. Naval gunfire from *Bayern* and *Emden* instead silenced the Russian battery, but later that day, when the tempo of the landings on Ösel slowed, Admiral Schmidt put ashore at Toffri a small party of sailors, who demolished the guns. The party then withdrew back to the fleet. Three days later, on the 15th, at 9 AM, a party of sailors led by Lieutenant von Ahlefeldt, who had captured Pamerort, returned and occupied Toffri. His force met no serious resistance.[43]

For the most part, the Germans had good intelligence concerning Dagö. They knew before the invasion that the Russians had a regiment of infantry, the 427th (Pudozhsky), on the island in addition to the naval artillerymen (the Second Coastal Battalion) manning the guns at the four batteries on Dagö. Prisoners captured on Ösel and Moon confirmed the German intelligence.[44] On the very northern tip of Dagö, at Cape Tahkona, the Russians had a 12" (305mm) battery of four guns, Battery #39. Just to the east, at Lekhtma, sat Battery #38, four 6" (152mm) guns, covering the northern entrance to the Moon Sound. In the west, on the Daggerort Peninsula, was Battery #47, with four 6 inch (152mm) guns. Finally, there was a battery at Toffri, guarding the west entrance of the Soela Sound. There is a discrepancy concerning the number of guns at Toffri. German records state eight guns were located there, confirmed in two separate reports: the first from the aerial photography unit conducting reconnaissance before the invasion and a second from a post-invasion damage assessment that says four guns were destroyed; four remained serviceable. The leading Russian historian states that there was only one battery at Toffri, #34, of 120mm guns.[45]

Schmidt and von Kathen became concerned about Toffri and Dagö Island. German progress in crossing from Ösel to Moon had come to a halt when the storm troops could not cross the causeway to Moon. The best alternative was to cross the Small Sound with infantry in small boats. This assault had its risks, which substantially increased if the Germans could not be sure of complete control of the Soela Sound and the Kassar Inlet.

If Russian naval vessels caught the German infantry crossing the Small Sound, the Germans would not have a chance. The shallow water of Kassar Inlet and uncertainty about mines precluded the Germans from using large ships. The Germans compensated by flooding the inlet with torpedo boats and other small craft. The Russians, who knew the waters, employed fewer but larger ships, such as cruisers and destroyers, in the Kassar Inlet. Finally, the Russian bases from which reinforcements could be dispatched (Kuivast and Rogokyul) were closer to the inlet and the Small Sound than the German base at Tagga Bay. The Russians recognized the German disadvantage in having to stage raids all the way through the Soela Sound into the Kassar Inlet with smaller craft, and they staunchly resisted the German advances. A balance had so far prevailed, but if Toffri returned to Russian hands, the Germans might find themselves unable to enter the Soela Sound with any vessels. With a regiment of soldiers on Dagö, the Russians could at any moment drive off von Ahlefeldt's party. On the other hand, if the Germans captured all of Dagö, the Kassar Inlet would be completely under German artillery coverage from shore batteries. The inlet would be a German lake.[46] No Russian ships would dare to enter, and the German infantry could then cross to Moon Island at will.

Admiral Schmidt notified the Admiralty and High Command on the 16th that he and General von Kathen recommended taking Dagö. Holding only the southern part of the island did not guarantee permanent mastery of the sound. The admiral also stated he could not guarantee entry into the Soela Sound or Kassar Inlet from Pamerort alone. If the Russians controlled most of Dagö, they could drive out German forces at the island's south cape and cross over to Ösel anytime they wished. Schmidt asked for authority to take the entire island, and stated he could accomplish this with the forces he had.[47] The High Command agreed, and the next day he received permission.[48]

THE GERMAN BRIDGEHEAD AT SERRO

Schmidt and von Kathen wasted no time. In fact, they jumped the gun by a few hours, apparently receiving a back channel communiqué which indicated that approval was coming. The naval officer in charge of transporting the soldiers from Ösel to Dagö received word at noon on the 17th to pick up the first group of troops at Murika Bay.[49] He arrived at 2:30 PM and embarked some eighty-five combat engineers from the Pioneer Landing

Company (PILAKO) along with forty-five additional soldiers. The Second Cycle Battalion arrived later to help Lieutenant von Ahlefeldt's force. By nightfall, they had linked up with Lieutenant von Ahlefeldt, whose force had fought off several Russian attacks during the day. That same day, Colonel von Kaweczynski marched his Seventeenth Infantry Regiment from Orrisar to Murika Bay, on the west side of Cape Pamerort, for embarkation. The next day, the regiment and a battery of field artillery went to Dagö to widen the bridgehead. Some of the units embarked for Dagö in the dark, and the weather was execrable, leading to delays and confusion. When some of the regiment arrived at Dagö, leaders discovered that instead of their own equipment, they had taken along captured Russian materiel. In all, the Germans hastily shipped some 3,600 men and 560 horses to Dagö for this operation.[50]

RUSSIAN COLLAPSE

Ironically, the Russians anticipated that the Germans would overrun Dagö from the south, but once the enemy landed on the island in force (the 17th of October), the Russians panicked, and their defenses fell to pieces. Russian soldiers and sailors at Serro had hemmed in the German bridgehead near Toffri all that day. At the very moment the Serro garrison bravely took on the Germans, Colonel Veselago, commander of the 427th Infantry Regiment and the garrison on Dagö, ordered Battery #47 on the Daggerort Peninsula and the units near it to abandon and demolish their positions and retreat to the fortifications running across the base of the Tahkona Peninsula. The soldiers took this order to mean all was lost. They panicked, and what should have been an orderly retreat became a rout. Rather than moving in an organized manner to the defense line at the base of the Tahkona Peninsula, the units instead fled to Kertel, where they simply milled about. The aviation unit at Hohenholm burned its facility, then likewise headed for Kertel. Unfortunately, Colonel Veselago could not, or would not, restore order. On the very south end of the island, at Serro, a small force of Russians, led by Lieutenant Elachich, had hemmed in the larger force of Germans all day. When Elachich's men found out that Veselago had ordered a retreat, they too lost their discipline and cohesion. They ran for kilometers to the quay at Heltermaa on the extreme southeast corner of Dagö. Elachich reported that he had sent a patrol to Keinis to discover if the Germans were moving, but the five-man patrol reported seeing no enemy forces—just Russian soldiers fleeing to Heltermaa. Russian morale had collapsed. "I consider it impossible," radioed Elachich, "to reestablish [our] initial position . . . [at Serro] . . . if we do not replace the units we have with new ones."[51]

Shortly afterward, at 6 AM, Colonel Veselago radioed both General Ghenrikson and Admiral Sveshnikov, asking them to send ships to Heltermaa and Lekhtma to evacuate the Dagö garrison. Later that afternoon, Elachich radioed to say he was departing Serro for Kertel. Fog and rain had reduced visibility to almost nothing, he added. Once he got to Kertel, he said, he would try to organize some patrols to see what the Germans were doing. Instead, Elachich returned to the area with some soldiers and reestablished an observation post near Serro. He noted that as he traveled along the entire east coast of Dagö, from Lekhtma to Keinis, he had seen no sign of the Germans. Nonetheless, most of the Russian sailors and soldiers on Dagö were fleeing to Kertel. "It is necessary," he said, "to stop the panic."[52]

THE DAGÖ GARRISON MUTINIES

The Germans moved the Seventeenth Infantry Regiment from Ösel to Dagö on the 18th, which allowed Lieutenant Elachich time to stabilize matters and steady his sailors. At 8:15 PM, he notified Admiral Razvozov's staff that two of his batteries were fully manned and operational. The morale of the gunners, he said, was "excellent." He also said that he thought he could restore Battery 47 (Daggerort). A half-hour later, Colonel Veselago shattered any optimism Razvozov's staff had after Lieutenant Elachich's reports. All his soldiers, explained Veselago, had fled to Kertel and Heltermaa, hoping to find transport to the mainland. Only Elachich's two batteries were battle-ready. Excluding those, Veselago reported he had no units capable of offering resistance. Not that it mattered, however, because the Germans were nowhere to be seen. The Russians had collapsed before the enemy showed up. A couple of hours later, Veselago radioed that matters had worsened. "The island is open to the enemy. . . . The morale of the troops is depressed; violence [against the officers] is possible."[53]

Admiral Razvozov did provide some help. He sent Captain Second Rank Bergshtresser with three steamers from Rogokyul to Heltermaa. Only the *Elba* made the round trip, bringing back to Rogokyul an "echelon" of soldiers. The second ship, the *Toledo*, ran aground, and its crew abandoned it. The third steamer also bottomed out, but its crew refloated it and went back to Rogokyul.[54] Of course, the one ship proved totally inadequate, and Colonel Veselago radioed Admiral Razvozov at 3 AM begging for more ships and proposing to evacuate the island completely. The garrison had collapsed, with the soldiers threatening the officers.[55]

In contrast to this alarming report, Lieutenant Elachich radioed a half hour later to note it was raining heavily, but no enemy ships were in sight. He also asked that if ships came to evacuate the garrison, they bring with them a reliable company to defend the batteries while Veselago's units withdrew. The lieutenant indicated he would try to organize volunteers for this task, but he later radioed and admitted that his effort had failed. While waiting for a trustworthy unit, Elachich said he would wire the guns at the batteries for demolition. Blowing them up, of course, would be a last-ditch effort. At 10 that morning (the 19th), the lieutenant reported that fog had cut visibility to zero, but the enemy had still not arrived.[56]

At 1:45 PM, Veselago again cried for ships, stating that "a mutiny is beginning. It's necessary to urgently send transports to Heltermaa and Kertel. Unit vehicles, weapons and field guns have been abandoned. Depots have been destroyed. Only new [and] disciplined troops can save the situation at the batteries. The fate of the officers depends on the resolution of this issue. They're all in danger of death."[57]

Tempering this alarming message came several more that night from Elachich indicating not all units had mutinied or given up. He also said he had blown up the guns at Cape Daggerort at 4 PM. Close to midnight, the signal officer of the garrison on Dagö radioed to say Batteries 38 and 39 (Lehktma and Cape Tahkona) were still operable and the morale of the gunners was high. He and his men had elected to remain until the end. He wanted authority to blow the guns if necessary.[58]

Just a few kilometers to the east, soldiers of the garrison on Worms Island panicked when they heard that the Germans had moved to Dagö. Admiral Razvozov's orders to blow up the shore facilities at Hapsal and Rogokyul led them to do the same to the guns and facilities at Battery 30 (four 6" guns) on the island. When an officer radioed this news to Admiral Razvozov's staff, he confessed that he did not know who authorized the destruction. The same officer later reported that rioting sailors had burned down their barracks facilities. Early the next morning, the sergeant major at Worms advised the fleet headquarters that the commander of Battery 30 and his crews were leaving in small boats for the mainland.[59]

KERTEL

Meanwhile, the Germans had begun to move and were closing on Kertel. Bogs in the middle of the island prevented them from marching directly north to Cape Tahkona. They had to stick to the coast road, which ran along the eastern side of the island, eventually turning north to Lehktma and the cape. A secondary road some 10 kilometers inland (west) branched off at the Keinis Church and ran parallel to the main highway. Heading north on the 19th, Colonel von Kaweczynski divided his task force into two columns at the Keinis Church crossroads, with one group heading north to the village of Ristiwelja (Ristivalja), and the other marching northeast to the Grossenhof Estate. The units met little resistance, and bivouacked in these locations that night. On the 20th, the Germans resumed the march north. Von Kaweczynski ordered his columns to converge on Kertel, the town where the main and secondary coast roads rejoined. The eastern German force, marching from Grossenhof through Tempa on the main coast road, first encountered the Russians at a manor near Pardas at 6:30 in the morning. The Second Cycle Battalion quickly overran an enemy rear guard detachment, capturing most of the defenders. The battalion's Second Company meanwhile captured the pier area at Heltermaa after a forty-five-minute fight. By 10 AM, the Germans were in the town of Kertel.[60]

The arrival of the Germans in Kertel caused panic. The Russians streamed northward to Lekhtma and Tahkona, followed by the German cyclists. Around 10:30, the station at Tahkona radioed Admiral Razvozov's staff to report that the Germans were in Kertel. About a thousand Russians cowered in Lekhtma. The gunners at Lekhtma had somehow turned their weapons around and were lobbing shells toward Kertel and the Germans. In spite of this ingenuity, the officer at Tahkona in charge of the battery there, Warrant Officer Manklevich, sought permission to demolish his own guns, although the Germans were still not in sight. Manklevich ominously asked that two torpedo boats be sent to evacuate him and his gunners.[61]

Once through the bombardment at Kertel, the German cyclists headed north and captured the batteries at Lektma and Cape Tahkona by early afternoon, overcoming light resistance. The Seventeenth Regiment's Third Battalion swung west at Kertel and marched across the base of the Tahkona Peninsula, occupying the manor at Hohenholm in the afternoon without facing any resistance. The Russians had burned their nearby airfield facilities. On the 21st, the German infantry occupied the shattered ruins of Battery 47 on Daggerort. No one was there to resist.[62]

Later that night, reports about the fate of the island trickled in to Razvozov's headquarters. At 11:30 PM, Lieutenant Elachich, calling from Worms, reported that he had left Kertel under enemy fire at 10 AM, but he claimed the Russians still held the village. He was wrong. A few minutes later, Colonel Veselago notified Razvozov's headquarters that he and his garrison had arrived on Worms Island. Worms is only a two- to three-hour sail from Lekhtma; thus Veselago had remained with the gun crews until the very end. About a thousand sailors and soldiers accompanied him, including the crews from Batteries 34, 38, and 39, and a few men from 47. He also had two men from the island's government and a few soldiers from his own 427th Regiment. The rest, he said, "were killed, captured or ran away."[63]

Actually, the Russians succeeded in evacuating most of the 427th Regiment. On the 25th of October, a Captain Calnitsky, identifying himself as the regiment's commander, reported that the unit had arrived in Narva on the 24th after "an eight-day resistance." He claimed the unit left Dagö only when ordered, and its strength as of the 24th of October numbered "50 officers, one doctor, one priest, 2 officials, and 2,100 soldiers with rifles and 23 machine-guns."[64] Back on Dagö, a demolition party under Captain Second Rank Nikolaev and Engineer Gornov had taken care of the guns in the two batteries at the north end of the island. At 11:55 PM, Colonel Veselago reported that Dagö, "is occupied by the enemy."[65]

The Germans knew the island was theirs, and they duly informed Berlin and Bad Kreuznach on the 20th about their success. Admiral Schmidt and General von Kathen indicated that some mopping up remained. It was not until the early morning of the 23rd of October that Berlin received the final message, "Dagö is in German hands."[66]

Admiral Nicholas Ottovich Essen. *Russian Central Naval Museum, HB-040009/1.*

Rear Admiral Alexander Vladimirovich Razvozov. *Russian Central Naval Museum,*
037819.

Rear Admiral Prince Mikhail Borisovich Cherkassky. *Russian Central Naval Museum, p-032955.51.*

Vice Admiral M. K. Bakhirev (with newspaper) and Captain P. M. Plenn. *Russian Central Naval Museum* , *HB-06188*.

Captain Pavel Ottovich Shishko (on right). *Russian Central Naval Museum, HB-08917.*

Russian 12" guns at Zenel. *Russian Central Naval Museum, HB-08535.*

Russian torpedo boats at Kuivast. *Russian Central Naval Museum, HB-0919.1.*

The *Grom. Russian Central Naval Museum, b-4264-p.*

The *Grom* on fire. *Russian Central Naval Museum, 037139/1.*

Sketch made by a crew member of the gunboat *Chrabry* (right) attempting to tow the sinking *Grom* from the Kassar Wiek. *Russian Central Naval Museum, HB-03273/2.*

The battleship *Slava*, 1911. *Russian Central Naval Museum , 038904.*

The *Grom* shortly before sinking. *SM Torpedo Boat B 110, 62.*

Cruiser *Bayan*, Vice Admiral Bakhirev's flagship. *Russian Central Naval Museum, HB-06959.1*

Torpedo boat *Sliny* (or *Storoschevoi*) and minesweeper *Minrep* evacuating crew from the *Slava*. *Russian Central Naval Museum, HB-03640.*

The *Slava* grounded. Its crew is being evacuated. *Russian Central Naval Museum,*
037236.4.

Slava under fire from 12" German guns. *Russian Central Naval Museum, 031971/7.*

Slava burning after the Russians blew it up. *Russian Central Naval Museum,* *03791.9.*

THE NAVAL BATTLE FOR THE BALTIC ISLANDS

THE MOST IMPORTANT mission the German navy faced during the campaign for the Baltic Islands was the safe transport of the landing force to the islands and its successful lodgment ashore. With that done, the navy then had to provide artillery support to the army's operations. Given the compelling need for speed and surprise, army forces landed without their usual accompaniment of artillery and heavy weapons. Ordinarily, this would be a recipe for disaster, but the navy had assured General von Kathen that its ships would hug the coast of the islands and provide fire support. To accomplish this task on the north side of Ösel, the navy had to break into the Kassar Inlet through the narrow and shallow Soela Sound between Pamerort on Ösel and Cape Toffri on Dagö Island, then drive the Russians from the inlet. An attack through the northern end of the Moon Sound into the Kassar Inlet presented even greater challenges than coming through the Soela Sound. The Russians had mined the opening of the northern end of the Moon Sound, and the entrance lay within range of long-range coastal artillery on Dagö and Worms islands. In addition, any attackers ran the risk of having the Baltic Fleet emerge from the Gulf of Finland, cutting the German fleet's vulnerable lines of communication. To provide support on the south side of Ösel called for passing the gantlet of mines and guns dominating the Irbe Straits. The Germans had to force their way through the straits and into the Gulf of Riga. Once there, they could follow and support the army's advance on the south shore of Ösel.

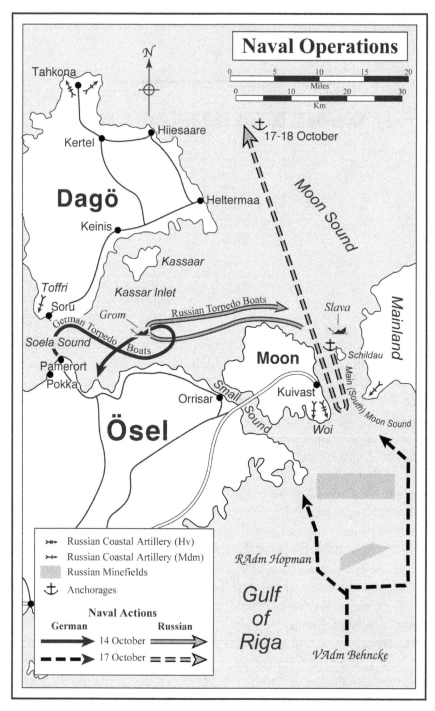

Map 9. Naval Operations

The Germans expected the Russians to contest their entry into both the Kassar Inlet and the Gulf of Riga.

BREAKING INTO THE KASSAR INLET

Von Tschischwitz and Volkmann both hoped that the Forty-second Division's troops could move inland with sufficient speed to catch the Russians before they could leave Arensburg and escape to Moon Island. Volkmann expected Colonel Matthiass's brigade to interdict the Arensburg–Orrisar road before the enemy left the island's capital. If the Russians escaped, the Germans could still claim victory by virtue of taking the island, but it would not amount to the decisive blow both von Estorff and Volkmann knew was expected of them. Their ace in the hole was the Second Cycle Battalion. Along with Captain von Winterfeld's storm troopers, the cyclists would take the north shore route along the coast of Ösel to Orrisar, using speed to gain surprise in order to offset their small numbers. The drawback was that if this card had to be played, because the division failed to block the Russian retreat from the center of the island to the east, then the cycle troops would have to hold the causeway against overwhelming numbers. Under any circumstances such a task would be daunting for a small unit; for one that had sacrificed its usual complement of machine guns and artillery for speed, the job was too much. The army planners acknowledged the dilemma, and came up with a solution.

General von Kathen wanted the navy to sail along the north coast of the island, near the cyclists, using the ships' guns to provide artillery support.[1] This task meant that German naval forces would have to enter the Kassar Inlet, the huge body of water to the northeast of the island, circumscribed by the narrow Soela Sound in the west, Dagö Island to the north, Ösel to the south, and Moon Island to the east. On the surface, this plan seemed straightforward, but it had several difficulties that were best overcome in phases. The only entrance to Kassar Inlet that the Germans could realistically use was the Solea Sound between Dagö and Ösel islands. The sound, which ran through shoals and rocks, was tortuous and narrow as well as shallow. Ordinarily it was well marked by a buoy system, but the Russians had removed most markers to prevent its use, and the Germans anticipated having to locate and mark the channel. Once inside Kassar Inlet, the waters were shallow, and large shoals extended into the inlet from most of Ösel's north shore. The Germans had access to prewar charts of this area, and it was clear the depth of the bay ruled out using large ships. Only small craft, torpedo boats, and destroyers with a shallow draft could navigate safely. In addition, the Germans could expect that weather and shifting sands had changed the boundaries of many areas that were marked on prewar charts. Finally, the Germans assumed that the Russians had mined both the inlet and the Soela Sound, making both even more hazardous. The shallow waters ruled out sending in a submarine to conduct a reconnaissance for mines.

To confuse the Russians about where the actual assault was, the XXIII Corps staged a secondary landing at Pamerort. The Germans had initially believed there was a Russian battery or fortification there, just as there was on the opposite side of the sound, at Toffri on Dagö Island. While aerial reconnaissance photographs taken on 1 October threw this into doubt,[2] the navy remained determined to send a landing party ashore. Taking the cape would serve to silence a fort if there was one, and it also allowed the Germans to establish a station on the cape both to observe the Soela Sound and to give warning if any Russians came from the east, threatening the forces at Tagga Bay. Finally, there was a telephone cable that ran through the village and then went underwater to Dagö. If the Germans seized the area, they could tap into or cut the cable and disrupt the enemy's communications. Taking the cape and village also permitted the Germans to send von Winterfeld's storm troopers and the cyclists toward Orrisar, and it enabled German vessels to enter the Solea Sound in order to provide fire support for their comrades advancing along the coast.

At the same time, German planners had great concern about the battery across the sound at Toffri on Dagö Island. The navy did not have sufficient landing craft to mount simultaneous landings at Tagga Bay, Pamerort, and Toffri. Putting sailors or soldiers ashore at Toffri rated third priority; thus the operation plan called for silencing the batteries at Toffri with naval gunfire, and when landing craft became available, to go ashore later and ensure its destruction.[3]

Once the Germans had silenced Toffri and any guns at Pamerort, their small craft could enter the Soela Sound and accompany the troops moving along the north shore road. Navy units had to find the navigable channel through the sound, ascertain its depth, sweep it for mines, and mark it with buoys. After all that was accomplished, the German naval craft could link up with the soldiers moving on the north shore of Ösel toward Orrisar and the causeway. When the army units reached St. Johannis, where the coastline turned south into the Small Sound, they planned to set up a landing facility. This St. Johannis site would become the staging point for the next phase of the operation, the crossing to Moon Island. In addition, the army would leave two artillery pieces at St. Johannis, where they could dominate the Small Sound, denying Russian vessels entry, while the Germans sent their smallest craft, A II torpedo boats, and their motorized launches to the bridgehead at Orrisar to assist von Winterfeld's detachment.[4] The torpedo boats mounted 88mm guns, and von Kathen and von Tschischwitz counted on them to help von Winterfeld hold on.[5] The mission of Commodore Heinrich's torpedo boat forces and the Pamerort landing party was to accomplish all these tasks.

At 4 AM on 12 October Commodore Heinrich left the fleet at Point White and sailed his own flagship, the cruiser *Emden*, and the battleship *Bayern* toward the Russian batteries at Toffri on the south side of Dagö Island. Both ships opened fire at 6:04. It did not take long for them to silence the Russians, and the German ships then headed south toward the landings at Pamerort. They passed some small trawlers with sounding equipment that Heinrich had sent earlier into the Soela Sound to determine the depth and location of its channel. As the *Emden* steamed by, the officer in charge of the vessels searching for the passage reported that he had not yet found the channel.[6]

When the Germans finally located the channel, they made the surprising discovery that the Russians had not mined it.[7] It was not an oversight; Russian torpedo boats routinely used the channel in order to get to their base at Kuivast. Going through the Soela Sound and the Kassar Inlet was much faster than sailing north around Dagö or south around Ösel. The absence of mines proved to be an extraordinary stroke of good fortune for the Germans. The channel was tricky and had many turns. Large vessels frequently ran aground, but smaller ones, especially the German torpedo boats, could transit the sound without fear of hitting mines on the bottom and enter the Kassar Inlet. Of course, the further east into the inlet the Germans ships went, the closer they came to the Russian fleet at Moon Island. Up to a point, the *Emden* and the other capital ships anchored at the west end of the Sound could provide covering fire, but it did not take long for the Germans to go beyond the range of their guns.

The first German warships, a torpedo boat and some minesweepers, went into the Soela Sound around 8 AM, carefully working their way east. At the same time, a German seaplane had landed next to the *Emden*, and the pilot told Commodore Heinrich that he saw no signs of enemy vessels in the Kassar Inlet. Around 9:30, however, smoke clouds appeared on the horizon to the east, and Heinrich ordered his boats back to the entrance to the sound, where the *Bayern* and *Emden* could protect them with their longer-range guns. Admiral Bakhirev had sent two destroyers (*Pogranichnik* and *Kondratenko*) from Kuivast into the Kassar Inlet as soon as he heard about the German landings. The older gunboat *Grozyashchy* later joined the two destroyers. When the Russians closed within range around 9:45 AM, both sides exchanged gunfire at long range, and the larger German ships drove off the Russians, who retreated carefully out of range and then watched the German actions.[8] At 11 AM, the head of the minesweeping force marking the Soela Sound reported to Commodore Heinrich that the buoys were in place, marking a channel 5 meters deep and 50 meters wide.[9] The Soela Sound was open.

THE CONTEST FOR THE KASSAR INLET

By midafternoon, Heinrich had assembled a dozen small craft, the larger ones from the Thirteenth Torpedo Boat Half-Flotilla that Admiral Schmidt had sent over from Tagga Bay.[10] Again, he attempted to force his way into the Kassar Inlet. Heinrich had five torpedo boats that he hoped would draw off any Russian destroyers, while six older, flat-bottom torpedo boats (A II models) under Commander von Rosenberg tried to skirt the north shore of Ösel and link up with von Winterfeld's forces moving toward the causeway at Orrisar. The flat-bottom boats could navigate the shallow waters of the Small Sound near the causeway. Around 4:40 PM, the Germans came through the Soela Sound and chased the two Russian destroyers and the gunboat *Grozyashchy* east toward Moon Island in a running battle. Russian reinforcements then arrived. The cruiser *Desna* appeared from the Moon Sound with four *Novik*-class destroyers. With the tables turned, and under fire from the heavy guns on *Desna*, the Germans beat a hasty retreat back toward the Soela Sound. With darkness closing, the Russians did not pursue. The *Grozyashchy* had taken several hits and suffered casualties of two killed and five wounded. The Germans claimed they broke off the action because they ran short of ammunition.[11]

Simultaneous with their efforts to penetrate into the Kassar Inlet via the Soela Sound, the Germans sent a landing party to ensure the permanent silence of the battery at Toffri on Dagö Island. The force landed without opposition at 11 AM and destroyed the Russians guns. They later withdrew this force, fearing its small numbers could not hold against a determined Russian counterattack.[12]

After meeting with his skippers late that night following the action with the Germans on the 12th, Bakhirev decided he would confront the enemy at the entrance to the Soela Sound the next morning.[13] As a consequence, on the morning of the 13th, at least eight Russian destroyers waited for the Germans to exit the Soela Sound. Once they saw the Russian ships, the Germans immediately turned back, and called for help from the *Emden*. Its covering fire proved ineffective in the morning. Later, strong winds and poor weather combined to ensure no further action took place between the two navies. The Germans, however, did not let the time go to waste. By nightfall, Heinrich had gathered a huge flotilla of torpedo boats at the west end of the Soela Sound and intended to enter the Kassar Inlet the next day in strength. He also brought up a battleship, the *Kaiser*, to provide effective support for his torpedo boats as they navigated the tricky Soela Sound.[14]

Bakhirev anticipated the Germans. Without elaboration he had told Admiral Razvozov on the night of the 12th that he would close the sound if he could not expel the Germans. A day later, on the night of the 13th–14th, he attempted to block the channel by sinking the steamer *Latvia* at the east end just before it widened and entered the Kassar Inlet. Success would keep the Germans out of the inlet for a long time. Taking no chances, he also ordered the minelayer *Pripyat* to accompany the *Latvia*. *Pripyat* was to seed mines in the channel just in case the block ship did not succeed. The ships left Rogokyul on the mainland the night of the 13th, but the effort failed. The *Latvia* accidentally ran aground as it left the harbor.[15] The *Pripyat* fared worse. Its crew mutinied as it entered the Kassar Inlet in the dark. The sailors cited a long list of complaints: the rain made arming the mines very difficult, and with all other torpedo boats having retreated east, the *Pripyat* was too exposed. The mutineers refused to carry out the mission. A day later with a different crew, *Pripyat* did go back and lay mines slightly further east, but the opportunity to seal the channel was lost.[16]

Preparing to enter the Kassar Inlet in force, Heinrich moved the battleship *Kaiser* to the west end of the Soela Sound on the night of the 13th, keeping it just behind Cape Pamerort and out of sight from any Russian vessels that might be loitering on their side of the entrance to the sound. He hoped to lure the Russian destroyers to the entrance. Having registered this point with the *Kaiser's* guns on the 13th, he could have it fire while it remained out of sight from the Russians.[17]

Expecting that the Germans would attempt to enter the Kassar Inlet as soon as the weather permitted, Bakhirev dispatched the *Novik*-class destroyers *Grom, Zabiyaka, Pobeditel, Konstantin* and the old gunboat *Chrabry* along with a few torpedo boats to the east end of the Soela Sound. They sat at anchor the morning of the 14th waiting for the Germans. By midday, Heinrich was ready to move into the Kassar Inlet, so he ordered the *Kaiser* to fire at the Russians. His ruse worked well. The battleship's first salvos landed unexpectedly in the midst of the Russian flotilla, causing consternation and confusion. *Kaiser*'s second shots smashed into the *Grom* while it weighed anchor, penetrating the engine room and the bottom of the hull. *Grom* caught fire and began to flood.[18] Its skipper, Lieutenant Anatoly Vaksmuth, notified Admiral Bakhirev, who dispatched another gunboat, the *Chivinetz*, to assist.[19]

Led by Heinrich, flying his flag in torpedo boat V100, the German flotilla of fifteen torpedo boats (ten from Lieutenant Commander Heinecke's Torpedo Boat Flotilla II, five from the Thirteenth Half-Flotilla) emerged from the Soela Sound and sped into the Kassar Inlet around 12:30. As they exited the sound, torpedo boat G101 ran hard aground and sat in the mud until dark. At 1 PM, the Germans saw the four Russian destroyers on the eastern horizon, and they opened fire at 1:22 PM at a range of 9,500 meters. Outside of one minor hit to the *Zabiyaka*, the firing did little damage because of the extreme range, the speed of the vessels, and the rainy weather.[20] Heinrich steamed in two columns. The Thirteenth Half-Flotilla with its five boats formed the northern line; Lieutenant Commander Heinecke's Second Flotilla with ten boats constituted the southern line.[21]

Just as the German force split into two lines, the Russians fled toward the Moon Sound, leaving the crippled *Grom* behind. It was listing and on fire. Its captain got its engines started several times, but he could not keep them running when he tried to engage the propellers. As the *Chrabry* approached the stricken destroyer to evacuate the crew, the men from the *Grom* panicked and jumped on to *Chrabry*'s deck and ran to its far side, huddling in terror and nearly capsizing the old gunboat. A few men leapt right into the water. Lieutenant Graf, on the nearby *Novik*, wrote afterward that when *Chrabry* came alongside, "the sailors, instead of passing [sic] the two ropes, threw themselves on the *Chrabry* like madmen. Nothing remained for the officers but to pass [sic] over also; the captain, who refused to leave his ship, was taken [off] by force. When the last men were leaving the *Grom*, she was in flames."[22] The *Chrabry* later attempted to tow the *Grom*, reducing drastically its speed and maneuverability, which made both ships an easy target for the Germans. As the German flotilla approached, the *Chrabry* gave up the effort in order to save itself.[23]

Heinrich and his vessels headed toward the burning *Grom*, but just before they arrived, they saw some dark objects in the water. They Germans avoided the objects, and tried to scout them out without stopping. Heinrich felt certain they were buoys, not mines.[24] Lieutenant Heinecke's B98 moved alongside the *Grom*, and the skipper sent over a prize crew, taking prisoner eight sailors who had been too frightened to jump over to the *Chrabry*. After giving three cheers for the kaiser, the Germans on the *Grom* raised their flag over the Russian Cross of St. Andrew, and the B98 took the prize in tow. It was the first enemy warship taken in combat by the German navy. A quick search turned up the *Grom*'s logbook and a current chart of the Kassar Inlet showing depths and, more importantly, revealing the absence of mines in the inlet. In addition, they found a signal codebook and another chart showing the location of the minefields at the south entrance to the Moon Sound. Meanwhile, Russian reinforcements attacked the B98. The *Chivinetz*, an obsolete monitor-like gunboat, arrived from Rogokyul, accompanied by all the torpedo boats remaining at Kuivast. Heinecke's flotilla tried to fend off the Russians with gunfire, and they laid down smoke screens to hide the two ships. The effort was in vain; B98 had to let the *Grom* go, and it capsized and sank a few minutes later. The officer in charge of the prize, Lieutenant Harsdorf von Enderndorf, had to swim for it when the ship went down.[25]

By 3 PM, the Germans had pushed the Russians to the east end of Kassar Bay. It was now the Germans' turn to come under attack from heavy artillery. As they neared the north end of Moon Island, the cruiser *Makarov* opened fire at them. The Germans' vessels quickly retreated out of range. Heinrich kept his ships in the area until dark to ensure that no Russians entered the Small Sound and scattered von Rosenberg's A II boats, which were engaged at the Orrisar–Moon Island causeway.[26] He then anchored his flotilla near Cape Fekerort, just east of the Soela Sound. German losses for the day were minor: G104 had taken a hit on its stern, while G101 finally showed up at dark with a bent propeller that vibrated badly when it tried to increase its speed. Both boats had to return to base for repair. Their ammunition was split among the remaining vessels.[27]

To the south, Commander von Rosenberg took advantage of the Russian focus on Heinrich's torpedo boats. His six scout boats (type A II) went into the Small Sound, looking for von Winterfeld's party. They arrived at the critical moment and provided von Winterfeld with ammunition just as his soldiers exhausted their supplies.[28]

On the 15th, the Germans observed Russian vessels in the Moon Sound, but none emerged into Kassar Inlet. The Russians did use their cruisers and capital ships anchored in the Moon Sound to fire over Moon Island and into the Small Sound. Both sides played cat and mouse. When the Germans approached close to Moon Island, the Russians would open fire and the Germans would retreat until the Russians stopped. The Germans would then move toward Moon, rekindling the cycle. When the weather cleared a bit, around noon, Heinrich moved his ships into the Kassar Inlet, trying to draw off the Russian fire from the Small Sound. In the same area where the *Grom* had sunk, he observed a mine, and as he ordered his minesweepers to determine whether it was floating or anchored, a huge detonation tore off the bow of Lieutenant Heinecke's boat, B98. Amazingly, the ship remained afloat and eventually returned to Tagga Bay under its own power.[29] The Germans swept the area and found no more mines. Heinrich radioed Admiral Schmidt, saying he was puzzled. His vessels had passed safely through the same area the day before, and the captured enemy maps showed the area to be free of mines, so he did not think the mine that blew up B98 was laid during the night of 14–15 October. The B98 was damaged close to the black objects Heinrich saw the day before during the attack on *Grom*. In all likelihood, the *Pripyat* left these mines when it returned the night of the 14th to mine the Soela Sound. None of the Germans knew about the *Pripyat*. In any event, the shallow water directed the force of the explosion upward, inflicting heavy losses on B98. Fifteen sailors were killed and five wounded.[30]

For the next couple of days, both sides in the Kassar Inlet watched each other and occasionally exchanged fire, all from great distances. The Germans noticed it took forty seconds from the muzzle flash of the Russian heavy coastal artillery or the ships' guns before the shells arrived, giving them plenty of time to move out of harm's way. The Russians were active on the eastern edge of the Kassar Inlet, but they did not contest the German supremacy inside it. On the morning of the 17th, the Germans observed the Russians firing—they saw the muzzle flashes and waited for the spouts of water that would come in forty seconds. When they saw no water spouts, they realized that the Russians were firing toward the southern end of the Moon Sound. This could only mean that German battleships were trying to enter the south end of the channel. Soon all the large Russian ships, cruisers and transports, led by two battleships flying huge battle flags per

Russian custom, emerged from behind Moon Island, heading north. The lead battleship, which they concluded was the *Slava*, suddenly stopped. A few minutes later, it blew up with a huge flash and bang. When the smoke had cleared, it had settled by the stern and the battle flag had disappeared. The Germans, without knowing entirely what had happened, recognized the signs of scuttling. After two years of heading the German Baltic Forces' "most wanted list," and evading every conceivable German effort to sink it using ships, submarines, planes, torpedo boats, and torpedo airplanes, *Slava* had brought about its own demise.[31]

BREAKING INTO THE GULF OF RIGA

The Russian leaders knew that if Zerel and the Sworbe Peninsula fell, the Germans would enter the Gulf of Riga and try to block the southern entrance to the Moon Sound. On the 15th, with the naval gunners at Zerel mutinying, Bakhirev feared the worst and called Admiral Razvozov. After bringing Razvozov up to date with the news that the guns there had fallen silent, Bakhirev added, "I consider the defense of the Moon Sound of primary importance. If we lose it, we'll lose our ability to land forces and transport supplies [to Moon and Ösel]."[32]

Admiral Hopman arrived at the Irbe Straits from Windau early on the morning of the 15th. He had three cruisers (*Kolberg, Straßburg,* and *Augsburg*), and he joined a number of his mine-clearing vessels, which had been there since the 12th of October, attempting to clear a passage through the Irbe Straits. They succeeded in sweeping and marking two 300-meter-wide passages through the straits.[33] He then tried to sneak by the Russian defenses. Russian artillery firing from Zerel stopped him. Vice Admiral Behncke returned with *König* and *Kronprinz* that morning from Putziger Wiek, where he had taken his Third Battleship Squadron to recoal. He joined Hopman's cruisers anchored along the Courland coast. He could not risk entering the gulf until he knew Zerel was silenced.[34] Later that night, Admiral Souchon radioed Schmidt, telling him that the big Russian guns at Zerel had fallen silent. "The enemy has surrendered Zerel," said Souchon, "and destroyed the equipment with explosives and gunfire." After considering this development, Behncke informed Admiral Schmidt that minesweeping operations in the Irbe Straits had progressed to the point where he planned to "push forward with all his forces at dawn toward Arensburg."[35]

Behncke was underway, having left at 5:15 AM on the 16th. Accompanying his two dreadnoughts were the three cruisers from Admiral Hopman's reconnaissance forces and a medley of support vessels, primarily mine-clearing vessels from the Second Mine Reconnaissance Flotilla of Lieutenant Commander Max Doflein. Just after passing the Sworbe Peninsula the Germans encountered a tugboat of some sort towing a huge barge filled with Russian soldiers. They had tried to escape from Zerel but had floundered at sea for a day or two under miserable conditions. The Germans captured both vessels and sent them to Arensburg.[36] A few hours later, Behncke received a radio message from Admiral Schmidt telling him "to attack Russian naval forces in the Moon Sound and the Gulf of Riga with everything you have."[37] The commander in chief's order called for a change both in plans and in course. While Behncke pondered the new orders, his force had to anchor twice while his minesweepers cleared a path through newly discovered minefields. He took advantage of one of the delays to have a skippers' meeting to discuss the new mission he had received that morning from Admiral Schmidt. He laid out his plan of attack for the Moon Sound. By 2:30 PM, Behncke resumed his progress northeast toward the Moon Sound. Before getting underway, he sent the support ships and the *Augsburg* north to Arensburg. He wanted the facilities there and at Rommassare safeguarded and made ready for the arrival of the transport fleet, which had left Tagga Bay that morning.

The Germans escaped damage when an enemy submarine attacked around 4:30 PM and the torpedoes missed. The submarine then accidentally surfaced between the two battleships. The astonished Germans at first thought it was one of their own because the net-cutting apparatus looked similar. The sailors gaped and said, "That can't be an enemy—one would have to be a bit crazy to attack from that position." By the time they recovered their wits, the enemy vessel had submerged. The sub's skipper was determined, however, and somehow maneuvered into a firing position. A half hour later a torpedo hit the *Indianola*, the tender for the minesweeping flotilla. It limped back to Arensburg.[38]

As the Germans approached the Moon Sound from the south, they could see the gun flashes from the heavy (10") battery at Woi on Moon Island. The fleet arrived at 8:30 and anchored 17 kilometers below the southern entrance to the Moon Sound.[39] Behncke convened another meeting on the *König* for all his captains and issued orders for the next morning's assault. The admiral recognized that the minefields below the entrance to the sound posed a serious obstacle. On the other hand, he knew there were two and their location. That information came from the chart found on the *Grom*. Behncke ordered his minesweepers to clear a passage diagonally from west to east through the southernmost field. He planned to bring his ships northeast through this minefield toward the Verder Peninsula on the mainland, then west toward Moon. This pattern would bring his ships within range of the enemy batteries at both places, as well as allowing all his large guns to bear. While the German mine-sweepers cleared the way through this minefield, however, they would have to endure enemy barrages. The German capital ships would be too far away to silence the enemy batteries. Behncke gave Admiral Hopman some minesweepers and directed him to take his two cruisers (*Straßburg*, *Kolberg*) northwest as far as possible into the Small Sound. Once there, Hopman was to engage the enemy batteries at Woi and support any army operations on Moon.[40]

The Germans spent an uncomfortable night, refueling and provision-ing the smaller vessels from the larger ones. It was nerve-wracking. Just before 4 AM, a radio message arrived from the *Moltke* advising Behncke that a north-south minefield existed in the middle of the Moon Sound.[41] This information necessitated a change in plans. Admiral Behncke brought Lieutenant Commander Weidgen, commander of the Third Mine Clear-ing Division and his immediate superior, Lieutenant Commander Doflein, of the Second Mine Reconnaissance Flotilla, on board his flagship. He told them he had decided to bypass the two known fields by sailing east, below them. He planned to turn north just before the Larina Bank, a shoal 10 kilometers east of the Estonian coast. This maneuver would necessitate passing east-northeast through the purported new minefield. On the other hand, it would bring the German ships to the coast and within range of the Russian land batteries on Moon and the mainland as well as the anchorage at Kuivast.[42]

THE BATTLE FOR MOON SOUND

Leaving their anchorage at 6 AM on the morning of the 17th, the Ger-mans soon encountered two *Novik*-class destroyers hugging the coast and speeding north ahead of them. Behncke took them under fire around 7 PM, without hitting either.[43] Admiral Bakhirev had dispatched the two destroyers to find the Germans, and they radioed Behncke's location as they escaped into the Moon Sound. Bakhirev recognized that the Germans planned to force the Moon Sound, and understanding the danger to his smaller ships and steamers, he ordered them to leave Kuivast immediately and anchor on the north side of Schildau Island, safely out of range. He then recalled the battleships *Slava* and *Graschdanin* from the north end of Moon, where they had spent the previous day firing on German vessels in the Kassar Inlet. As the Germans approached, the Russians discovered what they were up against. Their lookouts mistakenly identified the two battleships as *Kaiser*-class dreadnoughts. Behncke's ships came from the *König* class. This was an improved version of the *Kaiser* design, the major difference being in turret alignment, which allowed the *Königs* to bring all ten of their guns to bear on the enemy. The *Kaiser* class could engage only eight of ten guns. The lookouts also overestimated the size of Behncke's force, crediting it with a cruiser of the *Roon* class, four light cruisers, two aircraft tenders, and a number of minesweepers.[44]

At the same time, German observers identified the Russian ships at anchor near Kuivast: the *Slava*, the *Graschdanin*, a cruiser of the *Makarov* class (*Bayan*), several destroyers, and a number of transport steamers. Fifteen minutes later, one of the German ships sounded the alarm for mines, and the entire flotilla halted. Lieutenant Weidgen's vessels began their work, slowly sweeping channels for mines. Admiral Behncke wrote that after he watched their efforts for three-quarters of an hour, it dawned on him that the two Russian destroyers had obviously used an unmarked channel, so he ordered Lieutenant Commander Doflein to take his Third Mine Reconnaissance Half-Flotilla and find and mark the channel.[45]

After receiving reports about the approaching Germans, Bakhirev "decided to accept the battle, and, as much as it was possible, delay the enemy from capturing the southern Moon Sound." The admiral hoped to delay the Germans from entering the sound long enough to force them to return to their base to replenish coal and ammunition, a pause that would give the Russians time to recapture Ösel with fresh troops.[46] In 1916, the *Slava* had kept the Germans at bay for two or three days in the Irbe Straits, cleverly using the minefields and the shore batteries to its advantage. Bakhirev expected to use the minefields at the entrance to the Moon Sound Channel, along with the nearby 10" batteries at Woi, in a similar fashion. He told Admiral Razvozov that he had made this decision to fight "counting on our mine field, . . . but it turned out that the mine field was known to the enemy just as well as it was to us."[47]

With two of his staff, Captain Second Rank Muromtsov (operations officer) and Lieutenant Sokolov (flag lieutenant), Admiral Bakhirev boarded the cruiser *Bayan* at 7 AM and ordered his flag raised. A half hour later, in the middle of a German air raid[48] on Kuivast, the *Bayan* weighed anchor and headed south to meet the Germans. Alongside it were four destroyers (*Deyatelny, Delny, Storozhevoi,* and *Silny*) from the Eleventh Torpedo Boat Division. Behind them came the *Slava* and the *Graschdanin*, accompanied by destroyers from the Sixth Torpedo Boat Division.[49] The destroyers were not the most modern in the Russian fleet, and why Bakhirev chose them is not at all clear. The top-notch *Novik*-class destroyers were readily available.

At 8 AM the *Slava* opened fire at extremely long range. The Germans and the captain of the *Bayan* later stated that the *Slava* opened fire first; the captains of the *Slava* and the destroyer *Silny* claimed that the Germans initiated the shooting. Admiral Bakhirev's initial report is ambiguous, but his headquarters' after action report is not. That report says *Slava* opened up first. The *Slava* had had its guns upgraded in 1916, and it surprised everyone by outranging the German dreadnoughts.[50] In any event, once the firing started, the *Bayan* moved off to the side to let the *Slava* and the *Graschdanin* pass it, allowing an unobstructed view of the distant Germans.[51] Behncke ordered the lead German ships (minesweepers and several torpedo boats) and Hopman's two cruisers back toward his battleships. The two German battleships moved eastward and took the lead in the channel that Doflein's boats had started to clear, firing north at the Russians. At first, the *Slava* and the land batteries at Woi on Moon Island targeted the German minesweepers, but the Russians soon switched their aim to the *König* and *Kronprinz*. Despite the extreme range (20,400 meters), the Russian shells landed very close to the German ships—on occasion within 50 meters.[52] The Germans had to take the pounding. Behncke mistakenly thought that his ships were traversing a narrow passage through one of the minefields, allowing him no freedom to maneuver. In reality, his charts were incorrect, and he was just outside the field. Nonetheless, to avoid presenting an easy target, Behncke quickly reversed his course, trying to draw the Russian fire while his battleships retreated back out of range toward the west. The engagement was short—the Russians said the firing lasted for twenty minutes without their taking any hits. They thought that one of the German destroyers had hit a mine and sunk along with two torpedo boats. The Germans reported the Russian fire was accurate, but no vessels were lost.[53]

Behncke decided to break off the battle and wait southwest of the Larina Bank while Doflein's flotilla went back to ensure there were no

mines to the north—all the while under heavy fire from Russian land batteries. If Doflein could clear a passage, Behncke's ships would emerge from
the minefields well within range of all the Russian ships at Kuivast. As the
Germans moved back west out of the range of the Russian artillery, Bakhirev simultaneously reversed course and steamed northwest toward Kuivast,
hoping the Germans would follow him and run into the minefields. When
he realized that the enemy was not following, he ordered his fleet to stop.
They anchored just northeast of Paternoster Island, in front of the batteries
at Woi. "A signal from *Bayan*," wrote the captain of the *Silny*, "ordered the
crews to have lunch, but be ready to weigh anchor."[54]

While Behncke waited west of the Larina Bank, two minesweepers
(M67, M77) clearing the channel for him took a beating from the Russian
batteries. The small craft were damaged but remained in action.[55] When
the minesweepers finished, Behncke planned to run up along the Estonian
coastline toward the east side of the entrance to the Moon Sound at high
speed, hoping to catch the Russians off guard. Approaching from this direction meant a head-on attack and had the disadvantage of reducing his heavy
artillery by over half. In facing the enemy directly, only the forward two turrets could fire. Admiral Behncke hoped the surprise move might catch the
Russians off guard, for up to this point, he had run east and west courses,
which permitted all five of the turrets on the ship to bear on the enemy.[56]

Behncke and his two battleships resumed sailing toward the Estonian
mainland just before 10 AM As he moved east, he ordered Admiral Hopman
to break off from the formation and steam northwest with his cruisers into
the Small Sound. The Eighth Mine Sweeping Flotilla went with Hopman.[57] The two German capital ships turned and suddenly bolted north
at 10 AM, first at high, then at top, speed. Behncke opened fire thirteen
minutes later at a range of 16,500 meters.

Bakhirev could see the Germans coming so he was not completely
surprised, but when he realized they had safely bypassed his minefield, he
knew he was in serious trouble. If they slowed and turned to fire broadside,
they had him outgunned, twenty cannons to eight. He gave the order to
raise anchor once the German shells began to land near his ships, but he
had cut matters too close. *Graschdanin* took at least four hits, the *Slava* six.[58]
The Russian ships retreated north toward Schildau, returning fire. Bakhirev
understood that the situation was precarious. He now found himself dealing
with the same problem Behncke had faced earlier that morning: he was in
a narrow channel that offered no room to maneuver while under enemy
gunfire. In heading away from the enemy, the Russian ships could bring

only their aft guns to bear. In the *Slava's* case, it did not matter, because its forward turret would not move,[59] and the German shells had severed the link between the fire direction center and its rear turret. The officer in charge of the turret could still fire the guns, but accuracy suffered.

Captain Antonov of the *Slava* recognized that his ship had sustained mortal wounds. A 12" shell had landed in the water next to the bow of the ship and exploded, rupturing the forward turret magazine under the water-line and flooding it. All the damage control parties could do was close the watertight doors and let the compartment fill with seawater, which caused the ship to list eight degrees to port. Captain Antonov reduced the heel a few degrees after pumping seawater into ballast tanks on the starboard side of the ship, but the *Slava* was also down several feet by the bow. While it was not in immediate danger of sinking, the weight of the water in its forward compartments brought down its bow, making passage through the shallow Moon Sound channel impossible. The sound was Bakhirev's sole escape route, and he planned to use it within the hour.[60]

Everyone who saw the *Slava* suddenly list and go down at the bow knew it was hit badly. *Graschdanin* drew close, placing itself between the doomed ship and the German dreadnoughts, trying to provide some cover. Bakhirev had the *Bayan* turn to starboard (toward the Estonian mainland) in an effort to draw the German fire. He succeeded. The Germans shifted their aim to the cruiser. Its captain, Timirev, had kept it at a slow speed to avoid interfering with the retreat of the Russian battleships, but when eight salvoes of 12" shells came at him, he accelerated to 15 knots. Only one shell hit the *Bayan*, landing between the forward turret and the bridge, but splinters from the shell pierced the turret and set fire in the forward storage lockers and the conning room. It took over a day to extinguish the fire. Captain Timirev flooded the magazines, which lowered his draft in the bow by some 2.6 feet,[61] but his cruiser drew less water than the battleships and could still safely navigate the channel.

The Russian ships broke off fire as they sailed out of range, north past Schildau Island toward the narrow southern entrance to the Moon Sound. The batteries at Woi and Verder kept up their fire, however, so Behncke reversed course and shifted his guns to them. For forty-five min-utes (10:45–11:30 AM), he bombarded them and was rewarded by seeing explosions and fires. The Germans soon realized that they had not caused all the damage. The Russians planned to surrender or leave and were destroying the guns. The Germans anchored their ships, fearing to go any further north because of the presence of mines. The sighting of an enemy submarine caused Behncke to move his ships in a racetrack pattern so the submarine would not get a good shot at them. The big German ships steamed north and south in the channel below Verder, which they knew to be safe. The submarine did not reappear.[62]

On the opposite side of the lower sound, Admiral Hopman followed his minesweepers into the Small Sound between Ösel and Moon. While slowly approaching as his minesweepers cleared the route, Hopman's ships came under fire from the 10" batteries at Woi. When he drew within range, he returned fire, but the Russians soon ceased their shelling and destroyed their artillery. At 4 PM he sent a party of forty ashore, led by Lieutenant Kelm, who secured the battery at Woi until the arrival of the army later that night.[63]

At the south entrance to the Moon Sound, the *Bayan* stopped to give orders and provide cover, while all the smaller craft in the roadstead left for the Karilaid anchorage at the north end of the Sound. *Slava* could not escape because of its list. It had taken on too much water and could no longer navigate the Moon Sound channel. Admiral Bakhirev ordered Captain Antonov to sink it at the entrance to the channel.[64] While the engineers laid explosive charges, Bakhirev ordered several destroyers to take off the crew. *Silny* took off 141 panicked sailors, and the destroyer *Storozhevoi* and minesweeper *Minrep*, the rest. Captain Antonov departed last, after setting the fuses.[65] After the *Slava* exploded and burned, the destroyer *Turkmenetz Stavropolsky* fired torpedoes into it.[66]

Bakhirev ordered an evacuation of the Schildau roadstead. While the ships weighed anchor, their crews could see and hear large explosions on nearby Moon Island as well as at Verder on the Estonian mainland. Russian engineers were blowing up the shore batteries and facilities to prevent them from falling into German hands. They achieved only partial success.[67] The Russian fleet, led by *Graschdanin*, entered the Moon Sound Channel at 1:30 PM steaming north for the anchorage at Karilaid (Harilaid) Island, about 30 kilometers away, near the top end of the channel. At the south end of the channel, Bakhirev sank four ships (in addition to the *Slava*) to block the entrance to the sound. He had the *Pripyat* seed the area with mines as well. Bakhirev acknowledged that "in spite of the enemy planes dropping bombs, . . . [the] retreat was conducted in an excellent order." He also praised the ship's crew. While he wrote that comment from the *Bayan*, it was applicable to every Russian sailor that day. Captains Antonov and Timirev echoed these sentiments in their reports. Two and half hours later the fleet dropped anchor south of Karilaid Island.[68]

ESCAPE OF THE RUSSIAN FLEET

Bakhirev planned to escape to the north into the Gulf of Finland with his ships, but he had to wait until the channel north of his anchorage between Dagö and Worms was swept for mines.[69] His initial plan called for the larger ships to leave first, escorted by the *Admiral Makarov* and the *Diana* along with the *Novik*-class destroyers. When he mentioned this to his subordinates, they agreed. Escape into the Gulf of Finland, they said, would permit their vessels to fight with the rest of the fleet along the central defense position. Bakhirev thought otherwise; if he remained with some if not all of his forces, he could provide intelligence and delay the Germans, and the presence of naval forces in the upper reaches of the sound would enhance the morale of the Russian ground forces remaining in the area. If the Navy withdrew completely, the effect on the army would be "devastating." Nonetheless, as he later pointed out, all the talk was meaningless. Admiral Razvozov had given him order to evacuate the sound and head north into the Gulf of Finland.[70]

The Germans expected Bakhirev to head north. They had three opportunities to stop him. The first was to continue to pursue his battered fleet from the south with Behncke's dreadnoughts. Second, they could attempt to block his exit by attacking east into the Moon Sound from the Kassar Inlet. The final option was to attack the Russians when they emerged into the Baltic from the north end of the Moon Sound.

The mines between Moon Island and the mainland to the south of Kuivast kept Behncke's forces at a crawl, preventing him from keeping pressure on Bakhirev. He could not advance without unwarranted risk until his minesweepers cleared the way, and their progress was slow, hampered by bad weather, a boom in the channel, and a net barrier strung across the south entrance to the Moon Sound channel. The German minesweepers did not arrive at the wreck of the *Slava* until the 18th. Caution led them to tow Behncke's dreadnoughts into the Kuivast roadstead, and it took them two days.[71] Behncke correctly feared his battleships could not navigate the northern Moon Sound because they drew too much water. Furthermore, an examination of the entrance to the Moon Sound channel revealed that Bakhirev had done his work well: between the four sunken vessels and mines, the channel would not be opened for a long time.

Commodore Heinrich attempted the second means of stopping the Russians, attacking east into the Moon Sound from the Kassar Inlet to block the journey of the Russian fleet. Bakhirev expected this attack, and he had left the cruiser *Makarov* at the junction of the sound and Kassar Inlet on the morning of the 17th. The cruiser's 8" guns easily kept the Germans at bay when they tried to approach.[72] Heinrich was also not sure what had happened to the *Slava*. He thought the Russians were attempting to refloat it, so he sent three torpedo boats to finish it off the night of the 17th. En route, the S64 hit a German mine and sank. Most of the crew was rescued, but Heinrich called off the operation.[73]

The final and most logical approach for the Germans to stop the Russians was to seal off the north end of the Moon Sound, trapping the Russians in the narrow channel. This prospect must have given Bakhirev sleepless nights on the 17th and 18th of October. The Germans recognized the escape route and stationed no fewer than three submarines off the coast where the channel exited into the Baltic. Rain and high seas, along with Russian aircraft patrols, kept the submarines at bay.[74] During the late afternoon of the 17th, when he learned Bakhirev had fled to the north end of the Moon Sound, Admiral Schmidt ordered Admiral Souchon's Fourth Battleship Squadron to block that entrance, bottling up the Russians. The Germans knew that the Russians had mined the waters north of Dagö, so Schmidt ordered Admiral Reuter and his reconnaissance squadron to clear the way around Dagö Island for Souchon's ships.[75] Reuter had only the Fourth Minesweeping Half-Flotilla, which had an insufficient number of craft for the job. The remainder of the German mine-clearing capabilities were in the Kassar Inlet or the lower Moon Sound. Virtually no progress was made on the 18th because of poor weather, and at noon that day, Schmidt postponed the operation. In his unit diary, the admiral wrote there would be insufficient time to clear the way because his ships were needed to transport army forces to Dagö. The loss of precious mine-sweepers, the exhaustion of his crews, and the worsening weather further militated against clearing a route north of Dagö.[76]

On the 18th and 19th the Germans lost more small craft to mines, and it became clear to Schmidt that marking minefields and clearing passageways all around the islands had to take priority. At noon on the 18th, just as Schmidt decided to call of operations at Dagö, the Admiralty radioed its approval of his plan to encircle the Russian ships from the north, but the admiral realized it was unlikely that he could accomplish the task. "Any chance at success for the entire operation," he wrote, "depended on our forces being able to get to the northern entrance of the Moon Sound just before, or at least right after, the Russian ships . . . did." The prerequisite for success, he noted, was speed, but it also proved to be the Achilles' heel of the plan. The Germans could not clear a pathway for Souchon's squadron in time to prevent Bakhirev's escape into the open waters of the Baltic. Admiral Schmidt advised the Admiralty that he had postponed the operation, adding that unless circumstances changed dramatically for the better, he did not foresee carrying out the operation. At 6 PM that evening, the Admiralty concurred and ordered the operation cancelled.[77]

While Schmidt agonized over calling off the effort to hem in the Russians, Bakhirev made good his escape. Russian intelligence had broken the German code, and Admiral Razvozov knew what the Germans planned. Faced with this development, Admiral Razvozov had to get the ships out of the Moon Sound as soon as possible. He discussed the situation with General Cheremisov several times. He also knew that German submarines lay waiting for Bakhirev at the northern exit to the Moon Sound. The same submarines had laid mines near Stapelbotten, a sand bank northeast of the sound,[78] hoping to block any exit in that direction. General Cheremisov agreed on the afternoon of the 18th that Bakhirev needed to head for safety.[79]

Bakhirev wanted to break out of the sound on the 18th, but several factors held him back. General Cheremisov insisted on using some of his transports to assist in evacuating soldiers from Moon, and the Russians had not completed their efforts to block the Moon Sound. Bakhirev also had to search the northern end of the Moon Sound for mines and clear it before he could safely depart.[80]

With Bakhirev unable to depart from the Moon Sound on the 18th, Admiral Razvozov expected that the Germans would not miss their chance a second time. He ordered his main fleet be prepared to sortie from the Gulf of Finland into the Baltic to screen Bakhirev's escape. The official German history cites, without providing a source, the following message from Admiral Razvozov to Bakhirev: "In an emergency I will support you with all forces to include the battleship brigades." The Germans confess to not knowing if this was a ruse,[81] but the Russian records indicate Razvozov's staff took it seriously. The admiral's senior assistants told their counterparts at the northern front headquarters that plans called for one brigade of battleships to head for Porkkala, the other to Lapvik (Lappvik). "Our forces," said Captain Rengarten, Razvozov's executive officer, "intend to give battle with the [enemy] dreadnoughts." This statement prompted a flood of questions from Cheremisov's headquarters, indicating serious reservations about the turn of events,[82] and one officer told the Baltic

Fleet's liaison officer in a rather pointed memorandum that the mission of the Baltic Fleet was to protect the capital, fighting from behind battle positions. The risk of losing the fleet, a catastrophe that could influence the war's outcome, was not justified by Razvozov's noble attempt to save ships of little value. With Dagö in enemy hands, there was no forward battle position. Razvozov would have to accept battle in open water, which was exactly what Admiral Bakhirev did. A repetition of that sort of action under such conditions "can hardly be favorable to us."[83]

Bakhirev wanted to leave on the last vessel, and he had made arrangements to sail on a torpedo boat—the final one in the formation. At noon on the 19th, however, he received a radio message from Reval stating that the Germans were waiting and planned to cut off his escape. He passed this information on to his captains, adding to it an exhortation to be ready for action. He decided his leadership was needed, and moved his flag back to the *Bayan*.[84] Later that afternoon, the remnants of the Russian fleet steamed out of the northern entrance of the Moon Sound into the Gulf of Finland. Navigation in the dark and under blackout conditions so close to the coast was too dangerous, but Bakhirev timed his exit late in the day to take advantage of the dark. By departing Karilaid at 3 PM, his ships had sufficient daylight to navigate the treacherous channel, but as they emerged into the wide open Gulf of Finland, the falling darkness protected them, rendering the ships almost invisible. Bakhirev knew the location of the German submarines. Instead of exiting north into the well-marked shipping channel leading to Hango, he turned to starboard toward Odensholm Island and hugged the coast, leaving a trail of mines in his wake. The Battle of Moon Sound had ended.

By an odd coincidence, Lieutenant Karl Vesper of UC-58, whose favorable report on conditions in Tagga Bay launched Operation Albion, had the last say. Waiting north of the Moon Sound exit, Vesper radioed to the *Moltke* at 4:30 PM on the 19th of October that "two *Makaroff* [sic] and one *Gangut* class cruisers, enemy torpedo boats, and several steamers cleared the Moon Sound heading toward Odensholm Island. Not a chance of attacking them." A half hour later, Vesper transmitted again, "One *Slava* class ship, 3 minesweepers, 12 destroyers, and 4 steamers broke through to the north. Distance too great for a shot."[85]

CHAPTER TEN

CONCLUSION

AT DAWN ON the 20th of October, Bakhirev and his collection of ships steamed into the Russian naval facility at Lapvik, Finland, having made good their escape from the Moon Sound. The crews had no time to celebrate their good fortune. Skippers quickly moved the vessels to repair facilities in order to get them back to combat-ready status as soon as possible. Admiral Stark even sent two torpedo boats back to the islands, trying to rescue troops left on Dagö.[1] Meanwhile, the senior officers and leaders wrestled with the more important questions. What would the Germans do next? Would they land on the mainland? Would they come into the Gulf of Finland?

Two days earlier, when it was clear the islands were lost, Alexander Kerensky went to the northern front headquarters at Pskov. In addition to being the head of state, Kerensky had named himself supreme commander after dismissing General Kornilov in September. Kerensky convened a meeting late that night (the 18th) to discuss the military situation. He brought with him the naval minister, Admiral Verderevsky; Stankevich, a commissar from Stavka; and General Baranovski, an advisor whom General Knox called ambitious but inexperienced.

The supreme commander was clearly worried about the threat to his capital posed by the German successes, and the meeting, which lasted until 11 PM, reflected his concern. Admiral Verderevsky indicated a German attack at Reval would be fatal to the fleet and its defenses in that area. All expressed anxiety over the number and reliability of soldiers in the region. Nonetheless, Kerensky appeared satisfied with Cheremisov's handling of the crisis, only adding that he would order immediate strengthening of the northern front with soldiers taken from quiet spots elsewhere. He primarily wanted to beef up the garrison at Reval with a trustworthy division, and he hoped to send troops to Finland, which lay wide open. The main task, however, was the "urgent strengthening of our position on the line Reval-Pernau." He gave Cheremisov carte blanche to organize the defense of the region.[2]

Kerensky took the minutes for this meeting in his own hand, and they reflect the interesting fact that no one contested Verderevsky's statement about the fleet, or even asked what would happen if Reval fell. In light of the fact that the newest and best Russian ships had not been bloodied in the Moon Sound battles, Verderevsky's admission that the fleet could not halt a German advance in the middle of the Gulf of Finland should have been a major cause for alarm. Kerensky, however, passed over this startling revelation, probably because a meeting at an army headquarters was not the place to deal with naval issues.

Instead, Kerensky kept his attention solely on the army and the ground approaches to the capital. Cheremisov's execution of the response to the island invasion seems to have reassured him. To his credit, all during the crisis General Cheremisov had kept his focus on his main priority, namely the vast, undefended area behind his armies where his lines of communication to Reval and the capital ran.[3] If the Germans landed in Estonia, his flank would collapse, and certainly Reval would be lost. Its loss would mean the compromise of the main naval battle position in the Gulf of Finland, exposing Petrograd. Cheremisov had proven willing to commit reinforcements to the defense of the Baltic Islands, but once he concluded they could not be held, he cut his losses and protected his priorities: Petrograd and the northwest Russian region.

As soon as the Germans landed, Admiral Razvozov had asked General Cheremisov for assistance, and the general had responded promptly, pledging almost a division.[4] Over the next two days, these reinforcements converged in piecemeal fashion on Moon Island. At the same time, Cheremisov shuffled units in his rear areas, trying to cover the key roads leading into Reval. He issued a defense plan in case the islands were overrun, and the Germans crossed to the mainland.[5] With the mutiny of Battery #43 on Zerel, however, the picture on the islands changed. Unmolested by the Russian batteries, the German dreadnoughts waiting at the entrance to the gulf now steamed in, and both Cheremisov and Razvozov knew they would appear next at the entrance to the Moon Sound. Their guns could reach the Russian forces on Moon and the harbor at Kuivast. Cheremisov had immediately ordered Razvozov to evacuate his ground forces from the islands as quickly as possible.[6] Even as Bakhirev worried that the Germans would catch him when he exited from the northern end of the Moon Sound, Cheremisov nonetheless held him back, needing his transport ships to evacuate soldiers from Moon. Cheremisov knew these soldiers would be invaluable if the Germans crossed over to the mainland, and he had the disorganized units reconstituted as soon as they returned from the islands.[7] He also told Admiral Razvozov bluntly that the islands were lost and his mission now was to throw back any Germans who landed on the mainland and protect the roads to Reval.[8] He approved the destruction of the military facilities on the islands and the mainland. Fuel and supplies at Hapsal and Rogekyul went up in flames as Bakhirev's ships headed north.[9]

Cheremisov assigned General Ghenrikson to take charge of defenses on the shoreline as evidence of the coming invasion mounted. Cheremisov placed Ghenrikson directly underneath him—in effect, at the same level as his army commanders. Ghenrikson acted promptly, assigning responsibilities to various units. In addition to the scattered troops on the islands and the reinforcements committed to the defense of Moon, Ghenrikson also had the Forty-fifth Infantry and the Fourth Don Cossack Divisions to protect the rear areas.[10]

Admiral Razvozov also knew the islands were lost when Bakhirev abandoned Kuivast on the 17th. Securing the Gulf of Finland remained his top priority, despite the fact the Germans had now turned the southern flank of the forward defense position. All he could do was to hold the rest of the Baltic Fleet in readiness at the central defense position, the line running from Reval–Nargen Island–Porkkala–Helsingfors. He had planned to move his battleships from their anchorage at Helsingfors to the anchorage at Porkkala, a peninsula extending some 30 kilometers out into the Gulf of Finland below Helsingfors. Admiral Stark, in charge of the destroyers, told Razvozov's adjutant, Captain Petrov, that given the uncertainty of the German intentions or even their whereabouts, leaving so many warships in the crowded facilities at Lapvik was courting trouble. He and Admiral Pilkin (in charge of cruisers) recommended leaving the older, coal-burning destroyers there, but they urged him to move the *Novik*-class ships to Helsingfors and Porkkala. Ships and crews were exhausted, he said, just when it seemed likely the Baltic Fleet might have to fulfill its basic mission—denying the Germans entry into the Gulf of Finland. Razvozov accepted this recommendation. All but a few of the torpedo boats went to Helsingfors, but he kept the three cruisers in Lapvik and ordered them held on two-hour readiness.[11]

The Germans never advanced to the mainland, and Stavka must have realized for certain they were not going to once they began to send their ships back to the North Sea. While Kerensky had openly feared in his meeting at the northern front on the 18th that the Germans might focus their effort on the northern region, Russian intelligence already knew the Germans were transferring divisions to the west,[12] actions not exactly commensurate with further landings or a push to the capital. Perhaps Kerensky and his chief military advisor, General Dukhonin, counted on "General Winter" coming to the rescue, or maybe they discounted Verderevsky's grim assessment, because the navy had acquitted itself far better than the army in the Baltic Islands campaign. In an interview with the *Reval Observer*, General Dukhonin expressed concern for Reval, simply because it now was so close to the front. He categorically dismissed, however, as fanciful the idea that Petrograd faced danger. As long as Russia had naval forces in the Baltic, he said, "one cannot speak of a threat [to the capital] as an existing fact."[13]

He might have spoken a good deal less sanguinely had he known the admirals' assessment of the Baltic Fleet. Just one week later, on the 31st of October, Admiral Bakhirev and Admiral Stark wrote to Admiral Razvozov that the loss of the Baltic Islands had revealed that the army could no longer be counted upon. The soldiers had panicked and run. Only the peculiar conditions of life aboard ship, said Bakhirev, which significantly promote discipline and order when the ship is at sea or in battle, accounted for the navy's better performance in the Gulf of Riga. Nevertheless, Bakhirev believed that his forces had not accomplished much, and when the islands were lost, the navy's position became untenable. The only way the Baltic Fleet could now stop the Germans, the two explained, was to use its ships and lines of defense—the heavily fortified coastal artillery positions and minefields. Unfortunately, the sailors manning the fortifications had proven as unreliable as the army units. Bakhirev was blunt. The superiority of the German navy meant that "any operation the enemy launches in the Baltic theater will succeed." According to Bakhirev, even if the Germans did not undertake any further operations in the Baltic, without fundamental and rapid improvements in the nation as a whole, "by the beginning of the campaign of 1918, the Navy, as a fighting force, will not exist."[14] Admiral Razvozov said, "I agree completely," and forwarded the report to Admiral Verderevsky, the minister of the navy. Three of his other Baltic Fleet admirals, namely Zarubaev, Patton, and Cherkassky, he added, shared his opinion.[15]

Two days later, the principals met in Reval: Admiral Verderevsky, Admiral Razvozov, General Cheremisov, and Nicholas V. Nekrasov, governor-general of Finland. Nekrasov was the senior Russian official in Finland and had just completed negotiating a proposal for autonomy for that nation. The Provisional Government did not oppose Finland's seeking autonomy, and Russia could do nothing to halt it anyway. The military situation in Finland and the waters around it was hopeless. Admiral Verderevsky shared a draft he had written to the English naval attaché, thanking him for England's help and stating that Russia's "power of resistance has collapsed. . . . The Baltic Fleet has ceased to exist."[16]

On the 3rd of November, General Verkhovsky, the war minister, gave a similarly negative assessment of the army's status to a closed session of the State Council in Petrograd. An objective assessment of the army's status, said Verkhovsky, "forces us to acknowledge plainly and frankly that we cannot fight." He urged starting peace negotiations, indicating that if Russia did not have the means to get favorable terms, it must conclude peace on whatever terms the enemy gave. As shocked as the parliamentarians were at this news, they received a further jar when the general indicated the negotiations should start without Russia informing its allies. The final jolt came when the general indicated Russia would need a dictatorship following the war to restore order. Verkhovsky's candor cost him his job. Two days later, Kerensky fired him,[17] and two days after that, the Bolsheviks overthrew the Kerensky Government.

Three hundred twenty kilometers away, Admiral Schmidt, General von Kathen, and General von Hutier, the latter coming from Riga to Arensburg, had discussed taking Worms Island but decided against it following a lengthy meeting on the 22d of October. Admiral Behncke reported that the channels from the south to the island were well mined and blocked by sunken ships. It would take weeks, he said, to clear a passageway to Moon. From the west, the captured artillery on Dagö Island, now in German hands, could control the northern approaches to the island and the Moon Sound. Judging from the destruction the Russians had wreaked in the sound and at their former facilities at Hapsal and Rogokyul, it was clear that they had no intentions of returning. Everyone agreed that taking Worms served no purpose.[18] Instead, the High Command now proposed occupying the island of Kynö at the entrance to Pernau Bay and for the fleet to shell the coast near the front on the Aa River.[19] The navy had obliged, sending ships to bombard the Russians, but during another meeting in Arensburg on the next day, both General von Hutier and Admiral Schmidt backed away from the Kynö operation. Shelling it would suffice, they argued.

Most of the battleships had already left for Kiel or repair yards in Danzig, and the smaller ship units headed back to the west in their small flotillas. For example, the remaining boats in Heinecke's Second Flotilla escorted the battleships back to Kiel on the 24th of October.[20] High ranking officers, among them Prince Leopold, commander in chief, east, arrived to survey the scene. Not only did they tour the islands, but the navy took them out to the wreck of the *Slava*. On the 25th, Schmidt decided to move all the German ships from Kuivast to Arensburg. Kuivast lay within howitzer range of Verder, which was still in Russian hands, and while there was no sign of the enemy, Schmidt did not want to take unnecessary risks.[21]

Admiral Schmidt clearly wanted to return to Kiel as quickly as he could. The day Dagö fell, the 20th, he radioed Berlin, recommending that his fleet be discharged on the 25th, repeating the request the next day.[22] Finally, after a third request, the Admiralty agreed to disband his ad hoc command, effective on the 3rd of November. Schmidt returned to Kiel on the *Ostfriesland*, leaving Prince Henry, the commander in chief of the Baltic, in charge.[23] As he sailed home, Admiral Schmidt closed out the war diary of the Naval Task Force on the 4th of November 1917.

> With a grateful heart I lay down the authority entrusted to me as commander of the Naval Task Force for the operation against the Baltic Islands. I want to fully recognize and thank the vessel captains and their crews. All have done their best in this victorious achievement. Honor the dead who gave their lives! With God, onward for our all-gracious war lord and our beloved fatherland![24]

THE GERMAN OCCUPATION

After Admiral Schmidt left, only occupation forces remained. The High Command had quickly designated the units that would occupy the islands. General von Hutier's Eighth Army staff wanted a strong enough force to deter the Russians from returning.[25] They also wanted to leave most of the landing force in place, especially the Forty-second Division, because it had taken an enormous effort to bring the units to Ösel, and leaving them there was the expedient solution. The High Command disagreed. The

XXIII Corps Headquarters and the Forty-second Division were needed for combat, not garrison duties. In fact, the High Command had told the Admiralty on the 13th of October (the second day of the operation) that it had plans for the Forty-second Division and would ship it out the moment the operation ended.[26] The navy's liaison officer at Eighth Army confirmed this to Admiral Schmidt a week later.[27] In the long run, the Second Cycle Brigade remained on Dagö, and Colonel Berring's 255th Regiment stayed on Moon Island. Baron von Seckendorff, a retired major general, was appointed governor.[28] The occupation tied up the equivalent of a division on the islands and entangled German forces even further in the collapse of the Russian regime in 1918.

Only the ethnic Germans on the islands greeted the occupation forces warmly—perhaps too warmly. The German Balts clearly felt the victory belonged to them, and they now sat in the driver's seat. An intemperate *Te Deum* appeared in the German language *Arensburger Zeitung* of 17 November, the first appearance of the paper since the Russian government had closed its offices in 1915.[29] Despite the hopes of the German Balts, the islands did not prosper under German rule. According to one officer, attempts to exploit the islands failed miserably.[30] The November (Bolshevik) Revolution created even greater confusion. In Estonia, even moderate nationalists no longer saw themselves as part of Russia after the Bolshevik coup, and they hastened to take steps to achieve independence. At the same time, as Bolshevik depredations grew, the Germans now found themselves cast in many eyes as liberators from the Soviet yoke. In February 1918, when peace negotiations with the Bolsheviks at Brest-Litovsk collapsed, the Germans resumed fighting, taking the remainder of Latvia and Estonia before the Soviets threw in the towel. Just before the Germans advanced into Reval, a group of Estonian nationalists announced the formation of an independent Republic of Estonia. The "liberators" paid no attention, forcing the nascent government to go underground. Later in the year, the Soviet Government was forced to give up its claims to Estonia and Livonia, while the Treaty of Brest-Litovsk had already surrendered to Germany the Baltic Islands, Courland, and Riga, whose future would be determined by the Germans in concert with the inhabitants.[31]

Unable to influence anything once the Germans overran their country, Estonian nationalists turned to the Allies, who gave de facto recognition to the Estonian Republic in May 1918. Matters remained at that level until the Kaiserreich collapsed in November 1918. As German postwar ambitions to colonize the Baltic area emerged during the occupation, along with the

German tendency to view the local economies as donors for transfusions to the German war machine, native opposition hardened. At the same time, the German Balts remained completely insensitive to the notion of self-determination while utterly consumed by a fear of Bolshevism, and they petitioned to join the German Empire. When that empire collapsed on 9 November 1918, they had nowhere to turn.[32]

The Provisional Government of the Estonian Republic reappeared in Reval (now called Tallinn) on the 11th of November, and the Germans recognized it a week later. With the outbreak of revolution back home, German soldiers on Ösel established a soviet to run matters. Panic set in among the Baltic Barons on the island. They feared plundering and confiscation of their properties by the new Estonian government, and they advocated annexation to Germany. With the German defeat, that was impossible. The Arensburg Soviet of German forces on the islands meanwhile had sought shipping to take the troops back to Germany, and transports were due in December. With time running out, the Baltic Barons tried to form a *Landeswehr*, or militia, from the German units on the island. They asked for volunteers to remain, and some fifty officers and soldiers elected to stay. Most of these apparently had local female companions. Plans for the militia fell apart when Tallin sent a former tsarist colonel to form an Estonian militia in which Baltic Germans could not serve. Negotiations to form a purely Baltic-German militia failed, and the new Estonian regime said the Germans could not stay. The last German troops left in December 1918.[33] The rule of the Baltic Barons had ended.

ALBION IN PERSPECTIVE

The results, both strategic and tactical, of most engagements are usually obvious. One side is left on the field of battle claiming victory; the other has retreated, the empty side of the field speaking for itself. Unfortunately, even with the passage of time, the peculiar turn of events immediately after Albion has prevented a complete analysis.

Without question, Albion constituted a great battlefield success for the Germans. At both the tactical and operational levels, they achieved everything they set out to accomplish. Within ten days of departing Libau, they had taken the islands. Not only had they routed the defending Russian ground forces, they had captured most of them. The Russian 107th Infantry division ceased to exist, and all the naval batteries on the islands were in Germans hands, largely intact. The Russian fleet, while not destroyed and only mildly bloodied, had left the area, never to return. Severing or threatening of the Russian supply lines had forced them to withdraw. Von Winterfeld's stand at Orrisar and the arrival of the Forty-second Division at the causeway blocked the Russian line of retreat and led to a decisive victory over their ground forces. Admiral Behncke's triumph over Admiral Bakhirev's ships in the southern approaches to the Moon Sound had had the same effect.[34] With the lines of communication to the mainland threatened by Behncke's ships, the Russians had to withdraw from Moon Island. After these victories, the sea passage to Riga stood open to the Germans.

By First World War standards, casualties in Albion were low—almost negligible, in fact, given the scope of the operation. The Germans captured 20,130 Russians, along with 141 cannons, 130 machine guns, 2,000 horses, 2 armored cars, 28 private automobiles and trucks, 10 aircraft, and three boxes of money worth 365,000 rubles.[35] The Russians probably never knew how many soldiers and sailors they lost. The 107th and most of the 118th Infantry divisions were destroyed and captured on Ösel and Moon Islands. The Russians' naval losses were not high: an old battleship, the *Slava*, and one of their newest torpedo boats, the *Grom*. They succeeded in rescuing most of the crew from both vessels. A few other ships were damaged, but none badly.[36] The *Slava* had gone down bravely, fighting to the last, and earned its name, which means *Glory*.

The Germans knew their losses. From the army, 3 officers and 51 soldiers were killed, with an additional 6 officers and 135 men wounded.[37] The navy lost 4 officers and 152 sailors, with an additional 60 wounded. The Germans lost more naval craft than the Russians, but most were small torpedo boats. Prior to the operation, in clearing mines, two boats were sunk and an additional two damaged from mines. From the start of the operation on the 11th of October, two battleships suffered damages from mines— the *Bayern* and *Großer Kurfürst*. Both ships remained in the islands and continued to perform their missions. After they returned to Kiel, however, repairing them took months. Five boats of varying types were lost to mines, another two were severely damaged, and two that ran aground were ultimately sunk. The transport *Corsica* hit a mine and beached itself, and the minesweeping tender *Indianola* returned to harbor under its own steam after being hit by a torpedo from an English submarine.[38]

From a strategic standpoint, however, the jury remains out, and herein lies the problem of evaluating the significance of the operation. The Germans had ambitious goals: nothing less than effecting the withdrawal of

Russia from the war. This was never formally expressed in the orders for the operation, but Ludendorff made it clear that the operation had wider aims than taking a few islands, when he wrote, "the blow was aimed at Petrograd . . . it was bound to make a powerful impression there."[39] Field Marshal Hindenburg echoed his chief assistant. After the Germans took Riga, he wrote, the inhabitants of Petrograd grew fearful they were next, and many in Germany criticized the army for not following its success at Riga with a campaign to seize the Russian capital. Hindenburg dismissed taking the city as a fantasy, castigating critics for failing to understand the limits of space and time. Instead, he implied that the High Command had written off Russia, regarding its demise as a matter of time and believing that marching into the hinterland would tie up troops needed elsewhere and would serve no real purpose. With the situation in the west worsening daily, the pending campaign in Italy had top priority. In addition, an alternative method existed that promised to attain the same goal: an amphibious assault. Hindenburg made the decision to take the Baltic Islands, because "from that position we posed an immediate threat to the naval facilities at Reval and increased pressure on an already excited Petersburg with an economy of force effort."[40]

Whether the "powerful impression" or the "increased pressure on an already excited Petersburg" would ultimately have brought Russia to the table cannot be determined. The Provisional Government's war and naval ministers thought the end had arrived. When remarking that their forces could no longer fight, they had merely stated the obvious, namely that what Allen Wildman called a "soldiers' plebiscite" had sent "shockwaves back to the capital with the very clear message: peace must be obtained before winter sets in . . . or not a soldier would remain in the trenches; if the government were unwilling to treat for peace, the Soviet should take over, and if the Soviet leadership were reluctant, the Bolsheviks should be put in."[41]

Hindenburg was certain Albion had attained its objective: "With our last blows the colossus not only staggered, but he came apart and collapsed. But we had turned to another task."[42] Ludendorff was more non-committal, saying, "how far these last attacks [Riga, Baltic Islands] accelerated matters in Russia, I do not know."[43]

In candor, Albion did not topple the colossus, but it did remove the scales from everyone's eyes concerning any further military action. As Wildman stated, the military had voted, and the Bolsheviks knew what the results meant. They did not wait for others to bring about peace; instead, they overthrew the Provisional Government and sought an armistice.

After Albion, the fighting in the east ended, and after the Bolshevik Revolution two weeks later, local and unofficial truces broke out in many places. With fighting virtually at an end, the High Command knew the war in the east was over. Before Lenin's request for an armistice arrived late in the month, the Germans suggested to Austria-Hungary that it take over a larger part of the line in the east at some not too distant point. Shortly thereafter the Soviet Government proposed a cease-fire while negotiating peace terms, and "by the end of November, . . . troop trains were incessantly passing from East to West."[44]

With no respite from the war, the Germans did not seek to analyze to what degree, if any, Albion contributed to the victory in the east. Indeed, because of the momentous events that occurred in the west in 1918, the majority of German historical analysis focused there and on the defeat and German revolution.

The performance of the Russian Army during the Baltic Islands campaign left everything to be desired. Army leaders had to be disheartened, although they seem not to have taken the German threat to Petrograd as seriously as did their naval counterparts. Of course, they understood better than most what Hindenburg meant by the constraints of time and space. The Imperial Navy's crews had done well. Unfortunately, the naval coastal artillery batteries were more eager than the ground troops to avoid fighting. Knowing they faced a winter of inactivity and further Bolshevik-Soviet agitation, both navy and army leaders recognized the inevitable and bluntly admitted it was over. Bravery was fine, they admitted, but it could not replace an organized fighting force.[45] It is hard to imagine that the Albion experience did not play a major variable in that calculus. Albion had not caused the collapse of the Russian military forces, but it had illustrated that the Russian armed forces were through. The army had largely run from the Germans during the campaign. The navy had performed much better, but the admirals knew, and admitted, that it was a one-time shot. Albion had not created the conditions for the Russian collapse, but it had done what the Germans had hoped for; namely, it created an aura of overwhelming German military superiority that ultimately doomed any attempts at resistance.

Nonetheless, what would have happened had the Bolshevik Revolution not superseded everything is not known. Whether Albion shook Russia hard enough to bring about its collapse or posed a threat to Petrograd in the long run must remain moot. All that is certain is that Lenin had no intention of remaining in the war once he came to power. Lenin was determined to quit, and with that step, matters took on their own life, and events in Soviet Russia took on a greater significance than Russia's continuing in the war. The memory of Albion gradually faded.

In the immediate postwar period, Albion received scant notice. In Germany, historical research on the war in the 1920s had two focal points. For the army, the viability of the Schlieffen Plan and the circumstances surrounding the collapse in November 1918 commanded all attention. The debates in the navy raged over Admiral von Tirpitz's "risk theory" and what the proper strategy should have been. For both services, these were more than academic scuffles. The day would come when the Versailles Treaty limitations would end and the strategic concepts validated in these struggles would shape the rebuilding of Germany's armed forces.

The Allies naturally focused on those things they thought critical to their victory, and amphibious operations were not on that list. Their one effort at a joint army-navy undertaking, the Dardanelles, had come apart. No one really wanted to recall the disaster at Gallipoli.

In 1931, General von Tschischwitz published his history of the operation, *The Army and Navy during the Conquest of the Baltic Islands in October 1917.* While his is not an "official, government-sponsored" history, von Tschischwitz clearly had enjoyed access to the pertinent German and captured Russian records in compiling his work. He admitted that by the time of the operation, conquering the islands had no strategic military value. Enemy morale had fallen, and the frequency with which Russians had heretofore sacrificed themselves was receding rapidly. Consequently, he wrote, he expected no military advantages to accrue from the undertaking. On the other hand, "a certain psychological effect was expected from this blow directed against the Russian front—the *blow was aimed at Petrograd itself*" (emphasis in original). In that respect, he added, "in connection with other events, the loss of the Baltic Islands accelerated the fall . . . of the Kerenski Government."[46] In other words, the islands now had a strategic psychological value.

Clearly happy with the results at all levels, especially the strategic and operational results, von Tschischwitz did not overlook Albion's shortcomings,[47] even though the undertaking was an economy-of-force effort done on very short notice. The major problems, von Tschischwitz noted, came in the areas of communications, liaison officers, and joint training. The radio operators who went ashore were overtaxed since there were so few of them. Consolidating the message center on the *Moltke* made sense from a theoretical perspective, but in reality, the radiomen were simply overwhelmed by the volume of messages. Radio equipment was not compatible between the services. Liaison officers played a vital and greater role than usual because no one in the German military had ever conducted such an operation. Unfortunately, the tendency to slough off that assignment to relatively low-ranking officers slowed matters. Senior commanders found it difficult to accept that a lieutenant could represent a major headquarters. They wanted to talk to someone of comparable rank.[48]

The U.S. Army War College regarded von Tschischwitz's book as important and had it translated. The Command and General Staff School Press at Fort Leavenworth published it in 1933. The Marine Corps acquired copies for their library at Quantico, but there is no evidence Albion played a role in the development of Marine Corps amphibious doctrine.[49] Only the Army War College seems to have made much use of the operation in its curriculum. Instructors there dealt with joint operations in seminars and routinely used Gallipoli and Albion as case studies. Some prominent names whose fame came from amphibious warfare in the Pacific Theater in World War II appear in these seminars, among them Captain (later Fleet Admiral) William Halsey. Oddly, the Navy War College in Newport paid little attention to Albion.[50]

The Second World War eclipsed the First, both in memory and in history. From 1945 on, the more recent conflict commanded the focus of most military historians, to say nothing of the government agencies sponsoring military historical research. It was not until the 1970s, when a renaissance in First World War studies began, that Albion received some attention. Even then, treatment was almost backhanded. A leading historian of the German Imperial Navy, Holger Herwig, argued that general inactivity and unrest in the High Sea Fleet in June, a mutiny in August, inept handling of the mutiny's aftermath in the Reichstag by the Admiralty Staff, and a poor public image led to a compelling need for successful operations to dispel these negative images. Even the kaiser had suffered at the hands of "his navy." On a fleet visit in the summer of 1917, following the brutal winter of 1916–1917, better known in Germany as the "turnip winter," sailors greeted His Majesty with jeers of "Hunger!" instead of the usual cheer of "Hurrah!" Only a major undertaking and success could restore public confidence, and with the Baltic Sea offering the best prospects, Herwig indicates the navy "chose the islands of Ösel, Moon and Dagö in the Bay of Riga for attack." A. Harding Ganz, who first examined this issue using some of the German records, felt the High Sea Fleet's inactivity after Jutland contributed to the decision to mount the operation.[51] This latter argument carries more weight than worrying about the stain of a small mutiny in which the navy overplayed its hand. Levetzow, Meyer-Quitlingen, and Kiep implied as much when they told Admiral Keyserlingk that the navy should not be the one to turn down an undertaking of such magnitude. In addition, the operational and tactical reasons for the operation were quite sound, and one should recall that the navy had promoted such a strike since 1915 after its first foray into the Gulf of Riga. The navy had presented an impassioned argument to Ludendorff as recently as May 1917, and the disturbances in the fleet broke out much later, with the "mutiny" coming during the first week of August.

Moreover, the navy records for Operation Albion, which are quite complete, do not mention either the fleet's inactivity or the mutiny. The official German history does not credit the mutiny as a factor contributing to Albion.[52] As Keith Bird pointed out in his *German Naval History: A Guide to the Literature*,[53] the authors' goals in the official government account of World War I were to describe the positive accomplishments of the Kaiserliche Marine in order to justify the existence in the 1920s of the Reichsmarine and its eventual expansion. Such goals would naturally call for minimizing the mutinies and the fleet's inactivity. Gagern, Firle, and Rollmann used the same files as this author did for the writing of their "official" history, and there is no evidence they culled the records. The volume examining Albion was the last one printed in the official history. While a draft version of the volume concerning the last year of the Baltic Sea war was prepared by the 1940s, the war delayed its publication. It finally appeared in 1964, long after any reason existed to "hide" the shame of the mutinies. Both Gagern and Firle survived World War II, and they had ample opportunity between 1945 and the appearance in print of their history to amend the volume had they felt pressured in the 1920s or 1930s to reach a certain conclusion. Finally, the army's participation in Albion was essential, and it is difficult to envision Ludendorff suddenly releasing divisions so the navy could engage in some meaningful activity. Ludendorff came up with the soldiers for the invasion force when it suited his and the army's objectives, not the navy's.

Another observation from Holger Herwig stated that Albion amounted to a "classic case of overkill."[54] Such an argument overlooks the assumptions and premises of war and the operation itself. The large German fleet, with its ten capital ships, represented a deliberate choice to offset some of the disadvantages the Germans faced by having to use a relatively small and lightly armed ground force to seize the islands. In fact, the Germans had only a marginally larger assault force than the defenders, far below the norm of three or more attackers to one defender common to most offensives in the Great War. They recognized that the revolution had undermined most Russian units, but they could not be certain the units they faced would collapse until the moment of truth. They hedged their bets with firepower. It is not chance that the first principle of war is mass—"the first-est with the mostest" in the inimitable phrase of Nathan Bedford Forrest. The Germans did not have the capability of transporting to the islands an overwhelming mass of soldiers; they could and did bring an overwhelming mass of naval firepower. A German failure might have revived flagging Russian morale and prolonged the war in the East; a resounding German victory might finish off the Russian colossus. The Russians had some fight left in them, as Admiral Bakhirev and his crews proved. From the German perspective, anything less than overkill would be reckless. The Germans were not reckless. They "weighed, then ventured." And won.

CHAPTER ELEVEN

EPILOGUE

FOR THE GERMAN soldiers of the landing corps and sailors of the Naval Task Force, successful in battle, came a flurry of congratulatory messages. The kaiser, Field Marshal von Hindenburg, and General von Hutier all penned notes of praise. The services expressed their gratitude through awards and promotions. Prussia's highest award for wartime service and bravery, the *Pour le Mérite*, went to Colonel von Tschischwitz and Colonel Matthiass, the Sixty-fifth Infantry Brigade commander. General von Kathen and General von Estorff already had theirs—each had just received the medal for the capture of Riga in September—and Lieutenant Colonel Fischer, whose regiment played the key role in taking Zerel, also received one for the East Galician campaign along with the capture of Riga. For the navy, the awards went to Admiral Schmidt, Admiral Behncke, and Captain von Levetzow. Schmidt was the victor, von Levetzow the indefatigable taskmaster who freed the commander from the military mundane, and Behncke could claim a capital ship, albeit a tired one. The odd recipient (on account of his modest rank) was Commander Hugo von Rosenberg, the leader of the Baltic Sea Anti-submarine Reconnaissance Force. Von Rosenberg's submarine chasers and minesweepers had led the fleet safely to Ösel. His unceasing efforts in the Small Sound with his flotilla of flat-bottomed boats then saved the day for the Germans at Orrisar.[1]

For the Germans, the war continued. General Oskar von Hutier returned to the western front and added to his fame, commanding the

Eighteenth Army in the Spring Offensive of 1918. His divisions tore a huge gap in the Allied lines and forever associated his name with the eponymous infantry breakthrough tactics. General von Kathen and the XXIII Reserve Corps also returned to the western front in time to participate in the German counteroffensive at Cambrai (November 1917) and later in the great Spring Offensive. In July of 1918, von Kathen was given command of the Eighth Army in Riga, where he remained until his retirement in December 1918. In November, the Forty-second Division moved to Kowel in the Volhynia (south Poland); then in January 1918 it joined the exodus of divisions heading west. Assigned to the Sixth Army north of Lille, the division remained in action until the end. General von Estorff led the division until March 1918, when he took over the LX Army Corps in Lithuania. He remained in the army after the war, receiving command of the prestigious First Reichswehr Infantry Division in Königsberg. His career ended when he backed the wrong side during the Kapp Putsch in 1920. Colonel Matthiass received his promotion to brigadier general and remained with the Forty-second Division in heavy fighting until July 1918, when he was named to command the Twenty-fifth Reserve Infantry Division. During the postwar revolutionary disturbances in Germany, he apparently suffered a stroke while leading a brigade smashing a "Red Army" in Hamburg, and he died shortly thereafter in 1919. Artillery fire killed Lieutenant Colonel Fischer near Armentiers in July 1918. Captain Volkmann remained with the division until the end of the war, then joined the postwar Reichswehr. Like General von Estorff, he came out on the wrong side of the Kapp Putsch and had to leave the service. He later became an archivist for the army, publishing a number of histories of the war and several novels.

Schmidt returned to his battleship squadron in Kiel, and he was soon promoted from vice admiral to admiral. There was no available position for him, however, and because he had reached mandatory retirement age, he was placed on the inactive list. Souchon remained with his squadron until October 1918, when the kaiser named him commandant in Kiel to quell the fleet mutiny. His fiery temperament only worsened matters, and he was retired in March 1919. Admiral Behncke retained his squadron until September 1918, when Admiral Scheer named him state secretary, Tirpitz's old job. Behncke retired in February 1919, but he was recalled to lead the navy a year later, holding the post as chief of the navy until 1924. Von Levetzow went on to a more checkered career. One of Admiral Scheer's circle, he received as reward for Albion the command of the Second Reconnaissance Squadron in 1918 until August; he subsequently joined Scheer in

Berlin as his chief of staff. He remained in the navy after the war and made rear admiral, but was squeezed out after the Kapp Putsch. He became an advocate for the return of the monarchy in the 1920s, and when that went nowhere, he wandered into the ranks of the Nazis, becoming a Nazi delegate in the Reichstag, and later, police president of Berlin from 1933 to 1935. His reluctance to deal harshly with the Jews led to his dismissal.

There were no decorations or congratulatory messages for the Russians, and the Bolshevik coup on the 8th of November and Lenin's request for an armistice shortly thereafter abruptly ended the war in the east. The Tsentrobalt actually recommended Admiral Razvozov for promotion to vice admiral in November 1917, but the Soviets eliminated his position as fleet commander, and he retired. They temporarily reinstated him in March 1918, but soon arrested him and then let him go. For a short period he worked for a naval historical commission, but he fell victim to Soviet paranoia and was again arrested and died in jail in 1919. Admiral Bakhirev resigned in December 1917 when the Soviet Government refused to confirm Razvozov's position. Arrested, he died or was executed in prison. At his trial, he allegedly told the Reds, "I sympathize with no particular party, but I love Russia." After receiving the death sentence, he added, "Well, you are free to kill my body, but you cannot kill my spirit."[2] A special commission examined Admiral Sveshnikov's abandonment of his position at Arensburg and ordered his dismissal on the 7th of December 1917.[3]

The Bolshevik war commissar Krylenko, who took General Dukhonin's position as head of Stavka, had the general arrested, but on his way to Petrograd for questioning, a mob murdered him. Krylenko dismissed General Cheremisov and then arrested him in November, but he was released and immediately fled the country. He lived in Denmark and France. Of the fate of General Ivanov and General Kolbe, captured on Ösel, nothing is known. They certainly would have been repatriated after the war, but whether they returned to the Soviet Union is questionable. The Germans claimed to have captured a general on Moon Island, but nowhere in their literature do they ever list a name. General Martynov was the sole general officer there according to the Russian records, but his army file indicates he received command of the 120th Infantry Division in November 1917 and held that position until dismissed in May 1918. It would seem he escaped the Germans. It is possible that the Germans instead captured General Kreitner, a brigade commander of the Forty-fifth Division, whose unit was sent to reinforce the area. Kreitner's military service records end in the summer of 1917. General Ghenrikson remained in charge of the defense forces along the Estonian mainland and was given the "rights of a commander of a non-separate army" in December 1917. He was let go in March 1918, when the army was dismissed. Razvozov's chief of staff, Admiral Cherkassky, came from an old family and had the title of "prince." Dismissed in December 1917 by the Bolsheviks, he supposedly participated in the Civil War and fell in front of a Red firing squad. Captain Altvater, Admiral Razvozov's liaison at the northern front headquarters, went over to the Bolsheviks and represented them at the negotiations. Promoted to rear admiral, he died mysteriously in Moscow in 1919.[4] Pavel Ottovich Shisko, the commander of the Reval Death Battalion, was wounded and captured in the fighting on Moon Island. He returned to Russia immediately after the armistice and commanded a tank unit in General Yudenich's White Army forces. He emigrated to the United States in 1921, living most of the time in Connecticut, where he worked for the Electric Boat Company in Groton.

The participants did not entirely forget Albion. In October 1937, the Reichsarchiv sponsored an exhibit in the Zeughaus (Armory) in Berlin. Captured Russian artifacts as well as German ones, such as weapons, flags, documents, and uniforms, were displayed. Rear Admiral Rudolf Lahs, who had had commanded the Twelfth Torpedo Boat Half-Flotilla at the time of the operation, organized an anniversary dinner on the 10th of October. About twenty of the senior participants attended. Among them were Admirals Schmidt, Souchon, and Hopman, along with Captain von Levetzow and Commander Meyer-Quitlingen. From the army came General von Estorff and Colonels von Tschischwitz and Frotscher. The entrees consisted of Moon Soup, Baltic Beef, Russian Ice Cream, and Moon Mocha.[5]

APPENDIX: A WORD ON SOURCES

THE END OF the Soviet Union led to the opening of Russia's military and naval archives. Being unfamiliar with these sources, I inquired about access and the like. Given the confusion that results from any military retreat, the loss of the islands, and the overthrow of the Russian Provisional Government by the Bolsheviks a scant two weeks after the Baltic Islands campaign, followed by years of subsequent revolutionary turmoil, I feared the worst, namely that little or nothing would be available. David Glantz, expert on World War II, provided encouragement. The Russians, he said, are inveterate record keepers. The records will be there, and Westerners can now use them for research purposes. I engaged a research assistant, Ms. Elizaveta Zheganina, then a graduate student at St. Petersburg State University and now a Ph.D. candidate at Kansas State University. After preliminary inquiries, she advised me to write on letterhead to the administration at the Russian State Naval Archive, explaining my research interests and purpose and authorizing her to work on my behalf. While I followed her guidance, I did so with some trepidation. "It just can't be this easy," I thought, especially when the Russians see "The Military College of South Carolina" on the letterhead. But it was, and within a week she began to send me materials from the Naval Archive and later the corresponding army one in Moscow. She did the translations; the responsibility for accuracy and correct use is nevertheless mine. To my knowledge, this book is the first non-Soviet account to make use of this copious material.

David Glantz was correct. The Russians indeed are dutiful record keepers. The navy, which had responsibility for the defense of the islands, has fairly complete records. A great deal of essential material from the headquarters of the Baltic Fleet, the Chief of the Naval Defenses of the Gulf of Riga, and the Chief of the Defenses of the Baltic Islands Archipelago survived. I was not so lucky with army records. The largest army units involved, the 107th Infantry Division and elements of the 118th, were captured along with their records by the Germans. The Germans repatriated the prisoners after the war, but they kept the records they had captured.

After the war ended, the Soviets had little interest in writing about it, and no official history was produced. High-ranking tsarist officers became persona non grata, and many fled or were executed by the Soviet regime. Vice Admiral Mikhail Bakhirev did write a short memoir in 1918 or 1919, but it was not available in the West until recently. Former naval officers living abroad found it difficult to find publishers. They did form an association, and its members in 1958 produced a rebuttal to a Soviet historian's account that challenged their conduct, accusing them of having lost the battle through cowardice.

Ironically, the situation with German military records parallels that of the Russians. The German navy files are in good shape; the army's are almost nonexistent. The army kept its records at the Reichsarchiv in Potsdam. Unfortunately, in November 1944 a bomb raid destroyed the Reichsarchiv and most material inside it. The records of the majority of the senior headquarters along with most units (to include those that had participated in Albion) were lost. The captured Russian records from the First World War also went up in flames. Fortuitously, however, in the 1920s the United States Army had an arrangement with the Germans to permit a small team of two–three officers to travel to Berlin to copy the files of the German units that had fought against the Americans on the western front. Both of the major German army units in Albion, the XXIII Reserve Corps and the Forty-second Infantry Division, participated in the 1918 Spring Offensive. An enterprising but unknown American officer, when going through these records, had his interest piqued by the operation and made typescript copies of the materials relating to Albion. These files were incorporated into Record Group 165 of the U.S. National Archives. While the records are only those of the top-level headquarters, they nonetheless are invaluable.

Surprisingly, the German memoir literature on Albion is scanty. Colonel (later Lieutenant General) Erich von Tschischwitz, the chief of staff of the XXIII Reserve Corps, wrote two memoirs, which are listed in the bibliography. Both are invaluable for study of this topic. After the operation, both the commanders of the fleet and of the landing force wrote after-action summaries. While brief, they are important, as is a small article by the navigation officer, L. Kiep, written for the twentieth anniversary. Captain Erich Otto Volkmann, general staff officer for the Forty-second Infantry Division, wrote a novel about his experiences in the war. In *Die roten Streifen* (*The Red Stripes*), an illusion to the broad red stripes on the riding pants worn by general and general staff corps officers, he provides a detailed account of the operation. A condensed version of his work, focusing strictly on the island campaign, appeared under the title *Unternehmen Ösel.*

Volkmann's work is a novel, yet in every instance where records exist to verify his account, he is accurate. The book is essential to understanding the undertaking, but historians have overlooked it. Vice Admiral Friedrich Ruge, then an ensign serving on torpedo boat B110, participated in the operation. On his ship's return to Wilhelmshaven afterward, he wrote a one-hundred-page manuscript. When he tried to get it published, his commander turned him down, saying "naval officers don't publish." Ruge, who became an admiral in World War II and served later as the first head of the postwar Federal German Navy, eventually incorporated parts of his manuscript into a larger account of his wartime service called *SM Torpedo Boat B110,* which appeared in 1972. After his death, the original manuscript was published by Jörg Hillmann in 2005.

NOTES

ABBREVIATIONS

BA-MA	Bundersmilitararchiv, Freiburg i. Breisgau
NA	National Archives, Washington, DC
RGAVMF	Russian State Naval Archives St. Petersburg (Rossiiskii gosudarstvennyi arkhiv Voenno-Morskogo Flota)
RGVIA	Russian State Army Archives, Moscow (Rossiiskii gosudarstvennyi voenno istoricheskii arkhiv)

1. SUBMARINE UC-58, TAGGA BAY, 28 SEPTEMBER 1917

1. BA-MA, RM 47/127, Kriegstagebuch des Flottenverbands für Sonderunternehmung (hereafter referred to as KTB Sonderverband), entry 28.9.1918.

2. UC-59 was dispatched to Tagga Bay on the 20th of September, but two days later radioed that it had already run aground and the weather was too bad. Levetzow ordered her to push on anyway, given the importance of the mission. Four hours later it called in again and said it had turned back. See BA-MA, RM 47/127, KTB Sonderverband, entries for 20.9 and 22.9.1917.

3. BA-MA, RM47/126, Sonderverband, Gg 863 A 4., 6.10.1917. In a drawing later reproduced for the fleet, Vesper had sketched out the bay, the fishing camps, and the beacon, and noted "bei Kap Ninnast eine Pricke; Küste ganz friedlich."

4. BA-MA, RM47/127, KTB Sonderverband, 2.10.1917. The code name was assigned on the 17th of September. See RM47/126, Chef des Admiralstabes d. Marine, A. 26375, 17.9.1917.

2. THE STRATEGIC IMPORTANCE OF THE BALTIC ISLANDS

1. Holger H. Herwig, *The First World War: Germany and Austria-Hungary 1914–1918* (New York: Arnold, 1997), chapter 2; David G. Herrmann, *The Arming of Europe and the Making of the First World War* (Princeton: Princeton University Press, 1996), 135. Also Robert T. Foley, *German Strategy and the Path to Verdun: Erich von Falkenhayn and the Development of Attrition, 1870–1916* (Cambridge: Cambridge University Press, 2005).

2. Dennis E. Showalter, *Tannenberg: Clash of Empires* (Hamden, Conn.: Archon, 1991), 32ff.

3. Reinhard Scheer, *Germany's High Sea Fleet in the World War* (New York: Cassell, 1920), 2–25.

4. This arms race, the work of Grand Admiral Alfred Tirpitz, is well documented. The standard work is Volker R. Berghahn, *Der Tirpitz-Plan: Genesis und Verfall einer innenpolitischen Krisenstrategie* (Düsseldorf: Droste, 1971). A good review of the literature up to the 1970s is Holger H. Herwig, *Luxury Fleet: The Imperial German Navy, 1888–1918* (Boston: Allen and Unwin, 1980). An extremely readable account is Robert K. Massie, *Dreadnought: Britain, Germany, and the Coming of the Great War* (New York: Random House: 1991), and its successor by the same author, *Castles of Steel: Britain, Germany, and the Winning of the Great War at Sea* (New York: Random House, 2003), which carries the story forward through the 1916 Battle of Jutland and the end of the war.

5. See Gabriel V. Liulevicius, *War Land on the Eastern Front: Culture, National Identity and German Occupation in World War One* (Cambridge: Cambridge University Press, 2000).

6. Erich Ludendorff, *Ludendorff's Own Story, August 1914–November 1918* (New York: Harper, 1919), 1:284.

7. G. von Schoultz, *With the British Fleet: War Recollections of a Russian Naval Officer*, trans. Arthur Chambers (London: Hutchinson, n.d.), 66ff.

8. Paul von Hindenburg, *Aus meinem Leben* (Leipzig: Hirzel Verlag, Illustrierte Volksausgabe, 1934), 176ff.; Ludendorff, *Ludendorff's Own Story*, 2:1ff.

9. Ludendorff, *Ludendorff's Own Story*, 2:42.

10. Hindenburg, *Aus meinem Leben*, 201ff.

11. Ludendorff, *Ludendorff's Own Story*, 2:36–422, 92–97.

12. See map, "The Baltic Theater of Operations."

13. See Albert Hopman, *Das Kriegstagebuch eines deutschen Seeoffiziers* (Berlin: A. Scherl g.m.b.h. [c. 1925]), 122ff. Hopman commanded the German Baltic Sea Reconnaissance Forces. Also George M. Nekrasov, *Expendable Glory: A Russian Battleship in the Baltic, 1915–1917*, East European Monographs (New York: Columbia University Press, 2004), chapter 6, for a Russian view of the engagement.

14. 1862–1929. Joining the Navy in 1877, Henry rose through the ranks to become High Seas Fleet commander in 1906. He ran afoul of Admiral Tirpitz, head of the Naval Office, whose fleet-building policy led to the reconciliation of England with France and later Russia. Tirpitz had the ear of the kaiser, and Henry was shunted off to be inspector of the fleet. When the war broke out, he became commander in chief, Baltic, until that theater became inactive in early 1918.

15. The extensive correspondence is in the Federal Military Archive, Germany, BA-MA/RM5/5209, Admiralstab der Marine, Akten betr. Wissenwerts und Vorarbeiten für O-Plänen gegen Dagö und Ösel, 15. September 1915 bis 9. August 1917. (There is a microfilm copy in the U.S. National Archives, T1022, Roll 1235.) See Ernst Freiherr von Gagern, Rudolph Firle, and Heinrich Rollmann, *Der Krieg in der Ostsee*, vol. 3, *Von Anfang 1916 bis zum Kriegsende* (Frankfurt: E. S. Mittler and Sohn, 1964), 54–55. Two of the three editors of this official history, Kapitän von Gagern and Kapitänleutnant Firle, participated in the attack on the islands.

16. Hindenburg, *Aus meinem Leben*, 203–204.

17. Allan K. Wildman, *The End of the Russian Imperial Army*, vol. 1, *The Old Army and the Soldiers Revolt (March–April 1917)* (Princeton, N.J.: Princeton University Press, 1980), 64.

18. Bruce W. Menning, *Bayonets before Bullets: The Russian Imperial Army, 1861–1914* (Bloomington: Indiana University Press, 1992), 216ff.

19. 1857–1918. He served in Manchuria during the Russo-Japanese War, and then was the chief of staff of the Kiev Military District. When the war broke out, the district became the southwest front, and Alekseev planned the Russian offensive into Galicia. He became chief of staff in the Stavka when the tsar became commander in chief, 1915. He became commander in chief under the Provisional Government in March 1917, but resigned on 21 May owing to poor health.

20. 1848–1926. A cavalry officer, he first saw action in the Russo-Turk War of 1877–78. Promoted to general in 1898, and made war minister from 1909 to 1915, he improved Russian readiness somewhat. Venal and corrupt, he led a debauched life and counted many enemies, including Grand Duke Nicholas. Forced from office in 1915 owing to various materiel shortages, he was charged with treason in connection with the activities of one of his colonels, Miasoedov. In the fall of 1917 he fled to Finland and then Germany, where he died in 1926.

21. Menning, *Bayonets before Bullets*, 218–19.

22. Ibid., 239–40.

23. Ibid., 240ff. See map 4 in Herrmann, *Arming of Europe*, 133.

24. Menning, *Bayonets before Bullets*, 242–48. Also N. B. Pavlovich, "Introduction," *The Fleet in the First World War*, vol. 1, *Operations of the Russian Fleet*, trans. unknown (New Delhi: Amerind, 1979), 15–19.

25. Herrmann, *Arming of Europe*, 205–206, 214.

26. The figure for Austria-Hungary comes from Norman Stone, *The Eastern Front, 1914–1917* (New York: Scribner's Sons, 1975), 91. For Russia, David R. Jones cites 535,000. "From Imperial to Red Army: The Rise and Fall of the Bolshevik Military Tradition," in *Transformation in Russian and Soviet Military History. Proceedings of the 12th Military History Symposium USAF Academy, 1986* (Bolling, Md.: USAF Office of History, 1990). It is not clear what Jones's figure is, but it is probably deaths. Golovine estimates 1.2 million casualties, but his period runs until 1 May 1915. See Nicholas N. Golovine, *Russian Army in the World War* (New Haven: Yale University Press, 1931), 97.

27. Paul G. Halpern, *A Naval History of World War I* (Annapolis: Naval Institute Press, 1994), chapter 8 passim.

28. In fact, they did when the war broke out. The Baltic CINC had both Danish belts mined, although the Danes later added plenty of their own mines. See Halpern, *Naval History*, 183.

29. Halpern, *Naval History*, 180. N. B. Pavlovich, "Introduction," *The Fleet in the First World War*, 15–19.

30. Pavlovich, "Introduction," *The Fleet in the First World War*, 15–19.

31. 1844–1915.

32. Evgenii F. Podsoblyaev, "The Russian Naval General Staff and the Evolution of Naval Policy 1905–1914", trans. Francis King and John Biggart, *The Journal of Military History* 66 (January 2002): 42–44, 46–47.

33. 1856–1929.

34. Podsoblyaev, "Evolution of Naval Policy," 44, 51–52, 55–56.

35. Ibid., 53–54.

36. Ibid., 56–57.

37. See RGAVMF, Fond 417, File 4191, Ship Construction Program for 1912–1916; Baltic Fleet 1911–1915. At the completion of the large construction program, Russia would have 27 dreadnoughts, 12 battle cruisers, 24 small cruisers, and 108 destroyers, most

ear-marked for the Baltic Fleet. David W. Mitchell, *A History of Russian and Soviet Sea Power* (MacMillan: New York, 1974), 271ff.

38. Pertti Luntinen, *The Imperial Russian Army and Navy in Finland 1808–1918*. (Finnish Historical Society: Helsinki, 1997), 231–35.

39. Podsoblyaev, "Evolution of Naval Policy," 49–51.

40. Luntinen, *Russian Army and Navy in Finland*, 221–26; 235–52.

41. J. S. Cowie, *Mines, Minelayers and Minelaying* (Oxford: Oxford University Press, 1949), appendix 1, 200ff.

42. I. Achkasov, I. A. Kozlov, and I. N. Solov'ev, "Operations of the Russian Fleet in the Baltic Sea, 1914–1917" in Pavlovich, *The Fleet in the First World War*, 48–49; Podsoblyaev, "Evolution of Naval Policy," 58–60.

43. Achkasov, Kozlov, and Solov'ev, "Operations of the Russian Fleet," 50; Podsoblyaev, "Evolution of Naval Policy," 60–61.

44. The line is designated by numeral III (Central Position) on map 2. Podsoblyaev, "Evolution of Naval Policy," 61–62.

45. Halpern, *Naval History*, 180ff.; Achkasov, Kozlov, and Solov'ev, "Operations of the Russian Fleet," 50–56; Luntinen, *Russian Army and Navy in Finland*, 258; Podsoblyaev, "Evolution of Naval Policy," 62–65.

46. Menning, *Bayonets before Bullets*, 240.

47. Achkasov, Kozlov, and Solov'ev, "Operations of the Russian Fleet," 56ff.

48. Mitchell, *Russian and Soviet Sea Power*, 277.

49. Achkasov, Kozlov, and Solov'ev, "Operations of the Russian Fleet,'"46ff.

50. 1853–1930. He had commanded at Libau and the Baltic Fleet before becoming deputy naval minister in 1900 and naval minister in 1911 until 1917. He moved to France in 1924 and died there in 1930. His remains were returned to Russia in 2005.

51. Halpern, *Naval History*, 17; Pavlovich, "Introduction," *The Fleet in the First World War*, 22, 32–33, 45–48. Evan Mawdsley, *The Russian Revolution and the Baltic Fleet: War and Politics, February 1917–April 1918* (London: Macmillan, 1978), 85; and RGAVMF, F417/4191, Ship Construction Program for the Baltic Fleet for 1911–1915.

52. Mawdsley, *Revolution and Baltic Fleet*, 85.

53. Mitchell, *Russian and Soviet Sea Power*, 274ff.

54. The Russians promptly laid 2,124 mines in the Central Position in 1914. Halpern, *Naval History*, 183ff., 190ff. From November 1914 to February 1915, Essen's forces laid 1,598 mines along the coast of Germany, primarily across shipping lanes from Danzig and on German shipping routes to Sweden. See Achkasov, Kozlov, and Solov'ev, "Operations of the Russian Fleet," "85–120. There is a map on p. 121.

55. Achkasov, Kozlov, and Solov'ev, "Operations of the Russian Fleet," 77ff.

56. "'Ibid., 133–34.

57. "'Ibid., 77–78. The line is designated by numeral IV (Outer Position) on the map of "Russian Defenses in the Gulf of Finland."

58. Achkasov, Kozlov, and Solov'ev, "Operations of the Russian Fleet," 79, 133–34, 182–83. This area, the Baltic Islands archipelago, is designated by numeral V on the map of "Russian Defenses in the Gulf of Finland."

59. When the Russian pre-dreadnought *Slava* entered the Gulf at night via the Irbe Strait in 1915 in an effort to preempt a German entry, its crew accepted it was a one-way voyage, as the Moon Sound was too shallow and the Irbe Strait the sole entrance and exit, and it came under German fire. Nekrasov, *Expendable Glory*, 44, 52.

60. Mawdsley, *Revolution and the Baltic Fleet*, 3; Nekrasov, *Expendable Glory*, 64, 91; Achkasov, Kozlov, and Solov'ev, "Operations of the Russian Fleet," 186.

61. Mawdsley, *Revolution and Baltic Fleet*, 3.

62. Halpern, *Naval History*, 181.

63. Kriegsgeschichtlichen Forschungsanstalt des Heeres, *Der Weltkrieg, 1914–1918*, volume 12, *Die Kriegführung im Frühjahr 1917* (Berlin: E. S. Mittler and Sohn, 1939), 87ff.

64. Alfred Knox, *With the Russian Army, 1914–1917* (London: Hutchinson, 1921), 2:519–20; Maurice Paléologue, *An Ambassador's Memoirs*, trans. F. A. Holt, 3 vols. (1923; reprint, New York: Octagon Books, 1972), vol. 3, chapter 8 passim.

65. Kriegsgeschichtlichen Forschungsanstalt des Heeres, *Die Kriegführung im Frühjahr 1917*, 96–97.

66. Knox, *With the Russian Army*, 2:551–52.

67. Mawdsley, *Revolution and Baltic Fleet*, 84.

68. Golovine, *Russian Army in the World War*, 261.

69. Herwig, *First World War*, 326ff.; Knox, *With the Russian Army*, 2:517.

70. Herwig, *First World War*, 334.

71. Golovine, *Russian Army in the World War*, 273ff. Also Allan K. Wildman, *The End of the Russian Imperial Army*, vol. 2, *The Road to Soviet Power and Peace* (Princeton, N.J.: Princeton University Press, 1987), chapter 3.

72. Erich von Tschischwitz, *The Army and Navy during the Conquest of the Baltic Islands in October 1917: An Analytical Study Based on Actual Experience*, trans. Colonel Henry Hossfeld (Berlin: R. Eisenschmidt, 1931), 5. Colonel (later General) von Tschischwitz was chief of staff of the landing forces.

3. THE DECISION TO MOUNT OPERATION ALBION

1. BA-MA, 47/127, KTB Sonderverband, entries 15.9–20.9; Louis Kiep, "Vor 20 Jahren. Die Eroberung der baltischen Inseln," *Berliner Börsen Zeitung*, 10 October 1937.

2. BA-MA, RM47/126, Berlin, Kz. 53093, 17.9/1918, 2040 hrs. Confirmation, Kz. 43239, 18.9.1917, 1835 hrs.

3. 1865–1942. A captain and director of the Admiralty Staff when the war broke out, he commanded the Baltic Reconnaissance Forces from April 1915 to January 1916, moving back to the Admiralty Staff as chief of operations. In the summer of 1917 he returned again to his former position in the Baltic.

4. In 1914, the navy had stripped shore installations and formed two divisions of "naval infantry" to guard its shore stations in Flanders. The two divisions held the westernmost end of the front where it ran into the English Channel. See Mark Karau, *"Wielding the Dagger": The Marinekorps Flandern and the German War Effort, 1914–1918* (Westport, Conn.: Praeger, 2003).

5. Achkasov, Kozlov, and Solov'ev, "Operations of the Russian Fleet," 181.

6. NA, 1235/PG77462, BdAdO to OdO, 552c, 12.2.1916, and OdO to Admiralty, 17.2., 1201 A1.

7. 1869–1937. He had earlier commanded the battleships *Elsaß* and *Thüringen* in 1915, and was in charge of torpedoes until April 1916, when he became commander of the Baltic Reconnaissance Forces. In January 1917 he went to Helgoland and then ended up as the inspector of mine and barrier forces.

8. BA-MA, RM5/5209, OdO, B. G. 5956, 11.7.1916.

9. 1861–1922. Falkenhayn took over from Moltke after the First Marne Battle of September 1914. Associated with the German catastrophe at Verdun, Falkenhayn came under severe criticism after the war from his fellow officers. Hindenburg and Ludendorff took his place in August 1916. See Foley, *German Strategy and the Path to Verdun*. Falkenhayn

answered his critics in a peculiar memoir, *General Headquarters and its Critical Decisions 1914–1916* (London: Hutchinson, 1919).

10. NA, 1235/PG77462, 7.3.1916, Falkenhayn to Admiralty; Adm staff to Falkenhayn, 23.5.1916, A 7600 II; Falkenhayn to Admiralty, 25.3.1916.

11. BA-MA, RM5/5209, Bd.AdO, 30.6.1916; OdO, B. G. 5956, 11.7.1916.

12. BA-MA, RM5/5209, Bd.AdO, 30.6.1916; OdO, B. G. 5956, 11.7.1916; and Adm to OdO, 5.8.1916.

13. Hindenburg, *Aus meinem Leben*, 196–97.

14. Archduke Karl Franz Josef (1887–1922) became emperor in 1916, ruling until 1918. Fearful of Austria's capability to remain in the war, he secretly approached his brother-in-law, Sixtus of Parma y Bourbon, serving in the Belgian Army, and asked him to approach the Entente with a peace proposal that purported to give Alsace-Lorraine back to France. The proposal leaked, and the Germans became enraged at their ally. The embarrassing episode became known as the "Prince Sixtus Affair." Herwig, *First World War*, 317; Reichsarchiv, *Der Weltkrieg, 1914–1918*, vol. 12, *Frühjahr 1917*, 171.

15. NA, 1235/PG77462, "Erwägungen der die Möglichkeit einen militärischen Druck auf Russland aus zu üben durch Vorgehen auf Ösel." "O-Sache," Berlin, 11.5.1917.

16. See chapter 2, where the navy's forced entry into the gulf in 1915 is discussed. BA-MA, RM5/5209, Admiralstab der Marine, Akten betr. Wissenwerts und Vorarbeiten für O-Plänen gegen Dagö und Ösel, 15 September 1915 bis 9. August 1917.

17. At the onset of the war, Fleet Order #1 (30 July 1914) had instructed fleet commander Admiral von Ingenohl to engage only portions of the Royal Navy, and when it became clear in the first week of August that the British were not coming, Admiral von Pohl (head of the Admiralty), Chancellor Bethmann-Hollweg, and the kaiser curtailed the fleet's freedom to engage "in order to use it as a security at the peace table." Quoted in Herwig, *Luxury Fleet*, 159–60. Cf. Alfred von Tirpitz, *My Memoirs*, 2 vols. (New York: Dodd, Mead, 1919), 2:25ff.

18. NA/1236, Admiralstab der Marine, Akten betr. Operationen Ösel, 11.11.1917–4.4.1918. Notes for meetings on these dates. A complete set of minutes can be seen in BA-MA, RM5/5029, conversation minutes, at OHL, between Ludendorff and Holtzendorf et al., Gr. Hauptquartier, A 15297, "Niederschrift über die Besprechung im Großen Hauptquartier am 16. Mai 1917."

19. *Ludendorff's Own Story*, 2:35–42.

20. Ibid., 2:88.

21. Scheer, *Germany's High Sea Fleet*, 92.

22. BA-MA, RM5/5210, Holtzendorf's notes for *Immediatvortrag* (Briefing to Kaiser), A 26166 O II, dtd 14.9.1917, "Unternehmung gegen Ösel."

23. NA/1236, Admiralstab der Marine, Akten betr. Operationen Ösel, 11.11.1917–4.4.1918. Notes for meetings on these dates; and BA-MA, RM5/5210, Holtzendorf's notes for Immediatvortrag (Briefing to Kaiser), A 26166 O II, dtd 14.9.1917, "Unternehmung gegen Ösel."

24. *Ludendorff's Own Story*, 2:42, 89.

25. BA-MA, RM5/5210, Chef des Admiralstabs, 20.8, A 24567 O II, 20 August 1917.

26. Hindenburg, *Aus meinem Leben*, 203–204; *Ludendorff's Own Story*, 2:122.

27. BA-MA, RM5/5210, Holtzendorf's notes for *Immediatvortrag* (Briefing to Kaiser), A 26166 O II, dtd 14.9.1917, "Unternehmung gegen Ösel."

28. BA-MA, RM5/5210, Notes of a phone conversation of Adm Keyserlingk, 7.9.1917.

29. BA-MA, RM5/5210, Notes for 8.9.1917., Chef des Admiralstabs, 8.9.1917, 25821 O II, to RMA, Seetransportabtl; NA/PG77466, Telegram an Vertreter d. Admstabs. In Gr.H.Q. für Obstlt. Wetzell, 17(?).1.1918.

30. This was a very touchy point with Admiral Scheer, who wanted to see the Admiralty transformed into an operational headquarters like the Army Command. See Scheer's memoirs, *Germany's High Sea Fleet*, chapter 18, passim.

31. NA, T1022/Roll 1031 Admiralstab der Marine, Akten betr. O. Führer 1 Jan 1917–30 Sept 1918. Admiralty Staff Telegram A 26019 O II of 11.9.1917 to CINC Baltic.

32. BA-MA, RM47/126, Berlin, Admiralty, 1679, to High Sea Fleet. There is no date on the cable, but internal evidence dates it from this time.

33. NA, T1022/Roll 1031, AdM Akten Albion. Cable from *SMS Baden* to Admiralty, no date.

34. NA, T1022/Roll 1031, OdO 7852 A1; 12/9 7.5; Gagern, Firle, and Rollmann, *Krieg in der Ostsee*, 173. The bulk of the names were settled on by 13 September. See BA-MA, RM47/126, Entwurf einer A.K.O., 13.9.1917. Also Nachlaß Levetzow, N-239/16, undated memorandum listing duty assignments.

35. 1871–1939. Scheer, *Germany's High Sea Fleet*, 95; NA, Roll 1031, telegram from Scheer to Admiralty, n.d. For a brief biography that largely focuses on Levetzow's political career, see Gerhard Granier, *Magnus von Levetzow: Seeoffizier, Monarchist und Wegbereiter Hitlers: Lebensweg und ausgewählte Dokumente* (H. Boldt: Boppard am Rhein, 1982).

36. 1877–? See Kontreadmiral a.D. Albert Stoelzel, *Ehrenrangliste der Kaiserlich Deutschen Marine 1914–1918* (Marine-Offizier-Verband: Berlin, 1930), 156. Promoted to commander in 1919, then captain in 1920; he retired the same year.

37. 1881–? Entered service in 1900; retired in 1921 as lieutenant commander. He then attended the University of Berlin, earning his Dr. *rer. pol.* that year. He went into business, then became the chairman of the North German Lloyd Company board of directors. Also edited volume 1 of *Krieg in der Ostsee*. He was the "advisor" on the Turkish destroyer *Muvanet-i-Milet* that sank the *Goliath* in March 1915. Cf. Stoelzel, *Ehrenrangliste*, 189.

38. 1884–? Born in Glasgow. Entered service in 1904 and left in 1920 as a lieutenant commander. Afterward he earned a Dr. *rer. pol.* at Frankfurt and entered business, working for the Hamburg-Amerika Line and North German Lloyd. In a letter to Admiral Schmidt, 6 Oct. 1937, Kiep wrote to offer regrets that he could not attend the twentieth anniversary dinner of the undertaking. He then expressed his thanks for being selected to be on the admiral's staff and entrusted with such responsibility, as he was the youngest of the staff. BA-MA, Nachlaß Schmidt, N291/15. The *Ostfriesland* achieved notoriety as the battleship sunk by Billy Mitchell's Martin bombers. Cf. Stoelzel, *Ehrenrangliste*, 208.

39. 1867–1939.

40. Kiep, ""Die Eroberung der baltischen Inseln."

41. NA/PG77463, phone conversation notes; cables to OHL, AWA 25928 O II, 11.9.1917; meeting notes; and "Kriegsspiel: Der Wegnahme der Insel Ösel, 12.9 [1917]."

42. 1878–*xx*. Educated in the Cadet Academy, he joined the army in 1896. In 1914 he fought at Liège, then at the Marne, and finally Ypres. In the east, he served in a number of general staff positions, usually in charge of operations and planning. He had held that billet at OBEROST since November 1916. At the end of the war, he was General von Winterfeldt's assistant in the Political Section of the High Command and accompanied him to Compiègne to sign the Armistice. Hanns Möller-Witten, ed., *Geschichte der Ritter des Ordens "Pour le Mérite" im Weltkrieg* (Berlin: Bernard u. Graefe, 1935), "1:151–52.

43. Born 23 November 1879 in Halle. Completing the *Abitur*, or high school finishing certificate, was not common for army officers at that time. Volkmann's *Who's Who* entry does not list the years he attended the *Kriegsakademie*, but his position and the fact he named his larger novel *Die roten Streifen* (*The Red Stripes*, indicative of the General Staff Corps uniform) reveal his background. Promoted to major in 1918, he left the service in

1920, and worked for the Military Archive in Potsdam, writing a great number of histories of the war. See *Wer Ist's, 1935.*

44. Erich Otto Volkmann, *Unternehmen Ösel* (Hamburg: Hanseatische Verlagsanstalt, 1940), 245ff. This is an autobiographical work. In the novel he uses the name Erich Lindow for himself and Gen. v. Wietersberg for General Ludwig von Estorff, the commander of the Forty-second Infantry Division. This novel is actually an excerpt from a longer one, *Die roten Streifen: Roman eines Generalstabsoffiziers* (Hamburg: Hanseatische Verlagsanstalt, 1938). This longer and earlier novel carries protagonist Lindow from his youth through the war and into the postwar years, with adventures in the Freikorps period, the Kapp Putsch, and self-imposed exile in China and Chile. Because *Unternehmen Ösel* restricts itself to the war years and Albion, I have used this novel versus its longer version, *Die roten Streifen.* In every instance where it can be verified, the novel accurately reflects actual events.

45. Georg Alexander von Müller, *The Kaiser and His Court: The Diaries, Notebooks and Letters of Admiral Georg Alexander von Müller, Chief of the Naval Cabinet, 1914–1918,* ed. Walter Görlitz, trans. Mervyn Savill (New York: Harcourt, Brace and World, 1961), 15.

46. Kiep, "Die Eroberung der baltischen Inseln."

47. BA-MA, N-239/16, Nachlaß Levetzow, N-239/16, To Chef, Admiralstabes, A 26141 O, Behelfsführung in der Unternehmung gegen Ösel, n.d. [13.9.1917].

48. BA-MA, RM47/126, Entwurf einer A.K.O., 13.9.1917. At the bottom of the typed draft, someone in handwriting added Keyserlingk as "chief of staff" along with the time, 1430. Nothing ever came of this suggestion.

49. BA-MA, N-239/16, Nachlaß Levetzow, N-239/16, To Chef, Admiralstabes, A 26141 O, Behelfsführung in der Unternehmung gegen Ösel, n.d. [13.9.1917].

50. Müller, *Kaiser and His Court,* 301.

51. BA-MA, RM5/5210, "Bedenken gegen Unternehmung Ösel" 14.9.1917.

52. Müller, *Kaiser and His Court,* 301.Prince Henry's biographer, Harald Eschenburg, mistakenly places this episode in Riga on the 6th of September, the day the kaiser toured the newly captured city. Not until the 6th or 7th did the army propose the operation to Holtzendorf in Bad Kreuznach, thus Prince Henry could not have heard about the operation until a few days afterward when the special staff was assembled. Moreover, Admiral Müller's diary places the date of Henry's conversation with the kaiser between the 14th and the 17th. Müller was also at Riga on the 6th and makes no reference to Prince Henry being there, much less having a discussion with his brother. See Harald Eschenburg, *Prinz Heinrich von Preußen: Der Großadmiral im Schatten des Kaisers.* (Heide: Westholsteinische Verlagsanstalt, 1989), 173–74.

53. BA-MA, RM5/5210, notes for *Immediatvortrag,* A 26166 O II, dtd 14.9.1917, "Unternehmung gegen Ösel."

54. BA-MA, RM5/5210, undated draft, OHL Operationsabteilung. Handwritten note on the draft says Wetzell gave this to the navy on 15 October 1917. Also Kiep, " Die Eroberung der baltischen Inseln."

55. NA/PG77463, ObOst to OHL, RM 1 7114/17 15.9.1917; Halpern, *Naval History,* 214. The official German history says the suggestion came from Prince Leopold, but offers no evidence. See Gagern, Firle, and Rollmann, *Krieg in der Ostsee,* 3:168.

56. Granier, *Levetzow,* says Ernst Freiherr von Weizäcker, then flag lieutenant to Admiral Scheer, attributed Schmidt's appointment to Levetzow, 35n106. Schmidt had been Levetzow's tactical officer when the latter was a naval officer cadet.

57. Müller, *Kaiser and His Court,* 301.

58. NA/PG77463 for the typed draft of the order, signed by Hindenburg and Holtzendorf, dated 18 September. The day before, Ludendorff had telegrammed the High

Command's representative at court, Captain von Ilsemann, urging him to get the kaiser to act. Ludendorff suggested he work with the Admiralty, which probably accounts for the amazingly rapid appearance of the Hindenburg-Holtzendorf draft of the operation order. BA-MA, RM5/5210, Ia 4628, 17.9.1917.

59. Volkmann, *Unternehmen Ösel*, 68–69. One was actually completed and sent to a print shop. BA-MA, RM5/4079, Adm. #A VI S 630g.g., "Bestimmungen über die Abbeförderung der 42. Inf. Div. mit schwerer Artillerie" 18 September, Berlin.

60. Wilhelm left for a state visit on the 19th. In all likelihood he approved the order prior to departing Berlin, but he could have waited and had his approval telegraphed back to Berlin. See Müller, *Kaiser and His Court*, 301–302.

61. This was the warning Georg von Frundsberg whispered to Luther as he entered the Diet of Worms to face Charles V. To a German, it conveys the direst of warnings—a life or death matter.

62. Volkmann, *Unternehmen Ösel*, 67–68.

63. Kiep, " Die Eroberung der baltischen Inseln." In 1904, as the Russian Baltic Fleet left Europe to sail to Vladivostok, the nervous and edgy fleet fired on English trawlers plying their trade on the Dogger Bank off the east coast of England, thinking they were Japanese destroyers. The Russians later admitted to the mistake and paid an indemnity to the families.

64. BA-MA, RM 47/127, KTB Sonderverband entries 15.9–20.9. Kiep, " Die Eroberung der baltischen Inseln."

65. The order, copied in its entirety into the War Diary of the Special Naval Task Force, is dated the 18th, but the Admiralty did not send it to the task force staff at Libau until early hours on the 21st. It is inconceivable that the Admiralty would have "sat" for three days on an order of this importance. In all likelihood either the order was dated the 18th and the kaiser thought about it for a day or two and never changed the original date, or he signed it on the 18th and held it himself for a day or two. BA-MA, RM47/127, KTB Sonderverband, entry 21.9.1917, Kz. 53616.

4. THE ISLANDS AND THEIR DEFENSES

1. The differences among the three islands with respect to terrain and topography are minor. Dagö Island had an interior consisting almost entirely of bogs, and most of its population lived along its coastline.

2. The cobblestones still exist in a few streets in Arensburg, and the ride from Kielkond (Kielkona) to the former seaplane base is bone-jarring.

3. "Studies of the Defensive Characteristics of Ösel Island" by the 107th Infantry Division, printed in Tschischwitz, *Conquest of the Baltic Islands*, 103; and RGVIA, Fond 2031 Inventory Volume 1 File 103, Operation Order, 12th Army, to Commander of the 13th Army Corps, #04655, October 7, 1917, para. 20. The order was actually signed on 4 October but not issued until three days later.

4. Lothar Schücking,, *Ein Jahr auf Ösel: Beiträge zum System Ludendorff.* (Berlin-Steglitz: Fritz Würth Verlag, 1920), 2ff., 19ff. Schücking (1873–1942) was a former Social Democrat administrator in Prussia sent to Ösel in December 1917 as a judge. His memoir of a year on the island is a savage critique of the German rule.

5. Today 39,000 people live on Ösel, and urbanization has increased, with 16,000 now living in Arensburg.

6. Valdo Praust, *Estonian Manors*, http://www.mois.ee/kihel_n.shtml#saare (23 October 2005).

254   NOTES TO PAGES 58–64

7. Throughout Russia, the government shut down German-language publications, not just on Ösel. See Peter Gatrell, *A Whole Empire Walking: Refugees in Russia During World War I* (Bloomington: Indiana University Press, 1999), 23ff.

8. An interesting commentary on the "Baltic Baron" is given by Maurice Paléologue, ambassador of France to Russia, in his *An Ambassador's Memoirs*, volume 3, entry for Saturday, February 3, 1917.

9. Georg von Rauch, *The Baltic States: The Years of Independence; Estonia, Latvia, Lithuania, 1917–1940*, trans. Gerald Onn (Berkeley: University of California, 1974), 6–24. The standard work on the period before 1918 is R. Wittram, *Baltische Geschichte. Die Ostseelande Livland, Estland und Kurland, 1180–1918* (Munich, 1954).

10. Schücking, *Ein Jahr auf Ösel*, 2–3, 19ff. BA-MA, RM 47/127, Nachrichtenoffizier der OHL beim AOK 8, #6631, 23.9.1917, p. 5.

11. Rauch, *Baltic States*, 26–27, 39–40, 43ff.

12. Hydrographic data comes from the Estonian Maritime Administration Chart 305, Paldiski to Ventspils, scale 1:250000, 22 June 2004.

13. RGAVMF, F479/C905, Report on the Actions of the Cruiser *Admiral Makarov* in the Defense of the Baltic Islands, 30 October 1917, 166–70.

14. Halpern says the construction started in 1916 after the *Slava* held off the Germans in 1915. The 12" guns were sited to dominate the minefields. *Naval History*, 206–207.

15. Fedotoff-White (1889–1950) accompanied the Root Commission upon its arrival from the U.S. Led by former secretary of war Elihu Root, the senior military members were General Hugh Scott (1853–1934), army chief of staff, and Rear Admiral James H. Glennon, commander of the Washington Naval Shipyard. The team went from Rogokyul to Zerel, and while there underwent a German aerial attack. Fedotoff-White thought morale and discipline at Zerel were high. See Dimitri Fedotoff-White, *Survival through War and Revolution in Russia* (Philadelphia: University of Pennsylvania Press, 1939), 160–61.

16. Achkasov, Kozlov, and Solov'ev, "Operations of the Russian Fleet," "133–34, 156ff., 183. Jury Melkonov, *Batarei Moonzunda (Batteries of Moon Sound)* (Riga: RTC Bask, 2003) gives a range of 33.8 kilometers; John Lagerstedt and Markku Saari, *Land and Sea Fortress of Helsinki during the First World War*, http://www.novision.fi/viapori/easeet. htm, 10 November 2005, put the range over 40 kilometers. The German official history, *Krieg in der Ostsee*, claims 28.2 kilometers range at Zerel; 16.7 kilometers for Woi. See Appendix 9.

17. Sergei Nikolaevich Timirev, *Vospominanya Morskogo Ofitsera [Reminisces of a Naval Officer]: Baltiiskii flot vo vremia voiny i Revolutsii, 1914–1918 g.g.* (St. Petersburg: Tsitadel, 1998), 166.

18. Achkasov, Kozlov, and Solov'ev, "Operations of the Russian Fleet," 183; BA-MA, RM 47/127, Nachrichtenoffizier der OHL beim AOK 8, #6631, 23.9.1917, p. 5.

19. Menning, *Bayonets before Bullets*, 228.

20. Each artillery brigade had two artillery divisions of three batteries, each with eight guns. The terminology is confusing, as normally brigades are subordinate to divisions. See Menning, *Bayonets before Bullets*, 231, which gives the organization and equipment of a Russian infantry division.

21. RGVIA, F2031, History of 107th Infantry Division. The records of the division are in the Russian State Military Archives, Moscow, but there are none after April 1917. This seems to indicate that the transfer from the army to the navy was not really complete until the division headquarters actually moved to Arensburg in March 1917, at which time the unit's reports and records went through the Baltic Fleet. The unit's records were lost after the Germans captured them. Luntinen, *Russian Army and Navy in Finland*, 293–94, citing RGVIA, F2422, says the 107th Division, along with the 106th, was formed from

Russian militia units in Helsinki in 1915 and composed the 42nd Army Corps. Luntinen has the correct regimental numbers and names, but then says that in February 1916 the division "was divided in two" with the 116th Division being built from the 425th and 427th Regiments, and the 426th and 428th Regiments forming the basis for the 107th Division. RGVIA, F2031, does not show this development.

22. RGAVMF, F941–108, Description of Baltic Islands Operation, 12–18 October.

23. Born on 19 February 1866 in Lovich, Warsaw Province, son of a town official. Married to an officer's daughter, he had three sons and a daughter. The details of his career come from RGVIA, F409, record of service 5427, 1911; and F407, Inventory volume 1, case 101, p. 15.

24. A regular division of the Imperial Army, its peacetime garrison was Penza, a city some 480 kilometers east of Moscow. Three of its four regiments had Latvian names (178th Ust-Dvinsk Infantry Regiment, 179th Wenden Infantry Regiment, and 180th Windau Infantry Regiment), but it cannot be ascertained if these units recruited in that area. See Mark Conrad, *The Russian Army 1914*, http://home.comcast.net/~markconrad/RUSS1914. html#DIVISIONS.

25. RGAVMF, F716/114, Report by General Ivanov, 1 June 1916, 26ff.

26. RGVIA, F2031, History of 107th Infantry Division. The unit history says the 428th Infantry Regiment moved to the island as well, but other information indicates that if it went, it did not remain for long.

27. "Studies of the Defensive Characteristics of Ösel Island" by the 107th Infantry Division in Tschischwitz, *Conquest of Baltic Islands*, 116–17.

28. RGAVMF 479/905, Summary of Operations (Landing Operation12–20 October), 12 October—Day One of the Landing Operation, 41. RGVIA, F2422-1-4, Order 64, Headquarters 107th Infantry Division, 30 March 1917.

29. RGVIA, F2422-1-4, Order 64; RGAVMF, F941/108; Chief of Staff of the Baltic Islands Fortified Position, Description of Baltic Islands Operation, 12 October 1917. This document summarizes the division's orders and brings them up to date as of the day of the landing.

30. "Hundred" was the traditional Cossack cavalry organization, corresponding (roughly) to a squadron. A normal cavalry regiment had 777 men in four squadrons. The Cossacks were allowed to retain the designation "hundred." A Cossack regiment (*sotnii*) had six hundreds, which would mean each hundred numbered about 120 men. See Menning, *Bayonets before Bullet*, 27.

31. When the Germans captured Sworbe, they identified a Colonel Borsakowski as the commander of the 425th Infantry Regiment. They made no mention of a Colonel Sherekhovsky. See Erich von Tschischwitz, *Blaujacken und Feldgraue gen Ösel: Walter Flex' Heldentod* (Mylau: Buchdruckerei Carl Krüger, 1934), 100ff. The Russian records reflect this change as well. See RGAVMF, F941/108; Reek Report, part 2, 104–106.

32. Tschischwitz, *Blaujacken und Feldgraue gen Ösel*, 100. The Germans encountered an additional line of fortifications facing to the north across the peninsula at Anseküll (Anseküla), near where it joins the rest of the island.

33. RGVIA, F2422-1-4, Order 64, Headquarters 107th Infantry Division, 30 March 1917. All of these arrangements are confirmed in a document called "Description of Baltic Islands Operation, 12 October 1917," written by the Chief of Staff of the Baltic Islands Fortified Position, RGAVMF, F941/108. For the German assessment, see BA-MA, RM47/127, Nachrichtenoff. AOK8, G.6631, 23 September 1917

34. This regiment, and its sisters, the 470th and 471st infantry regiments, were organic units of the 118th Infantry Division. The division headquarters was already on Ösel, but the 470th and 471st remained on the mainland. Luntinen says the 428th Infantry

Regiment remained in Helsinki, was there during the 1917 March Revolution, then was at Hango in October, and finally was sent by the Petrograd Soviet to Moscow in November, allegedly to cement the Bolshevik coup there. See his *Russian Army and Navy in Finland*, 305, 324, 353.

35. RGAVMF, F941/108; Chief of Staff of the Baltic Islands Fortified Position, Description of Baltic Islands Operation, 12 October 1917. 107th Division Order #263, 11 October 1917. This order is dated the day before the landing; whether it reflected reality or was calling for repositioning is not certain, but the 428th Regiment does not appear in the battle.

36. RGAVMF, F941/108; Chief of Staff of the Baltic Islands Fortified Position, Description of Baltic Islands Operation, 12 October 1917. From 1916 to 1917, the regiments of the division had acquired 76 more machine guns (from a total of 36 in 1916 to 112 in 1917), reflecting the improved materiel situation of the Russian army in 1917. See RGVIA, F2422-1-39, Lists (registers, rolls) on the complement, payroll, and present composition of the Men and Horses According to the Tenure of Employment.

37. RGAVMF, F941/108; Chief of Staff of the Baltic Islands Fortified Position, Description of Baltic Islands Operation, 12 October 1917. This figure actually represents an improvement from the 1,200 effectives the regiment had when it moved to Ösel. See ibid., Vasiliev (HQ unk) to HQ Northern Front, #0597, 22 April 1917.

38. RGAVMF, F941/108, Reek Report, part 2, Report of 425th Infantry Regiment Paymaster Moginov, 104–106.

39. Melkonov, *Batteries of Moon Sound*, 6ff.; RGAVMF, F941/108; Chief of Staff of the Baltic Islands Fortified Position, Description of Baltic Islands Operation, 12 October 1917.

40. RGAVMF, F941/108; Chief of Staff of the Baltic Islands Fortified Position, Description of Baltic Islands Operation, 12 October 1917. Order to the Garrison of Dagö Island #28 from 23 September 1917.

41. RGAVMF, F941/108; Chief of Staff of the Baltic Islands Fortified Position, Description of Baltic Islands Operation, 12 October 1917.

42. Ibid., 46ff.

43. Ibid., Sveshnikov to the Admiralty Chief of Staff, #0392, 31 March 1917; Chief of Staff, Land Forces, to Sveshnikov, #478, 3 April 1917; Chief of Staff Land Forces to Sveshnikov, #5293/1912, 26 August 1917; and #5573/2005, 9 September 1917.

44. RGAVMF, F941/108; Chief of Staff of the Baltic Islands Fortified Position, Description of Baltic Islands Operation, 12 October 1917, 66–70.

45. 1879–1920. K. A. Zalesskii, *Pervaia mirovaia voina: biograficheskii entsikopedicheskii slovar'* (Moscow: Veche, 2000), 189–90; Mawdlesy, *Baltic Fleet*, 70. Mawdlesy says in 1916 Razvozov stood 182nd of 207 captains in the Russian Navy.

46. See Harald Graf, *The Russian Navy in War and Revolution From 1914 up to 1918 with 38 Photographs* (Munich: Oldenbourg, 1923), 163; For Razvozov's career, see Zalesskii, *Pervaia mirovaia voina*, 189–90.

47. Mikhail Koronatovich Bakhirev, *Otchet o Destviyah Morskih Sil Rizhskogo Zaliva, 25. Sentyabrya 7 Oktyabrya 1917 g.* (originally published in Petrograd, 1919; republished, St. Petersburg: Russian State Naval Archive, 1998), 11.

48. Graf, *Russian Navy*, 115.

49. Ibid., 115.

50. Ibid., 146; Mawdlesy, *Baltic Fleet*, p. 154.

51. The Russian expert, Achkasov, says Bakhirev had 116 vessels. The vast majority were minesweeping craft. See Achkasov, Kozlov, and Solov'ev, "Operations of the Russian Fleet," ""28. The Russian order of battle, taken from *Die Moon-Sund Unternehmung 1917*

(Leningrad: Marine Akademie USSR, 1928) is reproduced in Gagern, Firle, and Roll-mann, *Krieg in der Ostsee*, appendix 5, 420ff. Aerial photography told the Germans exactly what ships Bakhirev had. See RM47/126, Chef Sonderverband, Gg 626 O, 2.10.1917.

52. It was this engagement that led the Russians to begin work on emplacing 12" guns at Zerel, completed the next year.

53. Nekrasov, *Expendable Glory*, 64. The Baltic Fleet Order of Battle, dated 14 March 1917, is reproduced as appendix 1 in Gagern, Firle, and Rollmann, *Krieg in der Ostsee*, 407ff.

54. Wildman, *End of the Russian Imperial Army*, 1:105–20.

55. Norman E. Saul, *Sailors in Revolt: The Russia Baltic Fleet in 1917* (Lawrence: University of Kansas Press, 1978), 52–55.

56. Saul, *Sailors in Revolt*, 67, points out that enlisted sailors ran the fleet's communica-tion systems, and promptly passed on messages to their comrades in the ships' committees.

57. Wildman, *End of the Russian Imperial Army*, 1:212; Mawdsley, *Baltic Fleet*, 88. On the 12th of March, rioting sailors had murdered two dozen officers, including several admirals. Also see Graf, *Russian Navy*, 115ff. and 136–43; Saul, *Sailors in Revolt*, 59–80.

58. Order #1, dated 14 March 1917, is reproduced in its entirety along with an account of its origins in Wildman, *End of the Russian Imperial Army*, 1:182–92.

59. Quoted in Wildman, *End of the Russian Imperial Army*, 1:231.

60. Ibid., I, chapter 7, passim.

61. Kerensky's Order #8, "Rights . . ." is given in full in *The Russian Provisional Gov-ernment, 1917*, ed. Robert P. Browder and Alexander F. Kerensky (Stanford: Stanford Uni-versity Press, 1961), 2:880–83. Chapter 16 of this volume contains numerous documents relating to this theme. Also Mawdsley, *Baltic Fleet*, 36–41.

62. Saul, *Sailors in Revolt*, 98–99; Mawdsley, *Baltic Fleet*, 22–35.

63. Mawdsley, *Baltic Fleet*, 41–45; Saul, *Sailors in Revolt*, 82, has a diagram of the dual command structure.

64. Wildman, *End of the Russian Imperial Army*, 1:356, 346–62.

65. Ibid., vol. 2, chapters 1 and 2.

66. Saul, *Sailors in Revolt*, 117–36; Browder and Kerensky, *Provisional Government*, 2:942–87, provide a number of documents from this period, to include reinstating the death penalty at the front.

67. Mawdsley, *Baltic Fleet*, 86ff.

68. Browder and Kerensky, *Provisional Government*, "Excerpts from Protocols of the Conference of Government and Military Leaders," 2:989–1010; "Appointment of Kornilov as Supreme Commander," 31 July 1917. Cf. Wildman, *End of the Russian Imperial Army*, 2:106–107, for a description of the scene at the Twenty-eighth Division. For a discussion in detail about the breakdown of discipline and refusal to fight, see ibid., chapter 3, "The Revolt against the Offensive," 73–111.

69. Wildman, *End of the Russian Imperial Army*, 1:115; 278ff. On the "rotten corner," see Alexander F. Kerensky, *Russia and History's Turning Point* (New York: Stone and Pierce, 1965).

70. Graf, *Russian Navy*, 164; Saul, *Sailors in Revolt*, 146–49. For the details of the Kornilov Coup, see George Katkov, *The Kornilov Affair: Kerensky and the Break-up of the Russian Army* (New York: Longman, 1980).

71. 1882–1918. Fought in the Russo-Japanese War, and served on staff of Baltic Fleet during the First World War. Developed the forward position mine defense at the entrance to the Gulf of Finland that led to the greatest German disaster in the Baltic, the loss of seven destroyers to mines the night of 10–11 November 1916. Became acting chief of staff of the Baltic Fleet in March 1917. Timirev, *Vospominania Morskogo Ofitsera*, 140–41.

72. The gruesome details are recorded in Graf, *Russian Navy*, 164–68. Cf. extracts from the diary of Captain Rengarten (operations officer, Baltic Fleet) in Browder and Kerensky, *Provisional Government*, 3:1581–82.

73. See the remarkable editorials in *Izvestiya*, 16 September 1917, and the *Rabochaia Gazeta*, 25 September 1917, in Browder and Kerensky, *Provisional Government*, 1615–17.

74. Quoted from his diary in Mawdsley, *Baltic Fleet*, 81. Saul, *Sailors in Revolt*, 152–54, has Rear Admiral Prince Cherkassky (chief of staff) and Captain Rengarten (operations officer) accompanying Razvozov and handing in their resignations as well.

75. Achkasov, Kozlov, and Solov'ev, "Operations of the Russian Fleet," "229.

76. Military Intelligence Report from the Commander of the 6th Siberian Corps, n.d., October 1917; "Appeal for Order from the Central Executive Committee, Petrograd Soviet," in *Izvestiya*, 16 September 1917. Both in Browder and Kerensky, *Provisional Government*, 3:1615ff. The arrests and cleansing of counterrevolutionaries in the army is handled in Wildman's superb *End of the Russian Imperial Army*, 2:195–223. On anti-officer sentiment, ibid., 213–17.

77. Interview with *Russkoe Slovo*, 26 September 1917, and war minister Verkhovsky's Report, both in Browder and Kerensky, *Provisional Government*, 3:1620–23.

78. "Izvestija Moonzundskoi Ukreplennoi Pozitsii" # 8, 10 April 1917. This edition makes reference to the third meeting of the Moon Sound Soviet, held 7 April. The initial meeting obviously came sometime before that date. The first issue of the "Izvestija" was 24 March. I am grateful to Ms. Katrin Äär, archivist of the Kuresaare Bishop's castle, for making me aware of this "Izvestija" and its editor. The Library of the Academy of Sciences, St. Petersburg *(Biblioteka Akademii Nauk)*, has what may be the only surviving set of originals. Ms. Marina Alexandrova retrieved this material for me.

79. Ibid. # 34, 18 June; #43 4 July 1917.

80. Ibid., #42, 2 July 1917 has the full guidelines for the proposed soviet. See also issues # 43, 4 July and # 59, 11 August. Issue #63, 21 August, published the first proceedings of the new soviet, "Izvestija Soveta Voinskih i Rabotshih Deputatov Moonzundskoi Ukreplennoi pozitsii" or "Proceedings of the Soviet of Soldiers and Laborers Deputies of the Moon Sound Defensive Position." Commencing with Issue #64, 23 August, the paper adopted the full title for its remaining twenty issues rather than the previous and shorter "Proceedings of the Moon Sound Defensive Position."

81. RGAVMF, F941/108, part 3; BA-MA, RM47/127, Nachrichtenoff. AOK8, G.6631, 23 September 1917.

82. BA-MA, RM47/127, Nachrichtenoff. AOK8, G.6631, 23 September 1917.

83. Izvestija" Special Edition #4, 6 September 1917; # 71, 9 September 1917.

84. Ibid., Meeting 14 of the Executive Committee, 6 September 1917.

85. Ibid., Special Edition #5, 10 September; # 73, 15 September 1917.

86. RGAVMF, F941/108, Vasiliev to Headquarters, Northern Front (Captain Altvater), #0597, 22 April 1917.

87. Mawdsley, *Baltic Fleet*, 48; Nekrasov, *Expendable Glory*, 83–84.

88. Mawdsley, *Baltic Fleet*, 90.

89. Bakhirev, *Otchet*, 23ff.

90. Fedotoff-White, *Survival*, 165.

5. THE INVASION

1. Möller-Witten, *"Pour le Mérite,"* 1:549.

2. 1870–1938. "Weigh then venture" was the unofficial motto of the General Staff Corps. He wrote two books about the Baltic Islands campaign, *The Army and Navy during the Conquest of the Baltic Islands in October 1917: An Analytical Study Based on Actual Experience*, trans. Colonel Henry Hossfeld (Berlin: R. Eisenschmidt, 1931), and *Blaujacken und Feldgraue gen Ösel: Walter Flex' Heldentod* (Mylau: Buchdruckerei Carl Krüger, 1934). The quotation comes from General Kabisch, Tschischwitz's superior during the siege of Antwerp in 1914. See Möller-Witten, *Pour le Mérite*, 2:432ff.

3. Friedrich Ruge, "Die Öselfahrt auf Torpedoboot B110 (1917)," in *"Erleben— Lernen—Weitergeben" Friedrich Ruge (1894–1985)*, ed. Jörg Hillmann, *Kleine Schriften- reihe zur Militär- und Marinegeschichte*, Band 10 (Bochum: Verlag Dr. Dieter Winkler, 2005), 103–104.

4. 1872–?. Gygas apparently was also a pilot. At war's onset he commanded the First Naval Flying Detachment, then later the cruiser *Roon*. He commanded the *Moltke* from September 1916 until the end of the war, retiring in November 1919. He was given a brevet as rear admiral in 1920. See Stoelzel, *Ehrenrangliste*, 133–34.

5. BA-MA, RM 47/127, KTB Sonderverband, 11 October, entry 6 AM; Volkmann, *Unternehmen Ösel*, 73.

6. BA-MA, RM 47/127, KTB Sonderverband, 11 October 1917; Tschischwitz, *Blau- jacken und Feldgraue gen Ösel*, 25ff.

7. National Archives, RGS 165/320/box 153, 42d Inf Div, KTB, 27.9.1917. #4. Indirectly, BA-MA, RM 47/127, KTB Sonderverband, entry for 19 September 1917. This was to be the date by which the vessels were loaded and ready for departure.

8. Volkmann, *Unternehmen Ösel*, 245ff.

9. BA-MA, RM47/127, KTB Sonderverband, entry for 18 September 1917.

10. BA-MA, RM47/127, KTB Sonderverband, entry for 21 September 1917, copy therein of Admiralty Order, KZ 52616, paras. 8–9, n.d.

11. BA-MA, RM 47/127, KTB Sonderverband, entry for 22 September 1917.

12. Ibid.

13. Georg Frotscher, 1868–. From the Saxon Army, he had served in the Prussian General Staff before the war. When the war broke out, he was chief of staff, Nineteenth Army Corps in Leipzig, and remained with it in the west until January 1917, when he took command of Grenadier Reserve Regiment 100 at Arras. In March that year he moved to the staff of the governor general of Antwerp. On 9 September he went to Riga to become chief of staff, Eighth Army. In February 1918, he moved to General Eichhorn's army group in the Ukraine, then back to the west in July, promoted to brigadier general in charge of an infantry brigade (the 105th Reserve and the 245th Infantry Brigade). He served in the Reichswehr after the war, retiring in 1922.

14. BA-MA, RM 47/127, KTB Sonderverband, entry for 23 September 1917.

15. Volkmann, *Unternehmen Ösel*, 69–70.

16. For a short primer on this campaign, see Isabel Hull, "The Military Campaign in German Southwest Africa, 1904–1907," *Bulletin of the German Historical Institute* 37 (Fall 2005): 39–45.

17. Möller-Witten, *"Pour le Mérite,"* 1:283–84.

18. NA, RGS 165/320/box 153, 42d ID KTB, 26 September 1917. The unit was large. The OHL told the navy the cycle brigade strength was 144 officers; 5,199 soldiers; 734 horses; 4,597 bikes; 215 wagons; 51 autos; and 111 trucks.

19. Alfred Freiherr von Quadt-Wykradt-Hüchtenbruck, 1862–1928.

20. BA-MA, RM47/126, Flgrst. Windau, 4996, to KoFlieg, 1.10.1917; Koflieg to Chef, Sonderverband, G602 A.1, 1.101.1917.

21. BA-MA, RM 47/127, Sonderverband, Gg380/O, Sonderbefehl für des Landungskorps Rosenbergs bei die Batterie auf Kap Pamerort. 27.9.1917 and KTB Sonderverband, entry 27 September 1917. The navy claimed that Commander von Rosenberg originated the idea of the Pamerort attack. See Gagern, Firle, and Rollmann, *Krieg in der Ostsee*, 178.

22. BA-MA, RM 47/127, KTB Sonderverband, entry 29 September 1917.

23. Volkmann, *Unternehmen Ösel*, 71–72.

24. BA-MA, RM 47/127, KTB Sonderverband, entry 2 October 1917.

25. NA, RGS 165/320/box 153, 42d ID. KTB, 42 ID, Ia 1293 4.10.1917, Divisionsbefehl für Landungsabteilung Pamerort. This order superceded one dated 28 September, Ia 1233.

26. BA-MA, RM 47/127, KTB Sonderverband, entries for 3 and 8 October.

27. Volkmann, *Unternehmen Ösel*, 72.

28. Schmidt's operation order is in NA, T1022/Roll 238, Sonderverband, G 193 O, 25 September 1917.

29. There are some discrepancies in the exact number, but the after-action report of the Twenty-third Reserve Corps states 3,600 in the assault force and 1,650 cycle troops and 150 sailors for the Pamerort force. See NA, RGS 165/320/box 113, 5–6. Admiral Schmidt's figures in his report are much larger: an assault landing force of 4,500 men, and 3,000 cyclists for Pamerort. See BA-MA, Nachlaß Schmidt N-291/10, "Die Eroberung der Baltischen Inseln," 1090 II secret, 1917.

30. BA-MA, N-291/17, 19 August 1942, comments by Schmidt for a radio broadcast in honor of the twenth-fifth anniversary of the landings. Herwig in his *Luxury Fleet*, 177–78, says Jellicoe had 150 ships, Scheer 93 at Jutland in 1916. Of course, most of Schmidt's vessels were small minesweeping and related craft. Opposing him the Russians eventually fielded 116 vessels. See Achkasov, Kozlov, and Solov'ev, "Operations of the Russian Fleet," 28.

31. BA-MA, N291/50, (Landungskorps), Gk. Ic 4015, "Die Eroberung der baltischen Inseln," 27.12.1917, p. 6, and NA/165/320/box 153, 42d Inf Div, KTB 40ff., copy of XXIII Corps OPORD, Ia 202/9, 24 September 1917. The division's OPORD, 42 ID, Ia 1223, 27 September 1917, is in the same file, 81ff.

32. NA/165/320/box 153, 42d Inf Div, KTB 40ff., copy of XXIII Corps OPORD, Ia 202/9, 24 September 1917. The division's OPORD, 42 ID, Ia 1223, 27 September 1917, is in the same file, 81ff.

33. NA/165/320/box 153, 42 ID, Ia 1293 4.10.1917, "Divisionsbefehl für Landungsabteilung Pamerort."

34. NA/165/320/box 113, XXIII Corps, AAR, 27.12.1917.

35. Tschischwitz, *Conquest of the Baltic Islands*, 27–28. Admiral Schmidt's operation order is reproduced without heading or date in Gagern, Firle, and Rollmann, *Krieg in der Ostsee*, 180ff.

36. In addition to the small size of the harbor, it was also too shallow for the capital ships. Gagern, Firle, and Rollmann, *Krieg in der Ostsee*, p. 183.

37. Both the Admiralty and the High Command agreed that if they had to execute *Fall-J* during Albion, the Baltic Islands undertaking would be cancelled immediately and the steamers returned at once. BA-MA, Nachlaß Levetzow, N-239/16, Chef d. Admiralstabes, O 15 2, Berlin, 19.9.1917.

38. NA, 1032, AdM Akten Albion, Schlußbericht des Führers der Transportflotte, 29.11.1917.

39. G. von. Koblinsky, "The Conquest of the Baltic Islands," *U.S. Naval Institute Proceedings* 58, no. 2 (July 1932):"" 974ff. NA/PG76718 has messages from the Oberste Heeresleitung providing loading planning data for large units well after the ships were actually loaded. See also Gagern, Firle, and Rollmann, *Krieg in der Ostsee*, 187ff. Logisticians discovered, for example, that units in the east had far more horses authorized than those from the western front, from which the modeling data came.

40. The loading plan for the operation was finished before Volkmann left Berlin for Libau. See his *Unternehmen Ösel*, 68–69, and NA/1031, Adm. #A VI S 630g.g., "Bestimmungen über die Abbeförderung der 42. Inf. Div. mit schwerer Artillerie" 18 September 1917. The final loading plans are in NA/1031, AdM Akten Albion, Appendix 1 of Loading Guidelines, "Belegung der Schiffe."

41. NA, 1032, AdM Akten Albion, Schlußbericht des Führers der Transportflotte, 29.11.1917; and BA-MA, RM42/134, 42 ID, Ia 10304, 5.10.1917; and RM62/186, Bericht betr. Erfahrungen im Ueberfahren und Landen einer Marinelandungsabteilung auf Ösel, 16.11.1917.

42. Ruge, "Öselfahrt auf Torpedoboot B 110," 100ff.

43. NA/PG76718, KB 137, 30.9; and 1 Oct., Gp 636. Also, BA-MA, RM5/5210, Levetzow to Admiralty, O II© 1.10.1917. Ironically, the Forty-second Division thought the exercise was adequate. NA/42d Inf, KTB, 29. 9 [1917], 5.

44. BA-MA, RM42/135, PILAKO, BB 116, 3.10.1917, to Chef der Transportflotte, Kapt. v. Schlick.

45. NA, 1032, AdM Akten Albion, Schlußbericht des Führers der Transportflotte, 29.11.1917. On the Pioneer Landing Company (PILAKO), see NA/ 994, Pilako KTB, Anlage 3, Kriegstagebuch, Sonder-Bericht, attached to A VI S 9513 of RMA, 20.6.1918.

46. The navy officer was Lieutenant Ruge. See his "Öselfahrt auf Torpedoboot B110," 98. Also, Richard Stumpf, *War, Mutiny and the Revolution in the German Navy: The World War I Diary of Seaman Richard Stumpf*, trans. and ed. Daniel Horn (New Brunswick: Rutgers University Press, 1967), 357. When the operation failed to materialize immediately, owing to the weather delays, a disillusioned Stumpf wrote on 2 October, "I no longer believe in the whole swindle," 358.

47. NA/1236, XXIII Reserve Corps, 1A 4053, 11 December 1917, "Erfahrungen." [This was the corps after-action report.]

48. NA/42d Infantry Division, KTB entry for 30 Sept.

49. On mine operations, see Achkasov, Kozlov, and Solov'ev, "Operations of the Russian Fleet,"" 90ff.; Tschischwitz, *Conquest of the Baltic Islands*, 19ff.; Scheer, *Germany's High Sea Fleet*, 288; and Cowie, *Mines, Minelayers and Minelaying*, chapters 3–5; and Taprell Dorling, *Swept Channels: Being an Account of the Work of the Minesweepers in the Great War* (London: Hodder and Stoughton, 1935), chapter 2. On the internet, see http://www.globalsecurity.org/military/library/policy/navy/ nrtc/14160_ch8.pdf (accessed 11 November 2005).

50. BA-MA, RM 47/127, KTB Sonderverband, entries from 16.9; 20.9; and 21.9.1917.

51. BA-MA, RM 47/127, KTB Sonderverband, entry from 20 September; also Nachlaß Schmidt, N291/10, Erhardt Schmidt, "Die Eroberung der Baltischen Inseln," Top Secret, Berlin 1917, 13–14.

52. Franz Wieting, *Der Ostsee Krieg, 1914–1918* (Berlin: G. Braunbeck, 1918), 124.

53. BA-MA, RM 47/127, KTB Sonderverband, entries for 21, 22, 25–29 September, 2–5, and 7 October. Hopman, *Kriegstagebuch*, 244ff. Volkmann noted that the delays in clearing the mines led to fears the operation would be scrapped. See his *Unternehmen Ösel*, 72–73.

54. BA-MA, RM 47/127, KTB Sonderverband, OHL, Ia 4854, Ludendorff to 8th Army, 3 October 1917, entry for 4 October 1917.

55. 1857–1934. Hutier's mother was a Ludendorff; Erich (the quartermaster general) was his first cousin. Hutier enjoyed a normal career, passing into the General Staff Corps with the following accolade from his instructor, then Lieutenant Colonel von Hindenburg: "highly gifted young officer, of whom the greatest hopes are merited." He had commanded the Eighth Army since January 1917.

56. BA-MA, RM 47/127, KTB Sonderverband, entry for 5 and 6 October.

57. Ibid., entry for 6 and 7 October.

58. Ibid., entry 8 October 1917.

59. Tschischwitz, *Blaujacken und Feldgraue gen Ösel*, 25ff.; Gagern, Firle, and Rollmann, *Krieg in der Ostsee*, appendix 14.

60. Volkmann, *Unternehmen Ösel*, 74.

61. BA-MA, RM 47/127, KTB Sonderverband, entry of 2 October 1917. The German doctrine called for the brigade commander to have two, if not all three, of the division's infantry regiments under his control. He would direct the infantry engagement, while the division commander allocated assets such as artillery or reinforcements. Tschischwitz, *Conquest of the Baltic Islands*, 51, says Matthiass and his staff were on Heinecke's boats.

62. Ruge, "Öselfahrt auf B 110," 103.

63. Tschischwitz, *Blaujacken und Feldgraue gen Ösel*, 34.

64. BA-MA, Nachlaß Schmidt, N-291/10, Erhardt Schmidt, "Die Eroberung der Baltischen Inseln," Top Secret, Berlin 1917, 13–14, and Kiep, " Die Eroberung der baltischen Inseln."

65. Volkmann, *Unternehmen Ösel*, 74.

66. Möller-Witten, *Pour le Mérite*, 1:462–63; See Stoelzel, *Ehrenrangliste*, 163; Friedrich Ruge, *SM Torpedo Boat B110* (Windsor: Profile Publications, 1973), p. 56.

67. Kiep, " Die Eroberung der baltischen Inseln."

68. The Reichsmarine experimented with storing extra coal in bags on decks to cut down the number of support vessels. Major concerns were that the coal might interfere with operations or pose a safety risk, but neither fear materialized. See BA-MA, RM8/143, A.223/18, Ganz Geheim, Kriegserfahrungen des Kommandos der Hochseestreitkräfte, 30 Jan 1918.

69. Volkmann, *Unternehmen Ösel*, 78ff. Cf. Ruge, "Öselfahrt auf B110," 104, who confirms Heinecke's difficult decision made as the dawn began to break. See BA-MA, RM 47/126, "Tätigkeit der Motorruderbarkassen während der 'Albionunternehmung,'" 1.

70. Ruge, "Öselfahrt auf B110," 104–105.

71. Tschischwitz, *Blaujacken und Feldgraue gen Ösel*, 35ff.

72. "Kampf um die Taggebucht," Auf Vorposten. Wochenschau für die leichten Sestreitkräfte. Ösel Sonder Nummer, 9.12.1917. Contained in Admiral Schmidt's scrapbook in his Nachlaß, BA-MA, N-291/10.

73. Volkmann, *Unternehmen Ösel*, 78ff. BA-MA, RM 47/127, KTB Sonderverband, entry for 12 October.

74. Tschischwitz, *Blaujacken und Feldgraue gen Ösel*, 35ff. The colonel's conversation dovetails with the operation order, which stated that the ships would not open fire until given the command over the radio by the chief. See RM47/127, Chef Sonderverband, Gg 354 AO, Sonderbefehl f. die Beschiessung der Landbefestigungen. . . . 28.9.1917.

6. ÖSEL, 12–13 OCTOBER 1917: THE CENTRAL ISLAND

1. RGAVMF, F479/C906, Entry 12 October 1917, 0730, Lt. Prestin, 52.

2. RGAVMF, F479/904, Report of the Filzand Lighthouse Keeper to the Organization of Lighthouses of the Baltic Fleet, 17 October 1917. Toom ran the lighthouse from 1906 to 1941, achieving some fame for founding a bird sanctuary and study center on Filzand (Vilsandi) Island. A picture of Toom (1884–1943) and his family can be seen at http://www.loodus.ee/el/vanaweb/0008/toom.html. References to Toom's reports can be seen in F479/905, Commander of the Baltic Fleet, Materials on the Defense of the Baltic Islands, August 21–October 27, 1917, Day One, 12 October 1917, and one of his reports to the fleet commander is in F479/906, 11:28 AM, in which he reports the bombardment of the air station. Lt. Telepnev's report is in F479/906, with other references in F479/C905, report of 1115. From the opposite side, the guidance for the three vessels that bombarded the air station is in BA-MA, RM47/127, Flottenverband, Gg 811/O, 4.10.1917, Nachtrag zum O Befehl Nr. 1.

3. BA-MA, RM47/127, KTB Sonderverband, entry 12 October 1917; 0600; RM47/126, A telegram dated 1855, 12 October 1917, from Admiral Schmidt to Libau, says the assault landing party went ashore at 0545. Also Tschischwitz, *Blaujacken und Feldgraue gen Ösel*, 41ff. For a firsthand account of the landing, Ruge, "Öselfahrt auf B110," 104–105; and RM 47/126, "Tätigkeit der Motorruderbarkassen während der 'Albionunternehmung,'" 1–2.

4. BA-MA, RM8/127, Kriegstagebuch des I. Führers der Torpedobootsstreitkräfte, Nr. 4116, 1–17 Okt. 1917. In file RM 47/126, which contains the telegrams of situation reports, there is one recording the time *Bayern* reported hitting the mine as 0507. See also RM47/127, KTB Sonderverband, entry 0530 12 October 1917.

5. Wieting, *Der Ostsee Krieg*, 126.

6. BA-MA, RM47/1217, KTB Sonderverband, entry 12 October 1917. The *Corsica* did not immediately settle or list, leading those on the scene to think it had been hit from a shore battery.

7. Fedotoff-White, *Survival*, 165.

8. 1871–1937. An intellectual who had served largely on various staffs, he authored several books, including one on German tactics. He commanded a regiment in the East Prussian campaign (1914) and made brigadier general a year later. Sacked for dereliction of duty in late 1915, he returned in 1916 to command a brigade. After the March Revolution, he advanced fast, taking charge of a division, a corps, and finally an army. He ran afoul of General Kornilov, who thought he handled his forces rather unskillfully. Kerensky favored him and made him commander in chief of the northern front after the fall of Riga, promoting him to lieutenant general (general of infantry) as well. Zalesskii, *Pervaia mirovaia voina*, 220ff.

9. Wildman, *End of the Russian Imperial Army*, I, 115; 278ff.

10. 1886–1921. From a noble family, Parsky enjoyed a typical career after completing the Nicholas General Staff Academy with a first-class degree in 1893. During the Russo-Japanese War he served in the operations section of the Manchurian Army. In1910 he was promoted to brigadier general and commanded the Second Brigade of the Forty-sixth Infantry Division. In January 1915 he took over the Eightieth Infantry Division and received a second star a few months later. That year he also served in Kiev, as commander of the Fifty-fifth Division, and in 1916 of the Grenadier Guards Corps. In July 1917 he assumed command of the Twelfth Army at Riga, but he lost the city and twelve thousand men to the Germans in early September 1917. During the retreat from Riga, discipline in several of his units collapsed, culminating in a rout. From Zalesskii, *Pervaia mirovaia voina*, 172ff.

11. 1976–1917. He became an officer in 1895 in the Lithuanian Life Guards Regiment. In 1902 he completed the Nicholas General Staff Academy; following a brief stint in the Forty-second Infantry Division, he joined the staff of the Kiev Military District. He remained there in various positions until the war broke out. By then a colonel, he went to war with the Third Army staff as the intelligence officer. For most of 1915 he led the 165th (Lutsky) Infantry Regiment. In December 1915 he was promoted to brigadier and assigned to the headquarters of the southwest front. He later served as operations officer and chief of staff of the front and attained the rank of lieutenant general. In September 1917, Kerensky made him Stavka's chief of staff. See Zalesskii, *Pervaia mirovaia voina*, 110–11.

12. RGVIA, F2031-1-103, Dukhonin to Northern Front, #6757, 6 pm, 23 September 1917. General Dukhonin indicated that commander in chief Alexander Kerensky expected the fleet to hold out for only a few days, after which the weather would turn and favor the Russians.

13. RGAVMF, F479/904, Secret, From Commander, Northern Front, General Cheremisov, to Commander of the Fleet, #2735, September 25, 1917; From the Headquarters, Baltic Fleet, to the Chief of Naval Defense, #1578, 9 October 1917; To the Commander of the Baltic Fleet from the Commander of the Baltic Islands Position [Admiral Sveshnikov], 23 October 1917.

14. RGAVMF, F479/905, Bakhirev to Baltic Fleet, #148, 3 October 1917. F479/904, Baltic Fleet Headquarters to Sveshnikov (Naval Defense of Baltic Islands) #1578, 10 October 1917.

15. Tschischwitz, *Blaujacken und Feldgraue gen Ösel*, 53.

16. RGAVMF, F941/107, Conversation between Chief of Staff Captain Reek and Colonel Krusenshtieren, 5 pm, 12 October 1917.

17. RGAVMF, F479/905, Summary of Operations (Landing Operation 09.29–10.07) October 12–Day One of the Landing Operation. Entry 7:27.

18. Tschischwitz, *Blaujacken und Feldgraue gen Ösel*, 43.

19. RGAVMF, F479/906, Materials on the Defense of the Baltic Islands October 11–13, 1917. Cf. Artur Toom's report; BA-MA, RM 47/126, "Tätigkeit der Motorruderbarkassen während der 'Albionunternehmung,'" 1.

20. The account of the firing appears in both Tschischwitz's *Blaujacken und Feldgraue gen Ösel*, 37–38, and "Kampf um die Taggebucht," *Auf Vorposten. Wochenschau für die leichten Seestreitkräfte*. Ösel Sonder Nummer, 9 December 1917.

21. Tschischwitz, *Blaujacken und Feldgraue gen Ösel*, 45–46, says the Germans captured 3 officers and 30 men from the Hundsort fort. Russian reports claim a number of the Hundsort garrison did get to safety in Arensburg. See RGAVMF, F479/905, 13 October, Day 2 of the Landing Operation. Also BA-MA, RM47/1217, KTB Sonderverband, entry 12 October 1917. Long after the battle, a German survey damage crew discovered that only one gun of four on Hundsort was put out of action; at Ninnast all three guns remained functional. This coincides with Reek's report. For the survey damage report, see RM47/126, Meeting at Admiralty, with BMA Ösel, 5.11.1917, Defense Requirements for the Island.

22. RGAVMF, F941/108, 78–86, report of battle. This file contains the report of Captain Reek, Sveshnikov's chief of staff. Captain Reek's report of the battle contains accounts from both individuals and unit headquarters and will be cited extensively as the "Reek Report" along with time and date. It is thorough. The Russians claimed the gunners at Ninnast did return fire, albeit not for long. Also F941/107, Conversation between the Chief of Staff of the Baltic Islands Fortified Position, Captain Reek, and Colonel Kruzenstiern, Chief of Staff, Land Forces Defense, 3 pm, 12 October.

23. Ruge, "Öselfahrt auf B110," 104. Volkmann, *Upternehmen Ösel*, 79–80.

24. RGAVMF, F941/108, Reek Report, Part 2, 78–86. Death companies, battalions, and regiments were used for specially arduous or hazardous missions. According to Wildman, "a few entrepeneurs of the rear" convinced Kerensky and his new upreme ommander, General Alexei Brusilov, that units composed of volunteers who pledged to fight to the death, would be useful "to arouse the revolutionary, offensive spirit in the Army." They would inspire the wavering regular battalions and were given distinctive insignia and banners. The most famous was the Women's Battalion of Death, organized by Maria Bochkareva. Her battalion fought in the Kerensky or June Offensive and later defended the Winter Palace against the Bolsheviks in November 1917. She later wrote memoirs with Isaac Don Levine, *Yashka: My Life as a Peasant, Officer and Exile* (New York: Frederick A. Stokes, 1919). See Wildman, *End of the Russian Imperial Army*, 2:79.

25. Ruge, "Öselfahrt auf B110," 105, confessed it was hard to tell if the ship fire did any good—one could not see the Russians in the woods. Occasionally they could make out Russian field gun emplacements, and they silenced these. Also Ruge, *SM Torpedo Boat B110*, 59. Cf. Volkmann, *Unternehmen Ösel*, 79–80; and BA-MA, RM 47/126, "Tätigkeit der Motorruderbarkassen während der 'Albionunternehmung,'" 1–2.

26. Ruge, "Öselfahrt auf B110," 105ff.

27. RGAVMF, F941/108, Report, Part 2, 78–86, and F941/107, Reek Report, 12 October. Reek says only two division-level batteries were lost, not the four claimed by Tschischwitz. Reek of course was getting reports hot from the fighting, and the 107th Division was in disarray. Cf. Tschischwitz, *Blaujacken und Feldgraue gen Ösel*, 41ff.

28. Volkmann, *Unternehmen Ösel*, 79–80.

29. Wieting, *Der Ostsee Krieg*, 126. Black-white-red were the German imperial colors.

30. RGAVMF, F941/108, Reek Report, Part 2, 78–86.

31. Tschischwitz, *Blaujacken und Feldgraue gen Ösel*, 38.

32. Kiep, " Die Eroberung der baltischen Inseln." See BA-MA, RM47/126, Flottenverband, Gg 1550, 24 October 1917, 19. The Germans later discovered a map of this minefield when they occupied Sveshnikov's headquarters in Arensburg. See RM47/127 Kriegstagebuch des Führers der II Aufklärungsgruppe, [Reuter], GG 1180, 1–15 October, entry 12.10.1917.

33. Ruge, "Öselfahrt auf B110," 107.

34. 1869–1943. Reuter commanded cruisers and reconnaissance forces for most of the war. His chief claim to fame came from a postwar assignment. Designated commander of the portion of the High Sea Fleet interred at Scapa Flow, Reuter scuttled some 66 of his ships rather than turning them over to the Allies as the Versailles Treaty called for. He had the ships sunk the morning the treaty was signed, 21 June 1919.

35. RM47/127, Kriegstagebuch des Führers der II Aufklärungsgruppe, [Reuter], GG 1180, 1–15 Oktober, entry of 12.10.1917; Tschischwitz, *Blaujacken und Feldgraue gen Ösel*, 48.

36. RGAVMF, F479/904, Sveshnikov to Razvozov, 23 October 1917.

37. RGAVMF, F941/108, Reek Report, Part 2, 78–86.

38. Volkmann, *Unternehmen Ösel*, 81–82; Tschischwitz, *Blaujacken und Feldgraue gen Ösel*, 67–70. XXIII Reservekorps, Ic Nr. 4105 op geh. 27.12.1917, 6–7, in BA-MA, N-291/10, Nachlaß Schmidt.

39. Volkmann, *Unternehmen Ösel*, 81–82; Tschischwitz, *Blaujacken und Feldgraue gen Ösel*, 67–70.; Tschischwitz, *Conquest of the Baltic Islands*, 56–57.

40. The Russians claim they left Papensholm at 0200 on the 13th as German cycle troops approached. See RGAVMF, F479/905, 13 October, Day Two of the Landing

Operation, 2:14 AM. The Germans claim they took the air station by noon the first day. Cf. Tschischwitz, *Blaujacken und Feldgraue gen Ösel*, 46–47.

41. See Möller-Witten, *Pour le Mérite*, 2:20ff.

42. Wieting, *Der Ostsee Krieg*, 127.

43. Lieutenant Backer to Lieutenant Ruge, "Brief eines auf Ösel eingesetzten Offiziers vom Regiment 255," in Ruge, "Öselfahrt auf B110," 120. Backer did admit the food was good. He and his soldiers helped themselves to eggs, butter and "other treasures."

44. Volkmann, *Unternehmen Ösel*, 83. At 8 PM, the transport fleet commander reported having unloaded all the infantry and cyclists along with the machine gun companies, although not their transport. On the west side of the bay, 400 horses and 70 wagons had gone ashore; on the opposite side, 130 horses, 30 wagons. BA-MA, RM 47/127, KTB Sonderverband.

45. RGAVMF, F479/905. 12 October—Day One of the Landing Operation, entry 9:39 AM. This file is filled with situation reports from every imaginable spot on Ösel and Dagö. As the reports of the sightings poured in, the headquarters had to feel overwhelmed by the volume of reports arriving from all directions.

46. RGAVMF, F479/906, Bakhirev transmission, 12 October, 9:42.

47. RGAVMF, F479/904. Dated 12 October 1917 (9 AM).

48. Saul, *Sailors in Revolt*, 159–60.

49. RGVIA, F2301-1-105, Cheremisov to Razvozov, #3038, 11 AM, 12 October 1917, 6; F2301-1-106, From Chief of Staff of the Northern Front, #5236, date unk. (internal evidence, 12 October) to commanders of the 12th, 1st, 5th Armies, 42nd Army Corps, Higher Chief of Staff, Naval Higher Chief of Staff.

50. RGVIA, F2301-1-105, Kerensky telegrams #7202, #7203, 12 October 1917 in Chief of Staff, Northern Front, #5256 and #5257, 9. The *Petropavlovsk* crime refers to an incident occurring after the Kornilov Coup of September 1917. See chapter 4, p. 81.

51. RGAVMF, F9479/904, Sveshnikov to Razvozov, 23 October 1917, 88–91.

52. RGVIA, Fond 407/Inventory Volume I, case 98, 190. Born 15 June 1862; entered military service in 1880. His original regiment was the Lithuanian Life Guards Regiment, where his path would have crossed with that of General Dukhonin, now head of Stavka, and assigned to the regiment 1895–1900.

53. RGAVMF, F941/108, part 2, Reek Report, Report of 1st Battery Commander, 107th Infantry Division, 86–94.

54. RGAVMF, F941/108, part 2, Reek Report, 85–86.

55. RGAVMF, F479/904, Sveshnikov Report, 23 October, 88–91.

56. RGAVMF, 941/107, Reek to Krusenshtieren, 12 October, 3 PM; F479/C904, Sveshnikov Report, 23 October 1917.

57. RGAVMF, F479/C904, Sveshnikov Report, 23 October 1917.

58. Ibid. He says that the meeting was with the soviet only, that Ivanov and Kolbe did not report until 8 PM. Cf. 941/108, Reek Report, part 3, which states that the two generals were present at the 4 PM meeting and reported at length concerning the situation. Confusing the issue further, Reek's log says he relayed the contents of the meeting to Colonel Kruzenstiern, General Ghenrikson's deputy, at 3 PM. See F941/107.

59. RGAVMF, F479/906, secret, Cheremisov to Razvozov. Entry 9:21 PM, 12 October 1917.

60. Order #18, 107th Infantry Division, 12 October 1917, in RGAVMF, 941/108, Reek Report, part 2, 86–94.

61. RGAVMF, 941/108, Reek Report, part 3. Telegram #0252, To: Bakhirev, Commander of the Fleet, Chief of Staff 13th Corps, Chief of Staff 12th Army, and Chief of Staff of the Naval Fortress, 12 October 1917.

62. RGAVMF, 941/108, Reek Report, part 3. Telegram #12463, To: Chief of Staff of Land Forces, Admiral Bakhirev, Chief of Staff 12th Army and Chief of Staff 13th Corps, 12 October 1917.

63. RGAVMF, F479/C906, #274, Lt. Prestin to Naval Chief of Staff, entry 10:30. 12 October 1917, 194.

64. RGAVMF, 941/108, Reek Report, part 3. Telegram #02459, to Commander 107th Infantry Division, 12 October 1917.

65. RGAVMF, F479/904, Lt. Prestin to Baltic Fleet, #273, 10:30 PM 12 October 1917, 56.

66. RGAVMF, F479/904, Lt. Prestin to Baltic Fleet, #273, 10:30 PM 12 October. Most Russians left with the remnants of the 107th Division on the 12th, but a final few remained until just after 11 PM on 13 October; F479/905, 13 October, Day Two of Operation, entry of 1300; F479/906, #271, Prestin to Naval Staff, 10:25 PM, 12 October, 271.

67. RGAVMF, F479/904, Sveshnikov Report, 23 October 1917; F941/108, Reek Report, part 3. Telegram Razvozov to Sveshnikov, #1615 9:30 PM 12 October; Sveshnikov to Razvozov, #406, 13 October (no time), and narrative, 146–47.

68. RGAVMF, F479/906, Abstracts from the conversation between Commander of the Fleet and Sveshnikov, 13 October 1917.

69. RGAVMF, F479/904, Sveshnikov Report, 23 October 1917; F941/108, Reek Report, part 3. Telegram #02602, Sveshnikov to Bakhirev, 14 October 1917.

70. RGAVMF, F479/906, Cheremisov, #3055, to Commander of the Fleet, urgent and secret; copy to Higher Chief of Staff and Higher Naval Chief of Staff, 14 October 1917, 271.

71. RGVIA, F409/148–139, Inventory Volume 1, case 172714.

72. RGVIA, F 409, record of service 155–108, Inventory volume 1, case 177541. His service record (updated in 1917) notes that he was married, albeit a second marriage, to a general's widow. Perhaps a divorce explains the dismissal for domestic circumstances.

73. Ibid.

74. RGAVMF, F941/106, Order #1 to Baltic Islands Defense Position, 13 October 1917.

75. RGAVMF, F479/904, Sveshnikov Report, 23 October 1917.

76. Backer, "Brief eines auf Ösel eingesetzten Offiziers vom Regiment 255,"120; also BA-MA, Nachlaß Schmidt, N-291/10, XXIII Reservekorps, "Eroberung," 7. Tschischwitz, *Blaujacken und Feldgraue gen Ösel*, 67–70.

77. BA-MA, Nachlaß Schmidt, N-291/10, XXIII Reservekorps, "Eroberung," 7. Tschischwitz, *Blaujacken und Feldgraue gen Ösel*, 67–70. RGAVMF, F941/108, Reek Report, part 2, 86–94.

78. Volkmann, *Unternehmen Ösel*, 84–85.

79. Ibid.

80. Ibid., 85ff.

81. RGAVMF, F941/108, Reek Report, part 2, Report, Commander, 1st Battery, 107th Infantry Division, 86–94.

82. Ibid. The artillery men never made it to Orrisar. On the 14th, at Kybuasser, an evacuation party rescued them. See chapter 7 and RGAVMF, F479/C904, report of Laidunisky Lighthouse keeper, 18 October, 121–22.

83. Volkmann, *Unternehmen Ösel*, 84ff.

84. Ibid., 70–71. In fact, the Russians had abandoned the city by 2:30 PM. See reports in RGAVMF F479/905, Summary of Operations (Landing Operation 10.12–10.20), 13 October—Day Two of the Landing Operation; entry 14:35 and 15:00. General von Kathen's report says the Germans captured one colonel, two lieutenants, and 260 soldiers. The

colonel must have been Popow and the soldiers the ones who waved white flags while firing at the First Battery, 107th Infantry Division. See BA-MA, Nachlaß Schmidt, N-291/10, XXIII Reservekorps, "Eroberung," 7.

85. Volkmann, *Unternehmen Ösel*, 86ff.

86. Tschischwitz, *Blaujacken und Feldgraue gen Ösel*, 70ff.; Volkmann, *Unternehmen Ösel*, 86ff.

87. Volkmann, *Unternehmen Ösel* (87) 86ff.

88. Backer, "Brief eines auf Ösel eingesetzten Offiziers vom Regiment 255," 120.

89. Tschischwitz, *Blaujacken und Feldgraue gen Ösel*, 76ff.

90. Ibid., 72.

91. BA-MA, Nachlaß Schmidt, N-291/10, XXIII Reservekorps, "Eroberung," 8.

7. ÖSEL, 12–16 OCTOBER 1917: THE ISLAND'S ENDS

1. Tschischwitz, *Blaujacken und Feldgraue gen Ösel*, 99ff.; BA-MA, RM47/127, KTB Sonderverband, 8:20 am, 14 October.

2. BA-MA, RM47/127, KTB Sonderverband, 12 October 1917, entry for 9:30 PM. RGAVMF, F941/108, Reek Report, part 2, 86–94. The Russians claimed they held up the 131st for three hours.

3. Tschischwitz, *Blaujacken und Feldgraue gen Ösel*, 110–11. The Russians said they destroyed the facilities completely, but the German use of the station belies their assertion. See RGAVMF, F479/C905, Day One (12 October) of the Landing Operation, entry 1030; also Riga Bay Naval Forces Report, 95; and F479/C906, Lt. Telepnev's report, 1128 hours; and Lt. Prestin #0777, to Naval Chief of Staff, received at 12:45 PM.

4. Möller-Witten, *Pour le Mérite*, 1:310. For the Riga and East Galicia campaigns, see Kriegsgeschichtlichen Forschungsanstalt des Heeres, *Der Weltkrieg, 1914–1918*, vol. 13, *Die Kriegführung im Sommer und Herbst 1917. Die Ereignisse außerhalb der Westfront bis November 1918* (Berlin: E.S. Mittler and Sohn, 1942), 159–78; 191–200.

5. RGAVMF, F479/905, 13 October, Day Two of the Landing Operation, entry 15:29, radio message to Zerel.

6. BA-MA, RM47/126, Daily Report, v. Kathen to Libau, 13 October 1917; NA, RGS 165/320/box 113, AAR XXIII Reservekorps, 11–12.

7. 1864–1946. He is best known for his role in bringing Turkey into the war on the German side in 1914 with his clever handling of the *Breslau* and *Goeben*.

8. Tschischwitz, *Blaujacken und Feldgraue gen Ösel*, 98ff.

9. BA-MA, RM47/127, KTB Sonderverband, 8:20 AM, 14 October.

10. RGAVMF, F941/108, Reek Report, part 2, report of 425th Infantry Regiment Treasurer [Paymaster] Moginov, 105–106.

11. Tschischwitz, *Blaujacken und Feldgraue gen Ösel*, 100–101. RGAVMF, F941/108, Reek Report, part 2, report of 425th Infantry Regiment Treasurer Moginov, 105–106.

12. Tschischwitz, *Blaujacken und Feldgraue gen Ösel*, 99ff.

13. Ibid., 107–108; Hopman, *Kriegstagebuch*, 246–47. RGAVMF, F479/905, Summary of the Operation Irbe–Ösel. Day Four, October 15, entry 1400–1412; and F941/108, Reek Report, part 2, report of 425th Infantry Regiment Treasurer Moginov, 105–106.

14. 1883–1919. Served with distinction at the Battle of Port Arthur in the Russo-Japanese War, but spent all of the First World War at the northern front headquarters. Rumor had it that he was a natural son of Tsar Alexander III. He went over to the Bolsheviks and represented them during negotiations at Brest-Litovsk, then became commandant at Kronstadt. He died of a stroke in Moscow.

15. RGAVMF, F479/905, Summary of the Operation. Day Four (15 October), entries of 1400, 1509, 1550, and 1737. In the same file there is another report of this action. Titled "Actions of the Riga Bay Naval Forces during the German Troops Landing on the Baltic Island," it is a daily summary of the chronological entries. The author is unknown, but Bakhirev's headquarters put it together, and it constitutes his full report. Its date of origin is unknown, but it seems to have been written just after Bakhirev left the Gulf of Riga. It will be cited in the future as Actions of the Riga Bay Naval Forces. See the entry in this file for 15 October 1917; F479/C908, Bakhirev to Razvozov, message #237, October 16, 1917, 8:20 AM, 74. This report was filed on the 16th, but it clearly refers to events from the day before.

16. RGVIA, F2031/106, Kerensky to Cheremisov, #11043, 20 October 1917, 67.

17. RGAVMF, F479/905, Summary of the Operation. Day Four (15 October), entry of 1550.

18. The *Graschdanin* had not destroyed the battery. The gun crews actually did so by removing fire control apparatus. NA, 1032, Marinestation der Ostsee, O. 23244, 6.11.1917, confirms the destruction of fire control mechanisms, but says the guns were serviceable. Cf. BA-MA, RM47/126, Meeting at Admiralty, with BMA Ösel, 5.11.1917. Cf. Tschischwitz, *Blaujacken und Feldgraue gen Ösel*, 106ff.

19. Tschischwitz, *Blaujacken und Feldgraue gen Ösel*, 100–101.

20. RGAVMF, F479/905, Summary of the Operation Irbe—Ösel. Day Three and Four (14 October, entry for 23:20; 15 October, entry 0300).

21. RGAVMF, F941/108, Reek Report, part 2, report of 425th Infantry Regiment Paymaster Moginov, 105–106, and F479/905, Abstracts from the Conversation between Altvater (Northern Front, Pskov) and Cherkassky (Baltic Fleet, Revel), entry for 11 AM October 3, 1917.

22. Tschischwitz, *Blaujacken und Feldgraue gen Ösel*, 100–101.

23. Ibid., 100ff.

24. Ibid., 103ff.

25. Ibid., 107–108.

26. BA-MA, RM5/4078, Kz 59625, 16.10.1917.

27. Tschischwitz, *Blaujacken und Feldgraue gen Ösel*, 106ff.

28. Wieting, *Der Ostsee Krieg*, 133–34.

29. BA-MA, RM8/127, Kriegstagebuch des I. Führers der Torpedobootsstreitkräfte, Nr. 4116, 1–17 Okt. 1917. This is a copy; the original is in file RM47/127, but it is missing one of the pages that is fortunately in RM8/127. In file RM 47/126, which contains the telegrams of situation reports, there is one recording the time *Bayern* reported hitting the mine as 0507. See also BA-MA, RM47/127, KTB Sonderverband, entry 0530 12 October 1917 and 11 AM, 13 October 1917.

30. RM8/127, Kriegstagebuch des I. Führers der Torpedobootsstreitkräfte, Nr. 4116, 1–17 Okt. 1917; Tschischwitz, *Blaujacken und Feldgraue gen Ösel*, 56–57. The Russian report of the bombardment came in at 7:40. See RGAVMF, F479/905, 12 October—Day One of the Landing Operation, entry 7:41 AM, 41.

31. NA, RGS 165/320/box 113, XXIII AAR, 10–11. A tiny field artillery detachment of two guns and a caisson of ammunition was to accompany the force heading for Orrisar. Its destination was St. Johannis (Jani), a small village on a promontory overlooking the entrance to the Small Sound. The guns could block Russian vessels attempting to enter the sound. Unloading difficulties thwarted this plan. It took over 48 hours to unload the guns. See Tschischwitz, *Blaujacken und Feldgraue gen Ösel*, 60.

32. RGAVMF, F941/108, part 2, Reek Report, 78–86.

33. Unfortunately, little can be found about this officer. In the immediate postwar years, a Captain von Winterfeld figured prominently in illegal German rearming efforts, but Winterfeld is a common name.

34. Winterfeld's orders are contained in RM47/127, 42 ID, Ia 1233, Divisionsbefehl für Abteilung v. Winterfeld, n.d.

35. BA-MA, RM62/183, Kdo der S-Flotille, GB 3912, 9.10.1917.

36. Upon receiving word of the German landings, Sveshnikov sent his treasury, construction, and supply departments to the mainland. Apparently the treasury people were slow. See RGAVMF, F479/C904, Sveshnikov Report, 23 October 1917.

37. The Russians claimed that two armored cars, the Third Platoon of the Arensburg Cavalry, and a few stragglers from Orrisar were all they had defending the causeway. See RGAVMF, F941/108, part 2, Reek Report, 86–94. Also F479/C905, Report of the Gulf of Riga Naval Defense Forces, 13 October, Day Two of the Landing Operation. Entry 8:10 AM, 13 October, contains the reports of the failed German effort to cross the causeway. Entry for 1 PM that day cites the 40–man strength.

38. Tschischwitz, *Blaujacken und Feldgraue gen Ösel*, 58ff. Sveshnikov's headquarters had received reports all day that German cyclists were headed for Orrisar. The first confirmation the Germans had captured the town and causeway came around 11:30 PM on 12 October. See RGAVMF, F479/C906, entry 2330.

39. Tschischwitz, *Blaujacken und Feldgraue gen Ösel*, 58–63. For the Russian version, see RGAVMF, F941/108, part 2, Reek Report, 97–99.

40. Tschischwitz, *Blaujacken und Feldgraue gen Ösel*, 58–63.

41. Ibid. RGAVMF, F941/108, part 2, Reek Report, 97–99. The Russian report does not mention the effort to come across the causeway the night of the 13th; it merely says the fighting near the bridgehead lasted until 11 PM, with only a few Russians getting through to Moon Island.

42. Tschischwitz, *Blaujacken und Feldgraue gen Ösel*, 58–63. RGAVMF, F941/108, part 2, Reek Report, 100–102. The Russians were running low on ammunition as well.

43. Volkmann, *Unternehmen Ösel*, 88–89.

44. Gagern, Firle, and Rollmann, *Krieg in der Ostsee*, 177.

45. BA-MA, RM47/126, Flottenverband, Gg 1555 O, 24 October 1917. 14ff. RGAVMF, F479/905, Summary, Day Four (15 October), entry for 1310. Also Kriegstagebuch des I. Führers der Torpedobootsstreitkräfte, entry 14 October, entry 4:45 PM.

46. BA-MA, Kriegstagebuch des I. Führers der Torpedobootsstreitkräfte, entry 15 October, 2:30 AM, report from 42 Inf. Div. and XXIII Corps that 65th Brigade has been in action with the Russians since 3 PM on the 14th. Tschischwitz, *Conquest of the Baltic Islands*, 89.

47. RGAVMF, F941/108, Reek Report, part 2, Report of 3rd Battery Commander, 100–102.

48. Ibid.

49. Volkmann, *Unternehmen Ösel* 88ff.

50. Backer, "Brief eines auf Ösel eingesetzten Offiziers vom Regiment 255," 120.

51. Tschischwitz, *Blaujacken und Feldgraue gen Ösel*, 72–74; Volkmann, *Unternehmen Ösel*, 88–89.

52. RGAVMF, F941/108, Reek Report, part 2, Report of 3rd Battery Commander, 100–101. The captain identified Ivanov's headquarters as located in Sombi, but this village no longer exists. It is not on any of the maps that have survived from that period. Several elements of the captain's report and others witnesses place the bulk of the 107th Division in the village of Peude, which still exists. Not only is Peude within a few kilometers of the

causeway, but the Russians had placed their field hospital at the Oti Manor, part of the village. Sombi likely was a part of Peude or a tiny village that later was incorporated into it.

53. Backer, "Brief eines auf Ösel eingesetzten Offiziers vom Regiment 255," 120.

54. RGAVMF, F479/905, Bakhirev Report (?), 29 October 1917; F479/C908, Bakhirev to Razvozov, #239, 16 October, 10:20 PM; See also F941/108, Reek Report, part 2, Report of Lt. Kazansky, 1st Battery, 103–104. Nekrasov, *Expendable Glory*, 109–10.

55. Volkmann, *Unternehmen Ösel*, 91.

56. Tschischwitz, *Blaujacken und Feldgraue gen Ösel*, 79ff. Flex's company had stormed the estate at Peude around 1500 on 15 October, at which point the Russians began to surrender. Deputy Officer Weschkalnitz had gone forward to demand the surrender of a Russian officer. The Russian laid a hand on his shoulder and said, "No, you are my prisoner." Weschkalnitz jumped back and hurled himself behind a rock for cover as the Russians opened fire on him. Flex, seeing this, jumped on a Russian horse, grabbed a saber from its scabbard, and raced toward the Russians. Several opened fire, one round hitting Flex's abdomen. He fell from the horse, and despite his painful wound, somehow managed to stop his angry men from murdering the Russian who had shot him, saying, "Leave him—he only did his duty." The manor house at the Peude Estate had been used by the Russians as a field hospital, so Flex was taken there and treated by a Russian doctor. He was soon assisted by a German physician, and both agreed that because of the loss of blood and the weakness of the patient, an operation was out of the question. The bullet had done great internal damage. Flex died early in the afternoon of the 16th—the birthday of his youngest brother, Otto, who had been killed earlier in the war. The body was taken to a small pavilion in a park for burial. Originally the entire regiment was to have been present, but orders to march had come, and the regiment had departed, leaving only nine men for a burial detail.

57. RGAVMF, F941/108, Reek Report, part 2, Report of Lt. Kazansky, 1st Battery, 103–104.

58. RGAVMF, F479/C908, Bakhirev to Razvozov, #239, 16 October, 10:20 PM. Bakhirev's radio message said the village church where General Ivanov had fled before his capture was Geide. There is no village by that name, but the division was in Peude. The church there is large and made of stone, and would provide good cover from small arms fire. In Russian, the only difference between Peude (Геиде)and Geide (Пеиде) would be the first letter. The Russian letter for G is Г and for P is П. Perhaps the "P" was smeared or the second leg faded, making the P appear as a G. There was no village named Geide, and the 107th Division was definitely in Peude.

59. Volkmann, *Unternehmen Ösel*, 91–92.

60. BA-MA, N-291/50, Nachlaß Schmidt, XXIII Reservekorps, Ic Nr. 4105 op geh., 27 December 1917, 9.

61. BA-MA, RM/47/127, KTB Sonderverband, Entry 16 October 11 PM.

8. THE CAPTURE OF MOON AND DAGÖ ISLANDS

1. RGAVMF, F479/910, Abstracts from the Conversation between Captain Altvater in Pskov and Admiral Razvozov in Reval, October 15, 1917, 12 PM, 53–55; and F479/C904, conversation between Razvozov and Cherkassky, 14 October, 1:40 PM. See also RGVIA, F2031/1/106, Commander Northern Front, #5344, 15 October 1917, 125.

2. There is no date for the establishment of this headquarters; thus in all likelihood, General Cheremisov formed it on the eve of the battle. There is no reference to it in any correspondence preceding Albion, nor is there discussion about forming it during the

battle. Only Cheremisov would have had the authority to staff it with a general and colonel and to assign an infantry division (the 118th) to Razvozov.

3. RGAVMF, F941/108, Reek Report, part 3, 146ff.

4. RGVamF, F479/906, Cheremisov to Commander of the Fleet, urgent and secret, 14 October 1917.

5. RGVamF, F479/904, Sveshnikov Report, 23 October 1917; F941/108, part 3, #02606, Sveshnikov to Razvozov, 19 October 1907; #02067; Sveshnikov to Ghenrikson, 19 October 1917; Flag Officer Shents to Sveshnikov, n.d.

6. RGVIA, F409 (9 April 1869–) record of service 1933, 1913, Inventory volume 1, case 46384; F407, Inventory volume 1, Case 104, p. 166.

7. 1875–1941. From Tartu, he achieved fame by defending Estonia from the Red Army in 1918–19, eventually becoming a major general and later minister of defense. In the 1930s he was mayor of Tartu, then lord mayor of Tallinn (Reval). http://www.mil.ee/index_eng.php?s=ajalu; and http://www.okupatsioon.ee/english/photos/97-27aa2.html (31 August 2006). When the Soviets reoccupied the Baltic countries in 1940, they executed him.

8. In a vain effort to keep a handle on rising Baltic nationalism, Kerensky's Provisional Government had authorized the formation of Estonian regiments. Only one was formed, in May 1917, and its first engagement was with the Germans on Moon Island. See Rauch, *Baltic States*, 34; and http://www.mil.ee/index_eng.php?s=ajalugu (31 August 2006).

9. RGVIA, F2031-1-105, About the Occupation of Ösel by Germans in September and October 1917, Dates: 12–20 October, 1917, 146–47.

10. RGVIA, F2031-1-103, Commander of the 13th Army Corps, copy to Commander of the 6th Army Corps, #04655, September 24, 1917. Parsky signed this on the 21st, but did not publish it until three days later.

11. RGVamF, F479/905, Day 2 of Landings, 13 October 1917, entry for 1300.

12. RGAVMF, F479/C906, Conversation between Razvozov and Bakhirev, 14 October, 1300, p. 272; F941/108, Reek Report, Ghenrikson to Altvater, #019, 15 October 1917, 111–12; see also F479/C905, October 13, Day Two of the Landing Operation, entry for 1700, and October 15, Day Four of the Landing Operation, entry for 1200.

13. 1881–1967. See Rear Admiral Timirev, *Vospominania Morskogo Ofitsera*, 164. There is confusion about his rank at this time. One report says captain, second class; another, commander.

14. RGAVMF, F479/C905, October 1–Day Three of the Landing Operation, entry 1345; A Dispatch about the Military Operations of the Independent Reval Naval Death Battalion from 12 to 21 October 1917; F479/904, Captain of Destroyer *Silny*, To the Headquarters of the Commander of the Baltic Fleet, October 23, 1917, 115–16; F479/C906, Abstracts from the conversation between Count Cherkassky and Warrant Officer Lesgaft, 14 October, 1700, p. 100.

15. RGAVMF, F479/C904, abstracts of conversation between Razvozov and Cherkassky, 1:40 PM, 14 October 1917.

16. Actions of the Riga Bay Naval Forces; Abstracts from a conversation between Altvater (in Pskov) and Cherkassky (in Reval), 11 AM, 16 October, 121–23. Also F941/108, Reek Report, Kruzenstieren to Altvater, #041, 15 October 1917, 116.

17. RGAVMF, F941/108, Reek Report, report from battalion commander, 112–13. Internal evidence indicates the officer was most likely Lieutenant Colonel Rudnev, Third Battalion, 470th Dankovsky Infantry Regiment.

18. RGAVMF, F479/C905, Reval Naval Death Battalion Report from 12 to 21 October 1917.

19. RGAVMF, F941/108, Reek Report, report from battalion commander, 112–13.

20. Ibid.

21. Tschischwitz, *Blaujacken und Feldgraue gen Ösel*, 126.

22. RGAVMF, F941/108, Reek Report, Testimony of Lt. Rebane, 118ff. F479/C905, Reval Naval Death Battalion Report from 12 to 21 October 1917.

23. RGAVMF, F941/108, Reek Report, Lt. Colonel Rudnev, 122–23.

24. Actions of the Riga Bay Naval Forces, 15 October 1917.

25. Ibid., 95ff.

26. RGAVMF, F941/108, Reek Report, Captain Krotkov, 2d Battalion, 470th Infantry Regiment, 122–23.

27. Actions of the Riga Bay Naval Forces, 95ff.

28. See Tschischwitz, *Conquest of the Baltic Islands*, 171, for the order of battle.

29. NA, 1237, 42d ID, Ia 1394, 29.10.1917, "Erfahrungen bei der Eroberung der Inseln Ösel, Moon und Dagö," 5.

30. NA, RGS 165/320/box 113, XXIII Reserve Corps After Action Report, 16–17; BA-MA, 47/126, "Tätigkeit der Motorruderbarkassen während der 'Albionunternehmung,'" 1. Tschischwitz, *Conquest of the Baltic Islands*, 173ff.

31. RGAVMF, F479/C908, Conversation between Commander of the Fleet (Razvozow) and Commander-in-Chief of the Northern Front (Cheremisov), October 4, 263ff.

32. Ibid.

33. RGAVMF, F941/108, Reek Report, Lt. Colonel Rudnev, 122–23; and Captain Krotkov, 2d Battalion, 470th Infantry Regiment, 122–23; Lt. Rebane, 1st Battalion, Estonian Regiment, 124ff.

34. NA, RGS 165/320/box 113, XXIII Reservekorps After Action Report; Tschischwitz, *Conquest of the Baltic Islands*, 174ff. One of the officers leading the Germans across the Causeway was Prince Joachim of Prussia, a captain and the youngest son of the kaiser.

35. RGAVMF, F479/C905, Reval Naval Death Battalion Report from 12 to 21 October 1917.

36. RGAVMF, F941/108, Reek Report, Captain Krotkov, 2d Battalion, 470th Infantry Regiment, 122ff.

37. RGAVMF, F941/108, Reek Report, Lt. Rebane, 124–25.

38. Whoever wrote the report for the death battalion claimed incorrectly that Rudnev's regiment also vanished, fleeing and regrouping near Martynov's headquarters. RGAVMF, F479/C905, Reval Naval Death Battalion Report from 12 to 21 October 1917.

39. RGAVMF, F941/108, Reek Report, Lt. Colonel Rudnev and Captain Chelishev, 126ff.

40. Ibid. See also F479/C905, Report of 13th Torpedo Boat Division Commander (Captain 1st Rank Shevelev), 158–65, and Actions of the Riga Bay Naval Forces, 18 October 1917, 120–21. Nekrasov, *Expendable Glory*, 109–10, says he knew Shevelev when he (Nekrasov) was a teenager, and Shevelev claimed he commanded the Third Destroyer Division. Nekrasov said Soviet-era historians got it wrong when they said the captain commanded the Thirteenth Division, but the contemporary records clearly indicate the Thirteenth Division.

41. RGAVMF, F479/C905, Reval Naval Death Battalion Report from 12 to 21 October 1917; Tschischwitz, *Blaujacken und Feldgraue gen Ösel*, 129ff.; Backer, "Brief eines auf Ösel eingesetzten Offiziers vom Regiment 255," 120.

42. BA-MA, RM47/126, telegram from Schmidt to Admiralty, 1910, 18 October 1917 and RM5/4078, Kathen's telegram, Kz60517 to Admiralstab, 19.10 1612; Nachlaß Schmidt N-291/10, XXIII. Reservekorps, "Eroberung," 9. Estonian Defense Forces; Chronology, http://www.mil.ee/index_eng.php?s=ajalugu (31 August 2006).

43. BAMA, RM5/4078, Representative of Admiralty at OHL, 15 October, also Kz 59625, 16.10; Nachlaß Schmidt, N-291/10, "Die Eroberung der baltischen Inseln,"

Flottenverband Gg. 1555 O, 24 October 1917, 10–11. This is Admiral Schmidt's After Action Report. RGAVMF, F479/C905, Summary of Operations (Landing Operation 12–20 October)—Day One of the Landing Operation. The Russians reported the Germans took machine guns from Battery #34.

44. RM47/126, Sonderverband, G 1200 A 4., 17.10.1917, Report of interrogation.

45. See Melkonov, *Batarei Moonzunda (Batteries of Moon Sound)*, 7; and BA-MA, RM47/126, Flgrst. Windau, 4996, to KoFlieg, 1.10.1917. Achkasov also says the batteries were largely unprotected, and supposedly the range finder was the wrong model for the 12" guns. Achkasov, Kozlov, and Solov'ev, "Operations of the Russian Fleet," 229ff.

46. BA-MA, Nachlass Schmidt, N-291/10, Landungskorps, Ic 4105 op. geh., 27 December 1917, 10.

47. BAMA, RM5/4078, 16.10, Sonderverband to Admiralty.

48. BAMA, RM5/4078, Kz 60017, Vetrtr Adm in OHL, 17.10. 1630 hr.

49. BA-MA, RM42/135, Leiter der Dagö Unternehmung, Bericht ueber Ein- und Ausschiffung Murikabucht und Dagö vom 18.-27. Oktober 1917.

50. Ibid.; Nachlaß Schmidt, N-291/10, Landungskorps, Ic 4105 op. geh., 27 December 1917, 10; and "Die Eroberung der baltischen Inseln," Flottenverband Gg. 1555 O, 24 October 1917, 11.

51. RGAVMF, F479/C905, Summary of Operations (Landing Operation 12–20 October), October 18, Day 7 of the Landing Operation, 12 PM.

52. Ibid., 11:45 AM, 1:15, 4 and 3:40 PM entries.

53. Ibid., entries for 8:35 and 10:30 PM.

54. RGAVMF, F479/C905, entry October 18, 120–21. The number of soldiers in an echelon is unknown. General von Kathen claimed in his report that the Russians evacuated soldiers from Dagö on the 17th as well as the 18th. There is no evidence of this in the Russian files. See BA-MA, Nachlaß Schmidt, N-291/10, Landungskorps, Ic 4105 op. geh., 27 December 1917, 10.

55. RGAVMF, F479/C905, entry October 19, 0300.

56. Ibid., entries October 19, 1:30, 2:30, 5:50, and 8:00 AM.

57. Ibid., entry October 19, 145 PM.

58. Ibid., entries October 19, 2:30, and 9:15 PM.

59. Ibid., Summary of Operations (Landing Operation 12–20 October)—Day 8 (19 October), report from 4:20 and 5:40 PM; and Day 9 (20 October) 1:05 AM.

60. BA-MA, Nachlaß Schmidt, N-291/10, Landungskorps, Ic 4105 op. geh., 27 December 1917, 10.

61. RGAVMF, F479/C905, entries October 20, 8:15, 8:25, 9:30, and 10:59 AM.

62. Tschischwitz, *Blaujacken und Feldgraue gen Ösel*, 131; BAMA, RM5/4078, Berlin, Kz 60644. 19.10; Kz 61000 20.10. Kz 61199, 21.10.

63. RGAVMF, F479/C905, entries from October 20, 9:35, :55 PM.

64. RGVIA, 2031/1/106, Captain Calnitsky to Commander-in-Chief, Northern Front, 12:45 PM, 25 October 1917, 33. Cf. Calnitsky's figures with the morning report figure of 2,435 men on 12 October in RGAVMF, F941/108, Chief of Staff, Baltic Islands Fortified Position, 12 October 1917.

65. RGAVMF, F479/C905, entries from October 20, 2335, 2355 hours. See also 204–205, Conversation between Captains Rengarten and Altvater, 22 October, 10:25 AM. The Germans claimed to have captured about 750 Russians. See BA-MA, Nachlaß Schmidt, N-291/10, Landungskorps, Ic 4105 op. geh., 27 December 1917, 10.

66. BA-MA, RM 47/126, radiogram 1930, 20 October 1917, *Moltke* to Admiralty, 0648, 23 October; NA, 1031, Kz. 60935, 20 October 1917.

9. THE NAVAL BATTLE FOR THE BALTIC ISLANDS

1. BA-MA, N-291/10, XXIII Reservekorps. Ic. Nr. 4105, 27 December 1917, "Die Eroberung der baltischen Inslen," 3ff.; RM47/126, Flottenverband, Gg 1555 O, 24 October 1917, 7. This report is Schmidt's immediate summary of the operation.

2. BA-MA, RM47/126, Flgrst. Windau, 4996, to KoFlieg, 1.10.1917.

3. Tschischwitz, *Blaujacken und Feldgraue gen Ösel*, 85ff.

4. See BA-MA, RM47/127, Flottenverband, Gg B. 491/0, 29.9.1917, Anlage #2 to OpBefehl 2, Sonderbefehl für den Chef der Suchflotilla Rosenberg. Also Sonderverband, Gg 917/O, Nachtrag zum Sonderbefehl . . . des Landungskorps Rosenbergs gegen die Batterie auf Kapp Pamerort., 7.10.1917.

5. BA-MA, RM62/183, Kdo der S-Flotille, GB 3912, 9.10.1917; RM 47/127, KTB Sonderverband, entry 24 September 1917. RM 47/127, Gg380/O, Sonderbefehl für das Landungskorps Rosenbergs bei der Batterie auf Kap Pamerort. 27.9.1917; RM47/127, Sonderverband, Gg 193 O, Operationsplan, 25 September 1917.

6. BA-MA, RM8/127, Kriegstagebuch des I. Führers der Torpedobootsstreitkräfte, Nr. 4116, 1–17 Okt. 1917, entry 0620, 12 October 1917. Entries from 0500–0620 on 12 October are found in this file. Commodore Heinrich's logbook, but without the entries for the dates above, can be seen in file RM 47/127.

7. See Achkasov, Kozlov, and Solov'ev, "Operations of the Russian Fleet," "233.

8. RGAVMF, F479/905, Summary of Operations (Landing Operation 09.29–10.07), 12 October—Day One of the Landing Operation. Entry 10:30 PM, Bakhirev Reports. Bakhirev said he dispatched the destroyers as soon as he heard of the landings.

9. BA-MA, 47/127, Kriegstagebuch des I. Führers der Torpedobootsstreitkräfte, Nr. 4116, 1–17 Okt. 1917, 10 October 1917, entry 11 AM.

10. Ibid., 12 October 1917, entries 0925, 0945, 1015, 1023.

11. Ibid., 10 October 1917, entry 4:34 PM; RGAVMF, F479/905, Actions of the Riga Bay Naval Forces, 12 October 1917, 95–96. Entry 10:30 PM, Bakhirev Reports. Also see F479/906, Bakhirev Report, #218, to Razvozov, midnight, 12 October 1917, 197. This report, a page and a half long, was telegraphed to Razvozov the day of the engagement with the German battleships. See also Graf, *Russian Navy*, 148, and Tschischwitz, *Blaujacken und Feldgraue gen Ösel*, 85–88.

12. BA-MA, 47/127, Kriegstagebuch des I. Führers der Torpedobootsstreitkräfte, Nr. 4116, 1–17 Okt. 1917, 10 October 1917, entry 12:30 PM. The Germans discovered one gun had been destroyed from shelling; they blew up the remaining three. Also RGAVMF, F479/905, Summary of Operations (Landing Operation 12–25 October), 12 October—Day One of the Landing Operation. Entries 8:05, 9:19 AM, 12:45 and 12:55 PM. The Russian commander on Dagö confirmed the Toffri battery destruction the next day, entry for 13 October—Day Two, 1055 AM.

13. Ibid., Actions of the Riga Bay Naval Forces, 12 October 1917, 95.

14. Ruge, *SM Torpedo Boat B110*, 62.

15. RGAVMF, F479/906, phone conversation, Bakhirev to Razvozov, 1 PM, 13 October, 272.

16. RGAVMF, F479/905, Actions of the Riga Bay Naval Forces, 12–13 October 1917, 95ff. The admiral outlined his plan to Fleet Commander Razvozov, midnight, 12 October 1917, F479/906, #218 (p. 197) and a second conversation later that night. One of *Pripyat's* mines apparently damaged B 98 two days later.

17. BA-MA, 47/127, Kriegstagebuch des I. Führers der Torpedobootsstreitkräfte, Nr. 4116, 1–17 Okt. 1917, 13 October 1917, entry 5:45 PM.

18. RGAVMF, F479/905, Summary of Operations, Day Three (14 October), Report of Admiral Razvozov, entry of 8:30 PM. Also, Actions of the Riga Bay Naval Forces, 17

October 1917, 95ff., says *Grom* took a shell from the *Kaiser* in a mine storage compartment. An earlier entry recorded at 12:15 PM reported that *Grom* took nineteen hits, but this figure is nowhere else repeated and seems to be an entry made by some excited individual. Admiral Stark, commander of the Russian destroyer force, says *Grom* caught fire only when the Germans approached her. Otherwise his report duplicates the others. F479/C907, Report, Admiral Stark, #1747, 15 October, 8:23 AM, 179ff.

19. Graf, *Russian Navy*, 149–50.

20. Ruge, "Öselfahrt auf B110," 109; Graf, *Russian Navy*, 149–50.

21. BA-MA, 47/127, Kriegstagebuch des I. Führers der Torpedobootsstreitkräfte, Nr. 4116, 1–17 Okt. 1917, 14 October 1917, entry 1:38 PM.

22. Graf, *Russian Navy*, 150. When informed about *Grom's* sinking, Bakhirev was furious and complained about the cowardly crew for nearly causing the loss of the *Chrabry*.

23. RGAVMF, F479/905, Summary of Operations, Day Three, entries from around noon to about 3 PM. Cf. Actions of the Riga Bay Naval Forces, 14 October 1917, 95ff.

24. BA-MA, 47/127, Kriegstagebuch des I. Führers der Torpedobootsstreitkräfte, Nr. 4116, 1–17 Okt. 1917, 14 October 1917, entry 1:45 PM. These objects were very likely the mines that took out the B 98 the next day, and in all probability were the mines laid by *Pripyat* on the 13th. For a summary of what information the Germans gained from interrogating the eight prisoners, see BA-MA, RM47/126, Sonderverband, G 1227 A4, 15.10.1917.

25. Ruge, "Öselfahrt auf B110," 109; Tschischwitz, *Blaujacken und Feldgraue gen Ösel*, 90ff.

26. BA-MA, 47/127, Kriegstagebuch des I. Führers der Torpedobootsstreitkräfte, Nr. 4116, 1–17 Okt. 1917, 14 October 1917, entry 3:35 PM.

27. Ibid., entry 10:05 PM.

28. See chapter 8, p. 159.

29. BA-MA, 47/127, Kriegstagebuch des I. Führers der Torpedobootsstreitkräfte, Nr. 4116, 1–17 Okt. 1917, 15 October 1917, entry 12:05 PM. RGAVMF, F479/905, Actions of the Riga Bay Naval Forces, 14 October 1917, 95ff., indicates the *Pripyat* reported laying mines on a meridian that ran north from Pavasterort to the east end of the Soela Sound.

30. Ruge, "Öselfahrt auf B110," 111.

31. Ibid., 115.

32. RGAVMF, F479/C907, Phone call, #225, Bakhirev to Razvozov, 15 October 1917, 336; F479/C908, Phone call, #237, Bakhirev to Razvozov, 8:23 AM, 15 October 1917, 74.

33. Wieting, *Der Ostsee Krieg*, 127–33.

34. Tschischwitz, *Blaujacken und Feldgraue gen Ösel*, 104ff.

35. BA-MA, RM 47/127, KTB Sonderverband, 15 October, 7 PM; 8 PM entries.

36. Wieting, *Der Ostsee Krieg*, 134.

37. BA-MA, RM 47/127, KTB Sonderverband, 16 October, 8 AM; RM 47/126, Kommando, III Geschwader, B.N. Gg 535/0, 22 October 1917, 1–2. The Third Squadron received Schmidt's order to attack with all means at 11:50 AM, 16 October 1917.

38. Wieting, *Der Ostsee Krieg*, 134–35; BA-MA, RM 47/126, Kommando, III Geschwader, B.N. Gg 535/0, p. 2. The submarine proved to be the English boat C-26. See RGAVMF, F479/C905, Actions of the Riga Bay Naval Forces, 18 October 1917, 95–108. England had sent several submarines to the Baltic, and they formed a squadron, led by Commander F. N. A. Cromie, operating out of Hango and Reval. See Leslie H. Ashmore, *Forgotten Flotilla: British Submarines in Russia 1914–1919* (Portsmouth: Manuscript Press, 2001).

39. BA-MA, RM 47/126, Kommando, III Geschwader, B.N. Gg 535/0, p. 3; RM 47/127, KTB Sonderverband, 16 October, entry 9:19 PM.

40. BA-MA, RM 47/126, Kommando, III Geschwader, B.N. Gg 535/0, 22 October 1917, 2ff.

41. Ibid., 4–5. What the Germans did not know was that the Russian longitude measurements were 1.2 minutes different from the ones the Germans used on their charts. In addition, the location of the newly discovered minefield was given incorrectly, making it appear further south and east than it was in reality. See Gagern, Firle, and Rollman, *Krieg in der Ostsee*, 259–60.

42. BA-MA, RM 47/126, Kommando, III Geschwader, B.N. Gg 535/0, 22 October 1917, 2ff.; Gagern, Firle, and Rollman, *Krieg in der Ostsee*, 260.

43. Wieting, *Der Ostsee Krieg*, 138.

44. RGAVMF, F479/C904, Telephonogram #240 Bakhirev to Commander of the Baltic Fleet, 97ff. There is no date on this message, but it appears to have been written within a day or two of the battle.

45. BA-MA, RM 47/126, Kommando, III Geschwader, B.N. Gg 535/0, 22 October 1917, 5.

46. Bakhirev, *Otchet*, 53.

47. RGAVMF, F479/C904, Telephonogram #240 Bakhirev to Commander of the Baltic Fleet, 97ff.

48. See chapter 8, p. 213.

49. RGAVMF, F479/C904, Report, Captain of the Battleship *Slava* to Commander of the Baltic Fleet, October 17,1917; October 13, 1917; Report on the Battle of 17 October, Captain of Cruiser *Bayan* to Commander of the Baltic Fleet, October 26, 1917; F479/C905, 95ff. Four bombers dropped eight bombs each. Nekrasov, *Expendable Glory*, 102, has destroyers from the Sixth and Ninth divisions accompanying Bakhirev, but this error comes from using an obsolete order of battle. Cf. Gagern, Firle, and Rollman, *Krieg in der Ostsee*, Appendices 1 and 5.

50. RGAVMF, F479/C904, Report, Captain of the Battleship *Slava* to Commander of the Baltic Fleet, October 17, 1917; October 17, 1917; Report on the Battle of 17 October, Captain of Cruiser *Bayan* to Commander of the Baltic Fleet, October 26, 1917; Captain of Destroyer *Silny* to Commander of the Baltic Fleet, 7 November 1917; BA-MA, RM 47/126, Kommando, III Geschwader, B.N. Gg 535/0, 22 October 1917, 5. Wieting, *Der Ostsee Krieg*, 140ff., says the Russians fired first.

51. RGAVMF, F479/C904, Captain of Cruiser *Bayan* to Commander of the Baltic Fleet, October 26, 1917; Captain of Destroyer *Silny* to Commander of the Baltic Fleet, 7 November 1917.

52. BA-MA, RM 47/126, Kommando, III Geschwader, B.N. Gg 535/0, 22 October 1917, 6.

53. Ibid., 6–7; RGAVMF, F479/C904; Report, Captain of the Battleship *Slava* to Commander of the Baltic Fleet, 17 October; Actions of the Riga Bay Naval Forces, 95ff.

54. RGAVMF, F479/C904, Captain of Destroyer *Silny* to Commander of the Baltic Fleet, 7 November 1917, and Bakhirev's report, 17 October, along with those from the *Slava* and *Bayan*. The Russian time was 11:48 AM, making it time for lunch.

55. Gagern, Firle, and Rollman, *Krieg in der Ostsee*, 263. Captain Antonov of the *Slava* reported seeing two German minesweepers sinking. RGAVMF, F479/C904, Report, Captain of the Battleship *Slava* to Commander of the Baltic Fleet, October 17, 1917; October 13, 1917.

56. BA-MA, RM 47/126, Kommando, III Geschwader, B.N. Gg 535/0, 22 October 1917, 9.

57. Ibid., 6.

58. RGAVMF, F479/C904,, Report, Captain of the Battleship *Slava* to Commander of the Baltic Fleet, October 17,1917; October 17, 1917; Captain of Cruiser *Bayan* to Commander of the Baltic Fleet, October 26, 1917; Actions of the Riga Bay Naval Forces, 5 October 1917, 95ff., says *Bayan* and *Graschdanin* each took a hit; *Slava* three. Behncke reported that *König* hit the *Bayan* and the *Slava*, which listed heavily; *Kronprinz* claimed four hits on *Graschdanin*. See BA-MA, RM 47/126, Kommando, III Geschwader, B.N. Gg 535/0, 22 October 1917, 7.

59. Bakhirev's report indicates that the turret was out of commission before the ships anchored for lunch; Captain Antonov says the damage occurred in the "second" battle. Cf. RGAVMF, F479/C904, Telephonogram #240 Bakhirev to Commander of the Baltic Fleet, 97ff. with Report, Captain of the Battleship *Slava* to Commander of the Baltic Fleet, October 17, 1917; October 17, 1917.

60. RGAVMF, F479/C904, Report, Captain of the Battleship *Slava* to Commander of the Baltic Fleet, October 17, 1917. Nekrasov's account of this battle in his book *Expendable Glory* relies on émigré literature, saying Antonov wanted to continue the fight, but Bakhirev ordered a withdrawal on explicit orders from Admiral Razvozov. Antonov's report, written the day of the battle, makes no reference to any such order from the Baltic Fleet commander, nor does Bakhirev's. In fact, at the time of the battle Razvozov was on the phone telling General Cheremisov he was waiting to hear from Bakhirev, who was engaged with the Germans, before deciding whether he would try to hold Moon Island.

61. RGAVMF, F479/C904, Captain of Cruiser *Bayan* to Commander of the Baltic Fleet, October 26, 1917. Behncke had written that the cruiser accompanying the Russian battleships joined the firing late and without much energy, but it is clear that for most of the battle *Bayan*'s 8″ guns were outranged and it had deliberately kept its speed slow. Cf. BA-MA, RM 47/126, Kommando, III Geschwader, B.N. Gg 535/0, 22 October 1917, 7.

62. BA-MA, RM 47/126, Kommando, III Geschwader, B.N. Gg 535/0, 22 October 1917, 8.

63. Ibid., 9; Hopman, *Kriegstagebuch*, 250ff. Hopman claimed that Kelm persuaded the Russian brigade of 5,000 to surrender. This is not correct; the Russians were 8 kilometers to the north and being pushed further northeast by the 138th and 255th regiments. The story seems to have originated from Lieutenant Commander Wieting's book. He says Kelm took a party of 80 men ashore and secured the fortress at Woi. Kelm and his 80 men spent a nervous night in the close proximity of 5,000 enemy. See *Der Ostsee Krieg*, 143–44.

64. RGAVMF, F479/C904, Telephonogram #240 Bakhirev to Commander of the Baltic Fleet, 97ff.

65. RGAVMF, F479/C904, Captain of Destroyer *Silny* to Commander of the Baltic Fleet, 7 November 1917; Captain of the Minesweeper *Minrep* to Commander of the Baltic Fleet, 26 October; Nekrasov, *Expendable Glory*, 107ff.

66. Actions of the Riga Bay Naval Forces, 95ff.

67. BA-MA, RM47/126; a radio report on 20 October from a gunnery team at Woi says the five 10″ guns appeared serviceable, but four of five 6″ guns were destroyed.

68. RGAVMF, F479/C904, Telephonogram #240 Bakhirev to Commander of the Baltic Fleet, 97ff.; Report, Captain of the Battleship *Slava* to Commander of the Baltic Fleet, October 17,1917; October 17, 1917; Captain of Cruiser *Bayan* to Commander of the Baltic Fleet, October 26, 1917.

69. Graf, *Russian Navy*, 153ff.

70. Bakhirev, *Otchet*, 69–70.

71. BA-MA, RM 47/126, Kommando, III Geschwader, B.N. Gg 535/0, 22 October 1917, 10.

72. BA-MA, RM 47/127, Kriegstagebuch des I. Führers der Torpedobootsstreitkräfte, Nr. 4116, 1–17 Okt. 1917, entry 3 PM.

73. Ibid., 3:30 PM, 3:45 PM; RM47/126, Sonderverband, 18 October, entry 12:50 AM, entry 4 PM.

74. BA-MA, RM47/126, KTB Sonderverband, entry 19 October, 10 AM. Tschischwitz, *Conquest of the Baltic Islands,* 199–200, says there were four, but this is contradicted by Schmidt.

75. BA-MA, RM47/126, KTB Sonderverband, entry 17 October, 7 PM.

76. Ibid., entry 18 October, 12 PM; RM8/127, KTB des Führers der IIte Aufklärungs-gruppe, GG 1180, 17 October 1917, radio message from 1745; entries 18 and 19 October.

77. Ibid., RM47/126, KTB Sonderverband, entries 19 October, 12:17 and 6 PM.

78. RGAVMF, F479/C909, Abstracts of conversations between Razvozov and Captain Altvater (navy liaison at northern front headquarters); conversations between Altvater and Captain Rengarten (operations officer, Baltic Fleet) and Admiral Cherkassky, Baltic Fleet chief of staff, 103–104; 312–16; Gagern, Firle, and Rollmann, *Krieg in der Ostsee,* 287. In fact, the Russians capitalized on their information and sent two submarines to the waters near Cape Hundsort to ambush Souchon's battleships once they left Tagga Bay.

79. RGAVMF, F479/C909, Cheremisov to Razvozov, #3213, 18 October, 1:30 PM; Abstracts from the conversation between Altvater and Rengarten, 19 October 1917.

80. RGAVMF, F479/C909, Conversations between Altvater, Rengarten and Cherkas-sky, 312–16.

81. Gagern, Firle, and Rollmann, *Krieg in der Ostsee,* 287.

82. RGAVMF, F479/C909, Conversations between Altvater, Rengarten, and Cherkas-sky, 312–16.

83. RGVIA, 2003-1-532, 3 September 1917–30 January 1918. Report of Commander-in-Chief of the Northern Front and Correspondence about Battle Operations. To Naval Chief of Staff of the Northern Front, from B. Bubnov, #4908, 20 October 1917, 225. Of course, the Russian-German duel was not fought in exactly "open water."

84. Gagern, Firle, and Rollmann, *Krieg in der Ostsee,* 288.

85. BA-MA, RM47/126, KTB Sonderverband, entry made on 20 October; RM5/4078, UC58, Kz 60770.

10. CONCLUSION

1. RGAVMF, F479/905, Actions of the Riga Bay Naval Forces, 19 October 1917, states, "The entire squadron safely reached the northern shore." See also "Report on the Actions of Cruiser *Admiral Makarov* in the Defense of the Baltic Islands, 30 October, 1917," 166–70; F479/C910, Conversation between Stark and Rengarten, 20 October, 39; Conver-sation between Razvozov and Stark, unk. date (probably 21 October), 81. The Germans claimed one of Bakhirev's ships fell out coming from the Moon Sound—a freighter. See Gagern, Firle, and Rollman, *Krieg in der Ostsee,* 288.

2. RGVIA, F2003/532, Notes of meeting of 18 October 1917 at Northern Front Head-quarters, written October 19, 1917/ #10930. General Dukhonin, at Stavka, had anticipated this requirement, and had ordered a corps from the Rumanian front and another from the southwest front. See F2031/106, Stavka to Northern Front, #7351, 18 October.

3. Long before the German assault, Cheremisov had his subordinates developing defense plans for the area. For example, see Lieutenant General Parsky's (Twelfth Army commander) order to the Thirteenth Army Corps, #04655, 24 September 1917, in RGVIA F2031/103.

4. RGVIA F2031/105, To: Commander of the Fleet, Order #3038, 11 AM, 12 October 1917, 1.

5. RGVIA F2031/106, Cheremisov, Order #5344, to Commanders of the 1st, 5th, 12th Armies, Commander of the Fleet, 15 October 1917, 125; and Order #5379, same addressees, 17 October 1917.

6. RGAVMF, F479/C908, Conversation between Razvozov and Cheremisov, 17 October, 263–68. In an earlier conversation that day with Captain Altvater, Razvozov indicated he would ask for permission to evacuate Reval. He never indicated he received permission.

7. Ibid., 312–16. For a reconstitution order, merging the regiments from the 107th and 118th Divisions, see RGVIA, F2031/105, Cheremisov to Razvozov and Ghenrikson, #3277, 20 October, 44.

8. RGVIA, F2031/106, Order #3215, 18 October 1917, 32.

9. BA-MA, 47/127, KTB Sonderverband, entries on 21 and 22 October reveal the Russians had thoroughly seeded the Moon Sound with mines, blocked it with sunken ships in a number of places, and set fires that were still raging at the Rogekyul fuel farm.

10. RGVIA, F2031/105, Order #2, Land Forces of the Baltic Islands Position, Hapsal, October 16, 1917, 34–36.

11. RGVamF, F479/C910, Conversation between Stark and Rengarten, 20 October, 39; conversation between Razvozov and Stark, unk. date (probably 21 October), 81.

12. General Knox, the English attaché to Stavka, knew as early as the 18th of October that the Germans had moved seven divisions to the west in the last two weeks, including five from the Riga area. See his *With the Russian Army*, 698. Cf. Ludendorff, *Ludendorff's Own Story*, 2:97–99, who says four left.

13. *Reval Observer (Revelsky Nablyudatel)*, #229, Thursday, 25 October 1917.

14. RGAVMF, F479/C881, Report of the Committee of [Baltic Fleet] Flag Officers, Helsingfors, 31 October, 1917, signed by Bakhirev and Stark.

15. RGAVMF, F479/C881, Razvozov to Navy Minister, #1882, 31 October 1917. Admirals Zarubaev and Patton commanded battleship brigades in the Baltic Fleet; Cherkassky was still Baltic Fleet chief of staff.

16. Saul, *Sailors in Revolt*, 176.

17. Browder and Kerensky, *The Provisional Government*, "General Verkhosky's Testimony Recommending Peace Negotiations before a Joint Session of the Committees on Defense and Foreign Affairs of the State Council," 3 November 1917, 3:1742, and conversation between Kerensky and General Dukhonin, 4–5 November 1917, 3:1744–45.

18. BA-MA, 47/127, KTB Sonderverband, 23 October 1917.

19. Ibid., 21 October 1917; RM5/4078, Kz 62008, Admiralty to Chef Sonderverband, 25.10.

20. BA-MA, 47/127, KTB Sonderverband, 20 October 1917. Schmidt offered to release the *Kaiserin* and *König Albert* from waiting at Danzig to return to the North Sea (Kiel). The Admiralty agreed on 22 October, and ordered the return of the *Prinzregent Luitpold*, *Emden*, and *Bayern* as well. Also Ruge, *SM Torpedo Boat B110*, 66.

21. BA-MA, 47/127, KTB Sonderverband, 25 October 1917.

22. NA, RG 166, 1031, AdM Akten Albion, Schmidt to Berlin, KZ 60935, 20 October; BA-MA, RM 47/127, KTB Sonderverband, 21 October. See also RM 47/126, Note Flag Lt to Adm. Scheer, 27.10. 1917; 0835.

23. NA, RG 165, 1031, Schmidt to Adm Stab, 954, 31.10; 1032, Chef Adm Stab, O. 1074 II, 1.11.1917; BA-MA RM 47/126, SS Berlin, 1535, 1.11.1917.

24. BA-MA, RM8/127, KTB, 4 November 1917.

25. BA-MA, RM42/135, 8AOK Ia 3587/17 op to OBOST, durch Offiziere, 17.10.1917, to H.Gr Eichhorn. General von Kathen's comments, see BA-MA, RM42/134, XXIII Reserve Korps, Ia 621/10 op, Kathen to 8AOK, n.d.

26. BA-MA, RM5/4078, Chef Admiralstabs 13.10. to Kiel.

27. Ibid., RM5/4078, Kz 61182, 21.10.

28. Ibid., RM42/135, 8AOK Ia 3587/17 op to OBOST, durch Offiziere, 17.10.1917, to H.Gr Eichhorn. RM42/134, 8AOK to XXIII, Ia 622/10, 18.10.1917. Chef, Marine Kabinett to OdO, 24.10. and 25.10. OBOST wanted a retired admiral to serve as a naval advisor, but the Admiralty instead sent Commander Tegtmeyer from the Special Staff. A complete listing of what units were assigned to what island is given at Appendix 9, Gagern, Firle, and Rollmann, *Krieg in der Ostsee*, 428.

29. *Arensburger Zeitung*, 17 November 1917. "We have lived through hard times, and as we faced the worst, just in the nick of time came our salvation with the landing of the German troops on Ösel on the 12th of October, rescuing us from all sorts of mounting oppression. Enslaved by a short-sighted, ruthless despotism, threatened by utopian notions of an unwashed mob, we found ourselves on the edge of perdition. Our sacred properties stood in the balance. Our nationality, our mother-tongue, the faith of our fathers, the hundreds of years of our culture—it all faced destruction. Our economic existence stood threatened. As we read the most terrible accounts of abominations perpetrated by the inhuman Russian soldier-rabble in Latvia and the mainland, we were overcome by feelings of boundless thanks to the All Mighty who saved us from such horrors at the very last moment. Next to God we owe our thanks to the victorious German soldiers, who, through their brilliant strategy and bravery broke the yoke of our oppressors, and we confidently trust, have freed us for eternity from this darkness."

30. Schücking, *Ein Jahr auf Ösel*, passim.

31. Rauch, *Baltic States*, 43–46.

32. Ibid., 46–52. In Courland, OBEROST authorities made no attempt to govern through native Estonians. They relied totally on the Baltic Barons. Liulevicius, *War Land*, chapter 6, "Crisis."

33. Schücking, *Ein Jahr auf Ösel*, 110ff.

34. Tschischwitz, *Conquest of the Baltic Islands*, 204–205.

35. NA, RG 165/320/box 113, XXIII Reserve Corps; BA-MA, N-291/50, Nachlaß Schmidt, XXIII Reservekorps, Ic Nr. 4105, op. geh., 27 December 1917, 11.

36. RGAVMF, F479/C905, Actions of the Riga Bay Naval Defense Forces, 20 October 1917.

37. BA-MA, N-291/50, Nachlaß Schmidt, XXIII Reservekorps, Ic Nr. 4105, op. geh., 27 December 1917, 11.

38. Gagern, Firle, and Rollmann, *Krieg in der Ostsee*, Appendix 8.

39. Ludendorff, *Ludendorff's Own Story*, 2:122.

40. Hindenburg, *Aus meinem Leben*, 203–204. He hints that the Germans could have accomplished the deed had they thought it necessary and had they not had other fronts to worry about.

41. Wildman, *End of the Russian Imperial Army*, 2:225.

42. Hindenburg, *Aus meinem Leben*, 203–204.

43. Ludendorff, *Ludendorff's Own Story*, 2:122.

44. Ibid., 2:127, 129. The request for an armistice came on the 21st of November.

45. RGVAMF, F479/C881, Bakhirev to Razvozov, 31 October 1917. The latter agreed. See his note, same day, to the navy minister.

46. Tschischwitz, *Conquest*, 236, 244. In his next sentence, the author says "it enabled the Bolshevists [sic] to establish their power."

47. During the operation, Admiral Schmidt ordered his units to begin preparation of after action reports. He used them in his report. The army did the same, with both the Twenty-third Corps and the Forty-second Division preparing their own.

48. Tschischwitz, *Conquest of the Baltic Islands*, 206–35.

49. Jeter A. Isely and Philip A. Crowl, *The U.S. Marines and Amphibious War: Its Theory and Its Practice in the Pacific* (Princeton: Princeton University Press, 1951). A careful reading of chapters 2 and 3 will reveal the similarity between evolving U.S doctrine and the German practice in the Baltic, but Isley and Crowl never mention the German operation. Cf. Kenneth J. Clifford, *Amphibious Warfare Development in Britain and America from 1920–1940* (New York: Laurens, 1983). The English adopted many techniques used by the Germans, but there were some differences. The English, for example, did not believe daylight amphibious assaults could succeed until 1942.

50. Dr. Evelyn M. Cherpak, archivist, U.S. Navy War College, Newport, R.I., e-mail letter to author. Albion was not in their curriculum, but twice a Marine Corps colonel gave lectures on the operation.

51. Holger Herwig, *Luxury Fleet*, 236; and *The German Naval Officer Corps: A Social and Political History, 1890–1918* (London: Oxford, 1973), 224ff; A. Harding Ganz, "'Albion'—The Baltic Islands Operation," *Military Affairs* 42, no. 2 (1978): 91–97.

52. Gagern, Firle, and Rollmann, *Krieg in der Ostsee*, 161–62.

53. Courtland, N.Y., 1985, 29ff.

54. Herwig, *Luxury Fleet*, 236.

11. EPILOGUE

1. Biographical information and occasionally parts of the award citation can be found in Möller-Witten, *Pour le Mérite*. Each recipient is listed alphabetically.

2. Graf, *Russian Navy*, 147.

3. Timirev, *Vospominanya Morskogo Ofitsera*, 166.

4. General Max Hoffmann, the OBOST chief of staff who bullied Volkmann, claimed to have had many conversations with Altvater at Brest-Litovsk. Altvater, whom Hoffmann calls the "defender of the islands," stated that the Russian troops were so permeated with "Bolshevik propaganda" that it was impossible to think of a real defense. "The troops simply melted away before his eyes." See *The War of Lost Opportunities*, by General von Hoffmann (New York: International Publishers, 1925), 192. One or the other of these old warriors apparently had some memory problems. Altvater was never on the islands.

5. BA-MA, N-291/15, Nachlaß Schmidt, passim.

BIBLIOGRAPHY

PRIMARY SOURCES

German Federal Military Archive (Bundesmilitärarchiv), or BA-MA

N 239, Nachlaß Levetzow
N 291, Nachlaß Schmidt
RM5/4078, Albion, Bd. I, Angefangen 1.9.1917; Endet 29.10.1917.
RM5/4079, Albion, Bd. II, Angefangen 30.10.191; Endet 15.12.17
RM5/5209, Admiralstab der Marine, Akten betr. Wissenwerts und Vorarbeiten für O-Plänen
    gegen Dagö und Ösel, 15 September 1915 bis 9. August 1917.
RM5/5210, Pg 77463, Band II, 17.9.1917–28.9.1917.
RM5/5211–5214, various orders.
RM8/127, Reports from the I. Fuehrers der Torpedobootsstreitkräfte and subordinate
    squadrons.
RM8/143, A.223/18, Ganz Geheim, Kriegserfahrungen des Kommandos der Hochseestreit-
    kräfte (Vom 1. Januar bis 31. Dezember 1917).
RM42/134, Führer der Transportflottte III, Wichtige Akten Albion, Sept. 1917–Oct. 1917.
    has PG 90691 number.
RM42/135, Führer der Transportflottte III, Wichtige Akten Albion, Oct. 1917–Nov. 1917.
    has PG 90692 number.
RM47/126, Albion, Heft I.
RM47/127, Albion, Heft II.
RM62/183, Fall Albion, Allgemeines.
RM62/184, Taktische Befehle der S-Flotille, Fall Albion.
RM62/186, Kriegserfahrungen Albion.
RM112/188, Akten Gg V Albion (Koflieg).

Library of the Academy of Sciences, St. Petersburg (Biblioteka Akademii Nauk)

Proceedings of the Moon Sound Fortified Position (after issue 64 it took the title Proceed-
    ings of the Soviet of Military and Labor Deputies of the Moon Sound Fortified Posi-
    tion) "Izvestija Moonzundskoi ukreplennoi pozitsii," 1–84, March–October 1917.

U.S. National Archives

RGS 165/320/box 113, XXIII Reserve Corps, AWC transcription of files from Heeresarchiv, Potsdam, Capture of Ösel, Moon and Dagö [copied Jul 28, 1932]. (Cited as NA, followed by original document title.)

RGS 165/320/box 153, 42d Infantry Division, Army War College transcription of files from Heeresarchiv, Potsdam, Capture of Ösel, Moon and Dagö, folder II, Diary and Annexes, 42d ID, 21.9–31.10.1917, copied 7 Nov 1932.

T1022/Roll 238, Admiralstab der Marine, KTB des Flottenverbands für Sonder-unternehmungen, September–October 1917.

T1022, Roll 994 Admiralstab der Marine, Pg 76894, Bd. 2, the *Pionier Landungskompanie* (PILAKO).

T1022/Roll 1031 Admiralstab der Marine, Akten betr. O. Führer 1 Jan. 1917–30 Sept. 1918. PG 76718 vol 1., Akten betr. Albion, September 1917–31 Oktober 1917.

T1022/Roll 1032 Admiralstab der Marine, Akten betr. Albion, 1 Nov. 1917–30 Sept. 1918. PG 76719 vol. 1, Landings, signals, OPORDS, after-action reports, etc.

T1022, Roll 1235 Admiralstab der Marine, Akten betr. Wissenwerts und Vorarbeiten für O-Plänen gegen Dagö und Oesel, 15 September 1915 bis 9. August 1917. Also RM5/5209.

T1022, Roll 1236, Admiralstab der Marine, Akten betr. Operationen Oesel, 11.11.1917–4.4.1918.

T1022, Roll 1237, misc. including 42d ID, Ia 1394, 29.10.1917, "Erfahrungen bei der Eroberung der Inseln Oesel, Moon und Dago" and other unit After-Action Reports.

Russian State Naval Archives St. Petersburg
(Rossiiskii Gosudarstvennyi arkhiv Voenno-Morskogo Flota) or RGAVMF

Fond 417, File 4191, Ship Construction Program for 1912–1916; Ship Construction Program for the Baltic Fleet for 1911–1915.

Fond 479, File 881, Commander of the Baltic Fleet, Correspondence on . . . Action Plans . . . Armed Revolt in Finland . . . Closing of Newspaper *Volna (Wave)* and Other Issues, January 25–December 30, 1917.

Fond 479, Case 904, Commander of the Baltic Fleet, Materials on the Defense of the Baltic Islands, April 4–December 7, 1917.

Fond 479, Case 905, Commander of the Baltic Fleet, Materials on the Defense of the Baltic Islands, August 21–October 27, 1917.

Fond 479, Case 906, Commander of the Baltic Fleet, Materials on the Defense of the Baltic Islands, September 28–30, 1917.

Fond 479, Case 907, Commander of the Baltic Fleet, Materials on the Defense of the Baltic Islands, October 1–2, 1917.

Fond 479, Case 908, Commander of the Baltic Fleet, Materials on the Defense of the Baltic Islands, October 3–4, 1917.

Fond 479, Case 909, Commander of the Baltic Fleet, Operations, Materials on the Defense of the Baltic Islands, October 5–6, 1917.

Fond 479, Case 910, Commander of the Baltic Fleet, Operations, Materials on the Defense of the Baltic Islands, October 7–10, 1917

Fond 716, File 113, Naval Headquarters of the Head Commander-in-Chief (*Stavka*) Report on the Inspection by General Ivanov of the Naval Fortress of Emperor Peter the Great, Oesel Island and the Coast from Reval to Pernau with an Enclosure. Began—1916, ended—1916.

Fond 716, File 114, Naval Headquarters of the Head Commander-in-Chief (*Stavka*) Report on the Inspection by General Ivanov of Oesel Island and Organization of its Defense with an Enclosure of Maps and Diagrams. Began—1916, ended—1916.

Fond 941, Case 106, Battle Orders of the Commanders during the Operation (Commander of the Baltic Islands Fortified Position).

Fond 941, Case 108, Description of Baltic Islands Operation (Commander of the Baltic Islands Fortified Position).

Russian State Army Archives, Moscow
(Rossiiskii gosudarstvennyi voenno istoricheskii arkhiv) or RGVIA

107th Infantry History Synopsis.

Fond 2031, File 103, Headquarters of the Commander-in-Chief of the Northern Front, Preparation for the possible German Advances in the Fall 1917 and Concentration of our Forces, September 1917.

Fond 2031, File 105, Headquarters of the Commander-in-Chief of the Northern Front, About the Occupation of Oesel by Germans in September and October 1917, Dates: September 29–October 7, 1917.

Fond 2031, File 106, On the Preparation for the German Troop Landing on the Shores of Riga Bay (Moonzund Operation) September 30–October 7.

Fond 2031, File 506 *Northern Front, September 16, 1917*, Map.

Fond 2422, File 4, Orders to the 107th Infantry Division, March 17, 1917.

Fond 2422, File 39, Headquarters of the 107th Infantry Division. Lists (registers, rolls) on the complement, payroll, and present composition. . . . May 1, 1916–June 30, 1916.

Army War College

366–A-11, [Cmdr] Stiles, Wm. C. I. et al., "The German Operations against the Baltic Islands," Lecture, Army War College, 4 March 1930.

386–5, [Maj] King, C. K., et al., "A Critical Analysis of the Joint Operations in the World War at the Baltic Islands and along the Belgian Coast." Student Committee, 29 March 1932.

406–14, [Captain] Halsey, Wm. F., "Joint Operations." Student Committee, 24 February 1934.

6–1936–7, [Commander] Hinckley, R. M., "Plans and Execution of Plans in Joint Operations." Student Committee, 31 January 1936.

398–5B, [Commander] Robertson, M. C., "Oesel Island, October 10–24, 1917." Student Committee, 25 January 1933.

5–1938–1, [Commander] Umstead, S., "Coastal Frontier Defense and Joint Overseas Operations." Student Committee, 19 March 1938.

Mimeograph 92–140, Edmonds, James E. "A Study of Combined Operations."

Ministry of Defense Papers, #2 DEFE 2/806, Brigadier General J. E. Edmonds, R.E. (Ret.), "The Capture of the Batlic Islands, Oesel, Moon and Dago, October 1917."

PRIMARY PUBLISHED SOURCES

Ashmore, Leslie H. *Forgotten Flotilla: British Submarines in Russia 1914–1919*. Portsmouth: Manuscript Press, 2001.

Backer [Lieutenant]. "Brief eines auf Ösel eingesetzten Offiziers vom Regiment 255, Leutnant Backer aus dem Elsaß an Friedrich Ruge," in *"Erleben — Lernen — Weitergeben"* *Friedrich Ruge (1894–1985)*, ed. Jörg Hillmann. *Kleine Schriftenreihe zur Militär- und Marinegeschichte*, Band 10, Bochum: Verlag Dr. Dieter Winkler, 2005.

Bakhirev, Mikhail Kornotovich (Vice Admiral), *Otchet o Destviyah Morskih Sil Rizhskogo Zaliva, 25. Sentyabrya–7 Oktyabrya 1917 g.* [Report on Activity of the Gulf of Riga Naval Forces, 25 September–7 October 1917]. St. Petersburg: Russian State Naval Archive, 1998.

Bastian, Korvettenkapitän. "Die Eroberung der baltischen Inseln." Herausgegeben von Eberhard von Mantey, *Unsere Marine im Weltkrieg 1914–1918*. Berlin: Vaterländischer Verlag, 1927. (Cited as Bastian, "Eroberung.")

Behncke, Paul (Admiral). *Unsere Marine im Weltkriege und ihr Zusammenbruch*. Berlin: K. Curtius, n.d.

Berchem, Beda von. "The German Oesel Expedition in 1917." *U.S. Naval Institute Proceedings* 59 (Dec. 1933): 1720.

Bochkareva, Maria, and Isaac Don Levine. *Yashka: My Life as a Peasant, Officer and Exile*. New York: Frederick A. Stokes, 1919.

Fedotoff-White, Dimitri. *Survival through War and Revolution in Russia*. Philadelphia: University of Pennsylvania Press, 1939.

Golovine, Nicholas N. *The Russian Army in the World War*. New Haven: Yale University Press, 1931.

Graf, Harald. "Answer to Bogdanov." Translated by Liza Zheganina, in *Morskiya Zapiska*, 1958.

———. *The Russian Navy in War and Revolution: From 1914 up to 1918 with 38 Photographs*. Munich: Oldenbourg, 1923.

Hindenburg, Paul von. *Aus meinem Leben*. Leipzig: Hirzel Verlag, Illustrierte Volksausgabe, 1934

Hoffmann, Max, Generalmajor, a.D., herausgegeben v. Karl Friedrich Nowak, *Die Aufzeichnungen des Generalmajors Max Hoffmann*. 2 vols. Berlin: Verlag für Kulturpolitik, 1929. In English, *War Diaries and Other Papers*. Translated from the German by Eric Sutton. London: M. Secker [1929].

———. *The War of Lost Opportunities, by General von Hoffmann*. New York: International Publishers, 1925.

Hopman, Albert. *Das ereignisreiche Leben eines "Wilhelminers": Tagebücher, Briefe, Aufzeichnungen 1901 bis 1920 von Albert Hopman*, im Auftrag des Militärgeschichtlichen Forschungsamtes herausgegeben von Michael Epkenhans. München: R. Oldenbourg, 2004.

———. *Das Kriegstagebuch eines deutschen Seeoffiziers*. Berlin: A. Scherl g.m.b.h., 1925.

Kerensky, Alexander F. *Russia and History's Turning Point*. New York: Stone and Pierce, 1965.

Kiep, Louis. "Vor 20 Jahren. Die Eroberung der baltischen Inseln." *Berliner Börsen Zeitung*, 10 October 1937.

Knox, Alfred. *With the Russian Army, 1914–1917*. London: Hutchinson, 1921.

Koblinsky, G. von. "The Conquest of the Baltic Islands." *U.S. Naval Institute Proceedings* 58, no. 2 (July 1932): 971ff.

Ludendorff, Erich. *Ludendorff's Own Story, August 1914–November 1918*. 2 vols. New York: Harper, 1919.

Müller, Georg Alexander von. *The Kaiser and His Court: The Diaries, Notebooks and Letters of Admiral Georg Alexander von Müller, Chief of the Naval Cabinet, 1914–1918*. Ed. Walter Görlitz, trans. Mervyn Savill. New York: Harcourt, Brace and World, 1961.

Paléologue, Maurice. *An Ambassador's Memoirs*. Trans. F. A. Holt. 3 vols. 1923. Reprint, New York: Octagon Books, 1972.

Ruge, Friedrich. "Der Öselfahrt auf Torpedoboot B110." In *"Erleben — Lernen — Weitergeben" Friedrich Ruge (1894–1985)*, ed. Jörg Hillmann. *Kleine Schriftenreihe zur Militär- und Marinegeschichte*, Band 10. Bochum: Verlag Dr. Dieter Winkler, 2005.

———. *SM Torpedo Boat B110*. Windsor: Profile Publications, 1973.

Scheer, Reinhard. *Germany's High Sea Fleet in the World War*. New York: Cassell, 1920.

Schoultz, G. von. *With the British Fleet: War Recollections of a Russian Naval Officer*. Trans. Arthur Chambers. London: Hutchinson, n.d.

Schücking, Lothar. *Ein Jahr auf Ösel: Beiträge zum System Ludendorff*. Berlin-Steglitz: Fritz Würth Verlag, 1920.

Stoelzel, Albert [Kontreadmiral], a.D. *Ehrenrangliste der Kaiserlich Deutschen Marine 1914–1918*. Marine-Offizier-Verband: Berlin, 1930.

Stumpf, Richard. *War, Mutiny and the Revolution in the German Navy: The World War I Diary of Seaman Richard Stumpf*. Trans. and ed. Daniel Horn. New Brunswick: Rutgers University Press, 1967.

Timirev, Sergei Nikolaevich. *Vospominanya Morskogo Ofitsera [Reminisces of a Naval Officer]: Baltiiskii flot vo vremia voiny i Revolutsii, 1914–1918 g.g.* St. Petersburg: Tsitadel, 1998.

Tirpitz, Alfred von. *My Memoirs*. 2 vols. New York: Dodd, Mead, 1919.

Tschischwitz, Erich von, Gen.d. Inf. a.D. *The Army and Navy during the Conquest of the Baltic Islands in October 1917: An Analytical Study Based on Actual Experience*. Trans. Colonel Henry Hossfeld. Berlin: R. Eisenschmidt, 1931.

———. *Blaujacken und Feldgraue gen Ösel: Walter Flex' Heldentod*. Mylau: Buchdruckerei Carl Krüger, 1934.

Trotha, Adolf von. *Volkstum und Staatsführung: Briefe und Aufzeichnungen aus den Jahren 1915–1920*. Berlin: Grossdeutsche Verlagsanstalt, 1928.

Volkmann, Erich Otto, *Die roten Streifen: Roman eines Generalstabsoffiziers*. Hamburg: Hanseatische Verlagsanstalt, 1938.

———. *Unternehmen Ösel*. Hamburg: Hanseatische Verlagsanstalt, 1940. This novel was excerpted entirely from its larger forerunner noted above, *Die roten Streifen*. It focuses on the war years, leaves out the romantic interests, and ends with the conquest of the islands. Simply because this novel restricts itself to the war years and Albion, I have used this novel versus its longer version, *Die roten Streifen*.

Wieting, Franz. *Der Ostsee Krieg, 1914–1918*. Berlin: G. Braunbeck, 1918.

SECONDARY SOURCES

Books

Berghahn, Volker R. *Der Tirpitz-Plan: Genesis und Verfall einer innenpolitischen Krisenstrategie*. Düsseldorf: Droste, 1971.

Brinkmann, Jürgen. *Die Ritter des Ordens 'Pour le Merite'*. Brinkemann: Bückeburg, 1982.

Browder, Robert P., and Alexander F. Kerensky, eds. *The Russian Provisional Government, 1917.* Stanford: Stanford University Press, 1961.

Clifford, Kenneth J. *Amphibious Warfare Development in Britain and America from 1920–1940.* New York: Laurens, 1983.

Cowie, J. S. *Mines, Minelayers and Minelaying.* Oxford: Oxford University Press, 1949.

Dorling, Taprell. *Swept Channels: Being an Account of the Work of the Minesweepers in the Great War.* London: Hodder and Stoughton, 1935.

Eschenburg, Harald. *Prinz Heinrich von Preußen: Der Großadmiral im Schatten des Kaisers.* Heide: Westholsteinische Verlagsanstalt, 1989.

Foley, Robert T. *German Strategy and the Path to Verdun: Erich von Falkenhayn and the Development of Attrition, 1870–1916.* Cambridge: Cambridge University Press, 2005.

Forstner, Georg-Günter Freiherr von. *Der Krieg in der Ostsee.* Berlin: Weise Verlag, 1938.

Fischer, Jörg-Uwe. *Admiral des Kaisers: Georg Alexander von Müller als Chef des Marinekabinetts Wilhelms II.* New York: P. Lang, 1992.

Gagern, Ernst Freiherr von, Rudolph Firle, and Heinrich Rollmann. *Der Krieg in der Ostsee.* Vol. 3, *Von Anfang 1916 bis zum Kriegsende.* Frankfurt: E. S. Mittler and Sohn, 1964.

Gatrell, Peter. *A Whole Empire Walking: Refugees in Russia during World War I.* Bloomington: Indiana University Press, 1999.

Granier, Gerhard. *Magnus von Levetzow: Seeoffizier, Monarchist und Wegbereiter Hitlers: Lebensweg und ausgewählte Dokumente.* H. Boldt: Boppard am Rhein, c1982.

Greger, Rene, and Watts, A. J. *The Russian Fleet, 1914–1917.* London: Allan, 1972.

Halpern, Paul G. *A Naval History of World War I.* Annapolis: Naval Institute Press, 1994.

Herrmann, David G. *The Arming of Europe and the Making of the First World War.* Princeton: Princeton University Press, 1996.

Herwig, Holger H. *The First World War: Germany and Austria-Hungary 1914–1918.* New York: Arnold, 1997.

———. *The German Naval Officer Corps: A Social and Political History, 1890–1918.* London: Oxford, 1973.

———. *Luxury Fleet: The Imperial German Navy, 1888–1918.* Boston: Allen and Unwin, 1980.

Imrie, Alex. *German Naval Air Service.* London: Arms and Armour Press, 1989.

Isely, Jeter A., and Philip A. Crowl. *The U.S. Marines and Amphibious War: Its Theory and Its Practice in the Pacific.* Princeton: Princeton University Press, 1951.

Jones, David R. "From Imperial to Red Army: The Rise and Fall of the Bolshevik Military Tradition." In *Transformation in Russian and Soviet Military History. Proceedings of the 12th Military History Symposium USAF Academy, 1986.* Bolling, Md.: USAF Office of History, 1990.

———. "The Imperial Army in World War I, 1914–1917." In *The Military History of Tsarist Russia,* ed. F. W. Kagan and Robin Higham. New York: Palgrave, 2002.

Karau, Mark. *"Wielding the Dagger": The Marinekorps Flandern and the German War Effort, 1914–1918.* Westport, Conn.: Praeger, 2003.

Kosinskii, A. M. *Moonzundskaia operatsiia Baltiiskogo flota 1917.* Leningrad, 1928.

Kriegsgeschichtlichen Forschungsanstalt des Heeres. *Der Weltkrieg, 1914–1918.* Vol. 12, *Die Kreigführung im Frühjahr1917.* Berlin: E. S. Mittler and Sohn, 1939.

———. *Der Weltkrieg, 1914–1918.* Vol. 13, *Die Kriegführung im Sommer und Herbst 1917. Die Ereignisse außerhalb der Westfront bis November 1918.* Berlin: E. S. Mittler and Sohn, 1942.

Liulevicius, Vejas Gabriel. *War Land on the Eastern Front: Culture, National Identity, and German Occupation in World War I*. Cambridge: Cambridge University Press, 2000.

Luntinen, Pertti. *The Imperial Russian Army and Navy in Finland 1808–1918*. Helsinki: Finnish Historical Society, 1997.

Marder, Arthur J. *From the Dreadnought to Scapa Flow: The Royal Navy in the Fisher Era, 1904–1919*. Vol. 3, *1917: Year of Decision*. London: Oxford University Press, 1969.

Massie, Robert K. *Dreadnought: Britain, Germany, and the Coming of the Great War*. New York: Random House, 1991.

———. *Castles of Steel: Britain, Germany, and the Winning of the Great War at Sea*. New York: Random House, 2003.

Mawdsley, Evan. *The Russian Revolution and the Baltic Fleet: War and Politics, February 1917–April 1918*. London: Macmillan, 1978.

Melkonov, Yury. *Batarei Moonzunda (Batteries of Moon Sound)*. Riga: RTC Bask, 2003.

Menning, Bruce W. *Bayonets before Bullets: The Russian Imperial Army, 1861–1914*. Bloomington: Indiana University Press, 1992.

Mitchell, Donald W. *A History of Russian and Soviet Sea Power*. New York: Macmillan, 1974.

Möller-Witten, Hanns, ed. *Geschichte der Ritter des Ordens "Pour le Mérite" im Weltkrieg*. 2 vols. Berlin: Bernard u. Graefe, 1935.

Nekrasov, George M. *Expendable Glory: A Russian Battleship in the Baltic, 1915–1917*. East European Monographs. New York: Columbia University Press, 2004.

Pavlovich, N. B. *The Fleet in the First World War*. Vol. 1, *Operations of the Russian Fleet*. Trans. unknown. New Delhi: Amerind, 1979.

Rauch, Georg von. *The Baltic States: The Years of Independence; Estonia, Latvia, Lithuania, 1917–1940*. Trans. Gerald Onn. Berkeley: University of California, 1974.

Robinson, Douglas. *The Zeppelin in Combat: A History of the German Naval Airship Division, 1912–1918*. 3rd ed. Sun Valley, Calif.: J. W. Caler, 1971.

Saul, Norman E. *Sailors in Revolt: The Russian Baltic Fleet in 1917*. Lawrence: University of Kansas Press, 1978.

Showalter, Dennis E. *Tannenberg: Clash of Empires*. Hamden, Conn.: Archon, 1991.

Stegemann, Bernd. *Die deutsche Marinepolitik 1916–1918*. Berlin: Duncker und Humblot, 1970.

Stone, Norman. *The Eastern Front, 1914–1917*. New York: Scribner's Sons, 1975.

Volkmann, Erich Otto. *Der Grosse Krieg 1914–1918: Kurzgefasste Darstellung auf Grund der amtlichen Quellen des Reichsarchivs*. Berlin: Reimar Hobbing, 1922. Volkmann (see above under primary sources) retired from the army as a major and joined the staff of the Reich Archive in Potsdam, which permitted him access to the unit records.

Woodward, David. *The Russians at Sea: A History of the Russian Navy*. New York: Praeger, 1970.

Wildman, Allan K. *The End of the Russian Imperial Army*. Vol. 1, *The Old Army and the Soldiers' Revolt (Mar–Apr 1917)*. Princeton, N.J.: Princeton University Press, 1980.

———. *The End of the Russian Imperial Army*. Vol. 2, *The Road to Soviet Power and Peace*. Princeton, N.J.: University Press, 1987.

Zalesskii, K. A. *Pervaia mirovaia voina: biograficheskii entsikopedicheskii slovar'*. Moscow: Veche, 2000.

Articles

Agnew, James B. "From Where Did Our Amphibious Doctrine Come?" *Marine Corps Gazette*, August 1979, p. 52.
Benda, Hasso v. "General der Infantrie Oskar von Hutier: Zu seinem 50. Todestag," 288–91. *Deutsches Soldaten Jahrbuch 1984*. Munich: Schild, 1984.
Edmonds, James [Brig. Gen. Sir]. "German Engineer Landing Companies in 1914–1918." *Royal Engineers Journal*, Mar. 1942, pp. 10–13.
———. "A German Landing. The Capture of the Baltic Islands, Oesel, Moon and Dagö, October 1917." *Army Quarterly*, July 1925, p. 270 (reproduced as a mimeo handout for AWC students and listed under subtitle in the AWC MS collection).
Faupel, Guillermo [Col., Argentina]. "The Taking of the Baltic Islands in October, 1917, As a Model of the Cooperation Between the Army and the Navy," trans. L. L. Pendleton. *Revista Militar* 43 (July–Dec. 1924).
Ganz, A. Harding, "'Albion'—The Baltic Islands Operation." *Military Affairs* 42, no. 2 (1978): 91–97.
Green, Fred M., and C. T. Lanham. "The Invasion and Capture of the Baltic Islands." *Coast Artillery Journal*, July–Aug. 1936, p. 243, and Sept.–Oct. 1936, p. 323. Also in *Infantry Journal*, July–Aug. 1936, p. 291, and Sept.–Oct. 1936, p. 418.
Herwig, Holger H. "Admirals versus Generals: The War Aims of the Imperial German Navy, 1914–1918." *Central European History* 5 (Sept. 1972): 203–28.
———. "German Policy in the Eastern Baltic Sea in 1918: Expansion or Anti-Bolshevik Crusade?" *Slavic Review* 32 (Jan. 1973): 339–57.
Hull, Isabel. "The Military Campaign in German Southwest Africa, 1904–1907." *Bulletin of the German Historical Institute* 37 (Fall 2005): 39–45.
Podsoblyaev, Evgenii F. "The Russian Naval General Staff and the Evolution of Naval Policy, 1905–1914." Trans. Francis King and John Biggart. *Journal of Military History* 66 (Jan. 2002): 37–70.
Zverev, B. I. "Moonzund Operation of 1917." In *The Modern Encyclopedia of Russian and Soviet History*, vol. 23, ed. Joseph L. Wieczynski.: Gulf Breeze, Fla.: Academic International Press, 1918.

Electronic Sources

Conrad, Mark. *The Russian Army 1914*. http://home.comcast.net/~markconrad/RUSS1914. html#DIVISIONS, 10 October 2005.
Estonian Defence Forces. *Chronology of the Defence Forces*. http://www.mil.ee/index_eng. php?s=ajalugu, 31 August 2006.
———. *Tönisson, Aleksander*. Biographical materials; photograph. http://www.mil.ee/ index_eng.php?s=ajalu; and http://www.okupatsioon.ee/english/photos/97–27aa2. html, 31 August 2006.
Lagerstedt, John, and Markku Saari. *Land and Sea Fortress of Helsinki during the First World War*. http://www.novision.fi/viapori/easeet.htm, 10 November 2005.
Praust, Valdo. *Estonian Manors*. http://www.mois.ee/kihel_n.shtml#saare, 23 October 2005.
Staff, Gary. *Russian Order of Battle—Units of the Sea Forces of the Riga Gulf*. 2002. http:// www.gwpda.org/naval/rigaob.htm, 29 July 2006.

INDEX

ARMY UNITS

German